ICC 700-2020
National Green Building Standard®

ICC 700-2020
National G een Building Standard®

First Printing: April 202

ISBN-13: 978-0-86718-779-3
eISBN-13: 978-0-86718-780-9

Disclaimer

This publication provides accurate information on th subject matter covered. The publisher is selling it with the understanding that the publisher is not providing legal, accountin , or other professional service. If you need legal advice or other expert assistance, obtain the services of a qualifi d professional experienced in the subject matter involved. The NAHB has used commercially reasonable efforts to ensure that the contents of this volume are complete and appear without error; however the NAHB makes no representation or warranti s regarding the accuracy and completeness of this document's contents. The NAHB specifi ally disclaims any implied warranti s of merchantability or fitn ss for a particular purpos . The NAHB shall not be liable for any loss of profit or a y other commercial damages, including but not limited to incidental, special, consequential or oth r damages. Reference herein to any specifi commercial products, process, or service by trade name, trademark, manufacturer, or otherwise does not necessarily constitu e or imply its endorsement, recommendation or favored status by the NAHB. The views and opinions of the author expressed in this publicatio do not necessarily state or reflect thos of the NAHB, and they shall not be used to advertis or endorse a product.

Trademarks:"National Association of Home Builders," "NAHB," "BuilderBooks," and the "NAHB" logo are registered trademarks of the National Association of Home Builders of the United States."National Green Building Standard" is a registered trademark of the National Association of Home Builders of the United States.

Trademarks: "ICC International Code Council," and the "International Code Council" logo are registered trademarks of the International Code Council, Inc.

Photo Credits
Left-hand Column: 1800 Broadway, Criterion Development Partners
Top Right: Laurelhurst, Urban Northwest Homes
Middle Right: 77 12th Street, Ron Hart
Bottom Right: The Yates, Saussy Burbank

PREFACE

INTRODUCTION

Green buildings are designed, constructed, and operated with a goal of minimizing their environmental footprint. In both new construction and renovation, the building and its site are designed in an integrated manner using environmentally preferable practices and materials from start to finish. Many green features also carry direct consumer benefits, such as lower monthly utility bills, greater comfort, reduced maintenance, and increased value. To provide a uniform national platform for recognizing and advancing green construction and development, in 2007, the National Association of Home Builders (NAHB) and the International Code Council (ICC) partnered to establish the first consensus-based green building standard. The joint effort culminated in the publication of the 2008 National Green Building Standard® (NGBS) that received approval from the American National Standards Institute (ANSI).

Using a points-based system, a home or building can attain a rating of Bronze, Silver, Gold, or Emerald—depending on the green practices included. Alternative to the points-based system, new single-family homes, townhouses, or duplexes can earn a Certified rating by using a new streamlined, mandatory checklist of green practices. For a building to attain any certification level, all applicable mandatory provisions must be implemented. The NGBS also requires that the builder or remodeler incorporate a minimum number of features in each of six categories (lot development, resource efficiency, energy efficiency, water efficiency, indoor environmental quality, and homeowner education) for each rating level. The scope of the NGBS includes all newly-constructed and remodeled single-family dwellings, townhomes, multifamily residential buildings, as well as residential land developments. Beginning with the 2020 NGBS, both the commercial and residential portions of mixed-use buildings can also be certified. Residential and mixed-use communities of all sizes and densities can be recognized for green practices that are incorporated into their design and construction.

The NGBS provides developers, builders, and remodelers with a credible definition of green building and a useful measurement of relative environmental ratings. The expansive point-based system offers a process that can accommodate varying climates, market conditions, construction types, and homebuyer preferences.

The NGBS was updated in 2012 and 2015 to incorporate advances in building science, reflect recent model code improvements, and add more choices for compliance. As with the original, these later versions were developed in accordance with the ANSI requirements, and the NGBS remains a leading consensus-based residential green building standard.

This collaboration of the leading codes and standards development organizations and their continued commitment to the ANSI process further solidified the standing of the NGBS as the national benchmark for green residential construction in the United States. With over 200,000 dwelling units certified to date nationwide, the 2020 NGBS incorporates process improvements and new practices that reflect its decade-long implementation in the field.

The 2020 NGBS features many updates with the potential to further transform residential construction. Its expanded scope includes assisted living, residential care, and group homes with an I-1 occupancy, as well as the commercial space of mixed-use buildings, making the standard relevant to more diverse use types. For renovation, the new prescriptive paths for energy and water consumption provide flexibility to demonstrate a building's improvement. And finally, the certified compliance path for single-family homes, townhomes, and duplexes offers a streamlined approach for single-family builders to gain recognition for the efficiency and green features of their homes.

DEVELOPMENT

The Consensus Committee for the 2020 National Green Building Standard®, consisting of 45 members, was assembled of those entities and interests that are affected by the provisions of the Standard. In addition, eight Task Groups were formed according to specific areas of technical expertise to serve as a resource to the Consensus Committee. The Task Groups included committee members and other subject area experts. The entire NGBS was open for the public to submit proposed changes before the Consensus Committee and Task Groups began their work on revising and expanding its provisions. The Consensus Committee met three times during 2017, 2018, and 2019 to discuss and take formal actions first on proposed changes and then on public comments. All meetings were open to the public to provide an opportunity to address the Consensus Committee. All committee actions were also balloted through formal letter ballots.

Overall, the Consensus Committee reviewed and acted upon nearly 700 proposed changes and public comments ranging from revisions to individual provisions to addition of new compliance options.

ANSI APPROVAL

The ICC 700-2020 National Green Building Standard® was approved by ANSI as an American National Standard on January 6, 2020.

MAINTENANCE

The development process for the National Green Building Standard® is managed by Home Innovation Research Labs, an ANSI-Accredited Standards Developer. The NGBS is revised on a continuous maintenance basis in accordance with ANSI requirements. Proposals for revising the 2020 edition of the National Green Building Standard® are welcome. Please visit the Home Innovation Research Labs website (www.homeinnovation.com/NGBS) for a proposal form and instructions.

DISCLAIMER

Home Innovation Research Labs, NAHB, ICC, their members, and those participating in the development of the NGBS accept no liability resulting from compliance or noncompliance with the provisions. Home Innovation Research Labs, NAHB, or ICC do not have the power or authority to enforce compliance with the contents of the NGBS. Similarly, neither NAHB nor ICC makes any representations or warranties regarding enforcement, application, or compliance with the NGBS or any part thereof.

2020 Consensus Committee on the
National Green Building Standard®

At the time of ANSI approval, the Consensus Committee consisted of the following members:

Chair	Robert D. Ross
Vice Chairs	Paula Marie Cino, Amy Schmidt
Committee Staff	Kevin Kauffman, Nay Shah, Vladimir Kochkin
ICC Staff Liaison	Allan Bilka

Committee Member	Representative
ACCA (U)	Donald Prather
Air-Conditioning, Heating and Refrigeration Institute (P)	Laura Petrillo-Groh
Alliance for Water Efficiency (G)	Thomas Pape
Aluminum Extruders Council, Glass Association of North America (P)	Thomas Culp
American Gas Association (P)	Paul W. Cabot
	Ted Williams (Alt.)
American Wood Council (P)	Loren Ross
BOMA International (U)	Andrew Klein
Building Quality (U)	Craig Conner
Charles R. Foster (P)	Charles R. Foster, III
Cherry Hills Village (G)	Hope Medina
City of Des Moines (G)	Sean S. Devlin
City of Winter Park (G)	Kristopher R. Stenger
Coconino County (G)	Steven White
Crescent Communities (U)	Gregory Curtis Coolidge
DuPont Building Innovations (P)	Theresa A. Weston
Edison Electric Institute (P)	Steven Rosenstock
G&R Construction Services LLC (U)	Robert D. Ross
Gas Technology Institute/Carbon Management Information Center (P)	Neil P. Leslie
Greenscapes Alliance (P)	Greg Johnson
Knez Construction (U)	William A. Sanderson
Kohler Company (P)	Cambria McLeod
	Shabbir Rawalpindiwala (Alt.)
Los Alamos County (G)	Lee Brammeier
Lutron Electronics (P)	Michael Jouaneh
Mathis Consulting Company (U)	R Christopher Mathis
National Multifamily Housing Council (U)	Paula Cino
North American Insulation Manufacturers Association (P)	Charles C Cottrell
	Merle McBride (Alt.)
P3 Builder Group (U)	John Barrows
PEG (U)	Matthew Cooper
Plastic Pipe and Fittings Association (PPFA) (P)	Michael Cudahy
Plumbing Manufacturers International (P)	Matt Sigler
Portland Cement Association (P)	Marc Allen Nard
Red Tree Builders (U)	Brandon Bryant
Steinberg Dickey Collaborative LLP (U)	Sanford Steinberg
Steven Winter Associates (U)	Karla Butterfield
Tempo Partners (U)	Aaron Gary
The Dow Chemical Company (P)	Amy Schmidt
	Lorraine Ross (Alt.)

Town of Truckee (G) .... Johnny Goetz
UL (P) .... Josh Jacobs
Urban Northwest Homes (U).. Jerud Martin
U.S. Department of Energy (G).. Jeremiah Williams
U.S. Department of Housing & Urban Development (G)..................................... Dana Bres
U.S. Environmental Protection Agency (G)... Bob Thompson
.... Robert L. Goo (Alt.)
Vinyl Siding Institute, Inc. (P)... Matthew Dobson
.... Nicholas Capezza
WDG Architecture (U) .... Eric Schlegel
Window & Door Manufacturers Association (P) .... Jeff Inks

Acknowledgement

The development of the 2020 National Green Building Standard® (NGBS) would not have been possible without the contributions of time, effort, and insight by the Consensus Committee members, and the individuals who participated on the Task Groups. The organizations that sponsored this NGBS development process—ICC and NAHB—recognize and appreciate these contributions, as well as those of everyone who participated in the public hearings and formal comment process.

There is no implied or explicit endorsement of the 2020 NGBS by Consensus Committee members or by any other individuals and organizations participating in its development.

INTEREST CATEGORIES

Membership by Interest Category	
General interest (G):	10
Producer Interest (P):	19
User Interest (U):	16
TOTAL:	**45**

TABLE OF CONTENTS

TABLE OF CONTENTS

SECTION 1

SCOPE & ADMINISTRATION

101 GENERAL

101.1 Title. The title of this document is the *National Green Building Standard*®, hereinafter referred to as "this Standard."

101.2 Scope. The provisions of this Standard shall apply to the design, construction, alteration, enlargement, and renovation of (1) all residential buildings, (2) residential portions of mixed-use buildings, or (3) mixed-use buildings where the residential portion is greater than 50% of the gross floor area. This Standard shall also apply to subdivisions, building sites, building lots, and accessory structures.

101.2.1 Residential designation. For the purpose of this standard, all Group R occupancies as defined by the International Building Code and all buildings within the scope of the International Residential Code shall be considered residential. Assisted living facilities, residential board and care facilities, and group homes classified as an I-1 occupancy as defined by the International Building Code shall also be considered residential.

101.3 Intent. The purpose of this Standard is to establish criteria for rating the environmental impact of design and construction practices to achieve conformance with specified performance levels for green residential buildings, renovation thereof, accessory structures, building sites, and subdivisions. This Standard is intended to provide flexibility to permit the use of innovative approaches and techniques. This Standard is not intended to abridge safety, health, or environmental requirements contained in other applicable laws, codes, or ordinances.

101.4 Referenced documents. The codes, standards, and other documents referenced in this Standard shall be considered part of the requirements of this Standard to the prescribed extent of each such reference. The edition of the code, standard, or other referenced document shall be the edition referenced in Chapter 14.

101.5 Appendices. Where specifically required by a provision in this Standard, that appendix shall apply. Appendices not specifically required by a provision of this Standard shall not apply unless specifically adopted.

102 CONFORMANCE

102.1 Mandatory practices. This Standard does not require compliance with any specific practice except those noted as mandatory.

102.2 Conformance language. The green building provisions are written in mandatory language by way of using the verbs "to be," "is," "are," etc. The intent of the language is to require the user to conform to a particular practice in order to qualify for the number of points assigned to that practice. Where the term "shall" is used, or the points are designated as "mandatory," the provision or practice is mandatory.

102.3 Documentation. Verification of conformance to green building practices shall be the appropriate construction documents, architectural plans, site plans, specifications, builder certification and sign-off, inspection reports, or other data that demonstrates conformance as determined by the Adopting Entity. Where specific documentation is required by a provision of the Standard, that documentation is noted with that provision.

102.4 Alternative compliance methods. Alternative compliance methods shall be acceptable where the Adopting Entity finds that the proposed green building practice meets the intent of this Standard.

SECTION 103 ADMINISTRATION

103.1 Administration. The Adopting Entity shall specify performance level(s) to be achieved as identified in Chapter 3 and shall provide a verification process to ensure compliance with this Standard.

INTENTIONALLY LEFT BLANK.

SECTION 2

DEFINITIONS

201 GENERAL

201.1 Scope. Unless otherwise expressly stated, the following words and terms shall, for the purposes of this Standard, have the meanings shown in this chapter.

201.2 Interchangeability. Words used in the present tense include the future; words stated in the masculine gender include the feminine and neuter; the singular number includes the plural and the plural, the singular.

201.3 Terms defined in other documents. Where terms are not defined in this Standard, and such terms are used in relation to the reference of another document, those terms shall have the definition in that document.

201.4 Terms not defined. Where terms are not defined through the methods authorized by this section, such terms shall have ordinarily accepted meanings such as the context implies.

SECTION 202 DEFINITIONS

ACCESSORY STRUCTURE. A structure, the use of which is customarily accessory to and incidental to that of the residential building; the structure is located on the same lot or site as the residential building; the structure does not contain a dwelling unit or a sleeping unit; and (1) is classified as Group U – Utility and Miscellaneous in accordance with the ICC International Building Code, or (2) is classified as accessory in accordance with the ICC International Residential Code, or (3) is classified as accessory to the residential use by a determination of the Adopting Entity.

ADDITION. An extension or increase in the conditioned space floor area or height of a building or structure.

ADOPTING ENTITY. The governmental jurisdiction, green building program, or any other third-party compliance assurance body that adopts this Standard and is responsible for implementation and administration of the practices herein.

ADVANCED FRAMING. Code compliant layout, framing and engineering techniques that minimize the amount of framing products used and waste generated to construct a building while maintaining the structural integrity of the building.

AFUE (Annual Fuel Utilization Efficiency). The ratio of annual output energy to annual input energy which includes any non-heating season pilot input loss, and for gas or oil-fired furnaces or boilers, does not include electrical energy.

AIR BARRIER. Material(s) assembled and joined together to provide a barrier to air leakage through the building envelope. An air barrier may be a single material or a combination of materials.

AIR HANDLER. A blower or fan used for the purpose of distributing supply air to a room, space, or area.

AIR INFILTRATION. The uncontrolled inward air leakage into a building caused by the pressure effects of wind or the effect of differences in the indoor and outdoor air density or both.

AIR, MAKE-UP. Air that is provided to replace air being exhausted.

ARCHITECTURAL COATINGS. A material applied onto or impregnated into a substrate for protective, decorative, or functional purposes. Such materials include, but are not limited to, primers, paints, varnishes, sealers, and stains. An architectural coating is a material applied to stationary structures or their appurtenances at the site of installation. Coatings applied in shop applications, sealants, and adhesives are not considered architectural coatings.

AREA OF HIGH INTERSECTION DENSITY. An area whose existing streets and sidewalks create at least 90 intersections per square mile (35 intersections per square kilometer).

AUTHORITY HAVING JURISDICTION (AHJ). An agency or agent responsible for enforcing this code.

BALANCED VENTILATION. Any combination of concurrently operating mechanical exhaust and mechanical supply whereby the total mechanical exhaust airflow rate is within 10% of the total mechanical supply airflow rate.

BIOBASED PRODUCT. A commercial or industrial material or product that is composed of, or derived from, in whole or in significant part, biological products or renewable agricultural materials, including plant, animal, and marine materials, or forestry materials.

BROWNFIELD (also EPA-Recognized Brownfield). A site in which the expansion, redevelopment or reuse of would be required to address the presence or potential presence of a hazardous substance, pollutant or contaminant. Brownfield sites include:

- EPA-recognized brownfield sites as defined in Public Law 107-118 (H.R. 2869) "Small Business Liability Relief and Brownfields Revitalization Act," 40 CFR, Part 300; and

- Sites determined to be contaminated according to local or state regulation.

(i.e.: Pub.L. 107-118, § 1, Jan. 11, 2002, 115 Stat. 2356, provided that: "This Act [enacting 42 U.S.C.A. § 9628, amending this section, 42 U.S.C.A. § 9604, 42 U.S.C.A. § 9605, 42 U.S.C.A. § 9607, and 42 U.S.C.A. § 9622, and enacting provisions set out as notes under this section and 42 U.S.C.A. § 9607] may be cited as the 'Small Business Liability Relief and Brownfields Revitalization Act'.")

CERTIFIED GEOTHERMAL SERVICE CONTRACTOR. A person who has a current certification from the International Ground Source Heat Pump Association as an installer of ground source heat pump systems or as otherwise approved by the Adopting Entity.

CLIMATE ZONE. Climate zones are determined based on Figure 6(1).

CLUSTER DEVELOPMENT. A design technique that concentrates residential buildings and related infrastructure at a higher density within specified areas on a site. The remaining land on the site can then be used for low intensity uses such as recreation, common open space, farmland, or the preservation of historical sites and environmentally sensitive areas.

COMMON AREA(S).

1. Areas within a site or lot that are predominantly open spaces and consist of non-residential structures, landscaping, recreational facilities, roadways and walkways, which are owned and maintained by an incorporated or chartered entity such as a homeowner's association or governmental jurisdiction; or

2. Areas of a multifamily building that are outside the boundaries of a dwelling unit or sleeping unit and are shared among or serve the dwelling units or sleeping units; including, but not limited to, hallways, amenity and resident services areas, parking areas, property management offices, mechanical rooms, and laundry rooms.

COMPONENT. See "Major Component" and/or "Minor Component".

COMPOST FACILITY. An outdoor bin or similar structure designed for the decomposition of organic material such as leaves, twigs, grass clippings, and vegetative food waste.

COMPRESSED NATURAL GAS (CNG) VEHICLE RESIDENTIAL FUELING APPLIANCE. A residential appliance that supplies compressed natural gas into a CNG vehicle.

CONDITIONED SPACE. An area, room or space that is enclosed within the building thermal envelope and that is directly or indirectly heated or cooled. Spaces are indirectly heated or cooled where they communicate through openings with conditioned spaces, where they are separated from conditioned spaces by uninsulated walls, floors or ceilings or where they contain uninsulated ducts, piping or other sources of heating or cooling.

CONSTRUCTED WETLAND. An artificial wetland system (such as a marsh or swamp) created as new and/or restored habitat for native wetland plant and wildlife communities as well as to provide and/or restore wetland functions to the area. Constructed wetlands are often created as compensatory mitigation for ecological disturbances that result in a loss of natural wetlands from (1) anthropogenic discharge for wastewater, stormwater runoff, or sewage treatment; (2) mines or refineries; or (3) development.

CONSTRUCTION WASTE MANAGEMENT PLAN. A system of measures designed to reduce, reuse, and recycle the waste generated during construction and to properly dispose of the remaining waste.

CONTINUOUS PHYSICAL FOUNDATION TERMITE BARRIER. An uninterrupted, non-chemical method of preventing ground termite infestation (e.g., aggregate barriers, stainless steel mesh, flashing, or plastic barriers).

COEFFICIENT OF PERFORMANCE (COP) – COOLING. The ratio of the rate of heat removal to the rate of energy input, in consistent units, for a complete refrigerating system of some specific portion of the system under designated operating conditions.

COEFFICIENT OF PERFORMANCE (COP) – HEATING. The ratio of the rate of heat delivered to the rate of energy input, in consistent units, for a complete heat pump system, including the compressor, and, if applicable, auxiliary heat, under designated operating conditions.

DAYLIGHT CONTROL. A device or system that provides automatic control of electric light levels based on the amount of daylight.

DEMAND CONTROLLED HOT WATER LOOP. A hot water circulation (supply and return) loop with a pump that runs "on demand" when triggered by a user-activated switch or motion-activated sensor.

DESUPERHEATER. An auxiliary heat exchanger that uses superheated gases from an air conditioner's or heat pump's vapor-compression cycle to heat water.

DIRECT-VENT APPLIANCE. A fuel-burning appliance with a sealed combustion system that draws all air for combustion from the outside atmosphere and discharges all flue gases to the outside atmosphere.

DRAIN-WATER HEAT RECOVERY. A system to recapture the heat energy in drain water and use it to preheat cold water entering the water heater or other water fixtures.

DURABILITY. The ability of a building or any of its components to perform its required functions in its service environment over a period of time without unforeseen cost for maintenance or repair.

DWELLING UNIT. A single unit providing complete, independent living facilities for one or more persons, including permanent provisions for living, sleeping, eating, cooking, and sanitation.

DYNAMIC GLAZING. Any fenestration product that has the fully reversible ability to change its performance properties, including U-factor, SHGC, or VT.

EER (Energy Efficiency Ratio). A measure of the instantaneous energy efficiency of electric air conditioning defined as the ratio of net equipment cooling capacity in Btu/h to total rate of electric input in watts under designated operating conditions. When consistent units are used, this ratio becomes equal to COP. (See also Coefficient of Performance.)

ENERGY MANAGEMENT CONTROL SYSTEM. An integrated computerized control system that is intended to operate the heating, cooling, ventilation, lighting, water heating, and/or other energy-consuming appliances and/or devices for a building in order to reduce energy consumption. Also known as Building Automation Control (BAC) or Building Management Control System (BMCS).

ENERGY MONITORING DEVICE. A device installed within a building or dwelling unit that can provide near real-time data on whole building, dwelling unit or sleeping unit energy consumption.

ENGINEERED WOOD PRODUCTS. Products that are made by combining wood strand, veneers, lumber or other wood fiber with adhesive or connectors to make a larger composite structure.

ENVIRONMENTAL IMPACT. See **LCA (Life Cycle Analysis/Assessment).**

ENVIRONMENTALLY SENSITIVE AREAS.

1. Areas within wetlands as defined by federal, state, or local regulations;
2. Areas of steep slopes;
3. "Prime Farmland" as defined by the U.S. Department of Agriculture;
4. Areas of "critical habitat" for any federal or state threatened or endangered species;
5. Areas defined by state or local jurisdiction as environmentally sensitive; or,
6. Shoreline buffers that have important environmental functions as identified by the state or local jurisdiction, e.g., shoreline stability, pollutant removal, streamside shading, ecological flow protection.

EROSION CONTROLS. Measures that prevent soil from being removed by wind, water, ice, or other disturbance.

EXISTING BUILDING. A building erected prior to the date of the current adopted building code, or one for which a legal building occupancy permit has been issued.

EXISTING SUBDIVISION. An area of land, defined as "Site" in this Chapter, that has received all development approvals and has been platted and all infrastructure is complete at time of application to this Standard.

FENESTRATION. Products classified as either vertical fenestration or skylights.

> **SKYLIGHT.** Glass or other transparent or translucent glazing material installed at a slope of less than 60 degrees (1.05 rad) from horizontal.

> **VERTICAL FENESTRATION.** Windows (fixed or movable), opaque doors, glazed doors, glazed block and combination opaque/glazed doors composed of glass or other transparent or translucent glazing materials and installed at a slope of at least 60 degrees (1.05 rad) from horizontal.

FENESTRATION PRODUCT, FIELD-FABRICATED. A fenestration product whose frame is made at the construction site of standard dimensional lumber or other materials that were not previously cut, or otherwise formed with the specific intention of being used to fabricate a fenestration product or exterior door. Field fabricated does not include site-built fenestration.

FENESTRATION PRODUCT, SITE-BUILT. A fenestration designed to be made up of field-glazed or field-assembled units using specific factory cut or otherwise factory-formed framing and glazing units. Examples of site-built fenestration include storefront systems, curtain walls, and atrium roof systems.

FLOOR AREA, GROSS. The floor area within the inside perimeter of the exterior walls of the building under consideration, exclusive of vent shafts and courts, without deduction for corridors, stairways, ramps, closets, the thickness of interior walls, columns or other features. The floor area of a building, or portion thereof, not provided with surrounding exterior walls shall be the useable area under the horizontal projection of the roof or floor above. The gross floor area shall not include shafts with no opening or interior courts.

FROST-PROTECTED SHALLOW FOUNDATION. A foundation that does not extend below the design frost depth and is protected against the effects of frost in compliance with SEI/ASCE 32-01 or the provisions for frost-protected shallow foundations of the IBC or IRC, as applicable.

GRADE PLANE. A reference plane representing the average of the finished ground level adjoining the building at all exterior walls. Where the finished ground level slopes away from the exterior walls, the reference plane shall be established by the lowest points within the area between the building and the lot line or, where the lot line is more than 6 ft. (1830 mm) from the building, between the structure and a point 6 ft. (1830 mm) from the building.

GREYFIELD SITE. A previously developed site with little or no contamination or perceived contamination.

GREYWATER. Untreated wastewater that has not come into contact with wastewater from water closets, urinals, kitchen sinks, or dishwashers. Greywater includes, but is not limited to, wastewater from bathtubs, showers, lavatories, clothes washers, and laundry trays.

GRID-INTERACTIVE BATTERY STORAGE (GIBS). A battery storage system that provides electric system grid operators such as utilities, independent system operators (ISOs) and regional transmission organizations (RTOs), with automatic control that is capable of receiving and automatically responding to a signal for charge and discharge.

GRID-INTERACTIVE ELECTRIC THERMAL STORAGE (GETS). An energy storage system that provides electric system grid operators such as utilities, independent system operators (ISOs) and regional transmission organizations (RTOs), with variable control of a building's space heating and service water heating end uses.

GROUND SOURCE HEAT PUMP. A system that uses the earth or subsurface water as a heat sink for air conditioning and as a heat source for heating.

HARDSCAPE. Asphalt, concrete, masonry, stone, wood, and other non-plant elements external to the building shell on a landscape.

HEAT PUMP. An appliance having heating or heating/cooling capability, and which uses refrigerants to extract heat from air, liquid, or other sources.

HIGH-EFFICACY LAMPS. Compact fluorescent lamps (CFL); light emitting diode (LED); T-8 or smaller diameter linear fluorescent lamps; or lamps with a minimum efficacy of:
1) 60 lumens per watt for lamps over 40 watts,
2) 50 lumens per watt for lamps over 15 watts to 40 watts, or 3) 40 lumens per watt for lamps 15 watts or less.

HISTORIC BUILDINGS. Buildings that are listed in or are eligible for listing in the National Register of Historic Places (NRHP) or designated as being of historic or architectural significance under an appropriate state or local law.

HSPF (Heating Seasonal Performance Factor). The total seasonal heating output of a heat pump, in Btu, divided by the total electric energy input during the same period, in watt-hours using a defined test methodology.

HYDROZONING. A landscape practice that groups plants with similar watering needs together in an effort to conserve water.

ICF (INSULATING CONCRETE FORMS). A concrete forming system using stay-in-place forms of rigid foam plastic insulation, a hybrid of cement and foam insulation, a hybrid of cement and wood chips, or other insulating material for constructing cast-in-place concrete walls.

IMPERVIOUS SURFACE. Hard-covered ground area that prevents/retards the entry of water into the soil at that location, resulting in water flowing to another location. (Also see HARDSCAPE)

INDIRECT-FIRED WATER HEATER. A water storage tank, typically with no internal heating elements, that is connected by piping to an external heating source such as a gas or oil-fired boiler.

INFILL. A location including vacant or underutilized land that may apply to either a site or a lot and is located in an area served by existing infrastructure such as centralized water and sewer connections, roads, drainage, etc., and the site boundaries are adjacent to existing development on at least one side.

INTEGRATED PEST MANAGEMENT. A sustainable approach to managing pests by combining biological, cultural, physical, and chemical tools in a way that minimizes economic, health, and environmental risks.

INVASIVE PLANTS. Plants for which the species are not native to the ecosystem under consideration and that cause, or are likely to cause, economic or environmental harm or harm to human, animal or plant health. For the purposes of compliance with this standard, invasive plants are those that are included on local, state, or regional lists of plants determined to cause environmental harm and shall not be limited to those plants covered by law or regulation.

JALOUSIE WINDOW. A window consisting of a series of overlapping horizontal frameless louvers which pivot simultaneously in a common frame and are actuated by one or more operating devices so that the bottom edge of each louver swings outward and the top edge swings inward during operation.

LANDSCAPE PRACTICE (LANDSCAPING). Any activity that modifies the visible features of an area of land. It may include:

1. Living elements, such as flora or fauna;
2. Natural elements such as terrain shape, elevation, or bodies of water;
3. Created or installed elements such as fences or other material objects;
4. Abstract elements such as the weather and lighting conditions.

LAVATORY FAUCET. A valve for dispensing hot and/or cold water to a basin used for washing hands and face, but not for food preparation.

LCA (Life Cycle Analysis/Assessment). An accounting and evaluation of the environmental aspects and potential impacts of materials, products, assemblies, or buildings throughout their life (from raw material acquisition through manufacturing, construction, use, operation, demolition, and disposal).

Level 2 Electric Vehicle Charging Station. A device that is used to supply electricity to a plug-in hybrid electric vehicle or a plug-in electric vehicle and is rated for use with 208 to 240 Volts AC input.

Level 3 Electric Vehicle Charging Station. A device that is used to supply electricity to a plug-in hybrid electric vehicle or a plug-in electric vehicle and is rated for use with 208 to 500 Volts, 3 phase electric AC input.

LOT. A portion or parcel of land considered as a unit.

LOW-IMPACT DEVELOPMENT. A storm water management approach that attempts to recreate the predevelopment hydrology of a site by using lot level topography and landscape to deter storm water runoff and promote soil infiltration and recharge.

LOW-VOC (PRODUCTS). Products or materials with volatile organic compound (VOC) emissions equal to or below the established thresholds as defined in the referenced VOC emissions requirements for each applicable section in this document. (Also see VOC.)

MAJOR COMPONENT.

1. All structural members and structural systems.

2. Building materials or systems that are typically applied as a part of over 50% of the surface area of the foundation, wall, floor, ceiling, or roof assemblies.

MANUFACTURED HOME CONSTRUCTION. Three-dimensional sections of the complete building, dwelling unit, or sleeping unit built in a factory in conformance with the HUD Manufactured Home Construction and Safety Standards (24 CFR, Part 3280) and transported to the jobsite to be joined together on a foundation.

MASS WALLS. Above-grade masonry or concrete walls having a mass greater than or equal to 30 pounds per square foot (146 kg/m^2), solid wood walls having a mass greater than or equal to 20 pounds per square foot (98 kg/m^2), and any other walls having a heat capacity greater than or equal to 6 Btu/ft$^2 \bullet °$F [266 J/(m$^2 \bullet$ K)] with a minimum of 50% of the required R-value on the exterior side of the wall's centerline.

MERV (Minimum Efficiency Reporting Value). Minimum efficiency-rated value for the effectiveness of air filters.

MINOR COMPONENT. Building materials or systems that are not considered a major component. (Also see Major Component.)

MIXED-USE BUILDING. A building that incorporates more than one use (e.g., residential, retail, commercial) in a single structure.

MIXED-USE DEVELOPMENT. A project that incorporates more than one use (e.g., residential, retail, commercial) on the same site.

MODULAR CONSTRUCTION. Three-dimensional sections of the complete building or dwelling unit built in a factory and transported to the jobsite to be joined together on a permanent foundation.

MULTIFAMILY BUILDING. A building containing multiple dwelling units or sleeping units and classified as R-2 under the IBC.

NET DEVELOPABLE AREA. The land on which buildings may be constructed. Any land where buildings cannot be constructed due to environmental restrictors or is used for infrastructure or public purposes such as parks, schools, etc., is not considered net developable area.

NEW CONSTRUCTION. Construction of a new building.

NON-RESIDENTIAL SPACES. Spaces not designated as residential in § 101.2.1.

OCCUPANCY SENSOR. Devices that generally use passive infrared and/or ultrasonic technology or a combination of multiple sensing technologies to automatically turn lights on and off or from one preset light level to another based on whether the sensor detects that a space is occupied.

ON-SITE RENEWABLE ENERGY SYSTEM. An energy generation system located on the building or building site that derives its energy from a renewable energy source.

OPEN SPACE. An area of land or water that (1) remains in its natural state, (2) is used for agriculture, or (3) is free from intensive development.

PANELIZED ASSEMBLIES. Factory-assembled wall panels, roof trusses, and/or other components installed on-site.

PERFORMANCE PATH. An alternative set of standards (to the Prescriptive Path) with defined performance metrics, as specified in Chapter 7 of this Standard.

PERMEABLE MATERIAL. A material that permits the passage of water vapor and/or liquid.

PLUMBING FIXTURE. A receptor or device that requires both a water-supply connection and a discharge to the drainage system, such as water closets, lavatories, bathtubs, and sinks.

PRECUT. Materials cut to final size prior to delivery to site and ready for assembly.

PRESCRIPTIVE PATH. A set of provisions in a code or standard that must be adhered to for compliance.

PRESERVATION. The process of applying measures to maintain and sustain the existing materials, integrity, and/or form of a building, including its structure and building artifacts.

PROGRAMMABLE COMMUNICATING THERMOSTAT. A whole building or whole dwelling unit/sleeping unit thermostat that can be monitored and controlled remotely.

PROJECTION FACTOR. The ratio of the overhang width to the overhang height above the door threshold or window sill (PF = A/B).

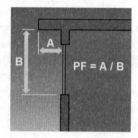

Projection Factor

R-VALUE (THERMAL RESISTANCE). The inverse of the time rate of heat flow through a body from one of its bounding surfaces to the other surface for a unit temperature difference between the two surfaces, under steady state conditions, per unit area ($h \cdot ft2 \cdot °F/Btu)[(m2 \cdot K)/W]$.

READILY ACCESIBLE. Capable of being reached quickly for operation, renewal, or inspection without requiring those to whom ready access is requisite to climb over or remove obstacles or to resort to portable ladders or access equipment.

RECLAIMED WATER. Non-potable water provided by a wastewater utility, treated to meet the requirements of the Authority Having Jurisdiction (AHJ) for the intended uses. The water may be sanitized to allow for above ground landscape irrigation or flush sanitary fixtures. May also be known as Recycled Water in some areas.

RECYCLE. To recover and reprocess manufactured goods into new products.

RECYCLED CONTENT. Resources containing post-consumer or pre-consumer (post-industrial) recycled content.

> **POST-CONSUMER RECYCLED CONTENT.** Proportion of recycled material in a product generated by households or by commercial, industrial, and institutional facilities in their role as end users of the product that can no longer be used for its intended purpose. This includes returns of material from the distribution chain.

> **PRE-CONSUMER (POST-INDUSTRIAL) RECYCLED CONTENT.** Proportion of recycled material in a product diverted from the waste stream during the manufacturing process. Pre-consumer recycled content does not include reutilization of materials such as rework, regrind, or scrap generated in a process and capable of being reclaimed within the same process that generated it.

REGIONAL MATERIAL. Material that originates, is produced, grows naturally, or occurs naturally within: (1) 500 miles (804.7 km) of the construction site if transported by truck, or (2) 1,500 miles (2,414 km) of the construction site if transported for not less than 80% of the total transport distance by rail or water. Products that are assembled or produced from multiple raw materials are considered regional materials if the weighted average (by weight or volume) of the distance the raw materials have been transported meet the distance criteria.

REMODELING. The process of restoring or improving an existing building, dwelling unit, sleeping unit, or property.

RENEWABLE ENERGY. Energy derived from renewable energy sources.

RENEWABLE ENERGY SOURCE. Energy derived from solar radiation, wind, hydropower, waves, tides, biogas, biomass, or geothermal energy.

REPLACEMENT. The act or process of replacing material or systems.

REUSE. To divert a construction material, product, component, module, or a building from the construction and demolition waste stream, without recycling the material, in order to use it again.

SEDIMENT CONTROLS. Practices used on building sites to minimize the movement of sand, soil, and particulates or dust from construction from reaching waterways.

SEER (Seasonal Energy Efficiency Ratio). The total cooling output of an electric air conditioner (or heat pump) during its normal annual usage period for cooling, in Btu, divided by the total electric energy input during the same period, in watt-hours (Wh), expressed as Btu/Wh. SEER is the cooling performance equivalent measurement of HSPF.

SHGC (Solar Heat Gain Coefficient). The ratio of the solar heat gain entering the space through the fenestration assembly to the incident solar radiation. Solar heat gain includes directly transmitted solar heat and absorbed solar radiation which is then reradiated, conducted, or convected into the space.

SIP (Structural Insulated Panel). A structural sandwich panel that consists of a light-weight foam plastic core securely laminated between two thin, rigid wood structural panel facings; a structural panel that consists of lightweight foam plastic and cold-formed steel sheet or structural cold-formed steel members; or other similar non-interrupted structural panels.

SITE. Any area of land that is or will be developed into two or more parcels of land intended for multiple ownership, uses, or structures and designed to be part of an integrated whole such as a residential subdivision, mixed-use development, or master-planned community. Site, as defined, generally contains multiple lots. (Also see LOT)

SLEEPING UNIT. A room or space in which people sleep, which can also include permanent provisions for living, eating, and either sanitation or kitchen facilities but not both. Such rooms and spaces that are also part of a dwelling unit are not sleeping units.

SMART APPLIANCE. A product that has the capability to receive, interpret, and act on a signal transmitted by a utility, third-party energy service provider, or home energy management device, and automatically adjust its operation depending on both the signal's contents and settings by the consumer. The product has this capability either built-in or added through an external device that easily connects to the appliance.

SOLID FUEL-BURNING APPLIANCE. A chimney connected device designed for purposes of heating, cooking, or both that burns solid fuel.

STEEP SLOPES. Slopes equal to or greater than 25 percent (≥ 25%).

STORY. That portion of a building included between the upper surface of a floor and the upper surface of the floor or roof next above.

STORY ABOVE GRADE. Any story having its finished floor surface entirely above grade plane, or in which the finished surface of the floor next above is:

- More than 6 ft. (1829 mm) above grade plane; or
- More than 12 ft. (3658 mm) above the finished ground level at any point.

STRUCTURAL SYSTEMS. Load-bearing elements and systems that transfer lateral and vertical loads to the foundation and may include, but are not limited to, load-bearing walls (interior or exterior), roofs, and other structural elements.

SUBDIVISION. A tract, lot, or parcel of land divided into two or more lots, plats, sites, or other divisions of land.

SWPPP (Stormwater Pollution Prevention Plan). A site-specific, written document or report that identifies required features specifically represented in the National Pollutant Discharge Elimination System (NPDES) Construction General Permit (CGP).

TERRAIN ADAPTIVE ARCHITECTURE. Architecture or landscape architecture where the design of the building or site has been specifically adapted to preserve unique features of the terrain.

UA. The total U-factor times area for a component or building.

URBAN. Areas within a designated census tract of 1,000 people per square mile or located within a Metropolitan Statistical Area primary city, as designated by the U.S. Census Bureau.

U-FACTOR (THERMAL TRANSMITTANCE). The coefficient of heat transmission (air to air) through a building envelope component or assembly, equal to the time rate of heat flow per unit area and unit temperature difference between the warm side and cold side air films (Btu/h • ft^2 • °F) [W/(m^2 • K)].

VAPOR RETARDER CLASS. A measure of the ability of a material or assembly to limit the amount of moisture that passes through that material or assembly. Vapor retarder class shall be defined using the desiccant method with Procedure A of ASTM E 96 as follows:

- Class I: 0.1 perm or less
- Class II: 0.1 < perm = 1.0 perm
- Class III: 1.0 < perm = 10 perm

VENTILATION. The natural or mechanical process of supplying conditioned or unconditioned air to, or removing such air from, any space.

VENTILATION AIR. That portion of supply air that comes from the outside (outdoors) plus any recirculated air that has been treated to maintain the desired quality of air within a designation space.

VOC (VOLATILE ORGANIC COMPOUNDS). A class of carbon-based molecules in substances and organic compounds that readily release gaseous vapors at room temperature as indoor pollutants and when reacting with other exterior pollutants can produce ground-level ozone.

WASTE HEAT. Heat discharged as a byproduct of one process to provide heat needed by a second process.

WATER FACTOR. The quantity of water, in gallons per cycle (Q), divided by a clothes washing machine clothes container capacity in cubic feet (C). The equation is WF=Q/C.

WATER-RESISTIVE BARRIER. A material behind an exterior wall covering that is intended to resist liquid water that has penetrated behind the exterior covering from further intruding into the exterior wall assembly.

WETLANDS. Areas that are inundated or saturated by the surface or groundwater at a frequency and duration sufficient to support, and that under normal circumstances do support, a prevalence of vegetation typically adapted for life in saturated soil conditions.

WILDLIFE HABITAT/CORRIDOR. An ecological or environmental area that is inhabited by a particular species of animal, plant, or other type of organism. It is the natural environment in which an organism lives or the physical environment that surrounds (influences and is utilized by) a species population.

WOOD-BASED PRODUCT. Any material that consists of a majority of wood or constituents derived from wood (e.g., wood fiber) as measured by either weight or volume.

SECTION 3

COMPLIANCE METHOD

301 GENERAL

301.1 Environmental rating levels. The building, project, site, and/or development environmental rating level shall consist of all mandatory requirements plus points assessed using the point system specified within this chapter. The rating level shall be in accordance with § 302, § 303, § 304, or § 305, as applicable. The designation for accessory structures shall be in accordance with § 306.

301.1.1 Non-residential spaces. Non-residential spaces in mixed-use buildings shall comply with Chapter 13 (Commercial Spaces) of this Standard or ICC IgCC Section 501.3.7.2 and Chapters 6-10, excluding Section 6.3.1.

301.2 Awarding of points. Points shall be awarded as follows:

(1) The maximum number of points that can be awarded for each practice is noted with that practice.

(2) Point allocation for multifamily buildings shall be as prescribed in § 304.

(3) The Adopting Entity shall allow the use of new and innovative products and practices deemed to meet the intent of this Standard. Points assigned for any new product or practice shall be determined by the Adopting Entity. A maximum of 20 points may be awarded at the discretion of the Adopting Entity. Innovative practices and products shall fall under Chapters 5-10 (Categories 1-6 in Table 303). Point values shall be determined by comparing the innovative product or practice to a product or practice already described in the Standard. The applicant shall supply demonstrable, quantified data to support the innovative product or practice and to determine the practice's functional equivalent in the Standard for the points to be awarded.

302 GREEN SUBDIVISIONS

302.1 Site design and development. The threshold points required for the environmental rating levels to qualify a new or existing subdivision as green under this Standard shall be in accordance with Table 302 and based on points in Chapter 4.

302.1.1 Site design and development obtaining thresholds in Table 302 are permitted to be verified, certified, and marketed as such prior to the verification of green buildings.

302.1.2 Developments are permitted to be marketed as a green subdivision. Developer shall provide clear explanation that the rating only applies to the development and not the buildings.

303 GREEN BUILDINGS

303.1 Compliance options. The criteria for new buildings shall be in accordance with § 303.2 for residential buildings, the residential portion of mixed-use buildings, or mixed-use buildings or § 303.3 for compliance for single-family homes, townhomes, and duplexes.

303.2 Buildings. The threshold points required for the environmental rating levels for a green building shall be in accordance with Table 303. To qualify for one of these rating levels, all of the following shall be satisfied:

(1) The threshold number of points, in accordance with Table 303, shall be achieved as prescribed in Categories 1 through 6. The lowest level achieved in any category shall determine the overall rating level achieved for the building.

(2) In addition to the threshold number of points in each category, all mandatory provisions of each category shall be implemented.

(3) In addition to the threshold number of points prescribed in Categories 1 through 6 (which corresponds to Chapters 5-10), the additional points prescribed in Category 7 shall be achieved from any

Table 302
Threshold Point Ratings for Site Design and Development

Green Subdivision Category		Rating Level Points			
		One Star	Two Stars	Three Stars	Four Stars
Chapter 4	Site Design and Development	95	122	149	176

Table 303
Threshold Point Ratings for Green Buildings

Green Building Categories			Rating Level Points [a] [b]			
			BRONZE	SILVER	GOLD	EMERALD
1.	Chapter 5	Lot Design, Preparation, and Development	50	64	93	121
2.	Chapter 6	Resource Efficiency	43	59	89	119
3.	Chapter 7	Energy Efficiency	30	45	60	70
4.	Chapter 8	Water Efficiency	25	39	67	92
5.	Chapter 9	Indoor Environmental Quality	25	42	69	97
6.	Chapter 10	Operation, Maintenance, and Building Owner Education	8	10	11	12
7.		Additional Points from Any Category	50	75	100	100
		Total Points:	231	334	489	611

[a] In addition to the threshold number of points in each category, all mandatory provisions of each category shall be implemented.

[b] For dwelling units greater than 4,000 sq. ft. (372 m²), the number of points in Category 7 (Additional Points from Any Category) shall be increased in accordance with Section 601.1. The "Total Points" shall be increased by the same number of points.

of the categories. Where deemed appropriate by the Adopting Entity based on regional conditions, additional points from Category 7 may be assigned to another category (or categories) to increase the threshold points required for that category (or categories). Points shall not be reduced by the Adopting Entity in any of the six other categories.

Exception: Where the builder is unable to control a majority of items in Chapter 5 due to timing and lack of relationship to the Lot Design, Preparation, and Development, green ratings on the home are permitted to be obtained by eliminating rating requirements and points from Chapter 5. Rating threshold requirements are permitted to be adjusted accordingly. Builders shall provide evidence of this impossibility to the Adopting Entity and provide disclaimer statement on marketing materials when this occurs.

303.3 Single-family homes, townhomes, and duplexes. Single-family homes, townhomes, and duplexes that meet all applicable requirements of Chapter 12 shall be deemed Certified.

304 GREEN MULTIFAMILY BUILDINGS

304.1 Multifamily buildings. All residential portions of a building shall meet the requirements of this Standard. Partial compliance shall not be allowed. Unless specifically addressed in other portions of this standard, all dwelling and sleeping units and residential common areas within a multifamily building shall meet all mandatory requirements. Where features similar to dwelling unit/sleeping unit features are installed in the common area, those features shall meet the standard of the dwelling and sleeping units. Green building practices for residential common areas may differ from

requirements for dwelling units/sleeping units. Points for the green building practices that apply to multiple units shall be credited once for the entire building. Where points are credited, including where a weighted average is used, practices shall be implemented in all dwelling and sleeping units, as applicable. Where application of a prescribed practice allows for a different number of points for different dwelling and sleeping units in a multifamily building, the fewer number of points shall be awarded, unless noted that a weighted average is used.

304.2 Alternative IgCC compliance. As an alternative, any multifamily or mixed-use building that complies with the ICC IgCC shall be designated as achieving the gold rating level. Additionally, acceptable air tightness of individual residential units shall be demonstrated by a blower door test. The testing and sampling procedure shall be in accordance with the ENERGY STAR Multifamily High Rise Program Testing and Verification Protocols, Version 1.0, Revision 03 - 2015, with an allowable maximum leakage of 0.3 cfm/sf of enclosure bounding the apartment at an induced pressure difference of 50 pascals.

305 GREEN REMODELING

305.1 Compliance. Compliance with § 305 shall be voluntary unless specifically adopted as mandatory by the Adopting Entity.

305.2 Whole-building rating criteria

305.2.1 Applicability. The provisions of § 305.2 shall apply to remodeling of existing buildings. In addition to the foundation, at least 50% of the structural systems of the existing building shall remain in place after the remodel for the building to be eligible for compliance under § 305.2. Recent new construction projects are not eligible for verification under the remodel path. Projects that would be eligible must have their Certificate of Occupancy at least 5 years prior to NGBS registration.

305.2.1.1 Additions. For a remodeled building that includes an addition, the entire building including the addition shall comply with the criteria of § 305.2. The total above-grade conditioned area added during a remodel shall not exceed 75% of the existing building's above-grade conditioned area. For multifamily buildings, the above-grade conditioned area shall be based on the entire building including all dwelling units/sleeping units and common areas.

305.2.2 Rating scope. The building rating achieved under § 305.2 and the associated compliance criteria apply to the entire building after the remodel including any additions.

305.2.3 Mandatory practices. Additions, alterations or repairs to an existing building, building system or portion thereof shall comply with the Mandatory requirements of Chapter 11. Unaltered portions of the existing building shall not be required to meet Mandatory requirements except when life safety or apparent moisture issues exist.

305.2.4 Rating level. A minimum rating level of Bronze shall be achieved in each of the following categories: Energy efficiency § 305.2.5), Water efficiency (§ 305.2.6), and Prescriptive practices (§ 305.2.7). The building rating level shall be the lowest rating level achieved in § 305.2.5, § 305.2.6, and § 305.2.7.

305.2.5 Energy efficiency. The building shall comply with § 305.2.5.1 or § 305.2.5.2.

305.2.5.1 Energy consumption reduction path. The energy efficiency rating level shall be based on the reduction in energy consumption resulting from the remodel in accordance with Table 305.2.5.1.

The reduction in energy consumption resulting from the remodel shall be based on the estimated annual energy cost savings or source energy savings as determined by a third-party energy audit and analysis or utility consumption data. The reduction shall be the percentage difference between the consumption per square foot before and after the remodel calculated as follows:

[(consumption per square foot before remodel – consumption per square foot after remodel)/ consumption per square foot before remodel]*100

The occupancy and lifestyle assumed and the method of making the energy consumption estimates shall be the same for estimates before and after the remodel. The building configuration for the after-remodel estimate shall include any additions to the building or other changes to the configuration of the conditioned space. For multifamily buildings, the energy consumption shall be based on the entire building including all dwelling units/sleeping units and common areas.

If a building can demonstrate through documentation approved by the Adopting Entity that the remodel activities started prior to project registration, the energy baseline (consumption per square foot before remodel) can be calculated based on data and building systems that was existing in the building up to 3 years prior project registration.

305.2.5.2 Prescriptive path. The building shall comply with Table 305.2.5.2 (Energy Rating Prescriptive Point Thresholds). Any practice listed in § 11.703 shall be eligible for contributing points toward Table 305.2.5.2 (Energy Rating Prescriptive Point Thresholds). The attributes of the existing building that were in compliance with the prescriptive practices of in § 11.703 prior to the remodel and remain in compliance after the remodel shall be eligible for contributing points to this section.

A building complying with § 305.2.5.2 Prescriptive Path for Energy shall obtain at least 30 points from § 11.703 and include a minimum of two practices from § 11.705.

Table 305.2.5.1
Energy Reduction Level Thresholds

	Rating Level			
	BRONZE	**SILVER**	**GOLD**	**EMERALD**
Reduction in energy consumption	15%	25%	35%	45%

Table 305.2.5.2
Energy Prescriptive Point Thresholds

	Rating Level			
	BRONZE	**SILVER**	**GOLD**	**EMERALD**
Section 11.703 prescriptive thresholds	30	45	60	70
Points from § 11.703. and § 11.706 shall not count towards the total points for § 305.2.7.				

Table 305.2.6.1
Water Reduction Level Thresholds

	Rating Level			
	BRONZE	**SILVER**	**GOLD**	**EMERALD**
Reduction in water consumption	20%	30%	40%	50%

Table 305.2.6.2
Water Prescriptive Point Thresholds

	Rating Level			
	BRONZE	**SILVER**	**GOLD**	**EMERALD**
Section 11.800 prescriptive thresholds	25	39	67	92
Points from § 11.801 through § 11.803 shall not count toward the total points for § 305.2.7.				

Points earned in § 11.705 and § 11.706 contribute to the energy points in Table 305.2.5.2 and support earning a higher certification level. Points from § 11.703, § 11.705 and § 11.706 do not count towards the required points in Table 305.2.7.

305.2.6 Water efficiency. The building shall comply with § 305.2.6.1 or § 305.2.6.2.

305.2.6.1 Water consumption reduction path. The water efficiency rating level shall be based on the reduction in water consumption resulting from the remodel in accordance with Table 305.2.6.1.

Water consumption shall be based on the estimated annual use as determined by a third-party audit and analysis or use of utility consumption data. The reduction shall be the percentage difference between the consumption before and after the remodel calculated as follows:

$$[(\text{consumption before remodel} - \text{consumption after remodel})/\text{consumption before remodel}]*100\%$$

The occupancy and lifestyle assumed and the method of making the water consumption estimates shall be the same for estimates before and after the remodel. The building configuration for the after-remodel estimate shall include any changes to the configuration of the building such as additions or new points of water use. For multifamily buildings, the water consumption shall be based on the entire building including all dwelling units and common areas.

Where a building can demonstrate through documentation approved by the Adopting Entity that the remodel activities started prior to project registration, the water baseline (consumption before remodel) shall be calculated based on data and building systems that existed in the building up to 3 years prior project registration.

305.2.6.2. Prescriptive path. The building shall comply with Table 305.2.6.2 (Water Rating Prescriptive Point Thresholds). Any practice listed in § 11.801 shall be eligible for contributing points toward Table 305.2.6.2 (Water Rating Prescriptive Point Thresholds). The attributes of the existing building that were in compliance with the prescriptive practices of in § 11.802 prior to the remodel and remain in compliance after the remodel shall be eligible for contributing points to this section.

305.2.7 Prescriptive practices. The point thresholds for the environmental rating levels based on compliance with the Chapter 11 prescriptive practices shall be in accordance with Table 305.2.7. Any practice listed in Chapter 11, except for § 11.701 through § 11.706 and § 11.801 through § 11.803 shall be eligible for contributing points to the prescriptive threshold ratings. The attributes of the existing building that were in compliance with the prescriptive practices of Chapter 11 prior to the remodel and remain in compliance after the remodel shall be eligible for contributing points to the prescriptive threshold ratings.

306 GREEN ACCESSORY STRUCTURES

306.1 Applicability. The designation criteria for accessory structures shall be in accordance with Appendix C.

306.2 Compliance. Compliance with Appendix C shall be voluntary unless specifically adopted as mandatory. If specifically adopted, the adopting entity shall establish rules for compliance with Appendix C.

Table 305.2.7
Prescriptive Threshold Point Ratings

	Rating Level			
	BRONZE	**SILVER**	**GOLD**	**EMERALD**
Chapter 11 prescriptive thresholds	88	125	181	225

SECTION 4

SITE DESIGN AND DEVELOPMENT

GREEN BUILDING PRACTICES	POINTS

400   SITE DESIGN AND DEVELOPMENT

400.0 Intent. This section applies to land development for the eventual construction of buildings or additions thereto that contain dwelling units/sleeping units. The rating earned under § 302 based on practices herein, applies only to the site as defined in Chapter 2. The buildings on the site achieve a separate rating level or designation by complying with the provisions of § 303, § 304, § 305, or § 306, as applicable.

401   SITE SELECTION

401.0 Intent. The site is selected to minimize environmental impact by one or more of the following:

401.1 Infill site. An infill site is selected. **7**

401.2 Greyfield site. A greyfield site is selected. **7**

401.3 Brownfield site. A brownfield site is selected. **8**

402   PROJECT TEAM, MISSION STATEMENT, AND GOALS

402.0 Intent. The site is designed and constructed by a team of qualified professionals trained in green development practices.

402.1 Team. A knowledgeable team is established and team member roles are identified with respect to green lot design, preparation, and development. The project's green goals and objectives are written into a mission statement. **4**

402.2 Training. Training is provided to on-site supervisors and team members regarding the green development practices to be used on the project. **3**

402.3 Project checklist. A checklist of green development practices to be used on the project is created, followed, and completed by the project team regarding the site. .... **M 4**

402.4 Development agreements. Through a developer agreement or equivalent, the developer requires purchasers of lots to construct the buildings in compliance with this Standard (or equivalent) certified to a minimum Bronze rating level. **6**

403   SITE DESIGN

403.0 Intent. The project is designed to avoid detrimental environmental impacts, minimize any unavoidable impacts, and mitigate impacts that do occur. The project is designed to minimize environmental impacts and to protect, restore, and enhance the natural features and environmental quality of the site.

To acquire points allocated for the design, the intent of the design is implemented.

GREEN BUILDING PRACTICES	M=Mandatory POINTS

403.1 Natural resources. Natural resources are conserved by one or more of the following:

(1) A natural resources inventory is used to create the site plan. .... **M 5**

(2) A plan to protect and maintain priority natural resources/areas during construction is created. (Also see § 404 for guidance in forming the plan.) .... **M 5**

(3) Member of builder's project team participates in a natural resources conservation program. **4**

(4) Streets, buildings, and other built features are located to conserve high priority vegetation. **5**

(5) Developer has a plan for removal or containment of invasive plants, as identified by a qualified professional, from the disturbed areas of the site. **3**

(6) Developer has a plan for removal or containment of invasive plants, as identified by a qualified professional, on the undisturbed areas of the site. **6**

403.2 Building orientation. A minimum of 75% of the building sites are designed with the longer dimension of the structure to face within 20 degrees of south. **6**

403.3 Slope disturbance. Slope disturbance is minimized by one or more of the following:

(1) Hydrological/soil stability study is completed and used to guide the design of all buildings on the site. **5**

(2) All or a percentage of roads are aligned with natural topography to reduce cut and fill.

    (a) greater than or equal to 10% to less than 25% **1**

    (b) greater than or equal to 25% to less than 75% **4**

    (c) greater than 75% **6**

(3) Long-term erosion effects are reduced by the use of clustering, terracing, retaining walls, landscaping, and restabilization techniques. **6**

403.4 Soil disturbance and erosion. A site Stormwater Pollution Prevention Plan (SWPPP) is developed in accordance with applicable stormwater Construction General Permits. The plan includes one or more of the following:

(1) Construction activities are scheduled to minimize length of time that soils are exposed. **4**

(2) Utilities are installed by alternate means such as directional boring in lieu of open-cut trenching. Shared easements or common utility trenches are utilized to minimize earth disturbance. Low ground pressure equipment or temporary matting is used to minimize excessive soil consolidation. ... **5**

(3) Limits of clearing and grading are demarcated. **4**

403.5 Stormwater management. The stormwater management system is designed to use low-impact development/green infrastructure practices to preserve, restore or mitigate changes in site hydrology due to land disturbance and the construction of impermeable surfaces through the use of one or more of the following techniques:

(1) A site assessment is conducted and a plan prepared and implemented that identifies important existing permeable soils, natural drainage ways and other water features, e.g., depressional storage, onsite to be preserved in order to maintain site hydrology. **7**

	M=Mandatory
GREEN BUILDING PRACTICES	**POINTS**

(2) A hydrologic analysis is conducted that results in the design and installation of a stormwater management system that maintains the predevelopment (stable, natural) runoff hydrology of the site through the development or redevelopment process. Ensure that post construction runoff rate, volume and duration do not exceed predevelopment rates, volume and duration. **10**

(3) Low-Impact Development/Green infrastructure stormwater management practices to promote infiltration and evapotranspiration are used to manage rainfall on the lot and prevent the off-lot discharge of runoff from all storms up to and including the volume of following storm events:

    (a) 80th percentile storm event **5**

    (b) 90th percentile storm event **8**

    (c) 95th percentile storm event **10**

(4) Permeable materials are used for driveways, parking areas, walkways and patios according to the following percentages:

Points for vegetative paving systems are only awarded for location receiving more than 20 in. per year of annual average precipitation.

    (a) greater than or equal to 10% to less than 25% (add 2 points for use of vegetative paving system) **2**

    (b) greater than or equal to 25 to less than 50% (add 4 points for use of vegetative paving system) ... **5**

    (c) greater than or equal to 50% (add 6 points for use of vegetative paving system) **10**

403.6 Landscape plan. A landscape plan is developed to limit water and energy use in common areas while preserving or enhancing the natural environment utilizing one or more of the following:

(1) A plan is formulated to restore or enhance natural vegetation that is cleared during construction. Landscaping is phased to coincide with achievement of final grades to ensure denuded areas are quickly vegetated. **6**

(2) On-site native or regionally appropriate trees and shrubs are conserved, maintained, and reused for landscaping to the greatest extent possible. **6**

(3) Non–invasive vegetation that is native or regionally appropriate for local growing conditions is selected to promote biodiversity. **7**

(4) EPA WaterSense Water Budget Tool or equivalent is used when implementing the site vegetative design. **10**

(5) Where turf is being planted, Turfgrass Water Conservation Alliance (TWCA) or equivalent third-party qualified water efficient grasses are used. **6**

(6) For landscaped vegetated areas, the maximum percentage of all turf areas is:

    (a) 0% **10**

    (b) greater than 0% to less than or equal to 20%... **8**

    (c) greater than 20% to less than or equal to 40%... **6**

    (d) greater than 40% to less than or equal to 60%... **4**

(7) To improve pollinator habitat, at least 10% of planted areas are composed of flowering and nectar producing plant species. Invasive plant species shall not be utilized. **6**

(8) Non-potable irrigation water is available to common areas **2**

M=Mandatory

GREEN BUILDING PRACTICES	POINTS

(9) Non-potable irrigation water is available to lots. **4**

(10) Plants with similar watering needs are grouped (hydrozoning). **4**

(11) Species and locations for tree planting are identified and utilized to increase summer shading of streets, parking areas, and buildings and to moderate temperatures. **5**

(12) Vegetative wind breaks or channels are designed as appropriate to local conditions. **4**

(13) On-site tree trimmings or stump grinding of regionally appropriate trees are used to provide protective mulch during construction or as base for walking trails, and cleared trees are recycled as sawn lumber or pulp wood. **4**

(14) An integrated common area pest management plan to minimize chemical use in pesticides and fertilizers is developed. **4**

(15) Plans for the common area landscape watering system include a weather-based or soil moisture-based controller. Required irrigation systems are designed in accordance with the IA Landscape Irrigation Best Management Practices **6**

(16) Trees that might otherwise be lost due to site construction are transplanted to other areas on-site or off-site using tree-transplanting techniques to ensure a high rate of survival. **4**

(17) Greywater irrigation systems are used to water common areas. Greywater used for irrigation conforms to all criteria of § 803.1. .... **7**

(18) Cisterns, rain barrels, and similar tanks are designed to intercept and store runoff. These systems may be above or below ground, and they may drain by gravity or be pumped. Stored water may be slowly released to a pervious area, and/or used for irrigation of lawn, trees, and gardens located in common areas. **6**

(19) Spray irrigation

    (a) Is not present on slopes steeper than 25% (i.e., where the land rises more than 1 ft. vertically for every 4 ft. horizontally). **2**

    (b) Has been tested in accordance with the ASABE/ICC 802, "Landscape Irrigation Sprinkler and Emitter Standard" and there is documentation of the sprinklers achieving a lower quarter distribution uniformity of at least 0.65. .... **2**

    (c) Is installed to eliminate low head/point drainage and runoff. **2**

    (d) Spray irrigation is not used **6**

403.7 Wildlife habitat.

(1) Measures are planned that will support wildlife habitat. **6**

(2) The site is adjacent to a wildlife corridor, fish and game park, or preserved areas and is designed with regard for this relationship. **3**

(3) Outdoor lighting techniques are utilized with regard for wildlife. **3**

403.8 Operation and maintenance plan. An operation and maintenance plan (manual) is prepared and outlines ongoing service of common open area, utilities (storm water, waste water), and environmental management activities. **6**

M=Mandatory

GREEN BUILDING PRACTICES	POINTS

403.9 Existing buildings. Following mitigation of any harmful materials, existing building(s) and structure(s) is/are preserved and reused, adapted, or disassembled for reuse or recycling of building materials.

(1) Building reuse or adaptation... **12**

(2) Disassemble for reuse or recycling of building materials. **10**

403.10 Existing and recycled materials. Existing pavements, curbs, and aggregates are salvaged and reincorporated into the development or recycled asphalt or concrete materials are used as follows. *[Points awarded for every 10% of total materials used for pavement, curb, and aggregate that meet the criteria of this practice. The percentage is consistently calculated on a weight, volume, or cost basis.]* .... **15 max**

(1) Existing pavements, curbs, and aggregates are reincorporated into the development. **3**

(2) Recycled asphalt or concrete with at least 50% recycled content is utilized in the project. **2**

403.11 Demolition of existing building. A demolition waste management plan is developed, posted at the jobsite, and implemented to recycle and/or salvage for reuse a minimum of 50% of the nonhazardous demolition waste.
[1 additional point awarded for every 10% of nonhazardous demolition waste recycled and/or salvaged beyond 50%.]... **5 [10 max]**

403.12 Environmentally sensitive areas. Environmentally sensitive areas are as follows:

(1) Environmentally sensitive areas are avoided as follows:

    (a) less than 25% of environmentally sensitive areas left undeveloped... **2**

    (b) greater than or equal to 25% to less than 75% of environmentally sensitive areas left undeveloped **4**

    (c) greater than or equal to 75% of environmentally sensitive areas left undeveloped **7**

(2) Environmentally sensitive areas are permanently protected by a conservation easement or similar mechanism. **10**

404   SITE DEVELOPMENT AND CONSTRUCTION

404.0 Intent. Environmental impact during construction is avoided to the extent possible; impacts that do occur are minimized, and any significant impacts are mitigated.

404.1 On-site supervision and coordination. On-site supervision and coordination is provided during clearing, grading, trenching, paving, and installation of utilities to ensure that specified green development practices are implemented. (also see § 403.4) **5**

404.2 Trees and vegetation. Designated trees and vegetation are preserved by one or more of the following:

(1) Fencing or equivalent is installed to protect trees and other vegetation... **4**

(2) Trenching, significant changes in grade, compaction of soil, and other activities are avoided in critical root zones (canopy drip line) in "tree save" areas... **5**

(3) Damage to designated existing trees and vegetation is mitigated during construction through pruning, root pruning, fertilizing, and watering... **4**

	M=Mandatory
GREEN BUILDING PRACTICES	**POINTS**

404.3 Soil disturbance and erosion. On-site soil disturbance and erosion are minimized by implementation of one or more of the following:

(1) Limits of clearing and grading are staked out prior to construction.	5
(2) "No disturbance" zones are created using fencing or flagging to protect vegetation and sensitive areas from construction vehicles, material storage, and washout.	4
(3) Sediment and erosion controls are installed and maintained.	5
(4) Topsoil is stockpiled and covered with tarps, straw, mulch, chipped wood, vegetative cover, or other means capable of protecting it from erosion for later use to establish landscape plantings.	5
(5) Soil compaction from construction equipment is reduced by distributing the weight of the equipment over a larger area by laying lightweight geogrids, mulch, chipped wood, plywood, OSB (oriented strand board), metal plates, or other materials capable of weight distribution in the pathway of the equipment.	4
(6) Disturbed areas are stabilized within the EPA-recommended 14-day period.	4
(7) Soil is improved with organic amendments and mulch.	4

404.4 Wildlife habitat. Measures are implemented to support wildlife habitat.

(1) Wildlife habitat is maintained.	5
(2) Measures are instituted to establish or promote wildlife habitat.	5
(3) Open space is preserved as part of a wildlife corridor.	6
(4) Builder or member of builder's project team participates in a wildlife conservation program.	5

405   INNOVATIVE PRACTICES

405.0 Intent. Innovative site design, preparation, and development practices are used to enhance environmental performance. Waivers or variances from local development regulations are obtained, and innovative zoning practices are used to implement such practices, as applicable.

405.1 Driveways and parking areas. Driveways and parking areas are minimized or mitigated by one or more of the following:

(1) Off-street parking areas are shared or driveways are shared; on-street parking is utilized; and alleys (shared common area driveways) are used for rear-loaded garages.	5
(2) In multifamily projects, parking capacity is not to exceed the local minimum requirements.	5
(3) Structured parking is utilized to reduce the footprint of surface parking areas.	
(a) greater than or equal to 25% to less than 50%	3
(b) greater than or equal to 50% to less than 75%	5
(c) greater than 75%	8

M=Mandatory

GREEN BUILDING PRACTICES	POINTS

405.2 Street widths.

(1) Street pavement widths are minimized per local code and are in accordance with Table 405.2. .... **6**

Table 405.2
Maximum Street Widths

Facility Type	Maximum Width
Collector street with parking (one side only)	31 feet
Collector street without parking	26 feet
Local access with parking (one side only)	27 feet
Local access street without parking	20 feet
Queuing (one-lane) streets with parking	24 feet
Alleys and queuing (one-lane) streets without parking	17 feet

For SI: 1 foot = 304.8 mm

(2) A waiver was secured by the developer from the local jurisdiction to allow for construction of streets below minimum width requirement. **8**

405.3 Cluster development. Cluster development enables and encourages flexibility of design and development of land in such a manner as to preserve the natural and scenic qualities of the site by utilizing an alternative method for the layout, configuration and design of lots, buildings and structures, roads, utility lines and other infrastructure, parks, and landscaping. **10**

405.4 Planning. Innovative planning techniques are implemented in accordance with the following:

(1) Innovative planning techniques are used or developed for permissible adjustments to population density, area, height, open space, mixed-use, or other provisions for the specific purpose of open space, natural resource preservation or protection and/or mass transit usage. Other innovative planning techniques may be considered on a case-by-case basis. **10**

(2) Provide common or public spaces of a minimum of 1/6 acre that are within 1/4 mile walk to 80% of planned and existing units and entrances to non-residential buildings. Both existing and newly constructed squares, parks, paseos, plazas, and similar uses qualify under this criterion. **10**

405.5 Wetlands. Constructed wetlands or other natural innovative wastewater or stormwater treatment technologies are used. **8**

405.6 Multi-modal transportation. Multi-modal transportation access is provided in accordance with one or more of the following:

(1) A site is selected with a boundary within one-half mile (805 m) of pedestrian access to a mass transit system or within five miles of a mass transit station with available parking. **5**

(2) A site is selected where all lots within the site are located within one-half mile (805 m) of pedestrian access to a mass transit system. **7**

(3) A system of walkways, bikeways, street crossings, or pathways designed to promote connectivity to existing and planned community amenities are provided.

   (a) Create a network of sidewalks and paths that provide a minimum level of connectivity of at least 90 bikeway or pathway intersections per square mile. **5**

   (b) Create a network of sidewalks and paths that provide a minimum level of connectivity of at least 140 bikeway or pathway intersections per square mile. **10**

GREEN BUILDING PRACTICES	M=Mandatory POINTS

(4) Dedicated bicycle parking and racks are indicated on the site plan and a minimum of six spaces are constructed for, multifamily buildings, and/or each developed common area.
[1 point awarded for every 6 spaces] .... **1 [6 max]**

(5) Bike sharing programs participate with the developer and facilities for bike sharing are planned for and constructed... **5**

(6) Car sharing programs participate with the developer and facilities for car sharing are planned for and constructed... **5**

(7) A site is selected within a census block group that, compared to its region, has above-average transit access to employment as calculated using the Transit Access Measures within the EPA's Smart Location Database:

    (a) Access is within the top quartile for the region **10**

    (b) Access is within the second quartile for the region **4**

(8) A site is selected within a census block group that, compared to its region, has above-average access to employment within a 45-minute drive as calculated using EPA's Smart Location Database:

    (a) Access is within the top quartile for the region **6**

    (b) Access is within the second quartile for the region **2**

405.7 Density. The average density on a net developable area basis is:

(1) greater than or equal to 7 to less than 14 dwelling units/sleeping units per acre (per 4,047 m²)........... **5**

(2) greater than or equal to 14 to less than 21 dwelling units/sleeping units per acre (per 4,047 m²)......... **7**

(3) greater than or equal to 21 dwelling units/sleeping units per acre (per 4,047 m²) **10**

405.8 Mixed-use development. (1) Mixed-use development is incorporated, or (2) for single-use sites 20 acres or less in size, 80% of the units are within 1/2 mile walk of 5 non-residential uses and where a system of walkways, bikeways, street crossings or pathways is designed to promote connectivity to those uses. **9**

405.9 Open space. The community is situated within 1/2 mile of an area of open space available to the public or a portion of the gross area of the community is set aside as open space.
[Points awarded for every 10% of the community set aside as open space. If open space outside of the community is included, a maximum of 3 points are awarded.] **2**

405.10 Community garden(s). Local food production for residents or area consumers. ....

    (a) A portion of the site of at least 250 sq. ft. is established as a community garden(s) for the residents of the site. *[1 point awarded per 250 sq. ft.]* .... **1 [3 max]**

    (b) Areas and physical provisions are provided for composting **1**

    (c) Signs designating the garden are posted **1**

M=Mandatory

GREEN BUILDING PRACTICES	POINTS

405.11 Insect mitigation. The site is designed to mitigate hazards from insect born disease.

To acquire points, the site must be documented to be at risk by an epidemiologist or qualified professional.

(a) Dense plant beds, shrubbery and woody plants are not planted within 5 ft. (1.5 m) of occupied buildings. **6**

(b) A minimum of a 5 ft. (1.5 m) border of paving, mulch, bare earth, or turfgrass is provided between woods or weedy areas and people trafficked or occupied areas, including playgrounds and dog parks. **5**

(c) Vegetation that is attractive to deer, as documented by a qualified professional, is not planted within 20 ft. (6 m) of buildings. **3**

(d) Paths or trails maintained through natural or non-maintained areas are a minimum of 5 ft. wide (1.5 m). **3**

(e) Conditions that are favorable to mosquito breeding, such as standing water, are not present on site. **2**

405.12 Smoking prohibitions. Signs are provided prohibiting smoking at the following locations:

(a) Smoking is prohibited within 25 ft. (7.5 m) of all building exterior doors and operable windows or building air intakes within 15 vertical feet (4.5 m) of grade or a walking surface. **3**

(b) Smoking is prohibited in common areas unless otherwise designated as smoking areas. **3**

INTENTIONALLY LEFT BLANK.

SECTION 5

LOT DESIGN, PREPARATION, AND DEVELOPMENT

GREEN BUILDING PRACTICES	POINTS

500   LOT DESIGN, PREPARATION, AND DEVELOPMENT

500.0 Intent. This section applies to lot development for the eventual construction of residential buildings, multifamily buildings, or additions thereto that contain dwelling units or sleeping units.

501 LOT SELECTION

501.1 Lot. Lot is selected in accordance with § 501.1(1) or § 501.1(2).

(1) A lot is selected within a site certified to this Standard or equivalent	15
(2) A lot is selected to minimize environmental impact by one or more of the following:	
(a) An infill lot is selected.	10
(b) A lot is selected that is a greyfield.	10
(c) An EPA-recognized brownfield lot is selected.	15

501.2 Multi-modal transportation. A range of multi-modal transportation choices are promoted by one or more of the following:

(1) A lot is selected within one-half mile (805 m) of pedestrian access to a mass transit system	6
(2) A lot is selected within five miles (8,046 m) of a mass transit station with provisions for parking.	3
(3) Walkways, street crossings, and entrances designed to promote pedestrian activity are provided. New buildings are connected to existing sidewalks and areas of development.	5

(4) A lot is selected within one-half mile (805 m) of six or more community resources. No more than two each of the following use category can be counted toward the total: Recreation, Retail, Civic, and Services. Examples of resources in each category include, but are not limited to the following:

Recreation: recreational facilities (such as pools, tennis courts, basketball courts), parks
Retail: grocery store, restaurant, retail store.
Civic: post office, place of worship, community center.
Services: bank, daycare center, school, medical/dental office, laundromat/dry cleaners. **4**

OR

A lot is selected within a census block group that, compared to its region, has above-average neighborhood walkability using an index within the EPA's Smart Location Database:

(a) Walkability is within the top quartile for the region..	5
(b) Walkability is within the second quartile for the region...	2

(5) Bicycle use is promoted by building on a lot located within a community that has rights-of-way specifically dedicated to bicycle use in the form of paved paths or bicycle lanes, or on an infill lot located within 1/2 mile of a bicycle lane designated by the jurisdiction.. **5**

GREEN BUILDING PRACTICES	M=Mandatory POINTS

(6) Dedicated bicycle parking and racks are indicated on the site plan and constructed for mixed-use and multifamily buildings:

    (a) Minimum of 1 bicycle parking space per 3 residential units. 2

    (b) Minimum of 1 bicycle parking space per 2 residential units. 4

    (c) Minimum of 1 bicycle parking space per 1 residential unit. 6

    (d) Bicycle enclosed storage is provided or parking spaces are covered or otherwise protected from the elements .... 2 Additional

(7) Select a lot in a community where there is access to shared vehicle usage such as carpool drop-off areas, car-share services, and shuttle services to mass transit. 5

(8) Lot is within 1/2 mile walking distance of where a bike sharing program is provided 5

502 PROJECT TEAM, MISSION STATEMENT, AND GOALS

502.1 Project team, mission statement, and goals. A knowledgeable team is established and team member roles are identified with respect to green lot design, preparation, and development. The project's green goals and objectives are written into a mission statement. 4

503 LOT DESIGN

503.0 Intent. The lot is designed to avoid detrimental environmental impacts first, to minimize any unavoidable impacts, and to mitigate for those impacts that do occur. The project is designed to minimize environmental impacts and to protect, restore, and enhance the natural features and environmental quality of the lot. *[Points awarded only if the intent of the design is implemented.]*

503.1 Natural resources. Natural resources are conserved by one or more of the following:

(1) A natural resources inventory is completed under the direction of a qualified professional. 5

(2) A plan is implemented to conserve the elements identified by the natural resource inventory as high-priority resources. 6

(3) Items listed for protection in the natural resource inventory plan are protected under the direction of a qualified professional. 4

(4) Basic training in tree or other natural resource protection is provided for the on-site supervisor. 4

(5) All tree pruning on-site is conducted by a certified arborist or other qualified professional. 3

(6) Ongoing maintenance of vegetation on the lot during construction is in accordance with TCIA A300 or locally accepted best practices 4

(7) Where a lot adjoins a landscaped common area, a protection plan from construction activities next to the common area is implemented. 5

(8) Developer has a plan to design and construct the lot in accordance with the International Wildland-Urban Interface Code (IWUIC). 6

Only applicable where the AHJ has not declared a wildland-urban interface area, but a fire protection engineer, certified fire marshal, or other qualified party has determined and documented the site as hazarded per the IWUIC.

GREEN BUILDING PRACTICES	M=Mandatory POINTS

503.2 Slope disturbance. Slope disturbance is minimized by one or more of the following:

(1) The use of terrain adaptive architecture. 5

(2) Hydrological/soil stability study is completed and used to guide the design of all buildings on the lot. 5

(3) All or a percentage of driveways and parking are aligned with natural topography to reduce cut and fill.

    (a) greater than or equal to 10% to less than 25%.............................. 1

    (b) greater than or equal to 25% to less than 75%.............................. 4

    (c) greater than or equal to 75%.. 6

(4) Long-term erosion effects are reduced through the design and implementation of clustering, terracing, retaining walls, landscaping, or restabilization techniques........................ 6

(5) Underground parking uses the natural slope for parking entrances. 5

503.3 Soil disturbance and erosion. Soil disturbance and erosion are minimized by one or more of the following: (also see § 504.3)

(1) Construction activities are scheduled such that disturbed soil that is to be left unworked for more than 21 days is stabilized within 14 days. 5

(2) At least 75% of total length of the utilities on the lot are designed to use one or more alternative means: 5

    (a) tunneling instead of trenching.

    (b) use of smaller (low ground pressure) equipment or geomats to spread the weight of construction equipment.

    (c) shared utility trenches or easements.

    (d) placement of utilities under paved surfaces instead of yards.

(3) Limits of clearing and grading are demarcated on the lot plan. 5

503.4 Stormwater management. The stormwater management system is designed to use low-impact development/green infrastructure practices to preserve, restore or mitigate changes in site hydrology due to land disturbance and the construction of impermeable surfaces through the use of one or more of the following techniques:

(1) A site assessment is conducted and a plan prepared and implemented that identifies important existing permeable soils, natural drainage ways and other water features, e.g., depressional storage, onsite to be preserved in order to maintain site hydrology. 7

(2) A hydrologic analysis is conducted that results in the design of a stormwater management system that maintains the pre-development (stable, natural) runoff hydrology of the site through the development or redevelopment process. Ensure that post construction runoff rate, volume and duration do not exceed predevelopment rates, volume and duration. 10

(3) Low-Impact Development/Green infrastructure stormwater management practices to promote infiltration and evapotranspiration are used to manage rainfall on the lot and prevent the off-lot discharge of runoff from all storms up to and including the volume of following storm events:

    (a) 80th percentile storm event 5

    (b) 90th percentile storm event 8

    (c) 95th percentile storm event 10

GREEN BUILDING PRACTICES	M=Mandatory POINTS

(4) Permeable materials are used for driveways, parking areas, walkways, patios, and recreational surfaces and the like according to the following percentages:

(a) greater than or equal to 10% to less than 25% (add 2 points for use of vegetative paving system) **2**

(b) greater than or equal to 25% to less than 50% (add 4 points for use of vegetative paving system) **5**

(c) greater than or equal to 50% (add 6 points for use of vegetative paving system) **10**

Points for vegetative paving systems are only awarded for locations receiving more than 20 in. per year of annual average precipitation.

(5) Complete gutter and downspout system directs storm water away from foundation to vegetated landscape area, a raingarden, or catchment system that provides for water infiltration...................... **3**

503.5 Landscape plan. A plan for the lot is developed to limit water and energy use while preserving or enhancing the natural environment. *[Where "front" only or "rear" only plan is implemented, only half of the points (rounding down to a whole number) are awarded for Items (1)-(8)]*

(1) A plan is formulated and implemented that protects, restores, or enhances natural vegetation on the lot.

(a) greater than or equal to 12% to less than 25% of the natural area **1**

(b) greater than or equal to 25% to less than 50% of the natural area **2**

(c) greater than or equal to 50% to less than 100% of the natural area **3**

(d) 100% of the natural area **4**

(2) Non-invasive vegetation that is native or regionally appropriate for local growing conditions is selected to promote biodiversity. **7**

(3) To improve pollinator habitat, at least 10% of planted areas are composed of native or regionally appropriate flowering and nectar producing plant species. Invasive plant species shall not be utilized. **3**

(4) EPA WaterSense Water Budget Tool or equivalent is used when implementing the site vegetative design. **5**

(5) Where turf is being planted, Turfgrass Water Conservation Alliance (TWCA) or equivalent as determined by the adopting entity third-party qualified water efficient grasses are used. **3**

(6) For landscaped vegetated areas, the maximum percentage of turf area is:

(a) greater than 40% to less than or equal to 60% **2**

(b) greater than 20% to less than or equal to 40% **3**

(c) greater than 0% to less than or equal to 20% **4**

(d) 0% **5**

(7) Plants with similar watering needs are grouped (hydrozoning) and shown on the lot plan.................. **5**

(8) Summer shading by planting installed to shade a minimum of 30% of building walls. To conform to summer shading, the effective shade coverage (five years after planting) is the arithmetic mean of the shade coverage calculated at 10 am for eastward facing walls, noon for southward facing walls, and 3 pm for westward facing walls on the summer solstice. **5**

(9) Vegetative wind breaks or channels are designed to protect the lot and immediate surrounding lots as appropriate for local conditions.. **5**

	M=Mandatory
GREEN BUILDING PRACTICES	**POINTS**

(10) Site or community generated tree trimmings or stump grinding of regionally appropriate trees are used on the lot to provide protective mulch during construction or for landscaping. **3**

(11) An integrated pest management plan is developed to minimize chemical use in pesticides and fertilizers. **4**

(12) Developer has a plan for removal or containment of invasive plants from the disturbed areas of the site................. **3**

(13) Developer implements a plan for removal or containment of invasive plants on the undisturbed areas of the site........................ **6**

503.6 Wildlife habitat. Measures are planned to support wildlife habitat and include at least two of the following:

(1) Plants and gardens that encourage wildlife, such as bird and butterfly gardens. **3**

(2) Inclusion of a certified "backyard wildlife" program. **3**

(3) The lot is adjacent to a wildlife corridor, fish and game park, or preserved areas and is designed with regard for this relationship. **3**

(4) Outdoor lighting techniques are utilized with regard for wildlife............................ **3**

503.7 Environmentally sensitive areas. The lot is in accordance with one or both of the following:

(1) The lot does not contain any environmentally sensitive areas that are disturbed by the construction. **4**

(2) On lots with environmentally sensitive areas, mitigation and/or restoration is conducted to preserve ecosystem functions lost through development and construction activities. **4**

503.8 Demolition of existing building. A demolition waste management plan is developed, posted at the jobsite, and implemented to recycle and/or salvage with a goal of recycling or salvaging a minimum of 50% of the nonhazardous demolition waste. *[1 additional point awarded for every 10% of nonhazardous demolition waste recycled and/or salvaged beyond 50%.]*........................ **5 [10 max]**

504   LOT CONSTRUCTION

504.0 Intent. Environmental impact during construction is avoided to the extent possible; impacts that do occur are minimized and any significant impacts are mitigated.

504.1 On-site supervision and coordination. On-site supervision and coordination are provided during on-the-lot clearing, grading, trenching, paving, and installation of utilities to ensure that specified green development practices are implemented. (also see § 503.3) **4**

504.2 Trees and vegetation. Designated trees and vegetation are preserved by one or more of the following:

(1) Fencing or equivalent is installed to protect trees and other vegetation........................ **3**

(2) Trenching, significant changes in grade, and compaction of soil and critical root zones in all "tree save" areas as shown on the lot plan are avoided........................ **5**

(3) Damage to designated existing trees and vegetation is mitigated during construction through pruning, root pruning, fertilizing, and watering........................ **4**

GREEN BUILDING PRACTICES	M=Mandatory POINTS

504.3 Soil disturbance and erosion implementation. On-site soil disturbance and erosion are minimized by one or more of the following in accordance with the SWPPP or applicable plan: (also see § 503.3)

(1) Sediment and erosion controls are installed on the lot and maintained in accordance with the stormwater pollution prevention plan, where required. 5

(2) Limits of clearing and grading are staked out on the lot. 5

(3) "No disturbance" zones are created using fencing or flagging to protect vegetation and sensitive areas on the lot from construction activity. 5

(4) Topsoil from either the lot or the site development is stockpiled and stabilized for later use and used to establish landscape plantings on the lot. 5

(5) Soil compaction from construction equipment is reduced by distributing the weight of the equipment over a larger area (laying lightweight geogrids, mulch, chipped wood, plywood, OSB, metal plates, or other materials capable of weight distribution in the pathway of the equipment). 4

(6) Disturbed areas on the lot that are complete or to be left unworked for 21 days or more are stabilized within 14 days using methods as recommended by the EPA or in the approved SWPPP, where required. 3

(7) Soil is improved with organic amendments or mulch. 3

(8) Utilities on the lot are installed using one or more alternative means (e.g., tunneling instead of trenching, use of smaller equipment, use of low ground pressure equipment, use of geomats, shared utility trenches or easements). 5

(9) Inspection reports of stormwater best management practices are available. 3

505   INNOVATIVE PRACTICES

505.0 Intent. Innovative lot design, preparation, and development practices are used to enhance environmental performance. Waivers or variances from local development regulations are obtained and innovative zoning is used to implement such practices.

505.1 Driveways and parking areas. Driveways and parking areas are minimized or mitigated by one or more of the following:

(1) Off-street parking areas or driveways are shared. Waivers or variances from local development regulations are obtained to implement such practices, if required. 5

(2) In a multifamily project, parking capacity does not exceed the local minimum requirements. 5

(3) Structured parking is utilized to reduce the footprint of surface parking areas.

    (a) greater than or equal to 25% to less than 50% 4

    (b) greater than or equal to 50% to less than 75% 5

    (c) greater than or equal to 75% 6

GREEN BUILDING PRACTICES	M=Mandatory POINTS

505.2 Heat island mitigation. Heat island effect is mitigated by the following.

(1) Hardscape: Not less than 50% of the surface area of the hardscape on the lot meets one or a combination of the following methods. **5**

    (a) Shading of hardscaping: Shade is provided from existing or new vegetation (within five years) or from trellises. Shade of hardscaping is to be measured on the summer solstice at noon.

    (b) Light-colored hardscaping: Horizontal hardscaping materials are installed with a solar reflectance index (SRI) of 29 or greater. The SRI is calculated in accordance with ASTM E1980. A default SRI value of 35 for new concrete without added color pigment is permitted to be used instead of measurements.

    (c) Permeable hardscaping: Permeable hardscaping materials are installed.

(2) Roofs: Not less than 75% of the exposed surface of the roof is vegetated using technology capable of withstanding the climate conditions of the jurisdiction and the microclimate conditions of the building lot. Invasive plant species are not permitted. **5**

505.3 Density. The average density on the lot on a net developable area basis is:

(1) greater than or equal to 7 to less than 14 dwelling units/sleeping units per acre (per 4,047 m^2) **4**

(2) greater than or equal to 14 to less than 21 dwelling units/sleeping units per acre (per 4,047 m^2) **5**

(3) greater than or equal to 21 to less than 35 dwelling units/sleeping units per acre (per 4,047 m^2) **6**

(4) greater than or equal to 35 to less than 70 dwelling units/sleeping units per acre (per 4,047 m^2) **7**

(5) greater than or equal to 70 dwelling units/sleeping units per acre (per 4,047 m^2) **8**

505.4 Mixed-use development.

(1) The lot contains a mixed-use building. **8**

505.5 Multifamily or mixed-use community garden(s). Local food production to residents or area consumers. **3**

    (a) A portion of the lot of at least 250 sq. ft. is established as community garden(s) for the residents of the site. *[3 points awarded per 250 sq. ft.]*.. **3 [9 max]**

    (b) Locate the project within a 0.5-mile walking distance of an existing or planned farmers market/ farm stand that is open or will operate at least once a week for at least five months of the year.. **3**

    (c) Areas and physical provisions are provided for composting. **1**

    (d) Signs designating the garden area are posted.. **1**

505.6 Multi-unit plug-in electric vehicle charging. Plug-in electric vehicle charging capability is provided for not fewer than 2% of parking stalls.
[An additional 2 points can be earned for each percentage point above 2% for a maximum of 10 points] ... **4 [10 max]**

Fractional values shall be rounded up to the nearest whole number. Electrical capacity in main electric panels supports Level 2 charging (208/240V- up to 80 amps or in accordance with SAE J1772). Each stall is provided with conduit and wiring infrastructure from the electric panel to support Level 2 charging (208/240V- up to 80 amps or in accordance with SAE J1772) service to the designated stalls, and stalls are equipped with either Level 2 charging AC grounded outlets (208/240V- up to 80 amps or in accordance with SAE J1772) or Level 2 charging stations (208/240V- up to 80 amps or in accordance with SAE J1772) by a third-party charging station.

GREEN BUILDING PRACTICES	M=Mandatory POINTS

505.7 Multi-unit residential CNG vehicle fueling. CNG vehicle residential fueling appliances are provided for at least 1% of the parking stalls. The CNG fueling appliances shall be listed in accordance with ANSI/CSA NGV 5.1 and installed in accordance with the appliance manufacturer's installation instructions. **4**

505.8 Street network. Project is located in an area of high intersection density. **5**

505.9 Smoking prohibitions. Signs are provided on multifamily and mixed-use lots prohibiting smoking at the following locations:

(a) Smoking is prohibited within 25 ft. (7.5 m) of all building exterior doors and operable windows or building air intakes within 15 vertical feet (4.5 m) of grade or a walking surface. **3**

(b) Smoking is prohibited on decks, balconies, patios and other occupied exterior spaces. **3**

(c) Smoking is prohibited at all parks, playgrounds, and community activity or recreational spaces... **3**

505.10 Exercise and recreational space. For multifamily buildings, on-site dedicated recreation space for exercise or play opportunities for adults and/or children open and accessible to residents is provided.

(a) A dedicated area of at least 400 sq. ft. is provided inside the building with adult exercise and/or children's play equipment. **3**

(b) A courtyard, garden, terrace, or roof space at least 10% of the lot area that can serve as outdoor space for children's play and /or adult activities is provided. **3**

(c) Active play/recreation areas are illuminated at night to extend opportunities for physical activity into the evening. **3**

§ SECTION 6

RESOURCE EFFICIENCY

GREEN BUILDING PRACTICES	POINTS

601   QUALITY OF CONSTRUCTION MATERIALS AND WASTE

601.0 Intent. Design and construction practices that minimize the environmental impact of the building materials are incorporated, environmentally efficient building systems and materials are incorporated, and waste generated during construction is reduced.

601.1 Conditioned floor area. Finished floor area of a dwelling unit or sleeping unit is limited. Finished floor area is calculated in accordance with ANSI Z765 for single family and ANSI/BOMA Z65.4 for multifamily buildings. Only the finished floor area for stories above grade plane is included in the calculation.
[For every 100 sq. ft. (9.29 m²) over 4,000 sq. ft. (372 m²), 1 point is to be added to rating level points shown in Table 303, Category 7 for each rating level.]

(1) less than or equal to 700 sq. ft. (65 m²)	**14**
(2) less than or equal to 1,000 sq. ft. (93 m²)	**12**
(3) less than or equal to 1,500 sq. ft. (139 m²)	**9**
(4) less than or equal to 2,000 sq. ft. (186 m²)	**6**
(5) less than or equal to 2,500 sq. ft. (232 m²)	**3**
(6) greater than 4,000 sq. ft. (372 m²)...	**M**

Multifamily Building Note: For a multifamily building, a weighted average of the individual unit sizes is used for this practice.

601.2 Material usage. Structural systems are designed, or construction techniques are implemented, to reduce and optimize material usage.	**9 max**
(1) Minimum structural member or element sizes necessary for strength and stiffness in accordance with advanced framing techniques or structural design standards are selected.	**3**
(2) Higher-grade or higher-strength of the same materials than commonly specified for structural elements and components in the building are used and element or component sizes are reduced accordingly........	**3**
(3) Performance-based structural design is used to optimize lateral force-resisting systems.....................	**3**

601.3 Building dimensions and layouts. Building dimensions and layouts are designed to reduce material cuts and waste. This practice is used for a minimum of 80% of the following areas:

(1) floor area..	**3**
(2) wall area...	**3**
(3) roof area...	**3**
(4) cladding or siding area	**3**
(5) penetrations or trim area...	**1**

	M=Mandatory
GREEN BUILDING PRACTICES	**POINTS**

601.4 Framing and structural plans. Detailed framing or structural plans, material quantity lists and on-site cut lists for framing, structural materials, and sheathing materials are provided. **4**

601.5 Prefabricated components. Precut or preassembled components, or panelized or precast assemblies are utilized for a minimum of 90% for the following system or building: .... **13 max**

(1) floor system **4**

(2) wall system **4**

(3) roof system **4**

(4) modular construction for the entire building located above grade **13**

(5) manufactured home construction for the entire building located above grade **13**

601.6 Stacked stories. Stories above grade are stacked, such as in 1½-story, 2-story, or greater structures. The area of the upper story is a minimum of 50% of the area of the story below based on areas with a minimum ceiling height of 7 ft. (2,134 mm). .... **8 max**

(1) first stacked story **4**

(2) for each additional stacked story **2**

601.7 Prefinished materials. Prefinished building materials or assemblies listed below have no additional site-applied finishing material are installed. .... **12 max**

    (a) interior trim not requiring paint or stain.

    (b) exterior trim not requiring paint or stain.

    (c) window, skylight, and door assemblies not requiring paint or stain on one of the following surfaces:
        i. exterior surfaces
        ii. interior surfaces

    (d) interior wall coverings or systems, floor systems, and/or ceiling systems not requiring paint or stain or other type of finishing application.

    (e) exterior wall coverings or systems, floor system, and/or ceiling systems not requiring paint or stain or other type of finishing application.

(1) Percent of prefinished building materials or assemblies installed:
[Points awarded for each type of material or assembly.]

    (a) greater than or equal to 35% to less than 50% **1**

    (b) greater than or equal to 50% to less than 90% **2**

    (c) greater than or equal to 90% **5**

601.8 Foundations. A foundation system that minimizes soil disturbance, excavation quantities, and material usage, such as frost-protected shallow foundations, isolated pier and pad foundations, deep foundations, post foundations, or helical piles is selected, designed, and constructed. The foundation is used on 50% or more of the building footprint. **3**

GREEN BUILDING PRACTICES	POINTS

602 ENHANCED DURABILITY AND REDUCED MAINTENANCE

602.0 Intent. Design and construction practices are implemented that enhance the durability of materials and reduce in-service maintenance.

602.1 Moisture management – building envelope

602.1.1 Capillary breaks

602.1.1.1 A capillary break and vapor retarder are installed at concrete slabs in accordance with IRC Sections R506.2.2 and R506.2.3 or IBC Sections 1907 and 1805.4.1. .... **M**

602.1.1.2 A capillary break between the footing and the foundation wall is provided to prevent moisture migration into foundation wall. **3**

602.1.2 Foundation waterproofing. Enhanced foundation waterproofing is installed using one or both of the following: **4**

(1) rubberized coating, or

(2) drainage mat

602.1.3 Foundation drainage

602.1.3.1 Where required by the IRC or IBC for habitable and usable spaces below grade, exterior drain tile is installed.. **M**

602.1.3.2 Interior and exterior foundation perimeter drains are installed and sloped to discharge to daylight, dry well, or sump pit.. **4**

602.1.4 Crawlspaces

602.1.4.1 Vapor retarder in unconditioned vented crawlspace is in accordance with the following, as applicable. Joints of vapor retarder overlap a minimum of 6 in. (152 mm) and are taped.

(1) Floors. Minimum 6-mil vapor retarder installed on the crawlspace floor and extended at least 6 in. up the wall and is attached and sealed to the wall.. **6**

(2) Walls. Dampproof walls are provided below finished grade. .... **M**

602.1.4.2 Crawlspace that is built as a conditioned area is sealed to prevent outside air infiltration and provided with conditioned air at a rate not less than 0.02 cfm (.009 L/s) per sq. ft. of horizontal area and one of the following is implemented:

(1) a concrete slab over 6-mil polyethylene sheeting, or other Class I vapor retarder installed in accordance with IRC Section 408.3 or Section 506. .... **8**

(2) 6-mil polyethylene sheeting, or other Class I vapor retarder installed in accordance with IRC Section 408.3 or Section 506. .... **M**

602.1.5 Termite barrier. Continuous physical foundation termite barrier provided:

(1) In geographic areas that have moderate to heavy infestation potential in accordance with Figure 6(3), a no or low toxicity treatment is also installed. **4**

(2) In geographic areas that have a very heavy infestation potential in accordance with Figure 6(3), in addition a low toxicity bait and kill termite treatment plan is selected and implemented. **4**

GREEN BUILDING PRACTICES	M=Mandatory POINTS

602.1.6 Termite-resistant materials. In areas of termite infestation probability as defined by Figure 6(3), termite-resistant materials are used as follows:

(1) In areas of slight to moderate termite infestation probability: for the foundation, all structural walls, floors, concealed roof spaces not accessible for inspection, exterior decks, and exterior claddings within the first 2 ft. (610 mm) above the top of the foundation.. **2**

(2) In areas of moderate to heavy termite infestation probability: for the foundation, all structural walls, floors, concealed roof spaces not accessible for inspection, exterior decks, and exterior claddings within the first 3 ft. (914 mm) above the top of the foundation... **4**

(3) In areas of very heavy termite infestation probability: for the foundation, all structural walls, floors, concealed roof spaces not accessible for inspection, exterior decks, and exterior claddings. **6**

602.1.7 Moisture control measures

602.1.7.1 Moisture control measures are in accordance with the following:

(1) Building materials with visible mold are not installed or are cleaned or encapsulated prior to concealment and closing. **2**

(2) Insulation in cavities is dry in accordance with manufacturer's instructions when enclosed (e.g., with drywall).. **M 2**

(3) The moisture content of lumber is sampled to ensure it does not exceed 19% prior to the surface and/or cavity enclosure. **4**

602.1.7.2 Moisture content of subfloor, substrate, or concrete slabs is in accordance with the appropriate industry standard for the finish flooring to be applied.. **2**

602.1.7.3 Building envelope assemblies are designed for moisture control based on documented hygrothermal simulation or field study analysis. Hygrothermal analysis is required to incorporate representative climatic conditions, interior conditions and include heating and cooling seasonal variation. .. **4**

602.1.8 Water-resistive barrier. Where required by the IRC, or IBC, a water-resistive barrier and/or drainage plane system is installed behind exterior veneer and/or siding. .... **M**

602.1.9 Flashing. Flashing is provided as follows to minimize water entry into wall and roof assemblies and to direct water to exterior surfaces or exterior water-resistive barriers for drainage. Flashing details are provided in the construction documents and are in accordance with the fenestration manufacturer's instructions, the flashing manufacturer's instructions, or as detailed by a registered design professional.

(1) Flashing is installed at all the following locations, as applicable: .... **M**

    (a) around exterior fenestrations, skylights, and doors;

    (b) at roof valleys;

    (c) at all building-to-deck, -balcony, -porch, and -stair intersections;

    (d) at roof-to-wall intersections, at roof-to-chimney intersections, at wall-to-chimney intersections, and at parapets;

    (e) at ends of and under masonry, wood, or metal copings and sills;

    (f) above projecting wood trim;

    (g) at built-in roof gutters; and

    (h) drip edge is installed at eave and rake edges.

GREEN BUILDING PRACTICES	

(2) All window and door head and jamb flashing is either self-adhered flashing complying with AAMA 711 or liquid applied flashing complying with AAMA 714 and installed in accordance with fenestration or flashing manufacturer's installation instructions. **2**

(3) Pan flashing is installed at sills of all exterior windows and doors. **3**

(4) Seamless, preformed kickout flashing or prefabricated metal with soldered seams is provided at all roof-to-wall intersections. The type and thickness of the material used for roof flashing including but not limited kickout and step flashing is commensurate with the anticipated service life of the roofing material. **3**

(5) A rainscreen wall design as follows is used for exterior wall assemblies. .... **4 max**

    (a) A system designed with minimum 1/4-in. air space exterior to the water-resistive barrier, vented to the exterior at top and bottom of the wall, and integrated with flashing details; or **4**

    (b) A cladding material or a water-resistive barrier with enhanced drainage, meeting 75% drainage efficiency determined in accordance with ASTM E2273. .... **2**

(6) Through-wall flashing is installed at transitions between wall cladding materials or wall construction types.................................... **2**

(7) Flashing is installed at expansion joints in stucco walls. **2**

602.1.10 Exterior doors. Entries at exterior door assemblies, inclusive of side lights (if any), are covered by one of the following methods to protect the building from the effects of precipitation and solar radiation. Either a storm door or a projection factor of 0.375 minimum is provided. Eastern- and western-facing entries in Climate Zones 1, 2, and 3, as determined in accordance with Figure 6(1) or Appendix A, have either a storm door or a projection factor of 1.0 minimum, unless protected from direct solar radiation by other means (e.g., screen wall, vegetation). *[2 points awarded per exterior door]* .... **2 [6 max]**

    (a) installing a porch roof or awning

    (b) extending the roof overhang

    (c) recessing the exterior door

    (d) Installing a storm door

602.1.11 Tile backing materials. Tile backing materials installed under tiled surfaces in wet areas are in accordance with ASTM C1178, C1278, C1288, or C1325. .... **M**

602.1.12 Roof overhangs. Roof overhangs, in accordance with Table 602.1.12, are provided over a minimum of 90% of exterior walls to protect the building envelope. **4**

Table 602.1.12
Minimum Roof Overhang for One- & Two-Story Buildings

Inches of Rainfall [1]	Eave Overhang (In.)	Rake Overhang (In.)
≤40	12	12
>41 and ≤70	18	12
>70	24	12

(1) Annual mean total rainfall in inches is in accordance with Figure 6(2).

For SI: 12 in. = 304.8 mm

GREEN BUILDING PRACTICES	M=Mandatory POINTS

602.1.13 Ice barrier. In areas where there has been a history of ice forming along the eaves causing a backup of water, an ice barrier is installed in accordance with the IRC or IBC at roof eaves of pitched roofs and extends a minimum of 24 in. (610 mm) inside the exterior wall line of the building................... **M**

602.1.14 Architectural features. Architectural features that increase the potential for water intrusion are avoided:

(1) All horizontal ledgers are sloped away to provide gravity drainage as appropriate for the application. ... **M 1**

(2) No roof configurations that create horizontal valleys in roof design. **2**

(3) No recessed windows and architectural features that trap water on horizontal surfaces. **2**

602.1.15 Kitchen and vanity cabinets. All kitchen and vanity cabinets are certified in accordance with the ANSI/KCMA A161.1 performance standard or equivalent. **2**

602.2 Roof surfaces. A minimum of 90% of roof surfaces, not used for roof penetrations and associated equipment, on-site renewable energy systems such as photovoltaics or solar thermal energy collectors, or rooftop decks, amenities and walkways, are constructed of one or more of the following:..................... **3**

(1) products that are in accordance with the ENERGY STAR® cool roof certification or equivalent.

(2) a vegetated roof system.

(3) Minimum initial SRI of 78 for low-sloped roof (a slope less than 2:12) and a minimum initial SRI of 29 for a steep-sloped roof (a slope equal to or greater than 2:12). The SRI is calculated in accordance with ASTM E1980. Roof products are certified and labeled.

602.3 Roof water discharge. A gutter and downspout system or splash blocks and effective grading are provided to carry water a minimum of 5 ft. (1524 mm) away from perimeter foundation walls. **4**

602.4 Finished grade

602.4.1 Finished grade at all sides of a building is sloped to provide a minimum of 6 in. (152 mm) of fall within 10 ft. (3048 mm) of the edge of the building. Where lot lines, walls, slopes, or other physical barriers prohibit 6 in. (152 mm) of fall within 10 ft. (3048 mm), the final grade is sloped away from the edge of the building at a minimum slope of 2%. .... **M**

602.4.2 The final grade is sloped away from the edge of the building at a minimum slope of 5%. **1**

602.4.3 Water is directed to drains or swales to ensure drainage away from the structure........................ **1**

603   REUSED OR SALVAGED MATERIALS

603.0 Intent. Practices that reuse or modify existing structures, salvage materials for other uses, or use salvaged materials in the building's construction are implemented.

603.1 Reuse of existing building. Major elements or components of existing buildings and structures are reused, modified, or deconstructed for later use.
[1 point awarded for every 200 sq. ft. (18.5 m²) of floor area.].. **1 [12 max]**

603.2 Salvaged materials. Reclaimed and/or salvaged materials and components are used. The total material value and labor cost of salvaged materials is equal to or exceeds 1% of the total construction cost.
[1 point awarded per 1% of salvaged materials used based on the total construction cost. Materials, elements, or components awarded points under § 603.1 shall not be awarded points under § 603.2.] .... **1 [9 max]**

GREEN BUILDING PRACTICES	POINTS

603.3 Scrap materials. Sorting and reuse of scrap building material is facilitated (e.g., a central storage area or dedicated bins are provided). **4**

604   RECYCLED-CONTENT BUILDING MATERIALS

604.1 Recycled content. Building materials with recycled content are used for two minor and/or two major components of the building.   **per Table 604.1**

Table 604.1
Recycled Content

Material Percentage Recycled Content	Points For 2 Minor	Points For 2 Major
25% to less than 50%	1	2
50% to less than 75%	2	4
more than 75%	3	6

605   RECYCLED CONSTRUCTION WASTE

605.0 Intent. Waste generated during construction is recycled.

605.1 Hazardous waste. The construction and waste management plan shall include information on the proper handling and disposal of hazardous waste. Hazardous waste is properly handled and disposed. ....   **M**

605.2 Construction waste management plan. A construction waste management plan is developed, posted at the jobsite, and implemented, diverting through reuse, salvage, recycling, or manufacturer reclamation, a minimum of 50% (by weight) of nonhazardous construction and demolition waste from disposal. For this practice, land-clearing debris is not considered construction waste. Materials used as alternative daily cover are considered construction waste and do not count toward recycling or salvaging.

For buildings following the new construction path that also have a renovation component, the waste management plan includes the recycling of 95% of electronic waste components (such as printed circuit boards from computers, building automation systems, HVAC, fire and security control boards) by an E-Waste recycling facility. **6**

Exceptions: 1) Waste materials generated from land clearing, soil and sub-grade excavation and vegetative debris shall not be in the calculations; and 2) a recycling facility (traditional or E-Waste) offering material receipt documentation is not available within 50 miles of the jobsite.

605.3 On-site recycling. On-site recycling measures following applicable regulations and codes are implemented, such as the following: **7**

   (a)   Materials are ground or otherwise safely applied on-site as soil amendment or fill. A minimum of 50% (by weight) of construction and land-clearing waste is diverted from landfill.

   (b)   Alternative compliance methods approved by the Adopting Entity.

   (c)   Compatible untreated biomass material (lumber, posts, beams, etc.) are set aside for combustion if a solid fuel-burning appliance per § 901.2.1(2) will be available for on-site renewable energy.

GREEN BUILDING PRACTICES	M=Mandatory POINTS

605.4 Recycled construction materials. Construction materials (e.g., wood, cardboard, metals, drywall, plastic, asphalt roofing shingles, or concrete) are recycled offsite. .... **6 max**

(1) a minimum of two types of materials are recycled **3**

(2) for each additional recycled material type **1**

606   RENEWABLE MATERIALS

606.0 Intent. Building materials derived from renewable resources are used.

606.1 Biobased products. The following biobased products are used: .... **8 max**

    (a) certified solid wood in accordance with § 606.2

    (b) engineered wood

    (c) bamboo

    (d) cotton

    (e) cork

    (f) straw

    (g) natural fiber products made from crops (soy-based, corn-based)

    (h) other biobased materials with a minimum of 50% biobased content (by weight or volume)

(1) Two types of biobased materials are used, each for more than 0.5% of the project's projected building material cost. **3**

(2) Two types of biobased materials are used, each for more than 1% of the project's projected building material cost. **6**

(3) For each additional biobased material used for more than 0.5% of the project's projected building material cost. .... **1 [2 max]**

606.2 Wood-based products. Wood or wood-based products are certified to the requirements of one of the following:

    (a) American Forest Foundation's *American Tree Farm System*® (ATFS)

    (b) Canadian Standards Association's *Sustainable Forest Management System Standards* (CSA Z809)

    (c) *Forest Stewardship Council* (FSC)

    (d) *Program for Endorsement of Forest Certification Systems* (PEFC)

    (e) *Sustainable Forestry Initiative*® *Program* (SFI)

    (f) National Wood Flooring Association's *Responsible Procurement Program* (RPP)

    (g) other product programs mutually recognized by PEFC

    (h) A manufacturer's fiber procurement system that has been audited by an approved agency as compliant with the provisions of ASTM D7612 as a responsible or certified source. Government or tribal forestlands whose water protection programs have been evaluated by an approved agency as compliant with the responsible source designation of ASTM D7612 are exempt from auditing in the manufacturers' fiber procurement system.

	M=Mandatory
GREEN BUILDING PRACTICES	**POINTS**

(1) A minimum of two responsible or certified wood-based products are used for minor components of the building. **3**

(2) A minimum of two responsible or certified wood-based products are used in major components of the building. **4**

606.3 Manufacturing energy. Materials manufactured using a minimum of 33% of the primary manufacturing process energy derived from (1) renewable sources, (2) combustible waste sources, or (3) renewable energy credits (RECs) are used for major components of the building. *[2 points awarded per material.]* .... **2 [6 max]**

607   RECYCLING AND WASTE REDUCTION

607.1 Recycling and composting. Recycling and composting by the occupant are facilitated by one or more of the following methods:

(1) A readily accessible space(s) for recyclable material containers is provided and identified on the floorplan of the house or dwelling unit or a readily accessible area(s) outside the living space is provided for recyclable material containers and identified on the site plan for the house or building. The area outside the living space shall accommodate recycling bin(s) for recyclable materials accepted in local recycling programs. **2**

(2) A readily accessible space(s) for compostable material containers is provided and identified on the floorplan of the house or dwelling unit or a readily accessible area(s) outside the living space is provided for compostable material containers and identified on the site plan for the house or building. The area outside the living space shall accommodate composting container(s) for locally accepted materials, or, accommodate composting container(s) for on-site composting. **4**

607.2 Food waste disposers. A minimum of one food waste disposer is installed at the primary kitchen sink. **1**

608   RESOURCE-EFFICIENT MATERIALS

608.1 Resource-efficient materials. Products containing fewer materials are used to achieve the same end-use requirements as conventional products, including but not limited to: *[3 points awarded per each material]* .... **3 [9 max]**

(1) lighter, thinner brick with bed depth less than 3 in. and/or brick with coring of more than 25%.

(2) engineered wood or engineered steel products.

(3) roof or floor trusses.

609   REGIONAL MATERIALS

609.1 Regional materials. Regional materials are used for major and/or minor components of the building. **10 max**

(1) Major component *[2 points awarded per each component]* **2**

(2) Minor component *[1 point awarded per each component]* **1**

For a component to comply with this practice, a minimum of 75% of all products in that component category must be sourced regionally, e.g., stone veneer category – 75% or more of the stone veneer on a project must be sourced regionally.

	M=Mandatory
GREEN BUILDING PRACTICES	**POINTS**

610 LIFE CYCLE ASSESSMENT

610.1 Life cycle assessment. A life cycle assessment (LCA) tool is used to select environmentally preferable products, assemblies, or, entire building designs. Points are awarded in accordance with § 610.1.1 or § 610.1.2. Only one method of analysis or tool may be utilized. The reference service life for the building is 60 years for any life cycle analysis tool. Results of the LCA are reported in the manual required in § 1001.1 or § 1002.1(1) of this Standard in terms of the environmental impacts listed in this practice and it is stated if operating energy was included in the LCA. .... **15 max**

610.1.1 Whole-building life cycle assessment. A whole-building LCA is performed in conformance with ASTM E2921 using ISO 14044 compliant life cycle assessment.. **15 max**

(1) Execute LCA at the whole building level through a comparative analysis between the final and reference building designs as set forth under Standard Practice, ASTM E2921. The assessment criteria includes the following environmental impact categories: **8**

    (a) Primary energy use

    (b) Global warming potential

    (c) Acidification potential

    (d) Eutrophication potential

    (e) Ozone depletion potential

    (f) Smog potential.

(2) Execute LCA on regulated loads throughout the building operations life cycle stage. Conduct simulated energy performance analyses in accordance with § 702.2.1 ICC IECC analysis (IECC Section 405) in establishing the comparative performance of final versus reference building designs. Primary energy use savings and global warming potential avoidance from simulation analyses results are determined using energy supplier, utility, or EPA electricity generation and other fuels energy conversion factors and electricity generation and other fuels emission rates for the locality or Sub-Region in which the building is located.. **5**

(3) Execute full LCA, including use-phase, through calculation of operating energy impacts (c) – (f) using local or regional emissions factors from energy supplier, utility, or EPA. **2**

610.1.2 Life cycle assessment for a product or assembly. An environmentally preferable product or assembly is selected for an application based upon the use of an LCA tool that incorporates data methods compliant with ISO 14044 or other recognized standards that compare the environmental impact of products or assemblies. .... **10 max**

M=Mandatory

GREEN BUILDING PRACTICES	POINTS

610.1.2.1 Product LCA. A product with improved environmental impact measures compared to another product(s) intended for the same use is selected. The environmental impact measures used in the assessment are selected from the following:

   (a) Primary energy use

   (b) Global warming potential

   (c) Acidification potential

   (d) Eutrophication potential

   (e) Ozone depletion potential

   (f) Smog potential

[Points are awarded for each product/system comparison where the selected product/system improved upon the environmental impact measures by an average of 15%.]

per Table 610.1.2.1 [10 max]

Table 610.1.2.1
Product LCA

4 Impact Measures	5 Impact Measures
POINTS	
2	3

610.1.2.2 Building assembly LCA. A building assembly with improved environmental impact measures compared to an alternative assembly of the same function is selected. The full life cycle, from resource extraction to demolition and disposal (including but not limited to on-site construction, maintenance and replacement, material and product embodied acquisition, and process and transportation energy), is assessed. The assessment includes all structural elements, insulation, and wall coverings of the assembly. The assessment does not include electrical and mechanical equipment and controls, plumbing products, fire detection and alarm systems, elevators, and conveying systems. The following types of building assemblies are eligible for points under this practice:

   (a) exterior walls

   (b) roof/ceiling

   (c) interior walls or ceilings

   (d) intermediate floors

The environmental impact measures used in the assessment are selected from the following:

   (a) Primary energy use

   (b) Global warming potential

   (c) Acidification potential

   (d) Eutrophication potential

   (e) Ozone depletion potential

   (f) Smog potential

[Points are awarded based on the number of types of building assemblies that improve upon environmental impact measures by an average of 15%.]

per Table 610.1.2.2 [10 max]

M=Mandatory

GREEN BUILDING PRACTICES	POINTS

Table 610.1.2.2
Building Assembly LCA

Number of Types of Building Assemblies	4 Impact Measures	5 Impact Measures
	POINTS	
2 types	3	6
3 types	4	8
4 types	5	10

611 PRODUCT DECLARATIONS

611.1 Product declarations. A minimum of 10 different products installed in the building project, at the time of certificate of occupancy, comply with one of the following sub-sections. Declarations, reports, and assessments are submitted and contain documentation of the critical peer review by an independent third party, results from the review, the reviewer's name, company name, contact information, and date of the review.. **5**

611.1.1 Industry-wide declaration. A Type III industry-wide environmental product declaration (EPD) is submitted for each product. Where the program operator explicitly recognizes the EPD as representative of the product group on a National level, it is considered industry-wide. In the case where an industry-wide EPD represents only a subset of an industry group, as opposed to being industry-wide, the manufacturer is required to be explicitly recognized as a participant by the EPD program operator. All EPDs are required to be consistent with ISO Standards 14025 and 21930 with at least a cradle-to-gate scope.

Each product complying with § 611.1.1 shall be counted as one product for compliance with § 611.1.

611.1.2 Product Specific Declaration. A product specific Type III EPD is submitted for each product. The product specific declaration shall be manufacturer specific for an individual product or product family. All Type III EPDs are required to be certified as complying, at a minimum, with the goal and scope for the cradle-to-gate requirements in accordance with ISO Standards 14025 and 21930.

Each product complying with § 611.1.2 shall be counted as two products for compliance with § 611.1.

612 INNOVATIVE PRACTICES

612.1 Manufacturer's environmental management system concepts. Product manufacturer's operations and business practices include environmental management system concepts, and the production facility is registered to ISO 14001 or equivalent. The aggregate value of building products from registered ISO 14001 or equivalent production facilities is 1% or more of the estimated total building materials cost. *[1 point awarded per percent.]*.. **1 [10 max]**

612.2 Sustainable products. One or more of the following products are used for at least 30% of the floor or wall area of the entire dwelling unit or the sleeping unit, as applicable. Products are certified by a third-party agency accredited to ISO 17065. .... **9 max**

(1) greater than or equal to 50% of carpet installed (by square feet) is certified to NSF 140 or equivalent. **3**

(2) greater than or equal to 50% of resilient flooring installed (by square feet) is certified to NSF 332 or equivalent. **3**

GREEN BUILDING PRACTICES	M=Mandatory POINTS

(3) greater than or equal to 50% of the insulation installed (by square feet) is certified to UL 2985 or equivalent. **3**

(4) greater than or equal to 50% of interior wall coverings installed (by square feet) is certified to NSF 342 or equivalent. **3**

(5) greater than or equal to 50% of the gypsum board installed (by square feet) is certified to UL 100 or equivalent. **3**

(6) greater than or equal to 50% of the door leafs installed (by number of door leafs) is certified to UL 102 or equivalent. **3**

(7) greater than or equal to 50% of the tile installed (by square feet) is certified to TCNA A138.1 Specifications for Sustainable Ceramic Tiles, Glass Tiles and Tile Installation Materials or equivalent.. **3**

612.3 Universal design elements. Dwelling incorporates one or more of the following universal design elements. Conventional industry construction tolerances are permitted. .... **12 max**

(1) Any no-step entrance into the dwelling which 1) is accessible from a substantially level parking or drop-off area (no more than 2%) via an accessible path which has no individual change in elevation or other obstruction of more than 1-1/2 in. in height with the pitch not exceeding 1 in 12; and 2) provides a minimum 32-in. wide clearance into the dwelling. **3**

(2) Minimum 36-in. wide accessible route from the no-step entrance into at least one visiting room in the dwelling and into at least one full or half bathroom which has a minimum 32-in. clear door width and a 30-in. by 48-in. clear area inside the bathroom outside the door swing. **3**

(3) Minimum 36-in. wide accessible route from the no-step entrance into at least one bedroom which has a minimum 32-in. clear door width. **3**

(4) Blocking or equivalent installed in the accessible bathroom walls for future installation of grab bars at water closet and bathing fixture, if applicable. **1**

(5) All interior and exterior door handles are levers rather than knobs. **1**

(6) All sink, lavatory and showering controls comply with ICC A117.1. .... **1**

(7) Interior convenience Power receptacles, communication connections (for cable, phone, Ethernet, etc.) and switches are placed between 15 in. and 48 in. above the finished floor. Additional switches to control devices and systems (such as alarms, home theaters and other equipment) not required by the local building code may be installed as desired. **1**

(8) All light switches are rocker-type switches or other similar switches that can be operated by pressing them (with assistive devices). Toggle-type switches may not be used. **1**

(9) Any of the following systems are automated and can be controlled with a wireless device or voice-activated device: HVAC, all permanently-installed lighting, alarm system, window treatments, or door locks. *[1 point awarded per system]* .... **1 [5 max]**

GREEN BUILDING PRACTICES	POINTS

613 RESILIENT CONSTRUCTION

613.1 Intent. Design and construction practices developed by a licensed design professional or equivalent are implemented to enhance the resilience and durability of the structure (above building code minimum design loads) so the structure can better withstand forces generated by flooding, snow, wind, or seismic activity (as applicable) and reduce the potential for the loss of life and property.

613.2 Minimum structural requirements (base design). The building is designed and constructed in compliance with structural requirements in the IBC or IRC as applicable... **2**

613.3 Enhanced resilience (10% above base design). Design and construction practices are implemented to enhance the resilience and durability of the structure by designing and building to forces generated by flooding, snow, wind, or seismic (as applicable) that are 10% higher than the base design............................ **3**

613.4 Enhanced resilience (20% above base design). Design and construction practices are implemented to enhance the resilience and durability of the structure by designing and building to forces generated by flooding, snow, wind, or seismic (as applicable) that are 20% higher than the base design............................ **5**

613.5 Enhanced resilience (30% above base design). Design and construction practices are implemented to enhance the resilience and durability of the structure by designing and building to forces generated by flooding, snow, wind, or seismic (as applicable) that are 30% higher than the base design............................ **10**

613.6 Enhanced resilience (40% above base design). Design and construction practices are implemented to enhance the resilience and durability of the structure by designing and building to forces generated by flooding, snow, wind, or seismic (as applicable) that are 40% higher than the base design............................ **12**

613.7 Enhanced resilience (50% above base design). Design and construction practices are implemented to enhance the resilience and durability of the structure by designing and building to forces generated by flooding, snow, wind, or seismic (as applicable) that are 50% higher than the base design............................ **15**

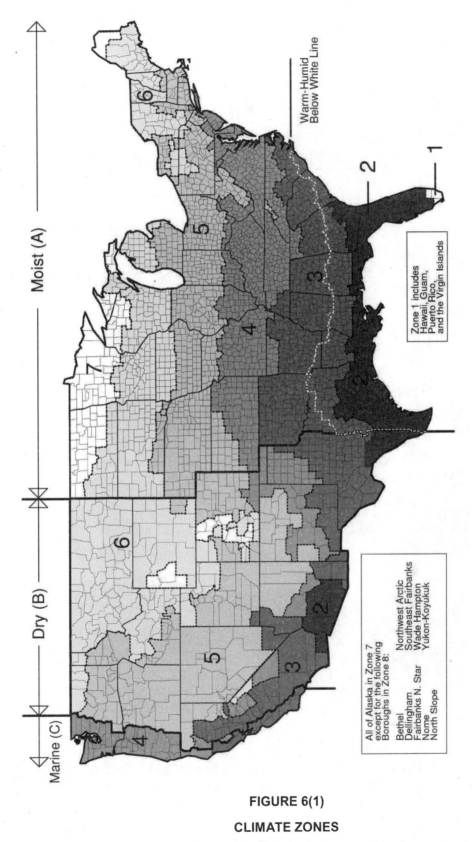

FIGURE 6(1)

CLIMATE ZONES

Reprinted with permission from the 2015 International Residential Code, a copyrighted work of the International Code Council, www.iccsafe.org.

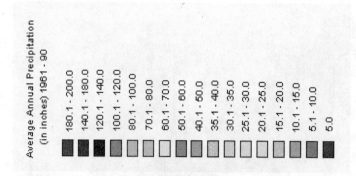

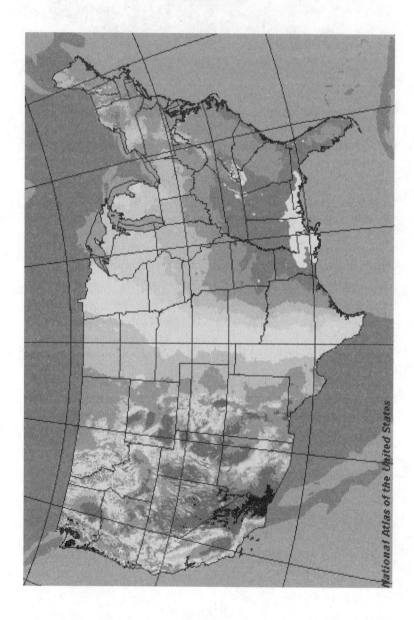

FIGURE 6(2)

AVERAGE ANNUAL PRECIPITATION (inches)

(Source: www.nationalatlas.gov)

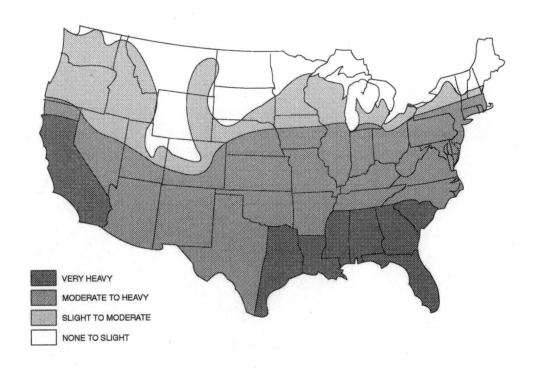

FIGURE 6(3)

TERMITE INFESTATION PROBABILITY MAP

Reprinted with permission from the 2015 International Residential Code, a copyrighted work of the International Code Council, www.iccsafe.org.

INTENTIONALLY LEFT BLANK.

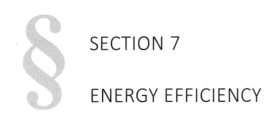

SECTION 7

ENERGY EFFICIENCY

GREEN BUILDING PRACTICES	POINTS

701 MINIMUM ENERGY EFFICIENCY REQUIREMENTS

701.1 Mandatory requirements. The building shall comply with § 702 (Performance Path), § 703 (Prescriptive Path), or § 704 (ERI Target Path). Items listed as "mandatory" in § 701.4 apply to all Paths. Unless otherwise noted, buildings in the Tropical Climate Zone shall comply with Climate Zone 1 requirements.

701.1.1 Minimum Performance Path requirements. A building complying with § 702 shall include a minimum of two practices from § 705, or a minimum of one practice from § 705 and a minimum of one practice from § 706.

701.1.2 Minimum Prescriptive Path requirements. A building complying with § 703 shall obtain a minimum of 30 points from § 703 and shall include a minimum of two practices from § 705, or a minimum of one practice from § 705 and a minimum of one practice from § 706.

701.1.3 ERI Target Path requirements. A building complying with § 704 shall obtain a minimum of 30 points from § 704 and shall include a minimum of two practices from § 705, or a minimum of one practice from § 705 and a minimum of one practice from § 706.

701.1.4 Alternative Bronze and Silver level compliance. As an alternative, any building that qualifies as an ENERGY STAR Version 3.0 Certified Home or ENERGY STAR Multifamily High Rise Version 1.0 Rev. 03 building or demonstrates compliance with the ICC IECC or IRC Chapter 11 achieves the Bronze level for Chapter 7. As an alternative, any building that qualifies as an ENERGY STAR Version 3.1 Certified Home or ENERGY STAR Multifamily High Rise Version 1.0 Rev. 03 (with the baseline at ASHRAE 90.1-2010) building achieves the Silver level for Chapter 7. As an alternative in the Tropical Climate Zone, any building that meets all the requirements in ICC IECC Section R401.2.1 (Tropical Zone) achieves the Silver level for Chapter 7. The buildings achieving compliance under § 701.1.4 are not eligible for achieving a rating level above Silver.

701.1.5 Alternative Gold level compliance. As an alternative, any building within the scope of the NGBS that complies with Chapter 7 of the ICC IgCC achieves the Gold level for Chapter 7. Additionally, acceptable air tightness of individual residential units shall be demonstrated by a blower door test. The testing and sampling procedure shall be in accordance with the ENERGY STAR Multifamily High Rise Program Testing and Verification Protocols, Version 1.0, Revision 03 - 2015, with an allowable maximum leakage of 0.3 cfm/sf of enclosure bounding the apartment at an induced pressure difference of 50 pascals.

701.1.6 Alternative Gold level compliance for tropical zones. One- or two-family dwelling in the tropical zone at an elevation less than 2,400 ft. (731.5 m) above sea level that complies with the following shall achieve the Gold level for Chapter 7:

(1) The residence complies with ICC IECC R401.2.1 Tropical zone.

(2) The residence includes a minimum of 2 kW of PV and a minimum of 6 kWh of battery storage.

(3) Any air conditioning has a minimum of 18 SEER.

GREEN BUILDING PRACTICES	M=Mandatory POINTS

(4) Solar, wind or other renewable energy source supplies not less than 90% of the energy for service water heating.

(5) Glazing in conditioned spaces has a solar heat gain coefficient of less than or equal to 0.25, or has an overhang with a projection factor equal to or greater than 0.30.

(6) The exterior roof/ceiling complies with at least two of the following:

    (a) Minimum roof reflectance and emittance in ICC IECC Table C402.3.

    (b) Roof or ceiling has insulation with an R-value of R-15 or greater.

    (c) Includes a radiant barrier.

(7) Walls comply with at least one of the following:

    (a) Walls have an overhang with a projection factor equal to or greater than 0.30.

    (b) Walls have insulation with an R-value of R-13 or greater.

    (c) Walls have a solar reflectance of 0.64.

(8) A ceiling fan is provided for bedrooms and the largest space that is not used as a bedroom; alternately a whole house fan is provided.

(9) Wiring sufficient for a Level 2 (208/240V 40-80 amp) electric vehicle charging station is installed on the building site.

701.2 Emerald level points. The Performance Path (§ 702) or the ERI Target Path (§ 704) shall be used to achieve the Emerald level.

701.3 Adopting entity review. A review by the Adopting Entity or designated third party shall be conducted to verify design and compliance with Chapter 7.

701.4 Mandatory practices

701.4.1 HVAC systems

701.4.1.1 HVAC system sizing. Space heating and cooling system is sized according to heating and cooling loads calculated using ACCA Manual J or equivalent. Equipment is selected using ACCA Manual S or equivalent. .... **M**

701.4.1.2 Radiant and hydronic space heating. Where installed as a primary heat source in the building, radiant or hydronic space heating system is designed, installed, and documented, using industry-approved guidelines and standards (e.g., ACCA Manual J, AHRI I=B=R, ACCA 5 QI, or an accredited design professional's and manufacturer's recommendation). .... **M**

701.4.2 Duct systems

701.4.2.1 Duct air sealing. Ducts are air sealed. All duct sealing materials are in conformance with UL 181A or UL 181B specifications and are installed in accordance with manufacturer's instructions. .... **M**

701.4.2.2 Ducts and Plenums. Building framing cavities are not used as ducts or plenums. .... **M**

701.4.2.3 Duct system sizing. Duct system is sized and designed in accordance with ACCA Manual D or equivalent. .... **M**

	M=Mandatory
GREEN BUILDING PRACTICES	**POINTS**

701.4.3 Insulation and air sealing.

701.4.3.1 Building thermal envelope air sealing. The building thermal envelope is durably sealed to limit infiltration. The sealing methods between dissimilar materials allow for differential expansion and contraction. The following are caulked, gasketed, weather-stripped or otherwise sealed with an air barrier material, suitable film, or solid material: .... **M**

    (a) All joints, seams and penetrations

    (b) Site-built windows, doors, and skylights

    (c) Openings between window and door assemblies and their respective jambs and framing

    (d) Utility penetrations

    (e) Dropped ceilings or chases adjacent to the thermal envelope

    (f) Knee walls

    (g) Walls, ceilings, and floors separating conditioned spaces from unconditioned spaces

    (h) Behind tubs and showers on exterior walls

    (i) Common walls between dwelling units or sleeping units

    (j) Attic access openings

    (k) Joints of framing members at rim joists

    (l) Top and bottom plates

    (m) Other sources of infiltration

701.4.3.2 Air barrier, air sealing, building envelope testing, and insulation. Building envelope air barrier, air sealing envelope tightness, and insulation installation is verified to be in accordance with this Section and § 701.4.3.2.1. Insulation installation other than Grade 1 is not permitted................................. **M**

(1) **Testing.** Building envelope tightness is tested. Testing is conducted in accordance with ASTM E779 using a blower door at a test pressure of 1.04 psf (50 Pa). Testing is conducted after rough-in and after installation of penetrations of the building envelope, including penetrations for utilities, plumbing, electrical, ventilation, and combustion appliances. Testing is conducted under the following conditions:

    (a) Exterior windows and doors, fireplace and stove doors are closed, but not sealed;

    (b) Dampers are closed, but not sealed, including exhaust, intake, make-up air, backdraft and flue dampers;

    (c) Interior doors are open;

    (d) Exterior openings for continuous ventilation systems and heat recovery ventilators are closed and sealed;

    (e) Heating and cooling systems are turned off;

    (f) HVAC duct terminations are not sealed; and

    (g) Supply and return registers are not sealed.

Multifamily Building Note: Testing by dwelling units, sleeping units, groups of dwelling units, groups of sleeping units, or the building as a whole is acceptable.

(2) **Visual inspection.** The air barrier and insulation items listed in Table 701.4.3.2(2) are field verified by visual inspection.

Table 701.4.3.2(2)
Air Barrier and Insulation Installation

COMPONENT	AIR BARRIER CRITERIA	INSULATION INSTALLATION CRITERIA
General requirements	A continuous air barrier shall be installed in the building envelope. The exterior thermal envelope contains a continuous air barrier. Breaks or joints in the air barrier shall be sealed.	Air-permeable insulation shall not be used as a sealing material.
Ceiling/attic	The air barrier in any dropped ceiling/soffit shall be aligned with the insulation and any gaps in the air barrier shall be sealed. Access openings, drop down stairs or knee wall doors to unconditioned attic spaces shall be sealed.	The insulation in any dropped ceiling/soffit shall be aligned with the air barrier.
Walls	The junction of the foundation and sill plate shall be sealed. The junction of the top plate and the top of exterior walls shall be sealed. Knee walls shall be sealed.	Cavities within corners and headers of frame walls shall be insulated by completely filling the cavity with a material having a thermal resistance of R-3 per inch minimum. Exterior thermal envelope insulation for framed walls shall be installed in substantial contact and continuous alignment with the air barrier.
Windows, skylights and doors	The space between window/doorjambs and framing, and skylights and framing shall be sealed.	
Rim joists	Rim joists shall include the air barrier.	Rim joists shall be insulated.
Floors (including above garage and cantilevered floors)	The air barrier shall be installed at any exposed edge of insulation.	Floor framing cavity insulation shall be installed to maintain permanent contact with the underside of subfloor decking, or floor framing cavity insulation shall be permitted to be in contact with the top side of sheathing, or continuous insulation installed on the underside of floor framing and extends from the bottom to the top of all perimeter floor framing members.
Crawl space walls	Exposed earth in unvented crawl spaces shall be covered with a Class I vapor retarder with overlapping joints taped.	Where provided instead of floor insulation, insulation shall be permanently attached to the crawlspace walls.
Shafts, penetrations	Duct shafts, utility penetrations, and flue shafts opening to exterior or unconditioned space shall be sealed.	
Narrow cavities		Batts in narrow cavities shall be cut to fit, or narrow cavities shall be filled by insulation that on installation readily conforms to the available cavity space.
Garage separation	Air sealing shall be provided between the garage and conditioned spaces.	
Recessed lighting	Recessed light fixtures installed in the building thermal envelope shall be sealed to the drywall.	Recessed light fixtures installed in the building thermal envelope shall be air tight and IC rated.
Plumbing and wiring		Batt insulation shall be cut neatly to fit around wiring and plumbing in exterior walls, or insulation that on installation readily conforms to available space shall extend behind piping and wiring.
Shower/tub on exterior wall	The air barrier installed at exterior walls adjacent to showers and tubs shall separate them from the showers and tubs.	Exterior walls adjacent to showers and tubs shall be insulated.
Electrical/phone box on exterior walls	The air barrier shall be installed behind electrical or communication boxes or air-sealed boxes shall be installed.	
HVAC register boots	HVAC register boots that penetrate building thermal envelope shall be sealed to the subfloor or drywall.	
Concealed sprinklers	When required to be sealed, concealed fire sprinklers shall only be sealed in a manner that is recommended by the manufacturer. Caulking or other adhesive sealants shall not be used to fill voids between fire sprinkler cover plates and walls or ceilings.	

a. In addition, inspection of log walls shall be in accordance with the provisions of ICC-400.

GREEN BUILDING PRACTICES	POINTS

701.4.3.2.1 Grade I insulation installations. Field-installed insulation products to ceilings, walls, floors, band joists, rim joists, conditioned attics, basements, and crawlspaces, except as specifically noted, are verified by a third-party as Grade I in accordance with the following: .... **M**

(1) Inspection is conducted before insulation is covered.

(2) Air-permeable insulation is enclosed on all six sides and is in substantial contact with the sheathing material on one or more sides (interior or exterior) of the cavity. Air permeable insulation in ceilings is not required to be enclosed when the insulation is installed in substantial contact with the surfaces it is intended to insulate.

(3) Cavity insulation uniformly fills each cavity side-to-side and top-to-bottom, without substantial gaps or voids around obstructions (such as blocking or bridging).

(4) Cavity insulation compression or incomplete fill amounts to 2% or less, presuming the compressed or incomplete areas are a minimum of 70% of the intended fill thickness; occasional small gaps are acceptable.

(5) Exterior rigid insulation has substantial contact with the structural framing members or sheathing materials and is tightly fitted at joints.

(6) Cavity insulation is split, installed, and/or fitted tightly around wiring and other services.

(7) Exterior sheathing is not visible from the interior through gaps in the cavity insulation.

(8) Faced batt insulation is permitted to have side-stapled tabs, provided the tabs are stapled neatly with no buckling, and provided the batt is compressed only at the edges of each cavity, to the depth of the tab itself.

(9) Where properly installed, ICFs, SIPs, and other wall systems that provide integral insulation are deemed in compliance with this section.

701.4.3.3 Multifamily air leakage alternative. Multifamily buildings four or more stories in height and in compliance with ICC IECC Section C402.5 (Air leakage-thermal envelope) are deemed to comply with § 701.4.3.1 and §701.4.3.2.

701.4.3.4 Fenestration air leakage. Windows, skylights and sliding glass doors have an air infiltration rate of no more than 0.3 cfm per sq. ft. (1.5 L/s/m^2), and swinging doors no more than 0.5 cfm per sq. ft. (2.6 L/s/m^2), when tested in accordance with NFRC 400 or AAMA/WDMA/CSA 101/I.S.2/A440 by an accredited, independent laboratory and listed and labeled. For site-built fenestration, a test report by an accredited, independent laboratory verifying compliance with the applicable infiltration rate shall be submitted to demonstrate compliance with this practice. This practice does not apply to field-fabricated fenestration products. .... **M**

Exception: For Tropical Zones Only, Jalousie windows are permitted to be used as a conditioned space boundary and shall have an air infiltration rate of not more than 1.3 cfm per sq. ft.

701.4.3.5 Lighting in building thermal envelope. Luminaires installed in the building thermal envelope which penetrate the air barrier are sealed to limit air leakage between conditioned and unconditioned spaces. All luminaires installed in the building thermal envelope which penetrate the air barrier are IC-rated and labeled as meeting ASTM E283 when tested at 1.57 psf (75 Pa) pressure differential with no more than 2.0 cfm (0.944 L/s) of air movement from the conditioned space to the ceiling cavity. All luminaires installed in the building thermal envelope which penetrate the air barrier are sealed with a gasket or caulk between the housing and the interior of the wall or ceiling covering...................................... **M**

	M=Mandatory
GREEN BUILDING PRACTICES	**POINTS**

701.4.4 High-efficacy lighting. Lighting efficacy in dwelling units or sleeping units is in accordance with one of the following: .... **M**

(1) A minimum of 75% of the total hard-wired lighting fixtures or the bulbs in those fixtures qualify as high efficacy or equivalent.

(2) Lighting power density, measured in watts/square foot, is 1.1 or less.

701.4.5 Boiler piping. Boiler piping in unconditioned space supplying and returning heated water or steam is insulated. .... **M**

702 PERFORMANCE PATH

702.1 Point allocation. Points from § 702 (Performance Path) shall not be combined with points from § 703 (Prescriptive Path) or § 704 (ERI Target Path). .... **M for § 702**

702.2 Energy performance levels

702.2.1 ICC IECC analysis. Energy efficiency features are implemented to achieve energy cost or source energy performance that meets the ICC IECC. A documented analysis using software in accordance with ICC IECC Section R405, or ICC IECC Section C407.2 through C407.5, applied as defined in the ICC IECC, is required. .... **M for § 702**

702.2.2 Energy performance analysis. Energy savings levels above the ICC IECC are determined through an analysis that includes improvements in building envelope, air infiltration, heating system efficiencies, cooling system efficiencies, duct sealing, water heating system efficiencies, lighting, appliances, and on-site renewable energy. Points are assigned using the following formula:

Points = 30 + (percent above ICC IECC) * 2

Multifamily Building Note: Modeling is completed building-wide using one of the following methods: whole building energy modeling, a unit-by-unit approach, or a building average of a unit-by-unit approach.

702.2.3 Tropical standard reference design. For the Tropical Climate Zone, the standard reference design shall use the specifications in ICC IECC Section R401.2.1 (Tropical Zone).

703 PRESCRIPTIVE PATH

703.1 Mandatory practices **30**

703.1.1 Building thermal envelope compliance. The building thermal envelope is in compliance with § 703.1.1.1 or § 703.1.1.2. .... **M for § 703**

Exception: Section 703.1.1 is not required for Tropical Climate Zone.

703.1.1.1 Maximum UA and SHGC. For ICC IECC residential buildings, the total building UA is less than or equal to the total maximum UA as computed by ICC IECC Section R402.1.5. The SHGC requirements for fenestration in Table R402.1.2 are also met. For ICC IECC commercial buildings, the total UA is less than or equal to the sum of the UA for ICC IECC Tables C402.1.4 and C402.4, including the U-factor times the area and C-factor or F-factor times the perimeter. The SHGC requirements for fenestration in Table C402.4 are also met. The total UA proposed and baseline calculations are documented. REScheck or COMcheck is deemed to provide UA calculation documentation.

GREEN BUILDING PRACTICES	M=Mandatory POINTS

703.1.1.2 Prescriptive R-values and fenestration requirements. The building thermal envelope is in accordance with the insulation and fenestration requirements of ICC IECC Table R402.1.2 or Table C402.1.3. The fenestration U-factors and SHGC's are in accordance with Table 703.2.5.1 or ICC IECC Table C402.4.

703.1.2 Building envelope leakage. The building thermal envelope is in accordance with ICC IECC R402.4.1.2 or C402.5 as applicable. .... **M for § 703**

Exception: Section 703.1.2 is not required for Tropical Climate Zone.

703.1.3 Duct testing. The duct system is in accordance with ICC IECC R403.3.2 through R403.3.5 as applicable. .... **M for § 703**

703.2 Building envelope

703.2.1 UA improvement. The total building thermal envelope UA is less than or equal to the baseline total UA resulting from the U-factors provided in Table 703.2.1(a) or ICC IECC Tables C402.1.4 and C402.4, as applicable. Where insulation is used to achieve the UA improvement, the insulation installation is in accordance with Grade 1 meeting § 701.4.3.2.1 as verified by a third-party. Total UA is documented using a REScheck, COMcheck, or equivalent report to verify the baseline and the UA improvement. .... **Per Table 703.2.1(b)**

Table 703.2.1(a)
Baseline U-Factors[a]

Climate Zone	Fenestration U-Factor	Skylight U-Factor	Ceiling U-Factor	Frame Wall U-Factor	Mass Wall U-Factor[b]	Floor U-Factor	Basement Wall U-Factor	Crawlspace Wall U-Factor[c]
1	0.50	0.75	0.035	0.084	0.197	0.064	0.360	0.477
2	0.40	0.65	0.030	0.084	0.165	0.064	0.360	0.477
3	0.35	0.55	0.030	0.060	0.098	0.047	0.091[c]	0.136
4 except Marine	0.35	0.55	0.026	0.060	0.098	0.047	0.059	0.065
5 and Marine 4	0.32	0.55	0.026	0.060	0.082	0.033	0.050	0.055
6	0.32	0.55	0.026	0.045	0.060	0.033	0.050	0.055
7 and 8	0.32	0.55	0.026	0.045	0.057	0.028	0.050	0.055

a. Non-fenestration U-factors shall be obtained from measurement, calculation, or an approved source.
b. Where more the half the insulation is on the interior, the mass wall U-factors is a maximum of 0.17 in Zone 1, 0.14 in Zone 2, 0.12 in Zone 3, 0.10 in Zone 4 except in Marine, and the same as the frame wall U-factor in Marine Zone 4 and Zones 5 through 8.
c. Basement wall U-factor of 0.360 in warm-humid locations.

GREEN BUILDING PRACTICES	POINTS

Table 703.2.1(b)
Points for Improvement in Total Building Thermal Envelope UA
Compared to Baseline UA

Minimum UA Improvement	Climate Zone							
	1[a]	2	3	4	5	6	7	8
	POINTS							
0 to <5%	0	0	0	0	0	0	0	0
5% to <10%	2	3	3	3	3	3	3	3
10% to <15%	3	6	5	6	6	6	5	7
15% to <20%	5	9	8	9	9	9	8	10
20% to <25%	6	12	10	12	12	12	11	13
25% to <30%	8	15	13	16	14	15	14	17
30% to <35%	10	18	16	19	17	18	16	20
≥35%	11	21	18	22	20	21	19	23

a. Tropical Climate Zone: Points are Climate Zone 1 points divided by 2 and rounded down

Exception: For the Tropical Climate Zone, crawl space, basement, and floor u-factors are excluded from the total building thermal envelope UA improvement calculation.

703.2.2 Mass walls. More than 75% of the above-grade exterior opaque wall area of the building is mass walls. ....

Per Table 703.2.2

Table 703.2.2
Exterior Mass Walls

Mass thickness	Climate Zone			
	1-4	5	6	7-8
	POINTS			
≥3 in. to <6 in.	1	0	0	0
>6 in.	3	2	2	0

703.2.3 A radiant barrier with an emittance of 0.05 or less is used in the attic. The product is tested in accordance with ASTM C1371 and installed in accordance with the manufacturer's instructions................

Per Table 703.2.3

Table 703.2.3
Radiant Barriers

Climate Zone	POINTS
Tropical	3
1	2
2-3	3
4-5	1
6-8	0

[In climate zones 1-3, 1 point maximum for multifamily buildings four or more stories in height.]

GREEN BUILDING PRACTICES	M=Mandatory POINTS

703.2.4 Building envelope leakage. The maximum building envelope leakage rate is in accordance with Table 703.2.4(a) or Table 703.2.4(b) and whole building ventilation is provided in accordance with § 902.2.1.. | **Per Table 703.2.4(a) or 703.2.4(b)**

Table 703.2.4(a)
Building Envelope Leakage

Max Envelope Leakage Rate (ACH50)	Climate Zone							
	1	2	3	4	5	6	7	8
	POINTS							
4	1	2	-	-	-	-	-	-
3	2	4	-	-	-	-	-	-
2	3	5	3	4	4	6	8	7
1	4	7	5	7	7	10	15	11

Table 703.2.4(b)
Building Envelope Leakage

Max Envelope Leakage Rate (ELR50)	Climate Zone							
	1	2	3	4	5	6	7	8
	POINTS							
0.28	1	2	-	-	-	-	-	-
0.23	2	4	-	-	-	-	-	-
0.18	3	5	3	4	4	6	8	7
0.13	4	7	5	7	7	10	15	11

Where ELR50 = CFM50 / Shell Area

CFM50 = cubic feet per minute at 50 Pa

Points not awarded if points are taken under § 705.6.2.1.

703.2.5 Fenestration

703.2.5.1 NFRC-certified (or equivalent) U-factor and SHGC of windows, exterior doors, skylights, and tubular daylighting devices (TDDs) on an area-weighted average basis do not exceed the values in Table 703.2.5.1. Area weighted averages are calculated separately for the categories of 1) windows and exterior doors and 2) skylights and tubular daylighting devices (TDDs). Decorative fenestration elements with a combined total maximum area of 15 sq. ft. (1.39 m^2) or 10% of the total glazing area, whichever is less, are not required to comply with this practice.. | **M for § 703**

| GREEN BUILDING PRACTICES | POINTS |

Table 703.2.5.1
Fenestration Specifications

Climate Zones	U-Factor	SHGC
	Windows and Exterior Doors (maximum certified ratings)	
1	0.50	0.25
2	0.40	0.25
3	0.32	0.25
4	0.32	0.40
5 to 8	0.30*	Any
	Skylights and TDDs (maximum certified ratings)	
1	0.75	0.30
2	0.65	0.30
3	0.55	0.30
4	0.55	0.40
5 to 8	0.55	Any

Exception: For Sun-tempered designs meeting the requirements of § 703.7.1, the SHGC is permitted to be 0.40 or higher on south facing glass.

Exception: A maximum U-factor of 0.32 shall apply in climate zones 5-8 to vertical fenestration products installed in buildings located: (i) above 4000 feet in elevation above sea level or (ii) in windborne debris regions where protection of openings is provided by fenestration as required under IRC section R301.2.1.2.

703.2.5.1.1 Dynamic glazing. Dynamic glazing is permitted to satisfy the SHGC requirements of Table 703.2.5.1 provided the ratio of the higher to lower labeled SHGC is greater than or equal to 2.4 and the dynamic glazing is automatically controlled to modulate the amount of solar gain into the space in multiple steps. Fenestration with dynamic glazing is considered separately from other fenestration and area-weighted averaging with fenestration that does not use dynamic glazing is not permitted. Dynamic glazing is not required to be automatically controlled or comply with minimum SHGC ratio when both the lower and higher labeled SHGC already comply with the requirements of Table 703.2.5.1.

703.2.5.2 The NFRC-certified (or equivalent) U-factor and SHGC of windows, exterior doors, skylights, and tubular daylighting devices (TDDs) are in accordance with Table 703.2.5.2(a), (b), or (c). Decorative fenestration elements with a combined total maximum area of 15 sq. ft. (1.39 m²) or 10% of the total glazing area, whichever is less, are not required to comply with this practice.

Per Table 703.2.5.2(a), or 703.2.5.2(b), or 703.2.5.2(c)

Table 703.2.5.2(a)
Enhanced Fenestration Specifications

Climate Zones	U-Factor Windows & Exterior Doors	SHGC Windows & Exterior Doors	U-Factor Skylights & TDDs	SHGC Skylights & TDDs	POINTS
1	0.40	0.25	0.60	0.28	1
2	0.40	0.25	0.60	0.28	1
3	0.30	0.25	0.53	0.28	2
4	0.30	0.40	0.53	0.35	3
5	0.27	Any	0.50	Any	3
6	0.27	Any	0.50	Any	4
7	0.27	Any	0.50	Any	4
8	0.27	Any	0.50	Any	4

Exception: For Sun-tempered designs meeting the requirements of § 703.7.1, the SHGC is permitted to be 0.40 or higher on south facing glass.

Table 703.2.5.2(b)
Enhanced Fenestration Specifications

Climate Zone	U-Factor Windows & Exterior Doors	SHGC Windows & Exterior Doors	U-Factor Skylights & TDDs	SHGC Skylights & TDDs	POINTS
1	0.38	0.25	0.55	0.28	2
2	0.38	0.25	0.53	0.28	3
3	0.30	0.25	0.50	0.28	4
4	0.28	0.40	0.50	0.35	4
5	0.25	Any	0.48	Any	4
6	0.25	Any	0.48	Any	5
7	0.25	Any	0.46	Any	5
8	0.25	Any	0.46	Any	4

Exception: For Sun-tempered designs meeting the requirements of § 703.7.1, the SHGC is permitted to be 0.40 or higher on south facing glass.

Table 703.2.5.2(c)
Enhanced Fenestration Specifications

Climate Zones	U-Factor Windows & Exterior Doors	SHGC Windows & Exterior Doors	U-Factor Skylights & TDDs	SHGC Skylights & TDDs	POINTS
4	0.25	0.40	0.45	0.40	6
5-8	0.22	Any	0.42	Any	6

[Points for multifamily buildings four or more stories in height are awarded at 3 times the point value listed in Table 703.2.5.2(c)]

703.2.5.2.1 Dynamic glazing. Dynamic glazing is permitted to satisfy the SHGC requirements of Tables 703.2.5.2(a), 703.2.5.2(b), and 703.2.5.2(c) provided the ratio of the higher to lower labeled SHGC is greater than or equal to 2.4, and the dynamic glazing is automatically controlled to modulate the amount of solar gain into the space in multiple steps. Fenestration with dynamic glazing is considered separately from other fenestration, and area-weighted averaging with fenestration that does not use dynamic glazing is not permitted. Dynamic glazing is not required to be automatically controlled or comply with minimum SHGC ratio when both the lower and higher labeled SHGC already comply with the requirements of Tables 703.2.5.2(a), 703.2.5.2(b), and 703.2.5.2(c).

703.3 HVAC equipment efficiency

703.3.0 Multiple heating and cooling systems. For multiple heating or cooling systems in one home, practices 703.3.1 through 703.3.6 apply to the system that supplies 80% or more of the total installed heating or cooling capacity. Where multiple systems each serve less than 80% of the total installed heating or cooling capacity, points under Sections 703.3.1 through 703.3.6 are awarded either for the system eligible for the fewest points or the weighted average of the systems. The weighted average shall be calculated in accordance with the following equation and be based upon the efficiency and capacity of the equipment as selected in accordance with ACCA Manual S with it loads calculated in accordance with ACCA Manual J.

Weighted Average $= [(E_{unit\ 1} * C_{unit\ 1}) + (E_{unit\ 2} * C_{unit\ 2}) + ... + (E_{unit\ n} * C_{unit\ n})] / (C_{unit\ 1} + C_{unit\ 2} + ... + C_{unit\ n})$

where:
E = Rated AHRI efficiency for unit
C = Rated heating or cooling capacity for unit
n = Unit count

GREEN BUILDING PRACTICES	POINTS

703.3.1 Combination space heating and water heating system (combo system) is installed using either a coil from the water heater connected to an air handler to provide heat for the building, dwelling unit or sleeping unit, or a space heating boiler using an indirect-fired water heater. Devices have a minimum combined annual efficiency of 0.80 and a minimum water heating recovery efficiency of 0.87. ....

4

703.3.2 Furnace and/or boiler efficiency is in accordance with one of the following:

(1) Gas and propane heaters:

Per Table 703.3.2(1)(a) or 703.3.2(1)(b)

Table 703.3.2(1)(a)
Gas and Propane Heaters

AFUE	Climate Zone							
	1	2	3	4	5	6	7	8
	POINTS							
≥90% AFUE	0	2	3	6	6	9	10	12
≥92% AFUE	0	2	4	7	8	10	12	14
≥94% AFUE	0	3	4	9	9	12	14	16
≥96% AFUE	1	3	5	10	10	14	16	19
≥98% AFUE	1	3	6	11	12	16	18	21

Table 703.3.2(1)(b)
Gas and Propane Heaters for Multifamily Buildings Four or More Stories in Height

AFUE	Climate Zone							
	1	2	3	4	5	6	7	8
	POINTS							
≥90% AFUE	0	4	4	8	8	10	11	13
≥92% AFUE	0	4	4	9	10	11	12	14
≥94% AFUE	0	5	5	10	11	12	14	16
≥96% AFUE	0	5	5	12	12	13	15	17
≥98% AFUE	0	6	6	13	13	14	16	18

(2) Oil furnace:

Per Table 703.3.2(2)

Table 703.3.2(2)
Oil Furnace

AFUE	Climate Zone							
	1	2	3	4	5	6	7	8
	POINTS							
≥85% AFUE	0	1	2	3	3	4	5	6
≥90% AFUE	0	2	3	6	6	9	10	12

(3) Gas boiler:

Per Table 703.3.2(3)

Table 703.3.2(3)
Gas Boiler

AFUE	Climate Zone							
	1	2	3	4	5	6	7	8
	POINTS							
≥85% AFUE	0	1	1	2	3	4	4	4
≥90% AFUE	0	1	2	4	6	7	8	6
≥94% AFUE	0	2	3	5	8	9	10	8
≥96% AFUE	0	2	4	6	9	11	12	10

GREEN BUILDING PRACTICES	M=Mandatory
	POINTS

(4) Oil boiler:

Table 703.3.2(4)
Oil Boiler

AFUE	Climate Zone							
	1	2	3	4	5	6	7	8
	POINTS							
≥85% AFUE	0	1	1	3	3	4	4	5
≥90% AFUE	1	2	3	5	6	7	9	10

Per Table 703.3.2(4)

703.3.3 Heat pump heating efficiency is in accordance with Table 703.3.3(1) or Table 703.3.3(2) or Table 703.3.3(3). Refrigerant charge is verified for compliance with manufacturer's instructions utilizing a method in ACCA 5 QI Section 4.3.

Per Table 703.3.3(1) or 703.3.3(2) or 703.3.3(3)

Table 703.3.3(1)
Electric Heat Pump Heating

Efficiency	Climate Zone					
	1	2	3	4	5	6-8[a]
	POINTS					
≥8.5 HSPF (11.5 EER)	0	1	1	2	2	2
≥9.0 HSPF (12.5 EER)	0	2	4	5	6	10
≥9.5 HSPF	0	3	7	7	11	18
≥10.0 HSPF	1	5	10	10	15	26
≥12.0 HSPF	1	6	11	11	17	28

Table 703.3.3(2)
Electric Heat Pump Heating for Multifamily Buildings Four or More Stories in Height

Efficiency	Climate Zone					
	1	2	3	4	5	6-8[a]
	POINTS					
≥8.5 HSPF (11.5 EER)	0	3	4	8	11	13

Table 703.3.3(3)
Gas Engine-Driven Heat Pump Heating

Efficiency	Climate Zone					
	1	2	3	4	5	6-8
	POINTS					
≥1.3 COP at 47°F	2	7	11	14	16	18

GREEN BUILDING PRACTICES	POINTS

703.3.4 Cooling efficiency is in accordance with Table 703.3.4(1) or Table 703.3.4(2). Refrigerant charge is verified for compliance with manufacturer's instructions utilizing a method in ACCA 5 QI Section 4.3.

Per Table 703.3.4(1) or 703.3.4(2)

Table 703.3.4(1)
Electric Air Conditioner and Heat Pump Cooling[a]

Efficiency	Climate Zone							
	1	2	3	4	5	6	7	8
	POINTS							
≥15 SEER (12.5 EER)	6	4	2	1	1	1	1	0
≥17 SEER (12.5 EER)	11	9	7	3	3	2	2	0
≥19 SEER (12.5 EER)	19	12	10	6	4	4	4	0
≥21 SEER	26	15	14	8	6	6	5	0
≥25 SEER	29	18	17	10	8	8	6	0

a. Tropical Climate Zone: where none of the occupied space is air conditioned and where ceiling fans are provided for bedrooms and the largest space which is not used as a bedroom, 20 points is awarded.

Table 703.3.4(2)
Gas Engine-Driven Heat Pump Cooling

Efficiency	Climate Zone					
	1	2	3	4	5	6-8
	POINTS					
>1.2 COP at 95°F	3	6	3	1	1	0

703.3.5 Water source cooling and heating efficiency is in accordance with Table 703.3.5. Refrigerant charge is verified for compliance with manufacturer's instructions utilizing a method in ACCA 5 QI Section 4.3.

Per Table 703.3.5

Table 703.3.5
Water Source Cooling and Heating

Efficiency	Climate Zone					
	1	2	3	4	5	6-8
	POINTS					
≥15 EER, ≥4.0 COP	14	18	22	30	37	37

703.3.6 Ground source heat pump is installed by a Certified Geothermal Service Contractor in accordance with Table 703.3.6. Refrigerant charge is verified for compliance with manufacturer's instructions utilizing a method in ACCA 5 QI Section 4.3.

Per Table 703.3.6

Table 703.3.6
Ground Source Heat Pump[a]

Efficiency	Climate Zone				
	1	2	3	4	5-8
	POINTS				
≥16.0 EER, ≥3.6 COP	1	1	2	16	22
≥24.0 EER, ≥4.3 COP	24	29	22	31	35
≥28.0 EER, ≥4.8 COP	42	46	35	42	44

a. The ground loop is sized to account for the ground conductance and the expected minimum incoming water temperature to achieve rated performance.

GREEN BUILDING PRACTICES	POINTS

703.3.7 ENERGY STAR, or equivalent, ceiling fans are installed. *[Points awarded per building.]* **1**

[For Tropical Climate Zone and Climate Zones 2B, 3B, and 4B: points awarded per fan where AC is not installed in the dwelling unit or sleeping unit (Max 8 points)]

Where points are awarded in § 703.3.8 for these specific climate zones, points shall not be awarded in § 703.3.7.

703.3.8 Whole-building or whole-dwelling unit or whole-sleeping unit fan(s) with insulated louvers and a sealed enclosure is installed. *[Points awarded per building.]* — **Per Table 703.3.8**

Table 703.3.8
Whole Dwelling Unit Fan

Climate Zone		
1-3, Tropical	4-6	7-8
POINTS		
4	3	0

703.4 Duct systems

703.4.1 All space heating is provided by a system(s) that does not include air ducts. — **Per Table 703.4.1**

Table 703.4.1
Ductless Heating System

Climate Zone					
1	2	3	4	5	6-8
POINTS					
0	2	4	6	8	8

[No points awarded for multifamily buildings four or more stories in height.]

703.4.2 All space cooling is provided by a system(s) that does not include air ducts. — **Per Table 703.4.2**

Table 703.4.2
Ductless Cooling System

Climate Zone					
1	2	3	4	5	6-8
POINTS					
8	8	4	2	1	0

[No points awarded for multifamily buildings four or more stories in height.]

703.4.3 Ductwork is in accordance with all of the following: — **Per Table 703.4.3**

(1) Building cavities are not used as return ductwork.

(2) Heating and cooling ducts and mechanical equipment are installed within the conditioned building space.

(3) Ductwork is not installed in exterior walls.

Table 703.4.3
Ducts

Climate Zone					
1	2	3	4	5	6-8
POINTS					
8	10	8	8	8	4

[No points awarded for multifamily buildings four or more stories in height.]

	GREEN BUILDING PRACTICES	M=Mandatory POINTS

703.4.4 Duct Leakage. The entire central HVAC duct system, including air handlers and register boots, is tested by a third party for total leakage at a pressure differential of 0.1 in. w.g. (25 Pa) and maximum air leakage is equal to or less than 6% of the system design flow rate or 4 cu-ft per minute per 100 sq. ft. of conditioned floor area.

Per Table 703.4.4

Table 703.4.4
Duct Leakage

Ductwork location	Climate Zone					
	1	2	3	4	5	6-8
	POINTS					
ductwork *entirely outside* the building's thermal envelope	4	5	4	3	2	1
ductwork *entirely inside* the building's thermal envelope	1	1	1	1	1	1
ductwork *inside and outside* the building's thermal envelope	3	4	3	2	1	1

Points not awarded if points are taken under § 705.6.2.3.

703.5 Water heating system

703.5.1 Water heater Uniform Energy Factor (UEF) is in accordance with the following:

[Where multiple systems are used, points awarded based on the system with the lowest efficiency.]

Water heater design is based on only 1 (one) water heater per dwelling unit, based on approved methods from ICC IPC, ASPE, or manufacturer specifications. All table values are based on water heaters with medium water draws as defined by the DOE test procedures (55 gallons per day).

(1) Gas water heating

Per Tables 703.5.1(1)(a) through 703.5.1(1)(e)

Table 703.5.1(1)(a)
Gas Water Heating
Storage Water Heater, Rated Storage Volume > 20 Gallons and ≤ 55 Gallons, Medium Water Draw

Uniform Energy Factor	Climate Zone							
	1	2	3	4	5	6	7	8
	POINTS							
0.65 to <0.78	2	2	2	2	2	2	2	1
≥0.78	3	3	3	3	3	3	3	2

Table 703.5.1(1)(b)
Gas Water Heating
Storage Water Heater, Rated Storage Volume > 55 Gallons and ≤ 100 Gallons, Medium Water Draw

Uniform Energy Factor	Climate Zone							
	1	2	3	4	5	6	7	8
	POINTS							
≥0.78	1	1	1	1	1	1	1	1

GREEN BUILDING PRACTICES	POINTS

Table 703.5.1(1)(c)
Gas Water Heating
Storage Water Heater with Input Rate Greater than 75,000 Btu/h (Commercial)

Thermal Efficiency	Climate Zone							
	1	2	3	4	5	6	7	8
	POINTS							
0.90 to < 0.95	6	6	5	3	3	3	3	2
≥0.95	7	7	5	4	4	4	4	2

Table 703.5.1(1)(d)
Gas Water Heating
Storage Water Heater with Input Rate Greater than 75,000 Btu/h (Commercial),
In Buildings with High-Capacity Service Water-Heating Systems
(1,000,000 Btu/h or Greater)

Thermal Efficiency	Climate Zone							
	1	2	3	4	5	6	7	8
	POINTS							
0.92 to < 0.95	1	1	1	1	1	1	1	1
≥0.95	2	2	2	2	2	2	2	1

Table 703.5.1(1)(e)
Gas Water Heating
Instantaneous Water Heater, Rated Storage Volume < 2 Gallons
and Input Rate of > 50,000 Btu/h, Medium Water Draw

Uniform Energy Factor	Climate Zone							
	1	2	3	4	5	6	7	8
	POINTS							
0.89 to < 0.94	2	2	2	1	1	1	1	1
≥0.94	3	3	2	2	2	2	2	1

(2) Electric water heating

Per Tables 703.5.1(2)(a) through 703.5.1(2)(e)

Table 703.5.1(2)(a)
Storage Water Heater, Rated Storage Volume ≥ 20 Gallons and ≤ 55 Gallons,
Medium Water Draw

Uniform Energy Factor	Climate Zone							
	1	2	3	4	5	6	7	8
	POINTS							
0.94 to <1.0	1	1	1	1	1	1	1	1
1.0 to <1.5	4	2	2	2	1	1	1	1
1.5 to <2.0	7	4	3	2	2	2	1	1
2.0 to <2.2	14	8	7	5	4	4	2	2
2.2 to <2.5	17	9	8	6	5	4	3	3
2.5 to <3.0	18	12	10	8	6	6	3	3
≥3.0	22	16	13	11	8	8	4	3

GREEN BUILDING PRACTICES

Table 703.5.1(2)(b)
Storage Water Heater, Rated Storage Volume ≥ 55 Gallons and ≤ 120 Gallons, Medium Water Draw

Uniform Energy Factor	Climate Zone							
	1	2	3	4	5	6	7	8
	POINTS							
2.2 to <2.5	6	4	3	3	2	2	1	1
2.5 to <3.0	7	5	4	3	3	3	2	2
3.0 to <3.5	8	5	5	4	3	3	3	2
≥3.5	9	6	6	5	4	4	3	2

Table 703.5.1(2)(c)
Electric Tabletop Water Heating
(Tabletop Water Heater, Rated Storage Volume ≥ 20 Gallons and ≤ 120 Gallons, Medium Water Draw)

Uniform Energy Factor	Climate Zone							
	1	2	3	4	5	6	7	8
	POINTS							
≥0.91	1	1	1	1	1	1	1	1

Table 703.5.1(2)(d)
Electric Instantaneous Water Heating[a]
(Instantaneous Electric Water Heater, Rated Storage Volume < 2 Gallons, Medium Water Draw)

Uniform Energy Factor or Thermal Efficiency[b]	Climate Zone							
	1	2	3	4	5	6	7	8
	POINTS							
≥0.97	2	2	2	2	2	2	2	2

a. Applies to any size water heater.
b. Electric instantaneous water heaters have either a Uniform Energy Factor (capacity less than or equal to 12 kW) or a Thermal Efficiency (capacity greater than 12 kW).

Table 703.5.1(2)(e)
Electric Grid Enabled Water Heating
(Grid Enabled Storage Water Heater, Rated Storage Volume ≥ 75 Gallons, Medium Water Draw)

Uniform Energy Factor	Climate Zone							
	1	2	3	4	5	6	7	8
	POINTS							
≥0.95	1	1	1	1	1	1	1	1

(3) Oil water heating

Per Table 703.5.1(3)

Table 703.5.1(3)
Oil Water Heating
(Oil Water Heating, < 50 Gallons, Medium Water Draw)

Uniform Energy Factor	Climate Zone							
	1	2	3	4	5	6	7	8
	POINTS							
≥0.62	1	1	1	1	1	1	1	1

GREEN BUILDING PRACTICES	POINTS

703.5.2 Desuperheater is installed by a qualified installer or is pre-installed in the factory. — Per Table 703.5.2

Table 703.5.2
Desuperheater

Climate Zone						
1	2	3	4	5	6	7-8
POINTS						
23	17	9	7	5	4	2

703.5.3 Drain-water heat recovery system is installed. *[Points awarded per building.]* .... — 2

703.5.4 Indirect-fired water heater storage tanks heated from boiler systems are installed. .... — 1

703.5.5 Solar water heater. SRCC (Solar Rating & Certification Corporation) OG 300 rated, or equivalent, solar domestic water heating system is installed. Solar Energy Factor (SEF) as defined by SRCC is in accordance with Table 703.5.5(a) and Table 703.5.5(b). — Per Table 703.5.5(a) or 703.5.5(b)

Table 703.5.5(a)
Storage Water Heater, Rated Storage Volume of Backup Water Heater
is ≥ 0.1 Gallon and ≤ 55 Gallons, Medium Water Draw

SEF	Climate Zone						
	Tropical &1	2	3	4	5	6	7-8
	POINTS						
SEF ≥ 1.3	1	2	3	5	6	7	6
SEF ≥ 1.51	2	2	4	6	9	10	10
SEF ≥ 1.81	2	3	5	9	13	14	14
SEF ≥ 2.31	4	5	8	14	19	21	20
SEF ≥ 3.01	5	7	11	21	27	31	30

Table 703.5.5(b)
Storage Water Heater, Rated Storage Volume of Backup Water Heater
is >55 Gallons, Medium Water Draw

SEF	Climate Zone						
	Tropical &1	2	3	4	5	6	7-8
	POINTS						
SEF ≥ 1.3	1	1	2	3	4	5	4
SEF ≥ 1.51	1	1	2	4	6	7	7
SEF ≥ 1.81	1	2	4	6	8	10	9
SEF ≥ 2.31	2	3	5	10	13	14	13
SEF ≥ 3.01	4	5	7	14	18	20	20

GREEN BUILDING PRACTICES	M=Mandatory POINTS

703.6 Lighting and appliances

703.6.1 Hard-wired lighting. Hard-wired lighting is in accordance with one of the following:

(1) A minimum percent of the total hard-wired interior luminaires or lamps qualify as ENERGY STAR, DesignLights Consortium (DLC), or applicable equivalent.

Per Table 703.6.1(1)

Table 703.6.1(1)
Hard-wired Lighting

Minimum percent of fixtures	Climate Zone							
	1	2	3	4	5	6	7	8
	POINTS							
95%	3	3	3	2	2	2	2	2

(2) A minimum of 80% of the exterior lighting wattage has a minimum efficacy of 61 lumens per watt or is solar-powered. **1**

(3) In multifamily buildings, common area lighting power density (LPD) is less than 0.51 Watts per square foot. **7**

703.6.2 Appliances. ENERGY STAR or equivalent appliance(s) are installed:

(1) Refrigerator

Per Table 703.6.2(1)

Table 703.6.2(1)
Refrigerator

Climate Zone							
1	2	3	4	5	6	7	8
POINTS							
1	1	1	1	1	1	1	1

(2) Dishwasher **1**

(3) Washing machine **4**

703.7 Passive solar design

703.7.1 Sun-tempered design. Building orientation, sizing of glazing, and design of overhangs are in accordance with all of the following:.. **4**

(1) The long side (or one side if of equal length) of the building faces within 20 degrees of true south.

(2) Vertical glazing area is between 5% and 7% of the gross conditioned floor area on the south face [also see § 703.7.1(8)] and glazing U-factors meet Table 703.2.5.2(a).

(3) Vertical glazing area is less than 2% of the gross conditioned floor area on the west face, and glazing meets Table 703.2.5.2(a).

(4) Vertical glazing area is less than 4% of the gross conditioned floor area on the east face, and glazing meets Table 703.2.5.2(a).

(5) Vertical glazing area is less than 8% of the gross conditioned floor area on the north face, and glazing meets Table 703.2.5.2(a).

GREEN BUILDING PRACTICES	POINTS

(6) Skylights, where installed, are in accordance with the following:

(a) shades and insulated wells are used, and all glazing meets Table 703.2.5.2(a).

(b) horizontal skylights are less than 0.5% of finished ceiling area.

(c) sloped skylights on slopes facing within 45 degrees of true south, east, or west are less than 1.5% of the finished ceiling area.

(7) Overhangs, adjustable canopies, awnings, or trellises provide shading on south-facing glass for the appropriate climate zone in accordance with Table 703.7.1(7):

Table 703.7.1(7)
South-Facing Window Overhang Depth

		Vertical distance between bottom of overhang and top of window sill				
		≤7' 4"	≤6' 4"	≤5' 4"	≤4' 4"	≤3' 4"
Climate Zone	1 & 2 & 3	2' 8"	2' 8"	2' 4"	2' 0"	2' 0"
	4 & 5 & 6	2' 4"	2' 4"	2' 0"	2' 0"	1' 8"
	7 & 8	2' 0"	1' 8"	1' 8"	1' 4"	1' 0"

For SI: 1 in. = 25.4 mm

(8) The south facing windows have an SHGC of 0.40 or higher.

(9) Return air or transfer grilles/ducts are in accordance with § 705.4.

Multifamily Building Note: The site is designed such that at least 40% of the multifamily dwelling or sleeping units have one south facing wall (within 15 degrees) containing at least 50% of glazing for entire unit, Effective shading is required for passive solar control on all south facing glazing. The floor area of at least 15 ft. from the south facing perimeter glazing is massive and exposed to capture solar heat during the day and reradiate at night.

703.7.2 Window shading. Automated solar protection or dynamic glazing is installed to provide shading for windows.. 1

703.7.3 Passive cooling design. Passive cooling design features are in accordance with at least three of the following: *[1 additional point awarded for each additional item.]* .... 3 [6 max]

(1) Exterior shading is provided on east and west windows using one or a combination of the following:

(a) vine-covered trellises with the vegetation separated a minimum of 1 ft. (305 mm) from face of building.

(b) moveable awnings or louvers.

(c) covered porches.

(d) attached or detached conditioned/unconditioned enclosed space that provides full shade of east and west windows (e.g., detached garage, shed, or building).

(2) Overhangs are installed to provide shading on south-facing glazing in accordance with § 703.7.1(7).

Points not awarded if points are taken under § 703.7.1.

GREEN BUILDING PRACTICES	POINTS

(3) Windows and/or venting skylights are located to facilitate cross and stack effect ventilation.

(4) Solar reflective roof or radiant barrier is installed in climate zones 1, 2, or 3 and roof material achieves a 3-year aged criteria of 0.50.

(5) Internal exposed thermal mass is a minimum of 3 in. (76 mm) in thickness. Thermal mass consists of concrete, brick, and/or tile fully adhered to a masonry base or other masonry material in accordance with one or a combination of the following:

   (a) A minimum of 1 sq. ft. (0.09 m^2) of exposed thermal mass of floor per 3 sq. ft. (2.8 m^2) of gross finished floor area.

   (b) A minimum of 3 sq. ft. (2.8 m^2) of exposed thermal mass in interior walls or elements per sq. ft. (0.09 m^2) of gross finished floor area.

(6) Roofing material is installed with a minimum 0.75 in. (19 mm) continuous air space offset from the roof deck from eave to ridge.

703.7.4 Passive solar heating design. In addition to the sun-tempered design features in § 703.7.1, all of the following are implemented: *[Points shall not be awarded in the Tropical Climate Zone]* **4**

(1) Additional glazing, no greater than 12%, is permitted on the south wall. This additional glazing is in accordance with the requirements of § 703.7.1.

(2) Additional thermal mass for any room with south-facing glazing of more than 7% of the finished floor area is provided in accordance with the following:

   (a) Thermal mass is solid and a minimum of 3 in. (76 mm) in thickness. Where two thermal mass materials are layered together (e.g., ceramic tile on concrete base) to achieve the appropriate thickness, they are fully adhered to (touching) each other.

   (b) Thermal mass directly exposed to sunlight is provided in accordance with the following minimum ratios:

      (i) Above latitude 35 degrees: 5 sq. ft. (0.465 m^2) of thermal mass for every 1 sq. ft. (0.093 m^2) of south-facing glazing.

      (ii) Latitude 30 degrees to 35 degrees: 5.5 sq. ft. (0.51 m^2) of thermal mass for every 1 sq. ft. (0.093 m^2) of south-facing glazing.

      (iii) Latitude 25 degrees to 30 degrees: 6 sq. ft. (0.557 m^2) of thermal mass for every 1 sq. ft. (0.093 m^2) of south-facing glazing.

   (c) Thermal mass not directly exposed to sunlight is permitted to be used to achieve thermal mass requirements of § 703.7.4 (2) based on a ratio of 40 sq. ft. (3.72 m^2) of thermal mass for every 1 sq. ft. (0.093 m^2) of south-facing glazing.

(3) In addition to return air or transfer grilles/ducts required by § 703.7.1(9), provisions for forced airflow to adjoining areas are implemented as needed.

GREEN BUILDING PRACTICES	POINTS

704 ERI TARGET PATH

704.1 ERI target compliance. Compliance with the energy chapter shall be permitted to be based on the EPA National ERI Target Procedure for ENERGY STAR Certified Homes. Points from § 704 (ERI Target) shall not be combined with points from § 702 (Performance Path) or § 703 (Prescriptive Path).

Dwelling ratings shall be submitted to a Rating Certification Body approved by the Adopting Entity for calculating points under this section.

704.2 Point calculation. Points for § 704 shall be computed based on Step "1" of the EPA National ERI Target Procedure. Points shall be computed individually for each building as follows:

Points = 30 + (ENERGY STAR National ERI Target - National ERI Points) * 2

705 ADDITIONAL PRACTICES

705.1 Application of additional practice points. Points from § 705 can be added to points earned in § 702 (Performance Path), § 703 (Prescriptive Path), § 704 (ERI Target Path), or § 701.1.4 (Alternative Bronze and Silver level compliance).

705.2 Lighting

705.2.1 Lighting controls

[Percentages for point thresholds are based on lighting not required for means of egress or security lighting as defined by local building codes.]

705.2.1.1 Interior lighting. In dwelling units or sleeping units, permanently installed interior lighting fixtures are controlled with an occupancy sensor, or dimmer:

(1) greater than or equal to 50% to less than 75% of lighting fixtures...	1
(2) a minimum of 75% of lighting fixtures.	2

705.2.1.2 Exterior lighting. Photo or motion sensors are installed on 75% of outdoor lighting fixtures to control lighting.
[Percentages for point thresholds do not include lighting equipped with photovoltaics.] **1**

705.2.1.3 Multifamily common areas

(1) In a multifamily building, occupancy sensors, or dimmers are installed in common areas (except corridors and stairwells).

(a) greater than or equal to 50% to less than 75% of lighting fixtures.	1
(b) a minimum of 75% of lighting fixtures.	2

(2) In a multifamily building, occupancy controls are installed to automatically reduce light levels in interior corridors and exit stairwells when the space is unoccupied. Light levels are reduced by:

(a) greater than or equal to 50% to less than 75% or to local minimum requirements	2
(b) a minimum of 75%	3

GREEN BUILDING PRACTICES	POINTS

705.2.1.4 In a multifamily building, occupancy controls are installed to automatically reduce light levels in garages and parking structures when the space is unoccupied. Light levels are reduced by:

(1) greater than or equal to 50% to less than 75% or to local minimum requirements **2**

(2) a minimum of 75%.. **3**

705.2.2 TDDs and skylights. A tubular daylighting device (TDD) or a skylight that meets the requirements of Table 703.2.5.2(a) is installed in rooms without windows. *[Points awarded per building.]* **2**

705.2.3 Lighting outlets. Occupancy sensors are installed for a minimum of 80% of hard-wired lighting outlets in the interior living space. **1**

705.2.4 Recessed luminaires. The number of recessed luminaires that penetrate the thermal envelope is less than 1 per 400 sq. ft. (37.16 m^2) of total conditioned floor area and they are in accordance with § 701.4.3.5. .... **1**

705.3 Induction cooktop. Induction cooktop is installed.. **1**

705.4 Return ducts and transfer grilles. Return ducts or transfer grilles are installed in every room with a door. Return ducts or transfer grilles are not required for bathrooms, kitchens, closets, pantries, and laundry rooms. **2**

705.5 HVAC design and installation

705.5.1 Meet one or both of the following:

(1) HVAC contractor is certified by the Air Conditioning Contractors of America's Quality Assured Program (ACCA/QA) or by an EPA-recognized HVAC Quality Installation Training Oversight Organization (H-QUITO) or equivalent. **1**

(2) HVAC installation technician(s) is certified by North American Technician Excellence, Inc. (NATE) or equivalent. **1**

705.5.2 Performance of the heating and/or cooling system is verified by the HVAC contractor in accordance with all of the following: **3**

(1) Start-up procedure is performed in accordance with the manufacturer's instructions.

(2) Refrigerant charge is verified by super-heat and/or sub-cooling method.

(3) Burner is set to fire at input level listed on nameplate.

(4) Air handler setting/fan speed is set in accordance with manufacturer's instructions.

(5) Total airflow is within 10% of design flow.

(6) Total external system static does not exceed equipment capability at rated airflow.

705.5.3 HVAC Design is verified by 3rd party as follows:

(1) The ENERGY STAR HVAC Design and Rater Design Review Checklists are completed and correct......... **3**

(2) HVAC Installation is inspected and conforms to HVAC design documents and plans........................... **3**

GREEN BUILDING PRACTICES	M=Mandatory POINTS

705.6 Installation and performance verification

705.6.1 Third-party on-site inspection is conducted to verify compliance with all of the following, as applicable. Minimum of two inspections are performed: one inspection after insulation is installed and prior to covering, and another inspection upon completion of the building. Where multiple buildings or dwelling units of the same model or sleeping units of the same model are built by the same builder, a representative sample inspection of a minimum of 15% of the buildings or dwelling units or sleeping units is permitted. **3**

(1) Ducts are installed in accordance with the IRC or IMC and ducts are sealed.

(2) Building envelope air sealing is installed.

(3) Insulation is installed in accordance with § 701.4.3.2.1.

(4) Windows, skylights, and doors are flashed, caulked, and sealed in accordance with manufacturer's instructions and in accordance with § 701.4.3.

705.6.2 Testing. Testing is conducted to verify performance.

705.6.2.1 Air leakage validation of building or dwelling units or sleeping units. A visual inspection is performed as described in § 701.4.3.2(2) and air leakage testing is performed in accordance with ASTM E779 or ASTM E1827.

Points awarded only for buildings where building envelope leakage testing is not required by ICC IECC. Points not awarded if points are taken under § 703.2.4.

(1) A blower door test. **3**

(2) Third-party verification is completed. **5**

705.6.2.2 HVAC airflow testing. Balanced HVAC airflows are demonstrated by flow hood or other acceptable flow measurement tool by a third party. Test results are in accordance with the following:

(1) Measured flow at each supply and return register meets or exceeds the requirements in ACCA 5 QI Section 5.2. .... **5**

(2) Total airflow meets or exceeds the requirements in ACCA 5 QI Section 5.2. .... **3**

705.6.2.3 HVAC duct leakage testing. One of the following is achieved:

Points awarded only for buildings where duct leakage testing is not required by ICC IECC. Points not awarded if points are taken under § 703.4.4.

(1) Duct leakage is in accordance with ICC IECC R403.3.3 and R403.3.4. .... **3**

(2) Duct leakage is in accordance with ICC IECC R403.3.3 and R403.3.4, and testing is conducted by an independent third party. **5**

	M=Mandatory
GREEN BUILDING PRACTICES	**POINTS**

705.6.3 Insulating hot water pipes. Insulation with a minimum thermal resistance (R-value) of at least R-3 is applied to the following, as applicable:
[Points awarded only where these practices are not required by ICC IECC.] 1

    (a) piping 3/4-in. and larger in outside diameter

    (b) piping serving more than one dwelling unit or sleeping unit

    (c) piping located outside the conditioned space

    (d) piping from the water heater to a distribution manifold

    (e) piping located under a floor slab

    (f) buried piping

    (g) supply and return piping in recirculation systems other than demand recirculation systems

705.6.4 Potable hot water demand re-circulation system.

705.6.4.1 Potable hot water demand re-circulation system is installed in a single-family unit. 1

705.6.4.2 Potable hot water demand re-circulation system(s) that serves every unit in a multifamily building is installed in place of a standard circulation pump and control. 2

705.7 Submetering system. In multifamily buildings, an advanced electric and fossil fuel submetering system is installed to monitor electricity and fossil fuel consumption for each unit. The device provides consumption information on a monthly or near real-time basis. The information is available to the occupants at a minimum on a monthly basis. 1

706   INNOVATIVE PRACTICES

706.1 Energy consumption control. A whole-building, whole-dwelling unit, or whole-sleeping unit device or system is installed that controls or monitors energy consumption. .... **3 max**

(1) programmable communicating thermostat with the capability to be controlled remotely 1

(2) energy-monitoring device or system 1

(3) energy management control system 3

(4) programmable thermostat with control capability based on occupant presence or usage pattern 1

(5) lighting control system 1

706.2 Renewable energy service plan. Renewable energy service plan is provided as follows:

(1) Builder selects a renewable energy service plan provided by the local electrical utility for interim (temporary) electric service, or purchases renewable energy certificates (RECs) to cover electricity used. The builder's local administrative office has renewable energy service or has otherwise been paired with RECs. Green-e Certified (or equivalent) is required for renewable electricity purchases.... 1

(2) The buyer of the building selects one of the following renewable energy service plans provided by the utility prior to occupancy of the building with a minimum two-year commitment.

    (a) less than 50% of the dwelling's projected electricity and gas use is provided by renewable energy.. 1

    (b) greater than or equal to 50% of the dwelling's projected electricity and gas use is provided by renewable energy 2

	M=Mandatory
GREEN BUILDING PRACTICES	**POINTS**

706.3 Smart appliances and systems. Smart appliances and systems are installed as follows:
[1 point awarded if at least 3 smart appliances are installed; 1 additional point awarded for 6 or more.] .. **1 [2 max]**

(1) Refrigerator

(2) Freezer

(3) Dishwasher

(4) Clothes Dryer

(5) Clothes Washer

(6) Room Air Conditioner

(7) HVAC Systems

(8) Service Hot Water Heating Systems

[Items (7) and (8) are permitted to count as two appliances each for the purpose of awarding points.]

Where points awarded in § 706.3, points shall not be awarded in § 706.7 and § 706.10.

706.4 Pumps

706.4.1 Pool, spa, and water features equipped with filtration pumps as follows:

(1) Electronically controlled variable-speed pump(s) is installed (full load efficiency of 90% or greater). .. **1**

(2) Electronically controlled variable-speed pump(s) is installed (full load efficiency of 90% or greater) in a pool **3**

706.4.2 Sump pump(s), with electrically commutated motors (ECMs) or permanent split capacitor (PSC) motors, is installed (full load efficiency of 90% or greater). **1**

706.5 On-site renewable energy system. One of the following options is implemented:

(1) Building is Solar-Ready in compliance with ICC IECC Appendix A Solar Ready Provisions. **1**

(2) An on-site renewable energy system(s) is installed on the property. .... **2 per kW**

(3) An on-site renewable energy system(s) and a battery energy storage system are installed on the property.
[2 points awarded per kW or renewable energy system plus 1 per each 2 kWh or battery energy storage system] .... **2 per kW**

Points awarded shall not be combined with points for renewable energy in another section of this chapter. Points shall not be awarded for solar thermal or geothermal systems that provide space heating, space cooling, or water heating, points for these systems are awarded in § 703. Where on-site renewable energy is included in § 702 Performance Path or 704 ERI Target Path, § 706.5 shall not be awarded. The solar-ready zone roof area in item (1) is area per dwelling unit. Points in item (2) and (3) shall be divided by the number of dwelling units.

Multifamily Building Note: Conditioned common area and non-residential space is excluded for the purpose of calculating number of units.

	M=Mandatory
GREEN BUILDING PRACTICES	**POINTS**

706.6 Parking garage efficiency. Structured parking garages are designed to require no mechanical ventilation for fresh air requirements. 2

706.7 Grid-interactive electric thermal storage system. A grid-interactive electric thermal storage system is installed.

(1) Grid-Interactive Water Heating System... 1

(2) Grid-Interactive Space Heating and Cooling System 1

Where points are awarded in § 706.7, points shall not be awarded in § 706.3 and § 706.10.

706.8 Electrical vehicle charging station. A Level 2 (208/240V 40-80 amp) or Level 3 electric vehicle charging station is installed on the building site. (Note: Charging station shall not be included in the building energy consumption.) 2

706.9 CNG vehicle fueling station. A CNG vehicle residential fueling appliance is installed on the building site. The CNG fueling appliances shall be listed in accordance with ANSI/CSA NGV 5.1 and installed in accordance to the appliance manufacturer's installation instructions. (Note: The fueling appliance shall not be included in the building energy consumption.).. 1

706.10 Automatic demand response. Automatic demand response system is installed that curtails energy usage upon a signal from the utility or an energy service provider is installed. 1

Where points are awarded in § 706.10, points shall not be awarded in § 706.3 and § 706.7.

706.11 Grid-interactive battery storage system. A grid-interactive battery storage system of no less than 6 kWh of available capacity is installed. 2

706.12 Smart ventilation. A whole-building ventilation system is installed with automatic ventilation controls to limit ventilation during periods of extreme temperature, extreme humidity, and/or during times of peak utility loads and is in accordance with the specifications of ASHRAE Standard 62.2-2010 Section 4. 1

706.13 Alternative refrigerant. Use of the following in mechanical space cooling systems for dwellings.

(1) Use alternative refrigerant with a GWP less than 1,000 1

(2) Do not use refrigerants.. 2

706.14 Third-party utility benchmarking service.

(1) For a multifamily building, the owner has contracted with a third-party utility benchmarking service with at least five (5) years of experience in utility data management and analysis to perform a monthly analysis of whole-building energy and water consumption for a minimum of one (1) year. ... 3

(2) The building owner commits to reporting energy data using EPA's ENERGY STAR Portfolio Manager for a minimum of three (3) years. 1

706.15 Entryway air seal. For multifamily buildings, where not required by the building or energy code, to slow the movement of unconditioned air from outdoors to indoors at the main building entrance, the following is installed:

(1) Building entry vestibule. 2

(2) Revolving entrance doors. 2

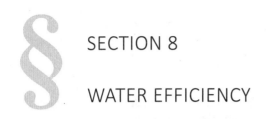

SECTION 8

WATER EFFICIENCY

GREEN BUILDING PRACTICES	POINTS

801 INDOOR AND OUTDOOR WATER USE

801.0 Intent. Implement measures that reduce indoor and outdoor water usage. Implement measures that include collection and use of alternative sources of water. Implement measures that treat water on site.

801.1 Mandatory requirements. The building shall comply with § 802 (Prescriptive Path) and § 803 (Innovative Practices) or § 804 (Performance Path). Points from § 804 (Performance Path) shall not be combined with points from § 802 (Prescriptive Path) or § 803 (Innovative Practices). The mandatory provisions of § 802 (Prescriptive Path) are required when using the Water Rating Index of § 804 (Performance Path) for Chapter 8 Water Efficiency compliance.

802 PRESCRIPTIVE PATH

802.1 Indoor hot water usage. Indoor hot water supply system is in accordance with one of the practices listed in items (1) through (5). The maximum water volume from the source of hot water to the termination of the fixture supply is determined in accordance with Tables 802.1(1) or 802.1(2). The maximum pipe length from the source of hot water to the termination of the fixture supply is 50 ft.

Where more than one water heater or where more than one type of hot water supply system, including multiple circulation loops, is used, points are awarded only for the system that qualifies for the minimum number of points. Systems with circulation loops are eligible for points only if pumps are demand controlled. Circulation systems with timers or aquastats and constant-on circulation systems are not eligible to receive points. Points awarded only if the pipes are insulated in accordance with § 705.6.3.

(1) The maximum volume from the water heater to the termination of the fixture supply at furthest fixture is 128 ounces (1 gallon or 3.78 liters). **8**

(2) The maximum volume from the water heater to the termination of the fixture supply at furthest fixture is 64 ounces (0.5 gallon or 1.89 liters). **12**

(3) The maximum volume from the water heater to the termination of the fixture supply at furthest fixture is 32 ounces (0.25 gallon or 0.945 liters). **20**

(4) A demand controlled hot water priming pump is installed on the main supply pipe of the circulation loop and the maximum volume from this supply pipe to the furthest fixture is 24 ounces (0.19 gallons or 0.71 liters). **24**

   (a) The volume in the circulation loop (supply) from the water heater or boiler to the branch for the furthest fixture is no more than 128 ounces (1 gallon or 3.78 liters). .... **4 Additional**

(5) A central hot water recirculation system is implemented in multifamily buildings in which the hot water line distance from the recirculating loop to the engineered parallel piping system (i.e., manifold system) is less than 30 ft. (9,144 mm) and the parallel piping to the fixture fittings contains a maximum of 64 ounces (1.89 liters) (115.50 cubic in.) (0.50 gallons)............................... **9**

GREEN BUILDING PRACTICES	POINTS

(6) Tankless water heater(s) with at least 0.5 gallon (1.89 liters) of storage are installed, or a tankless water heater that ramps up to at least 110°F within 5 seconds is installed. The storage may be internal or external to the tankless water heater. .... **1 Additional**

Table 802.1(1)
Maximum Pipe Length Conversion Table[a]

Nominal Pipe Size (in.)	Liquid Ounces per Foot of Length	Main, Branch, and Fixture Supply System Volume Category			Branch and Fixture Supply Volume from Circulation Loop
		128 ounces (1 gallons) [per 802.1(1)]	64 ounces (0.5 gallon) [per 802.1(2)]	32 ounces (0.25 gallon) [per 802.1(3)]	24 ounces (0.19 gallon) [per 802.1(4)]
		Maximum Pipe Length (feet)			
1/4[b]	0.33	50	50	50	50
5/16[b]	0.5	50	50	50	48
3/8[b]	0.75	50	50	43	32
1/2	1.5	50	43	21	16
5/8	2	50	32	16	12
3/4	3	43	21	11	8
7/8	4	32	16	8	6
1	5	26	13	6	5
1 1/4	8	16	8	4	3
1 1/2	11	12	6	3	2
2	18	7	4	2	1

a. Maximum pipe length figures apply when the entire pipe run is one nominal diameter only. Where multiple pipe diameters are used, the combined volume shall not exceed the volume limitation in § 802.1.

b. The maximum flow rate through 1/4 in. nominal piping shall not exceed 0.5 gpm. The maximum flow rate through 5/16 in. nominal piping shall not exceed 1 gpm. The maximum flow rate through 3/8 in. nominal piping shall not exceed 1.5 gpm.

Table 802.1(2)
Common Hot Water Pipe Internal Volumes

Size Nominal, In.	OUNCES OF WATER PER FOOT OF PIPE										
	Copper Type M	Copper Type L	Copper Type K	CPVC CTS SDR 11	CPVC SCH 40	CPVC SCH 80	PE-RT SDR 9	Composite ASTM F 1281	PEX CTS SDR 9	PP SDR 7.4 F2389	PP SDR 9 F2389
3/8	1.06	0.97	0.84	N/A	1.17	N/A	0.64	0.63	0.64	N/A	N/A
1/2	1.69	1.55	1.45	1.25	1.89	1.46	1.18	1.31	1.18	1.72	1.96
3/4	3.43	3.22	2.90	2.67	3.38	2.74	2.35	3.39	2.35	2.69	3.06
1	5.81	5.49	5.17	4.43	5.53	4.57	3.91	5.56	3.91	4.41	5.01
1 ¼	8.70	8.36	8.09	6.61	9.66	8.24	5.81	8.49	5.81	6.90	7.83
1 ½	12.18	11.83	11.45	9.22	13.2	11.38	8.09	13.88	8.09	10.77	12.24
2	21.08	20.58	20.04	15.79	21.88	19.11	13.86	21.48	13.86	17.11	19.43

GREEN BUILDING PRACTICES	M=Mandatory POINTS

802.2 Water-conserving appliances. ENERGY STAR or equivalent water-conserving appliances are installed.

(1) dishwasher	**2**
(2) clothes washer, or..	**13**
(3) clothes washer with an Integrated Water Factor of 3.8 or less.............................	**18**

Multifamily Building Note: Washing machines are installed in individual units or provided in common areas of multifamily buildings.

802.3 Water usage metering. Water meters are installed meeting the following:

(1) Single-Family Buildings: Water Usage Metering: ....

(a) Where not otherwise required by the local AHJ, installation of a meter for water consumed from any source associated with the building or building site.	**2 per unique use meter**
(b) Each water meter shall be capable of communicating water consumption data remotely for the dwelling unit occupant and be capable of providing daily data with electronic data storage and reporting capability that can produce reports for daily, monthly, and yearly water consumption. (Fire sprinkler systems are not required to be metered)..	**2 per sensor package**

(2) Multifamily Buildings: Water Usage Metering:

(a) Where not otherwise required by the local AHJ, installation of a meter for water consumed from any source associated with the building or building site.	**2 per unique use meter**
(b) Each water meter shall be capable of communicating water consumption data remotely for the dwelling unit occupant and be capable of providing daily data with electronic data storage and reporting capability that can produce reports for daily, monthly, and yearly water consumption. (Fire sprinkler systems are not required to be metered)..	**2 per sensor package**

Points earned in § 802.3(2) shall not exceed 50% of the total points earned for Chapter 8.

802.4 Showerheads. Showerheads are in accordance with the following:

(1) The total maximum combined flow rate of all showerheads in a shower compartment with floor area of 2,600 sq. in. or less is equal or less than 2.0 gpm. For each additional 1,300 sq. in. or any portion thereof of shower compartment floor area, an additional 2.0 gpm combined showerhead flow rate is allowed. Showerheads shall comply with ASME A112.18.1/CSA B125.1 and shall meet the performance criteria of the EPA WaterSense Specification for showerheads. Showerheads shall be served by an automatic compensating valve that complies with ASSE 1016/ASME A112.1016/CSA B125.16 or ASME A112.18.1/CSA B125.1 and is specifically designed to provide thermal shock and scald protection at the flow rate of the showerhead. *[4 points awarded for first compartment; 1 point for each additional compartment in dwelling]*.........	**4 [7 max]**

Points awarded per shower compartment. In multifamily buildings, the average of the points assigned to individual dwelling units or sleeping units may be used as the number of points awarded for this practice, rounded to the nearest whole number.

(2) All shower compartments in the dwelling unit(s) or sleeping unit(s) and common areas meet the requirements of 802.4(1) and all showerheads are in accordance with one of the following:

(a) maximum of 1.8 gpm	**6 Additional**
(b) maximum of 1.5 gpm	**10 Additional**

	M=Mandatory
GREEN BUILDING PRACTICES	**POINTS**

(3) Any shower control that can shut off water flow without affecting temperature is installed.
[1 Point awarded per shower control] .... **1 [3 max]**

For SI: 1 gallon per minute = 3.785 L/m

802.5 Faucets

802.5.1 Install water-efficient lavatory faucets with flow rates not more than 1.5 gpm (5.68 L/m), tested in compliance with ASME A112.18.1/CSA B125.1 and meeting the performance criteria of the EPA WaterSense High-Efficiency Lavatory Faucet Specification:

(1) Flow rate ≤ 1.5 gpm *[All faucets in a bathroom are in compliance]* .... **1 [3 max]**

> *[1 point awarded for each bathroom. In multifamily buildings, the average of the points assigned to individual dwelling units or sleeping units may be used as the number of points awarded for this practice, rounded to the nearest whole number.]*

(2) Flow rate ≤ 1.2 gpm *[All faucets in a bathroom are in compliance]* .... **2 [6 max]**

> *[2 points awarded for each bathroom. In multifamily buildings, the average of the points assigned to individual dwelling units or sleeping units may be used as the number of points awarded for this practice, rounded to the nearest whole number.]*

(3) Flow rate ≤ 1.5 gpm for all lavatory faucets in the dwelling unit(s) or sleeping unit(s) .... **6 Additional**

(4) Flow rate ≤ 1.5 gpm for all lavatory faucets in the dwelling unit(s), and at least one bathroom has faucets with flow rates ≤ 1.2 gpm .... **8 Additional**

(5) Flow rate ≤ 1.2 gpm for all lavatory faucets in the dwelling unit(s) .... **12 Additional**

802.5.2 Water-efficient residential kitchen faucets are installed in accordance with ASME A112.18.1/CSA B125.1. Residential kitchen faucets may temporarily increase the flow above the maximum rate but not to exceed 2.2 gpm.

(1) All residential kitchen faucets have a maximum flow rate of 1.8 gpm. **3**

(2) All residential kitchen faucets have a maximum flow rate of 1.5 gpm. .... **1 Additional**

802.5.3 Self-closing valve, motion sensor, metering, or pedal-activated faucet is installed to enable intermittent on/off operation. *[1 point awarded per fixture.]* .... **1 [3 max]**

802.5.4 Water closets and urinals are in accordance with the following:

Points awarded for § 802.5.4(2) or § 802.5.4(3), not both.

(1) Gold and Emerald levels: All water closets and urinals are in accordance with § 802.5.4. .... **M**

(2) A water closet is installed with an effective flush volume of 1.28 gallons (4.85 L) or less in accordance with ASME A112.19.2/CSA B45.1 or ASME A112.19.14 as applicable. Tank-type water closets shall be in accordance with the performance criteria of the EPA WaterSense Specification for Tank-Type Toilets.
[Points awarded per fixture. In multifamily buildings, the average of the points assigned to individual dwelling units or sleeping units may be used as the number of points awarded for this practice, rounded to the nearest whole number.] .... **4 [12 max]**

(3) All water closets are in accordance with § 802.5.4(2). **17**

GREEN BUILDING PRACTICES	M=Mandatory POINTS

(4) All water closets are in accordance with § 802.5.4(2) and one or more of the following are installed:

(a) Water closets that have an effective flush volume of 1.2 gallons or less.
[Points awarded per toilet. In multifamily buildings, the average of the points assigned to individual dwelling units or sleeping units may be used as the number of points awarded for this practice, rounded to the nearest whole number.] .... **2 Additional [6 Add'l max]**

(b) One or more urinals with a flush volume of 0.5 gallons (1.9L) or less when tested in accordance with ASME A112.19.2/CSA B45.1. .... **2 Additional**

(c) One or more composting or waterless toilets and/or non-water urinals. Non-water urinals shall be tested in accordance with ASME A112.19.2/CSA B45.1. .... **12 Additional**

802.6 Irrigation systems

802.6.1 Where an irrigation system is installed, an irrigation plan and implementation are executed by a qualified professional or equivalent. .... **M**

802.6.2 Irrigation sprinkler nozzles shall be tested according to ANSI standard ASABE/ICC 802 Landscape Irrigation Sprinkler and Emitter Standard by an accredited third-party laboratory. **6**

802.6.3 Drip irrigation is installed. .... **13 max**

(1) Drip irrigation is installed for all landscape beds. **4**

(2) Subsurface drip is installed for all turf grass areas. **4**

(3) Drip irrigation zones specifications show plant type by name and water use/need for each emitter *[Points awarded only if specifications are implemented.]* **5**

802.6.4 The irrigation system(s) is controlled by a smart controller or no irrigation is installed.
[Points are not additive.]

(1) Irrigation controllers shall be in accordance with the performance criteria of the EPA WaterSense program **10**

(2) No irrigation is installed and a landscape plan is developed in accordance with § 503.5, as applicable. **15**

802.6.5 Commissioning and water use reduction for irrigation systems.
[Points are not additive per each section.]

(1) All irrigation zones utilize pressure regulation so emission devices (sprinklers and drip emitters) operate at manufacturer's recommended operating pressure. **3**

(2) Where dripline tubing is installed, a filter with mesh size in accordance with the manufacturer's recommendation is installed on all drip zones. **3**

(3) Utilize spray bodies that incorporate an in-stem or external flow shut-off device. **3**

(4) For irrigation systems installed on sloped sites, either an in-stem or external check valve is utilized for each spray body. **3**

(5) Where an irrigation system is installed, a flow sensing device is installed to monitor and alert the controller when flows are outside design range. **3**

GREEN BUILDING PRACTICES	M=Mandatory POINTS

802.7 Rainwater collection and distribution. Rainwater collection and distribution is provided.

802.7.1 Rainwater is used for irrigation in accordance with one of the following:

(1) Rainwater is diverted for landscape irrigation without impermeable water storage **5**

(2) Rainwater is diverted for landscape irrigation with impermeable water storage in accordance with one of the following:

    (a) 50 – 499 gallon storage capacity **5**

    (b) 500 – 2,499 gallon storage capacity **10**

    (c) 2,500 gallon or larger storage capacity (system is designed by a professional certified by the ARCSA or equivalent).. **15**

    (d) All irrigation demands are met by rainwater capture (documentation demonstrating the water needs of the landscape are provided and the system is designed by a professional certified by the ARCSA or equivalent). **25**

802.7.2 Rainwater is used for indoor domestic demand as follows. The system is designed by a professional certified by the ARCSA or equivalent.

(1) Rainwater is used to supply an indoor appliance or fixture for any locally approved use.
[Points awarded per appliance or fixture.] .... **5 [15 max]**

(2) Rainwater provides for total domestic demand.. **25**

802.8 Sediment filters. Water filter is installed to reduce sediment and protect plumbing fixtures for the whole building or the entire dwelling unit. **1**

802.9 Water treatment devices.

802.9.1 Water softeners shall not be installed where the supplied water hardness is less than 8.0 grains per gallon measured as total calcium carbonate equivalents. Water softeners shall be listed to NSF 44 and a rated salt efficiency of 3,400 grains of total hardness per 1.0 pound of salt based on sodium chloride equivalency. Devices shall not discharge more than 4.0 gallons of water per 1,000 grains of hardness removed during the service or recharge cycle.

(1) No water softener. **5**

(2) Water softener installed to supply softened water only to domestic water heater. **2**

802.9.2 Reverse Osmosis (R/O) water treatment systems shall be listed to NSF 58 and shall include automatic shut-off valve to prevent water discharge when storage tank is full.

(1) No R/O system.. **3**

(2) Combined capacity of all R/O systems does not exceed 0.75 gallons. **1**

802.10 Pools and spas.

802.10.1 Pools and Spas with water surface area greater than 36 sq. ft. and connected to a water supply shall have a dedicated meter to measure the amount of water supplied to the pool or spa.

(1) Automated motorized non-permeable pool cover that covers the entire pool surface. **10**

GREEN BUILDING PRACTICES	M=Mandatory POINTS

803   INNOVATIVE PRACTICES

803.1 Reclaimed, grey, or recycled water. Reclaimed, grey, or recycled water is used as permitted by applicable code.

Points awarded for either § 803.1(1) or § 803.1(2), not both.
Points awarded for either § 803.6 or § 803.1, not both.

(1)   each water closet flushed by reclaimed, grey, or recycled water
[Points awarded per fixture or appliance.].. **5 [20 max]**

(2)   irrigation from reclaimed, grey, or recycled water on-site **10**

803.2 Reclaimed water, greywater, or rainwater pre-piping. Reclaimed, greywater, or rainwater systems are rough plumbed (and permanently marked, tagged or labeled) into buildings for future use. .... **3 per roughed in system**

803.3 Automatic leak detection and control devices. One of the following devices is installed. Where a fire sprinkler system is present, ensure the device will be installed to not interfere with the operation of the fire sprinkler system. **2**

(1)   automatic water leak detection and control devices.

(2)   automatic water leak detection and shutoff devices.

803.4 Engineered biological system or intensive bioremediation system. An engineered biological system or intensive bioremediation system is installed and the treated water is used on site. Design and implementation are approved by appropriate regional authority. **20**

803.5 Recirculating humidifier. Where a humidifier is required, a recirculating humidifier is used in lieu of a traditional "flow through" type. **1**

803.6 Advanced wastewater treatment system. Advanced wastewater (aerobic) treatment system is installed and treated water is used on site. *[Points awarded for either § 803.6 or § 803.1, not both.]* **20**

804   PERFORMANCE PATH

804.1 Performance Path. The index score for the Performance Path shall be calculated in accordance with Appendix D Water Rating Index (WRI) or equivalent methodology.

804.2 Water efficiency rating levels. In lieu of threshold levels for Chapter 8 in Table 303, rating levels for § 804.1 are in accordance with Table 804.2.

Table 804.2
Maximum WRI Scores for NGBS Certification in Chapter 8

BRONZE	SILVER	GOLD	EMERALD
70	60	50	40

804.3 Water efficiency NGBS points equivalency. The additional points for use with Table 303 from the Chapter 8 Water Efficiency Category are determined in accordance with Equation 804.3.

Equation 804.3
$$NGBS = WRI \times (-2.29) + 181.7$$

INTENTIONALLY LEFT BLANK.

SECTION 9

INDOOR ENVIRONMENTAL QUALITY

GREEN BUILDING PRACTICES	M=Mandatory POINTS

901 POLLUTANT SOURCE CONTROL

901.0 Intent. Pollutant sources are controlled.

901.1 Space and water heating options

901.1.1 Natural draft furnaces, boilers, or water heaters are not located in conditioned spaces, including conditioned crawlspaces, unless located in a mechanical room that has an outdoor air source and is sealed and insulated to separate it from the conditioned space(s). 5

Points are awarded only for buildings that use natural draft combustion space or water heating equipment.

901.1.2 Air handling equipment or return ducts are not located in the garage, unless placed in isolated, air-sealed mechanical rooms with an outside air source. 5

901.1.3 The following combustion space heating or water heating equipment is installed within conditioned space:

(1) all furnaces or all boilers

    (a) power-vent furnace(s) or boiler(s) 3

    (b) direct-vent furnace(s) or boiler(s) 5

(2) all water heaters

    (a) power-vent water heater(s) 3

    (b) direct-vent water heater(s) 5

901.1.4 Gas-fired fireplaces and direct heating equipment is listed and is installed in accordance with the NFPA 54, ICC IFGC, or the applicable local gas appliance installation code. Gas-fired fireplaces within dwelling units or sleeping units and direct heating equipment are vented to the outdoors. Alcohol burning devices and kerosene heaters are vented to the outdoors. .... M

901.1.5 Natural gas and propane fireplaces are direct vented, have permanently fixed glass fronts or gasketed doors, and comply with CSA Z21.88/CSA 2.33 or CSA Z21.50b/CSA 2.22b.................................... 7

901.1.6 The following electric equipment is installed:

(1) heat pump air handler in unconditioned space 2

(2) heat pump air handler in conditioned space 5

901.2 Solid fuel-burning appliances

901.2.1 Solid fuel-burning fireplaces, inserts, stoves and heaters are code compliant and are in accordance with the following requirements: .... M

(1) Site-built masonry wood-burning fireplaces use outside combustion air and include a means of sealing the flue and the combustion air outlets to minimize interior air (heat) loss when not in operation. 4

	M=Mandatory
GREEN BUILDING PRACTICES	**POINTS**

(2) Factory-built, wood-burning fireplaces are in accordance with the certification requirements of UL 127 and are an EPA Phase 2 Emission Level Qualified Model. **6**

(3) Wood stove and fireplace inserts, as defined in UL 1482 Section 3.8, are in accordance with the certification requirements of UL 1482 and are in accordance with the emission requirements of the EPA Certification and the State of Washington WAC 173-433-100(3). **6**

(4) Pellet (biomass) stoves and furnaces are in accordance with ASTM E1509 or are EPA certified............ **6**

(5) Masonry heaters are in accordance with the definitions in ASTM E1602 and IBC Section 2112.1. .... **6**

901.2.2 Fireplaces, woodstoves, pellet stoves, or masonry heaters are not installed. **6**

901.3 Garages. Garages are in accordance with the following:

(1) Attached garage

  (a) Doors installed in the common wall between the attached garage and conditioned space are tightly sealed and gasketed. .... **M 2**

  (b) A continuous air barrier is provided separating the garage space from the conditioned living spaces. **M 2**

  (c) For one- and two-family dwelling units, a 100 cfm (47 L/s) or greater ducted or 70 cfm (33 L/s) cfm or greater unducted wall exhaust fan is installed and vented to the outdoors and is designed and installed for continuous operation or has controls (e.g., motion detectors, pressure switches) that activate operation for a minimum of 1 hour when either human passage door or roll-up automatic doors are operated. For ducted exhaust fans, the fan airflow rating and duct sizing are in accordance with ASHRAE Standard 62.2-2007 Section 7.3. .... **8**

(2) A carport is installed, the garage is detached from the building, or no garage is installed..................... **10**

901.4 Wood materials. A minimum of 85% of material within a product group (i.e., wood structural panels, countertops, composite trim/doors, custom woodwork, and/or component closet shelving) is manufactured in accordance with the following: **10 max**

(1) Structural plywood used for floor, wall, and/or roof sheathing is compliant with DOC PS 1 and/or DOC PS 2. OSB used for floor, wall, and/or roof sheathing is compliant with DOC PS 2. The panels are made with moisture-resistant adhesives. The trademark indicates these adhesives as follows: Exposure 1 or Exterior for plywood, and Exposure 1 for OSB. .... **M**

(2) Particleboard and MDF (medium density fiberboard) is manufactured and labeled in accordance with CPA A208.1 and CPA A208.2, respectively. *[Points awarded per product group.]*.......................... **2**

(3) Hardwood plywood in accordance with HPVA HP-1. *[Points awarded per product group.]*.................... **2**

(4) Particleboard, MDF, or hardwood plywood is in accordance with CPA 4. *[Points awarded per product group.]*.. **3**

(5) Composite wood or agrifiber panel products contain no added urea-formaldehyde or are in accordance with the CARB Composite Wood Air Toxic Contaminant Measure Standard. *[Points awarded per product group.]*.. **4**

(6) Non-emitting products. *[Points awarded per product group.]* **4**

901.5 Cabinets. A minimum of 85% of installed cabinets are in accordance with one or both of the following: *[Where both of the following practices are used, only 3 points are awarded.]*

(1) All parts of the cabinet are made of solid wood or non-formaldehyde emitting materials such as metal or glass.. **5**

GREEN BUILDING PRACTICES	M=Mandatory POINTS

(2) The composite wood used in wood cabinets is in accordance with CARB Composite Wood Air Toxic Contaminant Measure Standard or equivalent as certified by a third-party program such as, but not limited to, those in Appendix B. **3**

901.6 Carpets. Wall-to-wall carpeting is not installed adjacent to water closets and bathing fixtures. .... **M**

901.7 Floor materials. The following types of finished flooring materials are used. The materials have emission levels in accordance with CDPH/EHLB Standard Method v1.1. Product is tested by a laboratory with the CDPH/EHLB Standard Method v1.1 within the laboratory scope of accreditation to ISO/IEC 17025 and certified by a third-party program accredited to ISO 17065, such as, but not limited to, those in Appendix B. *[1 point awarded for every 10% of conditioned floor space using one of the below materials. When carpet cushion meeting the emission limits of the practice is also installed, the percentage of compliant carpet area is calculated at 1.33 times the actual installed area.]*.. **1 [8 max]**

(1) Hard surface flooring: Prefinished installed hard-surface flooring is installed. Where post-manufacture coatings or surface applications have not been applied, the following hard surface flooring types are deemed to comply with the emission requirements of this practice:

    (a) Ceramic tile flooring

    (b) Organic-free, mineral-based flooring

    (c) Clay masonry flooring

    (d) Concrete masonry flooring

    (e) Concrete flooring

    (f) Metal flooring

(2) Carpet and carpet cushion are installed.

901.8 Wall coverings. A minimum of 10% of the interior wall surfaces are covered and a minimum of 85% of wall coverings are in accordance with the emission concentration limits of CDPH/EHLB Standard Method v1.1. Emission levels are determined by a laboratory accredited to ISO/IEC 17025 and the CDPH/EHLB Standard Method v1.1 is in its scope. The product is certified by a third-party program accredited to ISO 17065, such as, but not limited to, those in Appendix B. **4**

901.9 Interior architectural coatings. A minimum of 85% of the interior architectural coatings are in accordance with either § 901.9.1 or § 901.9.3, not both. A minimum of 85% of architectural colorants are in accordance with § 901.9.2.

Exception: Interior architectural coatings that are formulated to remove formaldehyde and other aldehydes in indoor air and are tested and labeled in accordance with ISO 16000-23, Indoor air – Part 23: Performance test for evaluating the reduction of formaldehyde concentrations by sorptive building materials.

901.9.1 Site-applied interior architectural coatings, which are inside the water proofing envelope, are in accordance with one or more of the following: **5**

(1) Zero VOC as determined by EPA Method 24 (VOC content is below the detection limit for the method)

(2) GreenSeal GS-11

(3) CARB *Suggested Control Measure for Architectural Coatings* (see Table 901.9.1)

Table 901.9.1
VOC Content Limits For Architectural Coatings[a,b,c]

Coating Category	LIMIT[d] (g/l)
Flat Coatings	50
Non-flat Coatings	100
Non-flat High-Gloss Coatings	150
Specialty Coatings:	
Aluminum Roof Coatings	400
Basement Specialty Coatings	400
Bituminous Roof Coatings	50
Bituminous Roof Primers	350
Bond Breakers	350
Concrete Curing Compounds	350
Concrete/Masonry Sealers	100
Driveway Sealers	50
Dry Fog Coatings	150
Faux Finishing Coatings	350
Fire Resistive Coatings	350
Floor Coatings	100
Form-Release Compounds	250
Graphic Arts Coatings (Sign Paints)	500
High Temperature Coatings	420
Industrial Maintenance Coatings	250
Low Solids Coatings	120[e]
Magnesite Cement Coatings	450
Mastic Texture Coatings	100
Metallic Pigmented Coatings	500
Multi-Color Coatings	250
Pre-Treatment Wash Primers	420
Primers, Sealers, and Undercoaters	100
Reactive Penetrating Sealers	350
Recycled Coatings	250
Roof Coatings	50
Rust Preventative Coatings	250
Shellacs, Clear	730
Shellacs, Opaque	550
Specialty Primers, Sealers, and Undercoaters	100
Stains	250
Stone Consolidants	450
Swimming Pool Coatings	340
Traffic Marking Coatings	100
Tub and Tile Refinish Coatings	420
Waterproofing Membranes	250
Wood Coatings	275
Wood Preservatives	350
Zinc-Rich Primers	340

a. The specified limits remain in effect unless revised limits are listed in subsequent columns in the table.

b. Values in this table are derived from those specified by the California Air Resources Board, Architectural Coatings Suggested Control Measure, February 1, 2008.

c. Table 901.9.1 architectural coating regulatory category and VOC content compliance determination shall conform to the California Air Resources Board Suggested Control Measure for Architectural Coatings dated February 1, 2008.

d. Limits are expressed as VOC Regulatory (except as noted), thinned to the manufacturer's maximum thinning recommendation, excluding any colorant added to tint bases.

e. Limit is expressed as VOC actual.

GREEN BUILDING PRACTICES	POINTS

901.9.2 Architectural coating colorant additive VOC content is in accordance with Table 901.9.2. *[Points for 901.9.2 are awarded only if base architectural coating is in accordance with § 901.9.1.]*.......... **1**

Table 901.9.2
VOC Content Limits for Colorants

Colorant	LIMIT (g/l)
Architectural Coatings, excluding IM Coatings	50
Solvent-Based IM	600
Waterborne IM	50

901.9.3 Site-applied interior architectural coatings, which are inside the waterproofing envelope, are in accordance with the emission levels of CDPH/EHLB Standard Method v1.1. Emission levels are determined by a laboratory accredited to ISO/IEC 17025 and the CDPH/EHLB Standard Method v1.1 in its scope of accreditation. The product is certified by a third-party program accredited to ISO 17065, such as, but not limited to, those found in Appendix B. **8**

901.10 Interior adhesives and sealants. A minimum of 85% of site-applied adhesives and sealants located inside the waterproofing envelope are in accordance with one of the following, as applicable.

(1) The emission levels are in accordance with CDPH/EHLB Standard Method v1.1. Emission levels are determined by a laboratory accredited to ISO/IEC 17025 and the CDPH/EHLB Standard Method v1.1 is in its scope of accreditation. The product is certified by a third-party program accredited to ISO 17065, such as, but not limited to, those found in Appendix B. **8**

(2) GreenSeal GS-36. .... **5**

(3) SCAQMD Rule 1168 in accordance with Table 901.10(3), excluding products that are sold in 16-ounce containers or less and are regulated by the California Air Resources Board (CARB) Consumer Products Regulations. **5**

901.11 Insulation. Emissions of 85% of wall, ceiling, and floor insulation materials are in accordance with the emission levels of CDPH/EHLB Standard Method v1.1. Emission levels are determined by a laboratory accredited to ISO/IEC 17025 and the CDPH/EHLB Standard Method v1.1 is in its scope of accreditation. Insulation is certified by a third-party program accredited to ISO 17065, such as, but not limited to, those in Appendix B. **4**

901.12 Furniture and furnishings. In a multifamily building, all furniture in common areas shall have VOC emission levels in accordance with ANSI/BIFMA e3-Furniture Sustainability Standard Sections 7.6.1 and 7.6.2, tested in accordance with ANSI/BIFMA Standard Method M7.1. Emission levels are determined by a laboratory accredited to ISO/IEC 17025 and the ANSI/BIFMA Standard Method M7.1 is in its scope of accreditation. Furniture and Furnishings are certified by a third-party program accredited to ISO 17065, such as, but not limited to, those in Appendix B................................... **2**

901.13 Carbon monoxide (CO) alarms. A carbon monoxide (CO) alarm is provided in accordance with the IRC Section R315. .... **M**

901.14 Building entrance pollutants control. Pollutants are controlled at all main building entrances by one of the following methods:

(1) Exterior grilles or mats are installed in a fixed manner and may be removable for cleaning................. **1**

(2) Interior grilles or mats are installed in a fixed manner and may be removable for cleaning. **1**

GREEN BUILDING PRACTICES	M=Mandatory POINTS

Table 901.10(3)
Site Applied Adhesive and Sealants VOC Limits[a,b]

ADHESIVE OR SEALANT	VOC LIMIT (g/l)
Indoor carpet adhesives	50
Carpet pad adhesives	50
Outdoor carpet adhesives	150
Wood flooring adhesive	100
Rubber floor adhesives	60
Subfloor adhesives	50
Ceramic tile adhesives	65
VCT and asphalt tile adhesives	50
Drywall and panel adhesives	50
Cove base adhesives	50
Multipurpose construction adhesives	70
Structural glazing adhesives	100
Single ply roof membrane adhesives	250
Architectural sealants	250
Architectural sealant primer	
Non-porous	250
Porous	775
Modified bituminous sealant primer	500
Other sealant primers	750
CPVC solvent cement	490
PVC solvent cement	510
ABS solvent cement	325
Plastic cement welding	250
Adhesive primer for plastic	550
Contact adhesive	80
Special purpose contact adhesive	250
Structural wood member adhesive	140

a. VOC limit less water and less exempt compounds in grams/liter

b. For low-solid adhesives and sealants, the VOC limit is expressed in grams/liter of material as specified in Rule 1168. For all other adhesives and sealants, the VOC limits are expressed as grams of VOC per liter of adhesive or sealant less water and less exempt compounds as specified in Rule 1168.

901.15 Non-smoking areas. Environmental tobacco smoke is minimized by one or more of the following:

(1) All interior common areas of a multifamily building are designated as non-smoking areas with posted signage. 1

(2) Exterior smoking areas of a multifamily building are designated with posted signage and located a minimum of 25 ft. from entries, outdoor air intakes, and operable windows. 1

902   POLLUTANT CONTROL

902.0 Intent. Pollutants generated in the building are controlled.

902.1 Spot ventilation

902.1.1 Spot ventilation is in accordance with the following:

(1) Bathrooms are vented to the outdoors. The minimum ventilation rate is 50 cfm (23.6 L/s) for intermittent operation or 20 cfm (9.4 L/s) for continuous operation in bathrooms.
[1 point awarded only if a window complying with IRC Section R303.3 is provided in addition to mechanical ventilation.] .... M [1 max]

GREEN BUILDING PRACTICES	M=Mandatory POINTS
(2) Clothes dryers (except listed and labeled condensing ductless dryers) are vented to the outdoors. ...	M
(3) Kitchen exhaust units and/or range hoods are ducted to the outdoors and have a minimum ventilation rate of 100 cfm (47.2 L/s) for intermittent operation or 25 cfm (11.8 L/s) for continuous operation.	8
902.1.2 Bathroom and/or laundry exhaust fan is provided with an automatic timer and/or humidistat:	**11 max**
(1) for first device	5
(2) for each additional device	2
902.1.3 Kitchen range, bathroom, and laundry exhaust are verified to air flow specification. Ventilation airflow at the point of exhaust is tested to a minimum of:	8
(a) 100 cfm (47.2 L/s) intermittent or 25 cfm (11.8 L/s) continuous for kitchens, and	
(b) 50 cfm (23.6 L/s) intermittent or 20 cfm (9.4 L/s) continuous for bathrooms and/or laundry	
902.1.4 Exhaust fans are ENERGY STAR, as applicable.	**12 max**
(1) ENERGY STAR, or equivalent, fans *[Points awarded per fan.]*................................	2
(2) ENERGY STAR, or equivalent, fans operating at or below 1 sone *[Points awarded per fan.]*	3
902.1.5 Fenestration in spaces other than those identified in § 902.1.1 through § 902.1.4 are designed for stack effect or cross-ventilation in accordance with all of the following:	3
(1) Operable windows, operable skylights, or sliding glass doors with a total area of at least 15% of the total conditioned floor area are provided.	
(2) Insect screens are provided for all operable windows, operable skylights, and sliding glass doors.	
(3) A minimum of two operable windows or sliding glass doors are placed in adjacent or opposite walls. If there is only one wall surface in that space exposed to the exterior, the minimum windows or sliding glass doors may be on the same wall.	
902.1.6 Ventilation for Multifamily Common Spaces. Systems are implemented and are in accordance with the specifications of ASHRAE 62.1 and an explanation of the operation and importance of the ventilation system is included in § 1002.1 and § 1002.2 of this Standard..................................	3
902.2 Building ventilation systems	
902.2.1 One of the following whole building ventilation systems is implemented and is in accordance with the specifications of ASHRAE Standard 62.2-2010 Section 4 and an explanation of the operation and importance of the ventilation system is included in either § 1001.1 or § 1002.2. *[*Mandatory where the maximum air infiltration rate is less than 5.0 ACH50]*	M *
(1) Exhaust or supply fan(s) ready for continuous operation and with appropriately labeled controls	3
(2) Balanced exhaust and supply fans with supply intakes located in accordance with the manufacturer's guidelines so as to not introduce polluted air back into the building	6
(3) Heat-recovery ventilator	7
(4) Energy-recovery ventilator	8
(5) Ventilation air is preconditioned by a system not specified above	10
902.2.2 Ventilation airflow is tested to achieve the design fan airflow in accordance with ANSI/RESNET/ICC 380 and § 902.2.1.	4

	M=Mandatory
GREEN BUILDING PRACTICES	**POINTS**

902.2.3 MERV filters 8 to 13 are installed on central forced air systems and are accessible. Designer or installer is to verify that the HVAC equipment is able to accommodate the greater pressure drop of MERV 8 to 13 filters. **2**

902.2.4 MERV filters 14 or greater are installed on central forced air systems and are accessible. Designer or installer is to verify that the HVAC equipment is able to accommodate the greater pressure drop of the filter used. **3**

902.3 Radon reduction measures. Radon reduction measures are in accordance with IRC Appendix F or § 902.3.1. Radon Zones as identified by the AHJ or, if the zone is not identified by the AHJ, as defined in Figure 9(1).

(1) Buildings located in Zone 1

    (a) a passive radon system is installed .... **M**

    (b) an active radon system is installed **12**

(2) Buildings located in Zone 2 or Zone 3

    (a) a passive radon system is installed **6**

    (b) an active radon system is installed **12**

902.3.1 Radon reduction option. This option requires § 902.3.1.1 through § 902.3.1.7.

902.3.1.1 Soil-gas barriers and base course. A base course in accordance with IRC Section 506.2.2 shall be installed below slabs and foundations. There shall be a continuous gas-permeable base course under each soil-gas retarder that is separated by foundation walls or footings. Between slabs and the base course, damp proofing or water proofing shall be installed in accordance with IRC Section 406. Punctures, tears and gaps around penetrations of the soil-gas retarder shall be repaired or covered with an additional soil-gas retarder. The soil-gas retarder shall be a continuous 6-mil (0.15 mm) polyethylene or an approved equivalent.

902.3.1.2 Soil gas collection. There shall be an unobstructed path for soil gas flow between the void space installed in the base course and the vent through the roof. Soil gases below the foundation shall be collected by a perforated pipe with a diameter of not less than 4 in. (10 cm) and not less than 5 ft. (1.5 m) in total length. A tee fitting or equivalent method shall provide two horizontal openings to the radon collection. The tee fitting shall be designed to prevent clogging of the radon collection path. Alternately the soil gas collection shall be by approved radon collection mats or an equivalent approved method.

902.3.1.3 Soil gas entry routes. Openings in slabs, soil-gas retarders, and joints such as, but not limited to, plumbing, ground water control systems, soil-gas vent pipes, piping and structural supports, shall be sealed against air leakage at the penetrations. The sealant shall be a polyurethane caulk, expanding foam or other approved method. Foundation walls shall comply with IRC Section 103.2.3. Sumps shall be sealed in accordance with IRC Section 103.2.2. Sump pits and sump lids intended for ground water control shall not be connected to the sub-slab soil-gas exhaust system.

902.3.1.4 Soil gas vent. A gas-tight pipe vent shall extend from the soil gas permeable layer through the roof. The vent pipe size shall not be reduced at any location as it goes from gas collection to the roof. Exposed and visible interior vent pipes shall be identified with not less than one label reading "Radon Reduction System" on each floor and in habitable attics.

GREEN BUILDING PRACTICES	POINTS

902.3.1.5 Vent pipe diameter. The minimum vent pipe diameter shall be as specified in Table 902.3.1.5.

Table 902.3.1.5
Maximum Vented Foundation Area

Maximum area vented	Nominal pipe diameter
2,500 ft² (232 m²)	3 in. (7.6 cm)
4,000 ft² (372 m²)	4 in. (10 cm)
Unlimited	6 in. (15.2 cm)

902.3.1.6 Multiple vented areas. In dwellings where interior footings or other barriers separate the soil-gas permeable layer, each area shall be fitted with an individual vent pipe. Vent pipes shall connect to a single vent that terminates above the roof or each individual vent pipe shall terminate separately above the roof.

902.3.1.7 Fan. Each sub-slab soil-gas exhaust system shall include a fan, or dedicated space for the post-construction installation of a fan. The electrical supply for the fan shall be located within 6 ft. (1.8 m) of the fan. Fan is not required to be on a dedicated circuit.

902.3.2 Radon testing. Radon testing is mandatory for Zone 1.

Exceptions: 1) Testing is not mandatory where the authority having jurisdiction has defined the radon zone as Zone 2 or 3; and 2) testing is not mandatory where the occupied space is located above an unenclosed open space.

(1) Testing specifications. Testing is performance as specified in (a) through (j). Testing of a representative sample shall be permitted for multifamily buildings only. 8

  (a) Testing is performed after the residence passes its airtightness test.

  (b) Testing is performed after the radon control system installation is complete. If the system has an active fan, the residence shall be tested with the fan operating.

  (c) Testing is performed at the lowest level within a dwelling unit which will be occupied, even if the space is not finished.

  (d) Testing is not performed in a closet, hallway, stairway, laundry room, furnace room, kitchen or bathroom.

  (e) Testing is performed with a commercially available test kit or with a continuous radon monitor that can be calibrated. Testing shall be in accordance with the testing device manufacturer's instructions.

  (f) Testing shall be performed by the builder, a registered design professional, or an approved third party.

  (g) Testing shall extend at least 48 hours or to the minimum specified by the manufacturer, whichever is longer.

  (h) Written radon test results shall be provided by the test lab or testing party. Written test results shall be included with construction documents.

  (i) An additional pre-paid test kit shall be provided for the homeowner to use when they choose. The test kit shall include mailing or emailing the results from the testing lab to the homeowner.

  (j) Where the radon test result is 4 pCi/L or greater, the fan for the radon vent pipe shall be installed.

(2) Testing results. A radon test done in accordance with 902.3.2(1) and completed before occupancy receives a results of 2 pCi/L or less. 6

GREEN BUILDING PRACTICES	M=Mandatory POINTS

902.4 HVAC system protection. One of the following HVAC system protection measures is performed. .... | 3

(1) HVAC supply registers (boots), return grilles, and rough-ins are covered during construction activities to prevent dust and other pollutants from entering the system.

(2) Prior to owner occupancy, HVAC supply registers (boots), return grilles, and duct terminations are inspected and vacuumed. In addition, the coils are inspected and cleaned and the filter is replaced if necessary.

(3) If HVAC systems are to be operated, during construction, all return grilles have a temporary MERV 8 or higher filter installed in a manner ensuring no leakage around the filter.

902.5 Central vacuum systems. Central vacuum system is installed and vented to the outside. .... | 3

902.6 Living space contaminants. The living space is sealed in accordance with § 701.4.3.1 to prevent unwanted contaminants.. | M

903   MOISTURE MANAGEMENT: VAPOR, RAINWATER, PLUMBING, HVAC

903.0 Intent. Moisture and moisture effects are controlled.

903.1 Plumbing

903.1.1 Cold water pipes in unconditioned spaces are insulated to a minimum of R-4 with pipe insulation or other covering that adequately prevents condensation. .... | 2

903.1.2 Plumbing is not installed in unconditioned spaces.. | 5

903.2 Duct insulation. Ducts are in accordance with one of the following.

(1) All HVAC ducts, plenums, and trunks are located in conditioned space. .... | 1

(2) All HVAC ducts, plenums, and trunks are located in conditioned space and all HVAC ducts are insulated to a minimum of R4. .... | 3

903.3 Relative humidity. In climate zones 1A, 2A, 3A, 4A, and 5A as defined by Figure 6(1), equipment is installed to maintain relative humidity (RH) at or below 60% using one of the following:
[Points not awarded in other climate zones.] .... | 7

(1) additional dehumidification system(s)

(2) central HVAC system equipped with additional controls to operate in dehumidification mode

904   INDOOR AIR QUALITY

904.0 Intent. IAQ is protected by best practices to control ventilation, moisture, pollutant sources and sanitation.

904.1 Indoor Air Quality (IAQ) during construction. Wood is dry before close-in (§ 602.1.7.1(3)), materials comply with emission criteria (§ 901.4-901.11), sources of water infiltration or condensation observed during construction have been eliminated, accessible interior surfaces are dry and free of visible suspect growth (per ASTM D7338 Section 6.3), and water damage (per ASTM D7338 Section 7.4.3). .... | 2

904.2 Indoor Air Quality (IAQ) Post Completion. Verify there are no moisture, mold, and dust issues per § 602.1.7.1(3), § 901.4 - 901.11, ASTM D7338 Section 6.3, and ASTM D7338 Section 7.4.3. .... | 3

	M=Mandatory
GREEN BUILDING PRACTICES	**POINTS**

904.3 Microbial growth & moisture inspection and remediation. A visual inspection is performed to confirm the following:

(1) Verify that no visible signs of discoloration and microbial growth on ceilings, walls or floors, or other building assemblies; or if minor microbial growth is observed (less than within a total area of 25 sq. ft. in homes or multifamily buildings, reference EPA Document 402-K-02-003 (A Brief Guide to Mold, Moisture, and Your Home) for guidance on how to properly remediate the issue. If microbial growth is observed, on a larger scale in homes or multifamily buildings (greater than 25 sq. ft.), reference EPA Document 402-K-01-001 (Mold Remediation in Schools and Commercial Buildings) for guidance on how to properly remediate the issue. .... **M**

(2) Verify that there are no visible signs of water damage or pooling. If signs of water damage or pooling are observed, verify that the source of the leak has been repaired, and that damaged materials are either properly dried or replaced as needed. .... **M**

905   INNOVATIVE PRACTICES

905.1 Humidity monitoring system. A humidity monitoring system is installed with a mobile base unit that displays readings of temperature and relative humidity. The system has a minimum of two remote sensor units. One remote sensor unit is placed permanently inside the conditioned space in a central location, excluding attachment to exterior walls, and another remote sensor unit is placed permanently outside of the conditioned space. **2**

905.2 Kitchen exhaust. A kitchen exhaust unit(s) that equals or exceeds 400 cfm (189 L/s) is installed, and make-up air is provided. **2**

905.3 Enhanced air filtration. Meet all of the following. **2**

(1) Design for and install a secondary filter rack space for activated carbon filters.

(2) Provide the manufacturer's recommended filter maintenance schedule to the homeowner or building manager.

905.4 Sound barrier. Provide room-to-room privacy between bedrooms and adjacent living spaces within dwelling units or homes by achieving an articulation index (AI) between 0 and 0.15 per the criteria below. .... **1 SF / 4 MF**

Articulation Index 0 to 0.05 = STC greater than 55 (NIC greater than 47)
Articulation Index 0.05 to 0.15 = STC 52 to 55 (NIC 44 to 47)

905.5 Evaporative coil mold prevention. For buildings with a mechanical system for cooling, ultraviolet lamps are installed on the cooling coils and drain pans of the mechanical system supplies. Lamps produce ultraviolet radiation at a wavelength of 254 nm so as not to generate ozone. Lamps have ballasts housed in a NEMA-rated enclosure. **2**

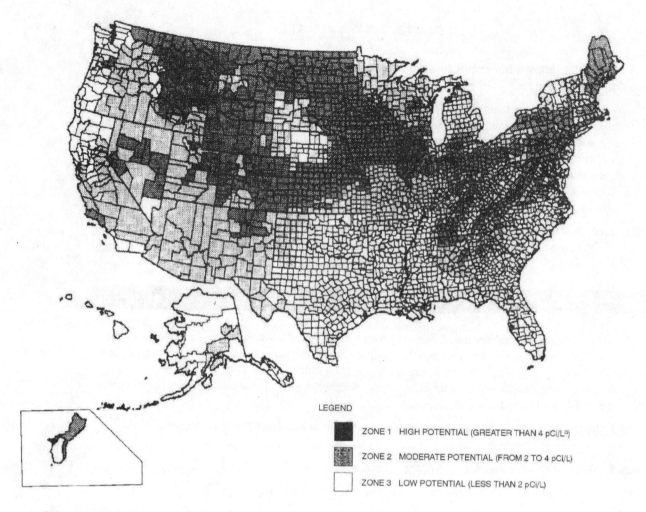

LEGEND

■	ZONE 1	HIGH POTENTIAL (GREATER THAN 4 pCi/L[a])
▨	ZONE 2	MODERATE POTENTIAL (FROM 2 TO 4 pCi/L)
□	ZONE 3	LOW POTENTIAL (LESS THAN 2 pCi/L)

a. pCi/L standard for picocuries per liter of radon gas. The U.S. Environmental Protection Agency (EPA) recommends that all homes that measure 4 pCi/L and greater be mitigated.

The EPA and the U.S. Geological Survey have evaluated the radon potential in the United States and have developed a map of radon zones designed to assist *building officials* in deciding whether radon-resistant features are applicable in new construction.

The map assigns each of the 3,141 counties in the United States to one of three zones based on radon potential. Each zone designation reflects the average short-term radon measurement that can be expected to be measured in a building without the implementation of radon control methods. The radon zone designation of highest priority is Zone 1. More detailed information can be obtained from state-specific booklets (EPA-402-R-93-021 through 070) available through state radon offices or from EPA regional offices.

FIGURE 9(1)
EPA MAP OF RADON ZONES

Reprinted with permission from the 2015 International Residential Code, a copyrighted work of the International Code Council, www.iccsafe.org.

SECTION 10

OPERATION, MAINTENANCE, AND BUILDING OWNER EDUCATION

	M=Mandatory
GREEN BUILDING PRACTICES	**POINTS**

1001	**HOMEOWNER'S MANUAL AND TRAINING GUIDELINES FOR ONE- AND TWO-FAMILY DWELLINGS**	

1001.0 Intent. Information on the building's use, maintenance, and green components is provided.

1001.1 Homeowner's manual. A homeowner's manual is provided and stored in a permanent location in the dwelling that includes the following, as available and applicable.
[1 point awarded per two items. Points awarded for non-mandatory items.] .... **1 [8 max]**

(1) A National Green Building Standard certificate with a web link and completion document. .... **M**

(2) List of green building features (can include the National Green Building Standard checklist)................ **M**

(3) Product manufacturer's manuals or product data sheet for installed major equipment, fixtures, and appliances. If product data sheet is in the building owners' manual, manufacturer's manual may be attached to the appliance in lieu of inclusion in the building owners' manual. .... **M**

(4) Maintenance checklist.

(5) Information on local recycling and composting programs.

(6) Information on available local utility programs that purchase a portion of energy from renewable energy providers.

(7) Explanation of the benefits of using energy-efficient lighting systems [e.g., compact fluorescent light bulbs, light emitting diode (LED)] in high-usage areas.

(8) A list of practices to conserve water and energy.

(9) Information on the importance and operation of the home's fresh air ventilation system.

(10) Local public transportation options.

(11) A diagram showing the location of safety valves and controls for major building systems.

(12) Where frost-protected shallow foundations are used, owner is informed of precautions including:

    (a) instructions to not remove or damage insulation when modifying landscaping.

    (b) providing heat to the building as required by the IRC or IBC.

    (c) keeping base materials beneath and around the building free from moisture caused by broken water pipes or other water sources.

(13) A list of local service providers that offer regularly scheduled service and maintenance contracts to ensure proper performance of equipment and the structure (e.g., HVAC, water-heating equipment, sealants, caulks, gutter and downspout system, shower and/or tub surrounds, irrigation system).

(14) A photo record of framing with utilities installed. Photos are taken prior to installing insulation, clearly labeled, and included as part of the building owners' manual.

(15) List of common hazardous materials often used around the building and instructions for proper handling and disposal of these materials.

GREEN BUILDING PRACTICES	POINTS

(16) Information on organic pest control, fertilizers, deicers, and cleaning products.

(17) Information on native landscape materials and/or those that have low water requirements.

(18) Information on methods of maintaining the building's relative humidity in the range of 30% to 60%.

(19) Instructions for inspecting the building for termite infestation.

(20) Instructions for maintaining gutters and downspouts and importance of diverting water a minimum of 5 ft. away from foundation.

(21) A narrative detailing the importance of maintenance and operation in retaining the attributes of a green-built building.

(22) Where stormwater management measures are installed on the lot, information on the location, purpose, and upkeep of these measures.

(23) Explanation of and benefits from green cleaning in the home.

(24) Retrofit energy calculator that provides baseline for future energy retrofits.

1001.2 Training of initial homeowners. Initial homeowners are familiarized with the role of occupants in achieving green goals. Training is provided to the responsible party(ies) regarding equipment operation and maintenance, control systems, and occupant actions that will improve the environmental performance of the building. These include: .... **M 8**

(1) HVAC filters

(2) Thermostat operation and programming

(3) Lighting controls

(4) Appliances operation

(5) Water heater settings and hot water use

(6) Fan controls

(7) Recycling and composting practices

(8) Whole-dwelling mechanical ventilation systems

1002   CONSTRUCTION, OPERATION, AND MAINTENANCE MANUALS AND TRAINING FOR MULTIFAMILY BUILDINGS

1002.0 Intent. Manuals are provided to the responsible parties (owner, management, tenant, and/or maintenance team) regarding the construction, operation, and maintenance of the building. Paper or digital format manuals are to include information regarding those aspects of the building's construction, maintenance, and operation that are within the area of responsibilities of the respective recipient. One or more responsible parties are to receive a copy of all documentation for archival purposes.

GREEN BUILDING PRACTICES	M=Mandatory POINTS

1002.1 Building construction manual. A building construction manual, including five or more of the following, is compiled and distributed in accordance with § 1002.0. *[Points awarded for non-mandatory items.]* .... | **1 per 2 items** |

(1) A narrative detailing the importance of constructing a green building, including a list of green building attributes included in the building. This narrative is included in all responsible parties' manuals. .... **M**

(2) A local green building program certificate as well as a copy of the *National Green Building Standard®*, as adopted by the Adopting Entity, and the individual measures achieved by the building............................ **M**

(3) Warranty, operation, and maintenance instructions for all equipment, fixtures, appliances, and finishes... **M**

(4) Record drawings of the building.

(5) A record drawing of the site including stormwater management plans, utility lines, landscaping with common name and genus/species of plantings.

(6) A diagram showing the location of safety valves and controls for major building systems.

(7) A list of the type and wattage of light bulbs installed in light fixtures.

(8) A photo record of framing with utilities installed. Photos are taken prior to installing insulation and clearly labeled.

1002.2 Operations manual. Operations manuals are created and distributed to the responsible parties in accordance with § 1002.0. Between all of the operation manuals, five or more of the following options are included. *[Points awarded for non-mandatory items.]* .... | **1 per 2 items** |

(1) A narrative detailing the importance of operating and living in a green building. This narrative is included in all responsible parties' manuals. .... **M**

(2) A list of practices to conserve water and energy (e.g., turning off lights when not in use, switching the rotation of ceiling fans in changing seasons, purchasing ENERGY STAR appliances and electronics). .... **M**

(3) Information on methods of maintaining the building's relative humidity in the range of 30% to 60%.

(4) Information on opportunities to purchase renewable energy from local utilities or national green power providers and information on utility and tax incentives for the installation of on-site renewable energy systems.

(5) Information on local and on-site recycling and hazardous waste disposal programs and, if applicable, building recycling and hazardous waste handling and disposal procedures.

(6) Local public transportation options.

(7) Explanation of the benefits of using compact fluorescent light bulbs, LEDs, or other high-efficiency lighting.

(8) Information on native landscape materials and/or those that have low water requirements.

(9) Information on the radon mitigation system, where applicable.

(10) A procedure for educating tenants in rental properties on the proper use, benefits, and maintenance of green building systems including a maintenance staff notification process for improperly functioning equipment.

(11) Information on the importance and operation of the building's fresh air ventilation system.

M=Mandatory

GREEN BUILDING PRACTICES	POINTS

1002.3 Maintenance manual. Maintenance manuals are created and distributed to the responsible parties in accordance with § 1002.0. Between all of the maintenance manuals, five or more of the following options are included. *[Points awarded for non-mandatory items.]* ....

1 per 2 items

(1) A narrative detailing the importance of maintaining a green building. This narrative is included in all responsible parties' manuals...

M

(2) A list of local service providers that offer regularly scheduled service and maintenance contracts to ensure proper performance of equipment and the structure (e.g., HVAC, water-heating equipment, sealants, caulks, gutter and downspout system, shower and/or tub surrounds, irrigation system).

(3) User-friendly maintenance checklist that includes:

(a) HVAC filters

(b) thermostat operation and programming

(c) lighting controls

(d) appliances and settings

(e) water heater settings

(f) fan controls

(4) List of common hazardous materials often used around the building and instructions for proper handling and disposal of these materials.

(5) Information on organic pest control, fertilizers, deicers, and cleaning products.

(6) Instructions for maintaining gutters and downspouts and the importance of diverting water a minimum of 5 ft. away from foundation.

(7) Instructions for inspecting the building for termite infestation.

(8) A procedure for rental tenant occupancy turnover that preserves the green features.

(9) An outline of a formal green building training program for maintenance staff.

(10) A green cleaning plan which includes guidance on sustainable cleaning products.

(11) A maintenance plan for active recreation and play spaces (e.g., playgrounds, ground markings, exercise equipment.

1002.4 Training of building owners. Building owners are familiarized with the role of occupants in achieving green goals. On-site training is provided to the responsible party(ies) regarding equipment operation and maintenance, control systems, and occupant actions that will improve the environmental performance of the building. These include: ....

M 8

(1) HVAC filters

(2) thermostat operation and programming

(3) lighting controls

(4) appliances operation

(5) water heater settings and hot water use

(6) fan controls

(7) recycling and composting practices

(8) Whole-dwelling mechanical ventilation systems

	M=Mandatory
GREEN BUILDING PRACTICES	**POINTS**

1002.5 Multifamily occupant manual. An occupant manual is compiled and distributed in accordance with § 1002.0. *[Points awarded for non-mandatory items.]*	**1 per 2 items**
(1) NGBS certificate	**M**
(2) List of green building features	**M**
(3) Operations manuals for all appliances and occupant operated equipment including lighting and ventilation controls, thermostats, etc.	**M**
(4) Information on recycling and composting programs.	
(5) Information on purchasing renewable energy from utility.	
(6) Information on energy efficient replacement lamps.	
(7) List of practices to save water and energy.	
(8) Local public transportation options.	
(9) Explanation of benefits of green cleaning.	
1002.6 Training of multifamily occupants. Prepare a training outline, video or website that familiarizes occupants with their role in maintaining the green goals of the project. Include all equipment that the occupant(s) is expected to operate, including but not limited to:	**1 per 2 items**
(1) Lighting controls	
(2) Ventilation controls	
(3) Thermostat operation and programming	
(4) Appliances operation	
(5) Recycling and composting	
(6) HVAC filters	
(7) Water heater setting and hot water use	

1003   PUBLIC EDUCATION

1003.0 Intent. Increase public awareness of the *National Green Building Standard®* and projects constructed in accordance with the NGBS to help increase demand for high-performance homes.

1003.1 Public education. One or more of the following is implemented:	**2 max**
(1) **Signage.** Signs showing the project is designed and built in accordance with the NGBS are posted on the construction site.	**1**
(2) **Certification Plaques.** NGBS certification plaques with rating level attainted are placed in a conspicuous location near the utility area of the home or, in a conspicuous location near the main entrance of a multifamily building.	**1**
(3) **Education.** A URL for the NGBS is included on site signage, builder website (or property website for multifamily buildings), and marketing materials for homes certified under the NGBS.	**1**

GREEN BUILDING PRACTICES	POINTS

1004   POST OCCUPANCY PERFORMANCE ASSESSMENT

1004.0 Intent. A verification system for post occupancy assessment of the building is intended to be a management tool for the building owner to determine if energy or water usage have deviated from expected levels so that inspection and correction action can be taken.

1004.1 Verification system. A verification system plan is provided in the building owner's manual (§ 1001 or § 1002). The verification system provides methods for demonstrating continued energy and water savings that are determined from the building's initial year of occupancy of water and energy consumption as compared to annualized consumption at least every four years.

(1) Verification plan is developed to monitor post-occupancy energy and water use and is provided in the building owner's manual. **1**

(2) Verification system is installed in the building to monitor post-occupancy energy and water use. **3**

1005   INNOVATIVE PRACTICES

1005.1 Appraisals. One or more of the following is implemented:

(1) Energy rating or projected usage data is posted in an appropriate location in the home, or public posting so that an appraiser can access the energy data for an energy efficiency property valuation. .. **2**

(2) An Appraisal Institute Form 820.05 "Residential Green and Energy Addendum" or Form 821 "Commercial Green and energy Efficient Addendum" that consider NGBS, LEED, ENERGY STAR certifications and equivalent programs, is completed for the appraiser by a qualified professional or builder to use in performing the valuation of the property. **2**

(3) NGBS certification information or one of the Appraisal Institute Forms cited in § 1005.1(2) is uploaded to a multiple listing service (MLS) or equivalent database so that appraisers can access it to compare property valuations. **2**

SECTION 11

REMODELING

GREEN BUILDING PRACTICES	M=Mandatory POINTS

Note: Where applicable, section numbering in Chapter 11 parallels a corresponding practice in a previous chapter.

11.500 LOT DESIGN, PREPARATION, AND DEVELOPMENT

11.500.0 Intent. This section applies to the lot and changes to the lot due to remodeling of an existing building.

11.501 LOT SELECTION

11.501.2 Multi-modal transportation. A range of multi-modal transportation choices are promoted by one or more of the following:

(1) The building is located within one-half mile (805 m) of pedestrian access to a mass transit system. ...   **6**

(2) The building is located within five miles (8,046 m) of a mass transit station with provisions for parking.   **3**

(3) The building is located within one-half mile (805 m) of six or more community resources. No more than two each of the following use category can be counted toward the total: Recreation, Retail, Civic, and Services. Examples of resources in each category include, but are not limited to the following: **4**

Recreation: recreational facilities (such as pools, tennis courts, basketball courts), parks.
Retail: grocery store, restaurant, retail store.
Civic: post office, place of worship, community center.
Services: bank, daycare center, school, medical/dental office, Laundromat/dry cleaners.

OR

A lot is selected within a census block group that, compared to its region, has above-average neighborhood walkability using an index within the EPA's Smart Location Database:

(a) Walkability is within the top quartile for the region..   **5**

(b) Walkability is within the second quartile for the region...   **2**

(4) The building is on a lot located within a community that has rights-of-way specifically dedicated to bicycle use in the form of paved paths or bicycle lanes, or is on an infill lot located within 1/2 mile of a bicycle lane designated by the jurisdiction. **5**

(5) Dedicated bicycle parking and racks are constructed for mixed-use and multifamily buildings:

(a) Minimum of 1 bicycle parking space per 3 residential units **2**

(b) Minimum of 1 bicycle parking space per 2 residential units **4**

(c) Minimum of 1 bicycle parking space per 1 residential unit. **6**

(d) Bicycle enclosed storage is provided or parking spaces are covered or otherwise protected from the elements ....   **2 Additional**

(6) The remodel includes the new development and implementation of a community scale bike sharing.   **3**

M=Mandatory

GREEN BUILDING PRACTICES	POINTS

(7) The remodel includes the new development and implementation of a community scale motorized vehicle sharing program. 5

11.502 PROJECT TEAM, MISSION STATEMENT, AND GOALS

11.502.1 Project team, mission statement, and goals. A knowledgeable team is established and team member roles are identified with respect to green lot design, preparation, and development. The project's green goals and objectives are written into a mission statement. 4

11.503 LOT DESIGN

11.503.0 Intent. The lot is designed to avoid detrimental environmental impacts first, to minimize any unavoidable impacts, and to mitigate for those impacts that do occur. The project is designed to minimize environmental impacts and to protect, restore, and enhance the natural features and environmental quality of the lot. *[Points awarded only if the intent of the design is implemented.]*

11.503.1 Natural resources. Natural resources are conserved by one or more of the following:

(1) A natural resources inventory is completed under the direction of a qualified professional. 5

(2) A plan is implemented to conserve the elements identified by the natural resource inventory as high-priority resources. 6

(3) Items listed for protection in the natural resource inventory plan are protected under the direction of a qualified professional. 4

(4) Basic training in tree or other natural resource protection is provided for the on-site supervisor. 4

(5) All tree pruning on-site is conducted by a certified arborist or other qualified professional. 3

(6) Ongoing maintenance of vegetation on the lot during construction is in accordance with TCIA A300 or locally accepted best practices. 4

(7) Where a lot adjoins a landscaped common area, a protection plan from the remodeling construction activities next to the common area is implemented. 5

(8) Developer has a plan to design and construct the lot in accordance with the International Wildland-Urban Interface Code (IWUIC). *[Only applicable where the AHJ has not declared a wildland-urban interface area, but a fire protection engineer, certified fire marshal, or other qualified party has determined and documented the site as hazarded per the IWUIC.]* 6

11.503.2 Slope disturbance. Slope disturbance is minimized by one or more of the following:

(1) The use of terrain-adaptive architecture. 5

(2) Hydrological/soil stability study is completed and used to guide the design of any additions to buildings on the lot. 5

(3) All or a percentage of new driveways and parking are aligned with natural topography to reduce cut and fill.

   (a) greater than or equal to 10% to less than 25% 1

   (b) greater than or equal to 25% to less than 75% 4

   (c) greater than or equal to 75% 6

GREEN BUILDING PRACTICES	M=Mandatory POINTS

(4) Long-term erosion effects are reduced through the design and implementation of clustering, terracing, retaining walls, landscaping, or restabilization techniques. **6**

(5) Underground parking uses the natural slope for parking entrances. **5**

11.503.3 Soil disturbance and erosion. Soil disturbance and erosion are minimized by one or more of the following: (also see § 11.504.3)

(1) Remodeling construction activities are scheduled such that disturbed soil that is to be left unworked for more than 21 days is stabilized within 14 days. **2**

(2) The new utilities on the lot are designed to use one or more alternative means: **2**

   (a) tunneling instead of trenching.

   (b) use of smaller (low ground pressure) equipment or geomats to spread the weight of construction equipment.

   (c) shared utility trenches or easements.

   (d) placement of utilities under paved surfaces instead of yards.

(3) Limits of new clearing and grading are demarcated on the lot plan. **5**

11.503.4 Stormwater Management. The stormwater management system is designed to use low-impact development/green infrastructure practices to preserve, restore or mitigate changes in site hydrology due to land disturbance and the construction of impermeable surfaces through the use of one or more of the following techniques:

(1) A site assessment is conducted and a plan prepared and implemented that identifies important existing permeable soils, natural drainage ways and other water features, e.g., depressional storage, onsite to be preserved in order to maintain site hydrology. **7**

(2) Low-Impact Development/Green infrastructure stormwater management practices to promote infiltration and evapotranspiration are used to manage rainfall on the lot and prevent the off-lot discharge of runoff from all storms up to and including the volume of following storm events:

   (a) 80th percentile storm event **5**

   (b) 90th percentile storm event **8**

   (c) 95th percentile storm event **10**

(3) Permeable materials are used for driveways, parking areas, walkways, patios, and recreational surfaces and the like according to the following percentages:

   (a) greater than or equal to 10% to less than 25% (add 2 points for use of vegetative paving system)..................................... **2**

   (b) greater than or equal to 25% to less than 50% (add 4 points for use of vegetative paving system)..................................... **5**

   (c) greater than or equal to 50% (add 6 points for use of vegetative paving system)..................................... **10**

   [Points for vegetative paving systems are only awarded for locations receiving more than 20 in. per year of annual average precipitation.]

(4) Complete gutter and downspout system directs storm water away from foundation to vegetated landscape area, a raingarden, or catchment system that provides for water infiltration. **8**

GREEN BUILDING PRACTICES	M=Mandatory POINTS

11.503.5 Landscape plan. A plan for the lot is developed to limit water and energy use while preserving or enhancing the natural environment. *[Where "front" only or "rear" only plan is implemented, only half of the points (rounding down to a whole number) are awarded for Items (1)-(8)]*

(1) A plan is formulated and implemented that protects, restores, or enhances natural vegetation on the lot.

    (a) greater than or equal to 12% to less than 25% of the natural area **1**

    (b) greater than or equal to 25% to less than 50% of the natural area **2**

    (c) greater than or equal to 50% to less than 100% of the natural area **3**

    (d) 100% of the natural area **4**

(2) Non-invasive vegetation that is native or regionally appropriate for local growing conditions is selected to promote. **4**

(3) To improve pollinator habitat, at least 10% of planted areas are composed of native or regionally appropriate flowering and nectar producing plant species. Invasive plant species shall not be utilized. **3**

(4) EPA WaterSense Water Budget Tool or equivalent is used when implementing the site vegetative design. **5**

(5) Where turf is being planted, Turfgrass Water Conservation Alliance (TWCA) or equivalent as determined by the adopting entity third-party qualified water efficient grasses are used. **3**

(6) For landscaped vegetated areas, the maximum percentage of all turf areas is:

    (a) greater than 40% to less than or equal to 60% **2**

    (b) greater than 20% to less than or equal to 40% **3**

    (c) greater than 0% to less than or equal to 20% **4**

    (d) 0% **5**

(7) Plants with similar watering needs are grouped (hydrozoning) and shown on the lot plan. **5**

(8) Summer shading by planting installed to shade a minimum of 30% of building walls. To conform to summer shading, the effective shade coverage (five years after planting) is the arithmetic mean of the shade coverage calculated at 10 am for eastward facing walls, noon for southward facing walls, and 3 pm for westward facing walls on the summer solstice. **5**

(9) Vegetative wind breaks or channels are designed to protect the lot and immediate surrounding lots as appropriate for local conditions. **4**

(10) Site- or community-generated tree trimmings or stump grinding of regionally appropriate trees are used on the site to provide protective mulch during construction or for landscaping. **3**

(11) An integrated pest management plan is developed to minimize chemical use in pesticides and fertilizers. **4**

(12) Developer has a plan for removal or containment of invasive plants from the disturbed areas of the site. .. **3**

(13) Developer implements a plan for removal or containment of invasive plants on the undisturbed areas of the site. **6**

	M=Mandatory
GREEN BUILDING PRACTICES	**POINTS**

11.503.6 Wildlife habitat. Measures are planned to support wildlife habitat and include at least two of the following:

(1) Plants and gardens that encourage wildlife, such as bird and butterfly gardens.	3
(2) Inclusion of a certified "backyard wildlife" program.	3
(3) The lot is adjacent to a wildlife corridor, fish and game park, or preserved areas and is designed with regard for this relationship.	3
(4) Outdoor lighting techniques are utilized with regard for wildlife.	3

11.503.7 Environmentally sensitive areas. The lot is in accordance with one or both of the following:

(1) The lot does not contain any environmentally sensitive areas that are disturbed during remodeling.	4
(2) On lots with environmentally sensitive areas, mitigation and/or restoration is conducted to preserve ecosystem functions lost through remodeling activities.	4

11.504   LOT CONSTRUCTION

11.504.0 Intent. Environmental impact during construction is avoided to the extent possible; impacts that do occur are minimized, and any significant impacts are mitigated.

11.504.1 On-site supervision and coordination. On-site supervision and coordination are provided during on-lot-lot clearing, grading, trenching, paving, and installation of utilities to ensure that specified green development practices are implemented. (also see § 11.503.3)	4

11.504.2 Trees and vegetation. Designated trees and vegetation are preserved by one or more of the following:

(1) Fencing or equivalent is installed to protect trees and other vegetation...	3
(2) Trenching, significant changes in grade, and compaction of soil and critical root zones in all "tree save" areas as shown on the lot plan are avoided...	5
(3) Damage to designated existing trees and vegetation is mitigated during construction through pruning, root pruning, fertilizing, and watering...	4

11.504.3 Soil disturbance and erosion implementation. On-site soil disturbance and erosion during remodeling are minimized by one or more of the following in accordance with the SWPPP or applicable plan: (also see § 11.503.3)

(1) Sediment and erosion controls are installed on the lot and maintained in accordance with the stormwater pollution prevention plan, where required...	5
(2) Limits of clearing and grading are staked out on the lot.	5
(3) "No disturbance" zones are created using fencing or flagging to protect vegetation and sensitive areas on the lot from construction activity..	5
(4) Topsoil from either the lot or the site development is stockpiled and stabilized for later use and used to establish landscape plantings on the lot.	5
(5) Soil compaction from construction equipment is reduced by distributing the weight of the equipment over a larger area (laying lightweight geogrids, mulch, chipped wood, plywood, OSB, metal plates, or other materials capable of weight distribution in the pathway of the equipment).	4

GREEN BUILDING PRACTICES	POINTS

(6) Disturbed areas on the lot that are complete or to be left unworked for 21 days or more are stabilized within 14 days using methods as recommended by the EPA, or in the approved SWPPP, where required. **3**

(7) Soil is improved with organic amendments and mulch. **3**

(8) Newly installed utilities on the lot are installed using one or more alternative means (e.g., tunneling instead of trenching, use of smaller equipment, use of low ground pressure equipment, use of geomats, shared utility trenches or easements). **5**

11.505 INNOVATIVE PRACTICES

11.505.0 Intent. Innovative lot design, preparation and development practices are used to enhance environmental performance. Waivers or variances from local development regulations are obtained, and innovative zoning is used to implement such practices.

11.505.1 Driveways and parking areas. Driveways and parking areas are minimized or mitigated by one or more of the following:

(1) Off-street parking areas or driveways are shared. Waivers or variances from local development regulations are obtained to implement such practices, if required. **5**

(2) In a multifamily project, parking capacity does not exceed the local minimum requirements. **5**

(3) Structured parking is utilized to reduce the footprint of surface parking areas.

    (a) greater than or equal to 25% to less than 50% **4**

    (b) greater than or equal to 50% to less than 75% **5**

    (c) greater than or equal to 75% **6**

11.505.2 Heat island mitigation. Heat island effect is mitigated by one or both of the following. **4**

(1) Hardscape: Not less than 50% of the surface area of the hardscape on the lot meets one or a combination of the following methods. **5**

    (a) Shading of hardscaping: Shade is provided from existing or new vegetation (within five years) or from trellises. Shade of hardscaping is to be measured on the summer solstice at noon.

    (b) Light-colored hardscaping: Horizontal hardscaping materials are installed with a solar reflectance index (SRI) of 29 or greater. The SRI is calculated in accordance with ASTM E1980. A default SRI value of 35 for new concrete without added color pigment is permitted to be used instead of measurements.

    (c) Permeable hardscaping: Permeable hardscaping materials are installed.

(2) Roofs: Not less than 75% of the exposed surface of the roof is vegetated using technology capable of withstanding the climate conditions of the jurisdiction and the microclimate of the building lot. Invasive plant species are not permitted. **5**

GREEN BUILDING PRACTICES	M=Mandatory POINTS

11.505.3 Density. The average density on the lot on a net developable area basis is:

(1) greater than or equal to 7 to less than 14 dwelling units/sleeping units per acre (per 4,047 m²) **4**

(2) greater than or equal to 14 to less than 21 dwelling units/sleeping units per acre (per 4,047 m²) **5**

(3) greater than or equal to 21 to less than 35 dwelling units/sleeping units per acre (per 4,047 m²) **6**

(4) greater than or equal to 35 to less than 70 dwelling units/sleeping units per acre (per 4,047 m²) **7**

(5) greater than or equal to 70 dwelling units/sleeping units per acre (per 4,047 m²)............................. **8**

11.505.4 Mixed-use development. **8**

(1) The lot contains a mixed-use building. **5**

11.505.5 Multifamily or mixed-use community garden(s). Local food production to residents or area consumers. **3**

    (a) A portion of the lot of at least 250 sq. ft. is established as community garden(s) for the residents of the site. *[3 points awarded per 250 sq. ft.]*.. **3 [9 max]**

    (b) Locate the project within a 0.5-mile walking distance of an existing or planned farmers market/ farm stand that is open or will operate at least once a week for at least five months of the year. **3**

    (c) Areas and physical provisions are provided for composting. **1**

    (d) Signs designating the garden area are posted. **1**

11.505.6 Multi-unit plug-in electric vehicle charging. Plug-in electric vehicle charging capability is provided for not fewer than 2% of parking stalls. *[An additional 2 points can be earned for each percentage point above 2% for a maximum of 10 points]* .... **4 [10 max]**

Fractional values shall be rounded up to the nearest whole number. Electrical capacity in main electric panels supports Level 2 charging (208/240V – up to 80 amps or in accordance with SAE J1772). Each stall is provided with conduit and wiring infrastructure from the electric panel to support Level 2 charging (208/240V – up to 80 amps or in accordance with SAE J1772) service to the designated stalls, and stalls are equipped with either Level 2 charging AC grounded outlets (208/240V – up to 80 amps or in accordance with SAE J1772) or Level 2 charging stations (208-240V – up to 80 amps or in accordance with SAE J1772) by a third-party charging station.

11.505.7 Multi-unit residential CNG vehicle fueling. CNG vehicle residential fueling appliances are provided for at least 1% of the parking stalls. The CNG fueling appliances shall be listed in accordance with ANSI/CSA NGV 5.1 and installed in accordance to the appliance manufacturer's installation instructions... **4**

11.505.8 Street network. Project is located in an area of high intersection density. **5**

11.505.9 Smoking prohibitions. Signs are provided on multifamily and mixed-use lots prohibiting smoking at the following locations:

    (a) Smoking is prohibited within 25 ft. (7.5 m) of all building exterior doors and operable windows or building air intakes within 15 vertical feet (4.5 m) of grade or a walking surface. **3**

    (b) Smoking is prohibited on decks, balconies, patios and other occupied exterior spaces. **3**

    (c) Smoking is prohibited at all parks, playgrounds, and community activity or recreational spaces. .. **3**

GREEN BUILDING PRACTICES	POINTS

11.505.10 Recreational space. For multifamily buildings, on-site dedicated recreation space for exercise or play opportunities for adults and/or children open and accessible to residents is provided.

(a) A dedicated area of at least 400 sq. ft. is provided inside the building with adult exercise and/or children's play equipment. **3**

(b) A courtyard, garden, terrace, or roof space at least 10% of the lot area that can serve as outdoor space for children's play and /or adult activities is provided. **3**

(c) Active play/recreation areas are illuminated at night to extend opportunities for physical activity into the evening. **3**

11.505.11 Battery storage system. A battery storage system of not less than 6 kWh of available capacity is installed that stores electric energy from an on-site renewable electric generation system or is grid-interactive or can perform both functions. **2**

11.601   QUALITY OF CONSTRUCTION MATERIALS AND WASTE

11.601.0 Intent. Design and construction practices that minimize the environmental impact of the building materials are incorporated, environmentally efficient building systems and materials are incorporated, and waste generated during construction is reduced.

11.601.1 Conditioned floor area. Finished floor area of a dwelling unit or sleeping unit after the remodeling is limited. Finished floor area is calculated in accordance with ANSI Z765 for single family and ANSI/BOMA Z65.4 for multifamily buildings. Only the finished floor area for stories above grade plane is included in the calculation. *[For every 100 sq. ft. (9.29 m^2) over 4,000 sq. ft. (372 m^2), 1 point is to be added the threshold points shown in Table 305.3.7 for each rating level.]*

(1) less than or equal to 700 sq. ft. (65 m^2)... **14**

(2) less than or equal to 1,000 sq. ft. (93 m^2)... **12**

(3) less than or equal to 1,500 sq. ft. (139 m^2)... **9**

(4) less than or equal to 2,000 sq. ft. (186 m^2)... **6**

(5) less than or equal to 2,500 sq. ft. (232 m^2)... **3**

(6) greater than 4,000 sq. ft. (372 m^2) .... **M**

Multifamily Building Note: For a multifamily building, a weighted average of the individual unit sizes is used for this practice.

11.601.2 Material usage. Newly installed structural systems are designed, or construction techniques are implemented, to reduce and optimize material usage.
[Points awarded only when the newly installed portion of each structural system comprises at least 25% of the total area of that structural system after the remodel] .... **9 max**

(1) Minimum structural member or element sizes necessary for strength and stiffness in accordance with advanced framing techniques or structural design standards are selected. **3**

(2) Higher-grade or higher-strength of the same materials than commonly specified for structural elements and components in the building are used and element or component sizes are reduced accordingly........ **3**

(3) Performance-based structural design is used to optimize lateral force-resisting systems. **3**

GREEN BUILDING PRACTICES	M=Mandatory POINTS

11.601.3 Building dimensions and layouts. Building dimensions and layouts are designed to reduce material cuts and waste. This practice is used for a minimum of 80% of the newly installed areas: *[Points awarded only when the newly installed area of the building comprises at least 25% of the total area of that element of the building after the remodel]*

(1) floor area.. 3

(2) wall area.. 3

(3) roof area.. 3

(4) cladding or siding area 3

(5) penetrations or trim area.. 1

11.601.4 Framing and structural plans. Detailed framing or structural plans, material quantity lists and on-site cut lists for newly installed framing, structural materials, and sheathing materials are provided.... 4

11.601.5 Prefabricated components. Precut or preassembled components, or panelized or precast assemblies are utilized for a minimum of 90% for the following system or building:
[Points awarded only when the newly installed system comprises at least 25% of the total area of that system of the building after the remodel] .... 13 max

(1) floor system 4

(2) wall system.. 4

(3) roof system 4

(4) modular construction for any new construction located above grade........................ 13

11.601.6 Stacked stories. Stories above grade are stacked, such as in 1½-story, 2-story, or greater structures. The area of the upper story is a minimum of 50% of the area of the story below, based on areas with a minimum ceiling height of 7 ft. (2,134 mm). .... 8 max

(1) first stacked story.. 4

(2) for each additional stacked story.. 2

11.601.7 Prefinished materials. Prefinished building materials or assemblies listed below have no additional site-applied finishing material are installed. .... 12 max

  (a) interior trim not requiring paint or stain.

  (b) exterior trim not requiring paint or stain.

  (c) window, skylight, and door assemblies not requiring paint or stain on one of the following surfaces:
      i. exterior surfaces
      ii. interior surfaces

  (d) interior wall coverings or systems, floor systems, and/or ceiling systems not requiring paint or stain or other type of finishing application.

  (e) exterior wall coverings or systems, floor systems, and/or ceiling systems not requiring paint or stain or other type of finishing application.

(1) Percent of prefinished building materials or assemblies installed:
    [Points awarded for each type of material or assembly.]

  (a) greater than or equal to 35% to less than 50% (after the remodel)................................ 1

  (b) greater than or equal to 50% to less than 90% (after the remodel)................................ 2

  (c) greater than or equal to 90% (after the remodel) 5

GREEN BUILDING PRACTICES	M=Mandatory POINTS

11.601.8 Foundations. A foundation system that minimizes soil disturbance, excavation quantities and material usage, such as frost-protected shallow foundations, isolated pier and pad foundations, deep foundations, post foundations, or helical piles is selected, designed, and constructed. The foundation is used on 25% or more of the building footprint after the remodel. **3**

11.602 ENHANCED DURABILITY AND REDUCED MAINTENANCE

11.602.0 Intent. Design and construction practices are implemented that enhance the durability of materials and reduce in-service maintenance.

11.602.1 Moisture management – building envelope

11.602.1.1 Capillary breaks

11.602.1.1.1 A capillary break and vapor retarder are installed at concrete slabs in accordance with IRC Sections R506.2.2 and R506.2.3 or IBC Sections 1910 and 1805.4.1.
*[*This practice is not mandatory for existing slabs without apparent moisture problem.]* .... **M***

11.602.1.1.2 A capillary break to prevent moisture migration into foundation wall is provided between the footing and the foundation wall on all new foundations, and on not less than 25% of the total length of the foundation after the remodel. **3**

11.602.1.2 Foundation waterproofing. Enhanced foundation waterproofing is installed on all new foundations, and on not less than 25% of the total length of the foundation after the remodel using one or both of the following: **4**

(1) rubberized coating, or

(2) drainage mat

11.602.1.3 Foundation drainage

11.602.1.3.1 Where required by the IRC or IBC for habitable and usable spaces below grade, exterior drain tile is installed.
*[*This practice is not mandatory for existing slabs without apparent moisture problem.]* .... **M***

11.602.1.3.2 Interior and exterior foundation perimeter drains are installed and sloped to discharge to daylight, dry well, or sump pit on all new foundations and not less than 25% of the total length of the foundation after the remodel. **4**

11.602.1.4 Crawlspaces.

11.602.1.4.1 Vapor retarder for all new unconditioned vented crawlspace foundations and not less than 25% of the total area after the remodel is in accordance with the following, as applicable. Joints of vapor retarder overlap a minimum of 6 in. (152 mm) and are taped.

(1) Floors. Minimum 6 mil vapor retarder installed on the crawlspace floor and extended at least 6 in. up the wall and is attached and sealed to the wall. **6**

(2) Walls. Dampproof walls are provided below finished grade.
    *[*This practice is not mandatory for existing walls without apparent moisture problem.]* .... **M***

GREEN BUILDING PRACTICES	M=Mandatory POINTS

11.602.1.4.2 For all new foundations and not less than 25% of the total area of the crawlspace after the remodel, crawlspace that is built as a conditioned area is sealed to prevent outside air infiltration and provided with conditioned air at a rate not less than 0.02 cfm (.009 L/s) per sq. ft. of horizontal area and one of the following is implemented:

(1) a concrete slab over 6 mil polyethylene sheeting or other Class I vapor retarder installed in accordance with IRC Section 408.3 or Section 506. .... **8**

(2) 6 mil polyethylene sheeting or other Class I vapor retarder installed in accordance with IRC Section 408.3 or Section 506.
[*This practice is not mandatory for existing foundations without apparent moisture problem.] .... **M***

11.602.1.5 Termite barrier. Continuous physical foundation termite barrier provided:

(1) In geographic areas that have moderate to heavy infestation potential in accordance with Figure 6(3), a no or low toxicity treatment is also installed. **4**

(2) In geographic areas that have a very heavy infestation potential in accordance with Figure 6(3), in addition a low toxicity bait and kill termite treatment plan is selected and implemented. **4**

11.602.1.6 Termite-resistant materials. In areas of termite infestation probability as defined by Figure 6(3), termite-resistant materials are used as follows:

(1) In areas of slight to moderate termite infestation probability: for the foundation, all structural walls, floors, concealed roof spaces not accessible for inspection, exterior decks, and exterior claddings within the first 2 ft. (610 mm) above the top of the foundation. **2**

(2) In areas of moderate to heavy termite infestation probability: for the foundation, all structural walls, floors, concealed roof spaces not accessible for inspection, exterior decks, and exterior claddings within the first 3 ft. (914 mm) above the top of the foundation. **4**

(3) In areas of very heavy termite infestation probability: for the foundation, all structural walls, floors, concealed roof spaces not accessible for inspection, exterior decks, and exterior claddings. **6**

11.602.1.7 Moisture control measures

11.602.1.7.1 Moisture control measures are in accordance with the following:

(1) Building materials with visible mold are not installed or are cleaned or encapsulated prior to concealment and closing. **2**

(2) Insulation in cavities is dry in accordance with manufacturer's instructions when enclosed (e.g., with drywall). .... **M 2**

(3) The moisture content of lumber is sampled to ensure it does not exceed 19% prior to the surface and/or cavity enclosure. **4**

11.602.1.7.2 Moisture content of subfloor, substrate, or concrete slabs is in accordance with the appropriate industry standard for the finish flooring to be applied. **2**

11.602.1.7.3 Building envelope assemblies that are designed for moisture control based on documented hygrothermal simulation or field study analysis. Hygrothermal analysis is required to incorporate representative climatic conditions, interior conditions and include heating and cooling seasonal variation. .. **4**

11.602.1.8 Water-resistive barrier. Where required by the IRC or IBC, a water-resistive barrier and/or drainage plane system is installed behind newly installed exterior veneer and/or siding and where there is evidence of a moisture problem. .... **M**

GREEN BUILDING PRACTICES	M=Mandatory POINTS

11.602.1.9 Flashing. Flashing is provided as follows to minimize water entry into wall and roof assemblies and to direct water to exterior surfaces or exterior water-resistive barriers for drainage. Flashing details are provided in the construction documents and are in accordance with the fenestration manufacturer's instructions, the flashing manufacturer's instructions, or as detailed by a registered design professional.

[Points awarded only when practices (2)-(7) are implemented in all newly installed construction and not less than 25% of the applicable building elements for the entire building after the remodel.]

(1) Flashing is installed at all the following locations, as applicable:
[*These practices are not mandatory for existing building elements without apparent moisture problem.] .... **M***

    (a) around exterior fenestrations, skylights and doors;

    (b) at roof valleys;

    (c) at all building-to-deck, -balcony, -porch, and -stair intersections;

    (d) at roof-to-wall intersections, at roof-to-chimney intersections, at wall-to-chimney intersections, and at parapets;

    (e) at ends of and under masonry, wood, or metal copings and sills;

    (f) above projecting wood trim;

    (g) at built-in roof gutters; and

    (h) drip edge is installed at eave and rake edges.

(2) All window and door head and jamb flashing is either self-adhered flashing complying with AAMA 711 or liquid applied flashing complying with AAMA 714 and installed in accordance with flashing fenestration or manufacturer's installation instructions. **2**

(3) Pan flashing is installed at sills of all exterior windows and doors **3**

(4) Seamless, preformed kickout flashing, or prefabricated metal with soldered seams is provided at all roof-to-wall intersections. The type and thickness of the material used for roof flashing including but not limited kickout and step flashing is commensurate with the anticipated service life of the roofing material. **3**

(5) A rainscreen wall design as follows is used for exterior wall assemblies .... **4 max**

    (a) a system designed with minimum ¼-in. air space exterior to the water-resistive barrier, vented to the exterior at top and bottom of the wall and integrated with flashing details, or **4**

    (b) a cladding material or a water-resistive barrier with enhanced drainage, meeting 75% drainage efficiency determined in accordance with ASTM E2273. .... **2**

(6) Through-wall flashing is installed at transitions between wall cladding materials, or wall construction types. **2**

(7) Flashing is installed at expansion joints in stucco walls **2**

M=Mandatory

GREEN BUILDING PRACTICES	POINTS

11.602.1.10 Exterior doors. Entries at exterior door assemblies, inclusive of side lights (if any), are covered by one of the following methods to protect the building from the effects of precipitation and solar radiation. Either a storm door or a projection factor of 0.375 minimum is provided. Eastern- and western-facing entries in Climate Zones 1, 2, and 3, as determined in accordance with Figure 6(1) or Appendix A, have either a storm door or a projection factor of 1.0 minimum, unless protected from direct solar radiation by other means (e.g., screen wall, vegetation).
[2 points awarded per exterior door] .... **2 [6 max]**

    (a) installing a porch roof or awning

    (b) extending the roof overhang

    (c) recessing the exterior door

    (d) Installing a storm door

11.602.1.11 Tile backing materials. Tile backing materials installed under tiled surfaces in wet areas are in accordance with ASTM C1178, C1278, C1288, or C1325.
*[*This practice is not mandatory for existing tile surfaces without apparent moisture problem.]* .... **M***

11.602.1.12 Roof overhangs. Roof overhangs, in accordance with Table 11.602.1.12, are provided over a minimum of 90% of exterior walls to protect the building envelope. **4**

Table 11.602.1.12

Minimum Roof Overhang for One- & Two-Story Buildings		
Inches of Rainfall [1]	Eave Overhang (In.)	Rake Overhang (In.)
≤40	12	12
>41 and ≤70	18	12
>70	24	12

(1) Annual mean total rainfall in inches is in accordance with Figure 6(2).
For SI: 12 in. = 304.8 mm

11.602.1.13 Ice barrier. In areas where there has been a history of ice forming along the eaves causing a backup of water, an ice barrier is installed in accordance with the IRC or IBC at roof eaves of pitched roofs and extends a minimum of 24 in. (610 mm) inside the exterior wall line of the building. .... **M**

11.602.1.14 Architectural features. Architectural features that increase the potential for the water intrusion are avoided:

(1) All horizontal ledgers are sloped away to provide gravity drainage as appropriate for the application. ... **M 1**

(2) No roof configurations that create horizontal valleys in roof design. **2**

(3) No recessed windows and architectural features that trap water on horizontal surfaces..................... **2**

11.602.1.15 Kitchen and vanity cabinets. All kitchen and vanity cabinets are certified in accordance with the ANSI/KCMA A161.1 performance standard or equivalent... **2**

GREEN BUILDING PRACTICES	POINTS

11.602.2 Roof surfaces. A minimum of 90% of roof surfaces, not used for roof penetrations and associated equipment, on-site renewable energy systems such as photovoltaics or solar thermal energy collectors, or rooftop decks, amenities and walkways, are constructed of one or more of the following: ... **3**

(1) products that are in accordance with the ENERGY STAR® cool roof certification or equivalent

(2) a vegetated roof system

(3) Minimum initial SRI of 78 for low-sloped roof (a slope less than 2:12) and a minimum initial SRI of 29 for a steep-sloped roof (a slope equal to or greater than 2:12). The SRI is calculated in accordance with ASTM E1980. Roof products are certified and labeled.

11.602.3 Roof water discharge. A gutter and downspout system or splash blocks and effective grading are provided to carry water a minimum of 5 ft. (1524 mm) away from perimeter foundation walls. **4**

11.602.4 Finished grade

11.602.4.1 Finished grade at all sides of a building is sloped to provide a minimum of 6 in. (152 mm) of fall within 10 ft. (3048 mm) of the edge of the building. Where lot lines, walls, slopes, or other physical barriers prohibit 6 in. (152 mm) of fall within 10 ft. (3048 mm), the final grade is sloped away from the edge of the building at a minimum slope of 2%. .... **M**

11.602.4.2 The final grade is sloped away from the edge of the building at a minimum slope of 5%. **1**

11.602.4.3 Water is directed to drains or swales to ensure drainage away from the structure. **1**

11.603   REUSED OR SALVAGED MATERIALS

11.603.0 Intent. Practices that reuse or modify existing structures, salvage materials for other uses, or use salvaged materials in the building's construction are implemented.

11.603.1 Reuse of existing building. Major elements or components of existing buildings and structures are reused, modified, or deconstructed for later use.
[1 Point awarded for every 200 sq. ft. (18.5 m²) of floor area.] .... **1 [12 max]**

11.603.2 Salvaged materials. Reclaimed and/or salvaged materials and components are used. The total material value and labor cost of salvaged materials is equal to or exceeds 1% of the total construction cost.
[1 Point awarded per 1% of salvaged materials used based on the total construction cost. Materials, elements, or components awarded points under § 11.603.1 shall not be awarded points under § 11.603.2.] . **1 [9 max]**

11.603.3 Scrap materials. Sorting and reuse of scrap building material is facilitated (e.g., a central storage area or dedicated bins are provided). **4**

	M=Mandatory
GREEN BUILDING PRACTICES	**POINTS**

11.604 RECYCLED-CONTENT BUILDING MATERIALS

11.604.1 Recycled content. Building materials with recycled content are used for two minor and/or two major components of the building.

Per Table 11.604.1

Table 11.604.1
Recycled Content

Material Percentage Recycled Content	Points For 2 Minor	Points For 2 Major
25% to less than 50%	1	2
50% to less than 75%	2	4
more than 75%	3	6

11.605 RECYCLED CONSTRUCTION WASTE

11.605.0 Intent. Waste generated during construction is recycled.

11.605.1 Hazardous waste. The construction waste management plan shall include information on the proper handling and disposal of hazardous waste. Hazardous waste is properly handled and disposed.......... **M**

11.605.2 Construction waste management plan. A construction waste management plan is developed, posted at the jobsite, and implemented, diverting through methods such as reuse, salvage, recycling, or manufacturer reclamation, a minimum of 50% (by weight) of nonhazardous construction and demolition waste from disposal. For this practice, land-clearing debris is not considered a construction waste. Materials used as alternative daily cover are considered construction waste and do not count toward recycling or salvaging. **6**

For remodeling projects or demolition of an existing facility, the waste management plan includes the recycling of 95% of electronic waste components (such as printed circuit boards from computers, building automation systems, HVAC, fire and security control boards), by an E-Waste recycling facility.

Exceptions: 1) Waste materials generated from land clearing, soil and sub-grade excavation and vegetative debris shall not be in the calculations; and 2) a recycling facility (traditional or E-Waste) offering material receipt documentation is not available within 50 miles of the jobsite.

11.605.3 On-site recycling. On-site recycling measures following applicable regulations and codes are implemented, such as the following: **7**

  (a) Materials are ground or otherwise safely applied on-site as soil amendment or fill. A minimum of 50% (by weight) of construction and land-clearing waste is diverted from landfill.

  (b) Alternative compliance methods approved by the Adopting Entity.

  (c) Compatible untreated biomass material (lumber, posts, beams etc.) are set aside for combustion if a Solid Fuel Burning Appliance per § 11.901.2.1(2) will be available for on-site renewable energy.

11.605.4 Recycled construction materials. Construction materials (e.g., wood, cardboard, metals, drywall, plastic, asphalt roofing shingles, or concrete) are recycled offsite. .... **6 max**

(1) a minimum of two types of materials are recycled **3**

(2) for each additional recycled material type **1**

GREEN BUILDING PRACTICES	M=Mandatory POINTS

11.606   RENEWABLE MATERIALS

11.606.0 Intent. Building materials derived from renewable resources are used.

11.606.1 Biobased products. The following biobased products are used: .... **8 max**

    (a)   certified solid wood in accordance with § 11.606.2

    (b)   engineered wood

    (c)   bamboo

    (d)   cotton

    (e)   cork

    (f)   straw

    (g)   natural fiber products made from crops (soy-based, corn-based)

    (h)   other biobased materials with a minimum of 50% biobased content (by weight or volume)

(1)   Two types of biobased materials are used, each for more than 0.5% of the project's projected building material cost. **3**

(2)   Two types of biobased materials are used, each for more than 1% of the project's projected building material cost. **6**

(3)   For each additional biobased material used for more than 0.5% of the project's projected building material cost. .... **1 [2 max]**

11.606.2 Wood-based products. Wood or wood-based products are certified to the requirements of one of the following recognized product programs:

    (a)   American Forest Foundation's American *Tree Farm System*® (ATFS)

    (b)   Canadian Standards Association's *Sustainable Forest Management System Standards* (CSA Z809)

    (c)   *Forest Stewardship Council* (FSC)

    (d)   *Program for Endorsement of Forest Certification Systems* (PEFC)

    (e)   *Sustainable Forestry Initiative ® Program* (SFI)

    (f)   *National Wood Flooring Association's Responsible Procurement Program* (RPP)

    (g)   other product programs mutually recognized by PEFC

    (h)   A manufacturer's fiber procurement system that has been audited by an approved agency as compliant with the provisions of ASTM D7612 as a responsible or certified source. Government or tribal forestlands whose water protection programs have been evaluated by an approved agency as compliant with the responsible source designation of ASTM D7612 are exempt from auditing in the manufacturer's fiber procurement system.

(1)   A minimum of two responsible or certified wood-based products are used for minor components of the building.. **3**

(2)   A minimum of two responsible or certified wood-based products are used in major components of the building.. **4**

GREEN BUILDING PRACTICES	M=Mandatory POINTS

11.606.3 Manufacturing energy. Materials are used for major components of the building that are manufactured using a minimum of 33% of the primary manufacturing process energy derived from renewable sources, combustible waste sources, or renewable energy credits (RECs). *[2 points awarded per material]* .... **2 [6 max]**

11.607   RECYCLING AND WASTE REDUCTION

11.607.1 Recycling and composting. Recycling and composting by the occupant are facilitated by one or more of the following methods:

(1) A readily accessible space(s) for recyclable material containers is provided and identified on the floorplan of the house or dwelling unitor a readily accessible area(s) outside the living space is provided for recyclable material containers and identified on the site plan for the house or building. The area outside the living space shall accommodate recycling bin(s) for recyclable materials accepted in local recycling programs **3**

(2) A readily accessible space(s) for compostable material containers is provided and identified on the floorplan of the house or dwelling unit or a readily accessible area(s) outside the living space is provided for compostable material containers and identified on the site plan for the house or building. The area outside the living space shall accommodate composting container(s) for locally accepted materials, or, accommodate composting container(s) for on-site composting. **4**

11.607.2 Food waste disposers. A minimum of one food waste disposer is installed at the primary kitchen sink. **1**

11.608   RESOURCE-EFFICIENT MATERIALS

11.608.1 Resource-efficient materials. Products containing fewer materials are used to achieve the same end-use requirements as conventional products, including but not limited to:
[3 points awarded per each material] .... **3 [9 max]**

(1) lighter, thinner brick with bed depth less than 3 in. and/or brick with coring of more than 25%.

(2) engineered wood or engineered steel products.

(3) roof or floor trusses.

11.609   REGIONAL MATERIALS

11.609.1 Regional materials. Regional materials are used for major and/or minor components of the building. *[2 points awarded per each major component and 1 per each minor component]* .... **10 max**

   (1) Major component *[2 points awarded per each component]* **2**

   (2) Minor component *[1 point awarded per each component]* **1**

For a component to comply with this practice, a minimum of 75% of all products in that component category must be sourced regionally, e.g., stone veneer category – 75% or more of the stone veneer on a project must be sourced regionally.

	M=Mandatory
GREEN BUILDING PRACTICES	**POINTS**

11.610   LIFE CYCLE ASSESSMENT

11.610.1 Life cycle assessment. A life cycle assessment (LCA) tool is used to select environmentally preferable products, assemblies, or, entire building designs. Points are awarded in accordance with § 11.610.1.1 or § 11.610.1.2. Only one method of analysis or tool may be utilized. A reference service life for the building is 60 years for any life cycle analysis tool. Results of the LCA are reported in the manual required in § 11.1001.1 or § 11.1002.1(1) of this Standard in terms of the environmental impacts listed in this practice and it is stated if operating energy was included in the LCA. .... **15 max**

11.610.1.1 Whole-building life cycle assessment. A whole-building LCA is performed in conformance with ASTM E2921 using ISO 14044 compliant life cycle assessment. .... **15 max**

(1) Execute LCA at the whole building level through a comparative analysis between the final and reference building designs as set forth under Standard Practice, ASTM E2921. The assessment criteria includes the following environmental impact categories: **8**

   (a) Primary energy use

   (b) Global warming potential

   (c) Acidification potential

   (d) Eutrophication potential

   (e) Ozone depletion potential

   (f) Smog potential

(2) Execute LCA on regulated loads throughout the building operations life cycle stage. Conduct simulated energy performance analyses in accordance with § 702.2.1 ICC IECC analysis (IECC Section 405) in establishing the comparative performance of final versus reference building designs. Primary energy use savings and global warming potential avoidance from simulation analyses results are determined using energy supplier, utility, or EPA electricity generation and other fuels energy conversion factors and electricity generation and other fuels emission rates for the locality or Sub-Region in which the building is located. **5**

(3) Execute full LCA, including use-phase, through calculation of operating energy impacts (c) – (f) using local or regional emissions factors from energy supplier, utility, or EPA. **2**

11.610.1.2 Life cycle assessment for a product or assembly. An environmentally preferable product or assembly is selected for an application based upon the use of an LCA tool that incorporates data methods compliant with ISO 14044 or other recognized standards that compare the environmental impact of products or assemblies. .... **10 max**

11.610.1.2.1 Product LCA. A product with improved environmental impact measures compared to another product(s) intended for the same use is selected. The environmental impact measures used in the assessment are selected from the following: **Per Table 11.610.1.2.1 [10 max]**

   (a) Primary energy use

   (b) Global warming potential

   (c) Acidification potential

   (d) Eutrophication potential

   (e) Ozone depletion potential

   (f) Smog potential

[Points awarded for each product/system comparison where the selected product/system improved upon the environmental impact measures by an average of 15%.]

GREEN BUILDING PRACTICES	POINTS

Table 11.610.1.2.1
Product LCA

4 Impact Measures	5 Impact Measures
POINTS	
2	3

11.610.1.2.2 Assembly LCA. An assembly with improved environmental impact measures compared to a functionally comparable assembly is selected. The full life cycle, from resource extraction to demolition and disposal (including but not limited to on-site construction, maintenance and replacement, material and product embodied acquisition, and process and transportation energy), is assessed. The assessment does not include electrical and mechanical equipment and controls, plumbing products, fire detection and alarm systems, elevators, and conveying systems. The following functional building elements are eligible for points under this practice:

Per Table 11.610.1.2.2 [10 max]

(a) exterior walls

(b) roof/ceiling

(c) interior walls or ceilings

(d) intermediate floors

The environmental impact measures used in the assessment are selected from the following:

(a) Primary energy use

(b) Global warming potential

(c) Acidification potential

(d) Eutrophication potential

(e) Ozone depletion potential

(f) Smog potential

[Points are awarded based on the number of functional building elements that improve upon environmental impact measures by an average of 15%.]

Table 11.610.1.2.2
Assembly LCA

	4 Impact Measures	5 Impact Measures
	POINTS	
2 functional building elements	3	6
3 functional building elements	4	8
4 functional building elements	5	10

	M=Mandatory
GREEN BUILDING PRACTICES	**POINTS**

11.611   PRODUCT DECLARATIONS

11.611.1 Product declarations. A minimum of 10 different products installed in the building project, at the time of certificate of occupancy, comply with one of the following sub-sections. Declarations, reports, and assessments are submitted and contain documentation of the critical peer review by an independent third party, results from the review, the reviewer's name, company name, contact information, and date of the review. **5**

11.611.1.1 Industry-wide declaration. A Type III industry-wide environmental product declaration (EPD) is submitted for each product. Where the program operator explicitly recognizes the EPD as representative of the product group on a National level, it is considered industry-wide. In the case where an industry-wide EPD represents only a subset of an industry group, as opposed to being industry-wide, the manufacturer is required to be explicitly recognized as a participant by the EPD program operator. All EPDs are required to be consistent with ISO Standards 14025 and 21930 with at least a cradle-to-gate scope.

[Each product complying with § 11. 611.1.1 shall be counted as one product for compliance with § 611.1]

11.611.1.2 Product Specific Declaration. A product specific Type III EPD is submitted for each product. The product specific declaration shall be manufacturer specific for an individual product or product family. All Type III EPDs are required to be certified as complying, at a minimum, with the goal and scope for the cradle-to-gate requirements in accordance with ISO Standards 14025 and 21930.

[Each product complying with § 11. 611.1.2 shall be counted as two products for compliance with § 611.1]

11.612   INNOVATIVE PRACTICES

11.612.1 Manufacturer's environmental management system concepts. Product manufacturer's operations and business practices include environmental management system concepts, and the production facility is registered to ISO 14001 or equivalent. The aggregate value of building products from registered ISO 14001 or equivalent production facilities is 1% or more of the estimated total building materials cost. *[1 point awarded per percent]*... **1 [10 max]**

11.612.2 Sustainable products. One or more of the following products are used for at least 30% of the floor or wall area of the entire dwelling unit or sleeping unit, as applicable. Products are certified by a third-party agency accredited to ISO 17065. .... **9 max**

(1) greater than or equal to 50% of carpet installed (by square feet) is certified to NSF 140 or equivalent. **3**

(2) greater than or equal to 50% of resilient flooring installed (by square feet) is certified to NSF 332 or equivalent. **3**

(3) greater than or equal to 50% of the insulation installed (by square feet) is certified to UL 2985 or equivalent. **3**

(4) greater than or equal to 50% of interior wall coverings installed (by square feet) is certified to NSF 342 or equivalent.. **3**

(5) greater than or equal to 50% of the gypsum board installed (by square feet) is certified to UL 100 or equivalent. **3**

GREEN BUILDING PRACTICES	POINTS

(6) greater than or equal to 50% of the door leafs installed (by number of door leafs) is certified to UL 102 or equivalent. **3**

(7) greater than or equal to 50% of the tile installed (by square feet) is certified to TCNA A138.1 Specifications for Sustainable Ceramic Tiles, Glass Tiles and Tile Installation Materials or equivalent.. **3**

11.612.3 Universal design elements. Dwelling incorporates one or more of the following universal design elements. Conventional industry tolerances are permitted. .... **12 max**

(1) Any no-step entrance into the dwelling which 1) is accessible from a substantially level parking or drop-off area (no more than 2%) via an accessible path which has no individual change in elevation or other obstruction of more than 1-1/2 in. in height with the pitch not exceeding 1 in 12; and 2) provides a minimum 32-in. wide clearance into the dwelling. **3**

(2) Minimum 36-in. wide accessible route from the no-step entrance into at least one visiting room in the dwelling and into at least one full or half bathroom which has a minimum 32-in. clear door width and a 30-in. by 48-in. clear area inside the bathroom outside the door swing. **3**

(3) Minimum 36-in. wide accessible route from the no-step entrance into at least one bedroom which has a minimum 32-in. clear door width. **3**

(4) Blocking or equivalent installed in the accessible bathroom walls for future installation of grab bars at water closet and bathing fixture, if applicable. **1**

(5) All interior and exterior door handles are levers rather than knobs. **1**

(6) All sink, lavatory and showering controls comply with ICC A117.1. .... **1**

(7) Interior convenience power receptacles, communication connections (for cable, phone, Ethernet, etc.) and switches are placed between 15 in. and 48 in. above the finished floor. Additional switches to control devices and systems (such as alarms, home theaters and other equipment) not required by the local building code may be installed as desired. **1**

(8) All light switches are rocker-type switches or other similar switches that can be operated by pressing them (with assistive devices) – no toggle-type switches may be used. **1**

(9) Anyone of the following systems are automated and can be controlled with a wireless device or voice-activated device: HVAC, all permanently installed lighting, alarm system, window treatments, or door locks. *[1 point awarded per system]* .... **1 [5 max]**

11.613 RESILIENT CONSTRUCTION

11.613.1 Intent. Design and construction practices developed by a licensed design professional or equivalent are implemented to enhance the resilience and durability of the structure (above building code minimum design loads) so the structure can better withstand forces generated by flooding, snow, wind, or seismic activity (as applicable) and reduce the potential for the loss of life and property.

11.613.2 Minimum structural requirements (base design). The building is designed and constructed in compliance with structural requirements in the IBC or IRC as applicable. **2**

11.613.3 Enhanced resilience (10% above base design). Design and construction practices are implemented to enhance the resilience and durability of the structure by designing and building to forces generated by flooding, snow, wind, or seismic (as applicable) that are 10% higher than the base design........ **3**

M=Mandatory

GREEN BUILDING PRACTICES	POINTS

11.613.4 Enhanced resilience (20% above base design). Design and construction practices are implemented to enhance the resilience and durability of the structure by designing and building to forces generated by flooding, snow, wind, or seismic (as applicable) that are 20% higher than the base design. **5**

11.613.5 Enhanced resilience (30% above base design). Design and construction practices are implemented to enhance the resilience and durability of the structure by designing and building to forces generated by flooding, snow, wind, or seismic (as applicable) that are 30% higher than the base design. **10**

613.13.6 Enhanced resilience (40% above base design). Design and construction practices are implemented to enhance the resilience and durability of the structure by designing and building to forces generated by flooding, snow, wind, or seismic (as applicable) that are 40% higher than the base design. **12**

11.613.7 Enhanced resilience (50% above base design). Design and construction practices are implemented to enhance the resilience and durability of the structure by designing and building to forces generated by flooding, snow, wind, or seismic (as applicable) that are 50% higher than the base design. **15**

11.701   MINIMUM ENERGY EFFICIENCY REQUIREMENTS

11.701.4 Mandatory practices

11.701.4.0 Minimum energy efficiency requirements. Additions, alterations, or renovations to an existing building, building system or portion thereof shall comply with the provisions of the ICC IECC as they relate to new construction without requiring the unaltered portion(s) of the existing building or building system to comply with the ICC IECC. An addition complies with the ICC IECC if the addition complies or if the existing building and addition comply with the ICC IECC as a single building. .... **M**

11.701.4.1 HVAC systems

11.701.4.1.1 HVAC system sizing. Newly installed or modified space heating and cooling system is sized according to heating and cooling loads calculated using ACCA Manual J, or equivalent. New equipment is selected using ACCA Manual S or equivalent. .... **M**

11.701.4.1.2 Radiant and hydronic space heating. Where installed as a primary heat source in the building, new radiant or hydronic space heating system is designed, installed, and documented, using industry-approved guidelines and standards (e.g., ACCA Manual J, AHRI I=B=R, ANSI/ACCA 5 QI, or an accredited design professional's and manufacturer's recommendation). .... **M**

11.701.4.2 Duct systems

11.701.4.2.1 Duct air sealing. Ducts that are newly installed, modified, or are exposed during the remodel are air sealed. All duct sealing materials are in conformance with UL 181A or UL 181B specifications and are installed in accordance with manufacturer's instructions. .... **M**

11.701.4.2.2 Ducts and plenums. Building framing cavities are not used as ducts or plenums. Existing building cavities currently used as supply ducts exposed during the remodel are lined. .... **M**

11.701.4.2.3 Duct system sizing. New or modified duct system is sized and designed in accordance with ACCA Manual D or equivalent. .... **M**

GREEN BUILDING PRACTICES	M=Mandatory POINTS

11.701.4.3 Insulation and air sealing

11.701.4.3.1 Building thermal envelope air sealing. The building thermal envelope exposed or created during the remodel is durably sealed to limit infiltration. The sealing methods between dissimilar materials allow for differential expansion and contraction. The following are caulked, gasketed, weather-stripped or otherwise sealed with an air barrier material, suitable film or solid material: .... **M**

   (a) All joints, seams and penetrations

   (b) Site-built windows, doors and skylights

   (c) Openings between window and door assemblies and their respective jambs and framing

   (d) Utility penetrations

   (e) Dropped ceilings or chases adjacent to the thermal envelope

   (f) Knee walls

   (g) Walls, ceilings, and floors separating conditioned spaces from unconditioned spaces

   (h) Behind tubs and showers on exterior walls

   (i) Common walls between dwelling units or sleeping units

   (j) Attic access openings

   (k) Joints of framing members at rim joists

   (l) Top and bottom plates

   (m) Other sources of infiltration

11.701.4.3.2 Air barrier, air sealing, building envelope testing and insulation. For portions of the building envelope that are exposed or created during the remodel, building envelope air tightness and insulation installation is verified to be in accordance with this Section and § 11.701.4.3.2.1. Insulation installation other than Grade 1 is not permitted. .... **M**

(1) **Testing.** Building envelope tightness is tested. Testing is conducted in accordance with ASTM E779 using a blower door at a test pressure of 1.04 psf (50 Pa). Testing is conducted after rough-in and after installation of penetrations of the building envelope, including penetrations for utilities, plumbing, electrical, ventilation and combustion appliances. Testing is conducted under the following conditions:

   (a) Exterior windows and doors, fireplace and stove doors are closed, but not sealed;

   (b) Dampers are closed, but not sealed, including exhaust, intake, make-up air, backdraft, and flue dampers;

   (c) Interior doors are open;

   (d) Exterior openings for continuous ventilation systems and heat recovery ventilators are closed and sealed;

   (e) Heating and cooling system(s) is turned off;

   (f) HVAC duct terminations are not sealed; and

   (g) Supply and return registers are not sealed.

Multifamily Building Note: Testing by dwelling units, sleeping units, groups of dwelling units, groups of sleeping units, or the building as a whole is acceptable.

(2) **Visual inspection.** The air barrier and insulation items listed in Table 11.701.4.3.2(2) are field verified by visual inspection.

Table 11.701.4.3.2(2)
Air Barrier and Insulation Installation

COMPONENT	AIR BARRIER CRITERIA	INSULATION INSTALLATION CRITERIA
General requirements	A continuous air barrier shall be installed in the building envelope. The exterior thermal envelope contains a continuous air barrier. Breaks or joints in the air barrier shall be sealed.	Air-permeable insulation shall not be used as a sealing material.
Ceiling/attic	The air barrier in any dropped ceiling/soffit shall be aligned with the insulation and any gaps in the air barrier shall be sealed. Access openings, drop down stairs or knee wall doors to unconditioned attic spaces shall be sealed.	The insulation in any dropped ceiling/soffit shall be aligned with the air barrier.
Walls	The junction of the foundation and sill plate shall be sealed. The junction of the top plate and the top of exterior walls shall be sealed. Knee walls shall be sealed.	Cavities within comers and headers of frame walls shall be insulated by completely filling the cavity with a material having a thermal resistance of R-3 per inch minimum. Exterior thermal envelope insulation for framed walls shall be installed in substantial contact and continuous alignment with the air barrier.
Windows, skylights and doors	The space between window/doorjambs and framing, and skylights and framing shall be sealed.	
Rim joists	Rim joists shall include the air barrier.	Rim joists shall be insulated.
Floors (including above garage and cantilevered floors)	The air barrier shall be installed at any exposed edge of insulation.	Floor framing cavity insulation shall be installed to maintain permanent contact with the underside of subfloor decking, or floor framing cavity insulation shall be permitted to be in contact with the top side of sheathing, or continuous insulation installed on the underside of floor framing and extends from the bottom to the top of all perimeter floor framing members.
Crawl space walls	Exposed earth in unvented crawl spaces shall be covered with a Class I vapor retarder with overlapping joints taped.	Where provided instead of floor insulation, insulation shall be permanently attached to the crawlspace walls.
Shafts, penetrations	Duct shafts, utility penetrations, and flue shafts opening to exterior or unconditioned space shall be sealed.	
Narrow cavities		Batts in narrow cavities shall be cut to fit, or narrow cavities shall be filled by insulation that on installation readily conforms to the available cavity space.
Garage separation	Air sealing shall be provided between the garage and conditioned spaces.	
Recessed lighting	Recessed light fixtures installed in the building thermal envelope shall be sealed to the drywall.	Recessed light fixtures installed in the building thermal envelope shall be air tight and IC rated.
Plumbing and wiring		Batt insulation shall be cut neatly to fit around wiring and plumbing in exterior walls, or insulation that on installation readily conforms to available space shall extend behind piping and wiring.
Shower/tub on exterior wall	The air barrier installed at exterior walls adjacent to showers and tubs shall separate them from the showers and tubs.	Exterior walls adjacent to showers and tubs shall be insulated.
Electrical/phone box on exterior walls	The air barrier shall be installed behind electrical or communication boxes or air-sealed boxes shall be installed.	
HVAC register boots	HVAC register boots that penetrate building thermal envelope shall be sealed to the subfloor or drywall.	
Concealed sprinklers	When required to be sealed, concealed fire sprinklers shall only be sealed in a manner that is recommended by the manufacturer. Caulking or other adhesive sealants shall not be used to fill voids between fire sprinkler cover plates and walls or ceilings.	

a. In addition, inspection of log walls shall be in accordance with the provisions of ICC-400.

GREEN BUILDING PRACTICES	POINTS

11.701.4.3.2.1 Grade I insulation installation. Field-installed insulation products to ceilings, walls, floors, band joists, rim joists, conditioned attics, basements, and crawlspaces, except as specifically noted, are verified by a third-party as Grade I in accordance with the following: .... **M**

(1)   Inspection is conducted before insulation is covered.

(2)   Air-permeable insulation is enclosed on all six sides and is in substantial contact with the sheathing material on one or more sides (interior or exterior) of the cavity. Air permeable insulation in ceilings is not required to be enclosed when the insulation is installed in substantial contact with the surfaces it is intended to insulate.

(3)   Cavity insulation uniformly fills each cavity side-to-side and top-to-bottom, without substantial gaps or voids around obstructions (such as blocking or bridging).

(4)   Cavity insulation compression or incomplete fill amounts to 2% or less, presuming the compressed or incomplete areas are a minimum of 70% of the intended fill thickness; occasional small gaps are acceptable.

(5)   Exterior rigid insulation has substantial contact with the structural framing members or sheathing materials and is tightly fitted at joints.

(6)   Cavity insulation is split, installed, and/or fitted tightly around wiring and other services.

(7)   Exterior sheathing is not visible from the interior through gaps in the cavity insulation.

(8)   Faced batt insulation is permitted to have side-stapled tabs, provided the tabs are stapled neatly with no buckling, and provided the batt is compressed only at the edges of each cavity, to the depth of the tab itself.

(9)   Where properly installed, ICFs, SIPs, and other wall systems that provide integral insulation are deemed in compliance with this section.

11.701.4.3.3 Multifamily air leakage alternative. Multifamily buildings four or more stories in height and in compliance with ICC IECC section C402.5 (Air leakage-thermal envelope) are deemed to comply with § 11.701.4.3.1 and § 11.701.4.3.2.

11.701.4.3.4 Fenestration air leakage. Newly installed Windows, skylights and sliding glass doors have an air infiltration rate of no more than 0.3 cfm per sq. ft. (1.5 L/s/m^2), and swinging doors no more than 0.5 cfm per sq. ft. (2.6 L/s/m^2), when tested in accordance with NFRC 400 or AAMA/WDMA/CSA 101/I.S.2/A440 by an accredited, independent laboratory and listed and labeled. For site-built fenestration, a test report by an accredited, independent laboratory verifying compliance with the applicable infiltration rate shall be submitted to demonstrate compliance with this practice. This practice does not apply to field-fabricated fenestration products... **M**

Exception: For Tropical Zones only, jalousie windows are permitted to be used as a conditioned space boundary and shall have an air infiltration rate of not more than 1.3 cfm per sq. ft.

11.701.4.3.5 Lighting and building thermal envelope. Newly installed luminaires installed in the building thermal envelope which penetrate the air barrier are sealed to limit air leakage between conditioned and unconditioned spaces. All luminaires are IC-rated and labeled as meeting ASTM E283 when tested at 1.57 psf (75 Pa) pressure differential with no more than 2.0 cfm (0.944 L/s) of air movement from the conditioned space to the ceiling cavity. All luminaires installed in the building thermal envelope which penetrate the air barrier are sealed with a gasket or caulk between the housing and the interior of the wall or ceiling covering. .... **M**

GREEN BUILDING PRACTICES	M=Mandatory POINTS

11.701.4.4 High-efficacy lighting. A minimum of 90% of newly installed hard-wired lighting fixtures or the bulbs in those fixtures shall be high efficacy .... **M**

11.701.4.5 Boiler piping. Boiler piping in unconditioned space supplying and returning heated water or steam that is accessible during the remodel is insulated. Exception: where condensing boilers are installed, insulation is not required for return piping.. **M**

11.701.4.6 Fenestration specifications. The NFRC-certified U-factor and SHGC of newly installed windows, exterior doors, skylights, and tubular daylighting devices (TDDs) do not exceed the values in Table 703.2.5.1. .... **M**

11.701.4.7 Replacement fenestration. Where some or all of an existing fenestration unit is replaced with a new fenestration product, including sash and glazing, the NFRC-certified U-factor and SHGC of the replacement fenestration unit do not exceed the values in Table 703.2.5.1. .... **M**

11.703 PRESCRIPTIVE PATH

11.703.1 Mandatory practices **30**

11.703.1.1 Building thermal envelope compliance. The building thermal envelope is in compliance with § 11.703.1.1.1 or § 11.703.1.1.2. .... **M for § 11.703**

Exception: Section 11.703.1.1 is not required for Tropical Climate Zone.

11.703.1.1.1 Maximum UA. For ICC IECC residential, the total building UA is less than or equal to the total maximum UA as computed by ICC IECC Section R402.1.5. For ICC IECC commercial, the total UA is less than or equal to the sum of the UA for ICC IECC Tables C402.1.4 and C402.4, including the U-factor times the area and C-factor or F-factor times the perimeter. The total UA proposed and baseline calculations are documented. REScheck or COMcheck is deemed to provide UA calculation documentation.

11.703.1.1.2 Prescriptive R-value and fenestration requirements. The building thermal envelope is in accordance with the insulation and fenestration requirements of ICC IECC R502.1.1.1. The SHGC is in accordance with the ICC IECC requirements.

11.703.1.2 Building envelope leakage. The building thermal envelope is in accordance with ICC IECC R502.1.1.1 or R503.1.1 as applicable.

Exception: Section 11.703.1.2 is not required for Tropical Climate Zone.

11.703.1.3 Duct testing. The duct system is in accordance with ICC IECC R403.3.2 through R403.3.5 as applicable.

GREEN BUILDING PRACTICES	POINTS

11.703.2 Building envelope

11.703.2.1 UA improvement. The total building thermal envelope UA is less than or equal to the baseline total UA resulting from the U-factors provided in Table 11.703.2.1(a) or ICC IECC Tables C402.1.4 and C402.4, as applicable. Where insulation is used to achieve the UA improvement, the insulation installation is in accordance with Grade 1 meeting § 11.701.4.3.2.1 as verified by a third-party. Total UA is documented using a REScheck, COMcheck, or equivalent report to verify the baseline and the UA improvement.

Per Table 11.703.2.1(b)

Table 11.703.2.1(a)
Baseline U-Factors[a]

Climate Zone	Fenestration U-Factor	Skylight U-Factor	Ceiling U-Factor	Frame Wall U-Factor	Mass Wall U-Factor[b]	Floor U-Factor	Basement Wall U-Factor	Crawlspace Wall U-Factor[c]
1	0.50	0.75	0.035	0.084	0.197	0.064	0.360	0.477
2	0.40	0.65	0.030	0.084	0.165	0.064	0.360	0.477
3	0.35	0.55	0.030	0.060	0.098	0.047	0.091[c]	0.136
4 except Marine	0.35	0.55	0.026	0.060	0.098	0.047	0.059	0.065
5 and Marine 4	0.32	0.55	0.026	0.060	0.082	0.033	0.050	0.055
6	0.32	0.55	0.026	0.045	0.060	0.033	0.050	0.055
7 and 8	0.32	0.55	0.026	0.045	0.057	0.028	0.050	0.055

a. Non-fenestration U-factors shall be obtained from measurement, calculation, or an approved source.
b. Where more the half the insulation is on the interior, the mass wall U-factors is a maximum of 0.17 in Zone 1, 0.14 in Zone 2, 0.12 in Zone 3, 0.10 in Zone 4 except in Marine, and the same as the frame wall U-factor in Marine Zone 4 and Zones 5 through 8.
c. Basement wall U-factor of 0.360 in warm-humid locations.

Table 11.703.2.1(b)
Points for Improvement in Total Building Thermal Envelope UA
Compared to Baseline UA

Minimum UA Improvement	Climate Zone							
	1[a]	2	3	4	5	6	7	8
	POINTS							
0 to <5%	0	0	0	0	0	0	0	0
5% to <10%	2	3	3	3	3	3	3	3
10% to <15%	3	6	5	6	6	6	5	7
15% to <20%	5	9	8	9	9	9	8	10
20% to <25%	6	12	10	12	12	12	11	13
25% to <30%	8	15	13	16	14	15	14	17
30% to <35%	10	18	16	19	17	18	16	20
≥35%	11	21	18	22	20	21	19	23

a. Tropical Climate Zone: Points are Climate Zone 1 points divided by 2 and rounded down

Exception: For the Tropical Climate Zone, crawl space, basement, and floor u-factors are excluded from the total building thermal envelope UA improvement calculation.

GREEN BUILDING PRACTICES	POINTS

11.703.2.2 Mass walls. More than 75% of the above-grade exterior opaque wall area of the building is mass walls.

Per Table 11.703.2.2

Table 11.703.2.2
Exterior Mass Walls

Mass thickness	Climate Zone			
	1-4	5	6	7-8
	POINTS			
≥3 in. to <6 in.	1	0	0	0
>6 in.	3	2	2	0

11.703.2.3 A radiant barrier with an emittance of 0.05 or less is used in the attic. The product is tested in accordance with ASTM C1371 and installed in accordance with the manufacturer's instructions.

Per Table 11.703.2.3

Table 11.703.2.3
Radiant Barriers

Climate Zone	POINTS
Tropical	3
1	2
2-3	3
4-5	1
6-8	0

[In climate zones 1-3, 1 point maximum for multifamily buildings four or more stories in height.]

11.703.2.4 Building envelope leakage. The maximum building envelope leakage rate is in accordance with Table 11.703.2.4(a) or Table 11.703.2.4(b) and whole building ventilation is provided in accordance with § 11.902.2.1.

Per Table 11.703.2.4(a) or 11.703.2.4(b)

Table 11.703.2.4(a)
Building Envelope Leakage

Max Envelope Leakage Rate (ACH50)	Climate Zone							
	1	2	3	4	5	6	7	8
	POINTS							
4	1	2	-	-	-	-	-	-
3	2	4	-	-	-	-	-	-
2	3	5	3	4	4	6	8	7
1	4	7	5	7	7	10	15	11

Table 11.703.2.4(b)
Building Envelope Leakage

Max Envelope Leakage Rate (ELR50)	Climate Zone							
	1	2	3	4	5	6	7	8
	POINTS							
0.28	1	2	-	-	-	-	-	-
0.23	2	4	-	-	-	-	-	-
0.18	3	5	3	4	4	6	8	7
0.13	4	7	5	7	7	10	15	11

Where ELR50 = CFM50 / Shell Area
CFM50 = cubic feet per minute at 50 Pa

[Points not awarded if points are taken under § 11.705.6.2.1.]

GREEN BUILDING PRACTICES

11.703.2.5 Fenestration

11.703.2.5.1 NFRC-certified (or equivalent) U-factor and SHGC of windows, exterior doors, skylights, and tubular daylighting devices (TDDs) on an area-weighted average basis do not exceed the values in Table 11.703.2.5.1. Area weighted averages are calculated separately for the categories of 1) windows and exterior doors and 2) skylights and tubular daylighting devices (TDDs). Decorative fenestration elements with a combined total maximum area of 15 sq. ft. (1.39 m^2) or 10% of the total glazing area, whichever is less, are not required to comply with this practice. ....

**M for §
11.703**

Table 11.703.2.5.1
Fenestration Specifications

Climate Zones	U-Factor	SHGC
	Windows and Exterior Doors (maximum certified ratings)	
1	0.50	0.25
2	0.40	0.25
3	0.32	0.25
4	0.32	0.40
5 to 8	0.30*	Any
	Skylights and TDDs (maximum certified ratings)	
1	0.75	0.30
2	0.65	0.30
3	0.55	0.30
4	0.55	0.40
5 to 8	0.55	Any

Exception: For Sun-tempered designs meeting the requirements of § 11.703.7.1, the SHGC is permitted to be 0.40 or higher on south facing glass.

Exception: A maximum U-factor of 0.32 shall apply in climate zones 5-8 to vertical fenestration products installed in buildings located: (i) above 4000 feet in elevation above sea level or (ii) in windborne debris regions where protection of openings is provided by fenestration as required under IRC section R301.2.1.2.

11.703.2.5.1.1 Dynamic glazing. Dynamic glazing is permitted to satisfy the SHGC requirements of Table 11.703.2.5.1 provided the ratio of the higher to lower labeled SHGC is greater than or equal to 2.4 and the dynamic glazing is automatically controlled to modulate the amount of solar gain into the space in multiple steps. Fenestration with dynamic glazing is considered separately from other fenestration and area-weighted averaging with fenestration that does not use dynamic glazing is not permitted. Dynamic glazing is not required to be automatically controlled or comply with minimum SHGC ratio when both the lower and higher labeled SHGC already comply with the requirements of Table 11.703.2.5.1.

GREEN BUILDING PRACTICES	POINTS

11.703.2.5.2 The NFRC-certified (or equivalent) U-factor and SHGC of windows, exterior doors, skylights, and tubular daylighting devices (TDDs) are in accordance with Table 11.703.2.5.2(a), (b), or (c). Decorative fenestration elements with a combined total maximum area of 15 sq. ft. (1.39 m²) or 10% of the total glazing area, whichever is less, are not required to comply with this practice.

Per Table
11.703.2.5.2(a),
or
11.703.2.5.2 (b),
or
11.703.2.5.2 (c)

Table 11.703.2.5.2(a)
Enhanced Fenestration Specifications

Climate Zones	U-Factor Windows & Exterior Doors	SHGC Windows & Exterior Doors	U-Factor Skylights & TDDs	SHGC Skylights & TDDs	POINTS
1	0.40	0.25	0.60	0.28	1
2	0.40	0.25	0.60	0.28	1
3	0.30	0.25	0.53	0.28	2
4	0.30	0.40	0.53	0.35	3
5	0.27	Any	0.50	Any	3
6	0.27	Any	0.50	Any	4
7	0.27	Any	0.50	Any	4
8	0.27	Any	0.50	Any	4

Exception: For Sun-tempered designs meeting the requirements of § 11.703.7.1, the SHGC is permitted to be 0.40 or higher on south facing glass.

Table 11.703.2.5.2(b)
Enhanced Fenestration Specifications

Climate Zone	U-Factor Windows & Exterior Doors	SHGC Windows & Exterior Doors	U-Factor Skylights & TDDs	SHGC Skylights & TDDs	POINTS
1	0.38	0.25	0.55	0.28	2
2	0.38	0.25	0.53	0.28	3
3	0.30	0.25	0.50	0.28	4
4	0.28	0.40	0.50	0.35	4
5	0.25	Any	0.48	Any	4
6	0.25	Any	0.48	Any	5
7	0.25	Any	0.46	Any	5
8	0.25	Any	0.46	Any	4

Exception: For Sun-tempered designs meeting the requirements of § 11.703.7.1, the SHGC is permitted to be 0.40 or higher on south facing glass.

Table 11.703.2.5.2(c)
Enhanced Fenestration Specifications

Climate Zones	U-Factor Windows & Exterior Doors	SHGC Windows & Exterior Doors	U-Factor Skylights & TDDs	SHGC Skylights & TDDs	POINTS
4	0.25	0.40	0.45	0.40	6
5-8	0.22	Any	0.42	Any	6

[Points for multifamily buildings four or more stories in height are awarded at 3 times the point value listed in Table 11.703.2.5.2(c)]

11.703.2.5.2.1 Dynamic glazing. Dynamic glazing is permitted to satisfy the SHGC requirements of Tables 11.703.2.5.2(a), 11.703.2.5.2(b), and 11.703.2.5.2(c) provided the ratio of the higher to lower labeled SHGC is greater than or equal to 2.4, and the dynamic glazing is automatically controlled to

GREEN BUILDING PRACTICES	POINTS

modulate the amount of solar gain into the space in multiple steps. Fenestration with dynamic glazing is considered separately from other fenestration, and area-weighted averaging with fenestration that does not use dynamic glazing is not permitted. Dynamic glazing is not required to be automatically controlled or comply with minimum SHGC ratio when both the lower and higher labeled SHGC already comply with the requirements of Tables 11.703.2.5.2(a), 11.703.2.5.2(b), and 11.703.2.5.2(c).

11.703.3 HVAC equipment efficiency

11.703.3.0 Multiple heating and cooling systems. For multiple heating or cooling systems in one home, practices 11.703.3.1 through 11.703.3.6 apply to the system that supplies 80% or more of the total installed heating or cooling capacity. Where multiple systems each serve less than 80% of the total installed heating or cooling capacity, points under Sections 11.703.3.1 through 11.703.3.6 are awarded either for the system eligible for the fewest points or the weighted average of the systems. The weighted average shall be calculated in accordance with the following equation and be based upon the efficiency and capacity of the equipment as selected in accordance with ACCA Manual S with it loads calculated in accordance with ACCA Manual J.

Weighted Average = $[(E_{unit\ 1}*C_{unit\ 1})+(E_{unit\ 2}*C_{unit\ 2})+...+(E_{unit\ n}*C_{unit\ n})] / (C_{unit\ 1}+C_{unit\ 2}+...+C_{unit\ n})$
where:
E = Rated AHRI efficiency for unit
C = Rated heating or cooling capacity for unit
n = Unit count

11.703.3.1 Combination space heating and water heating system (combo system) is installed using either a coil from the water heater connected to an air handler to provide heat for the building, dwelling unit or sleeping unit, or a space heating boiler using an indirect-fired water heater. Devices have a minimum combined annual efficiency of 0.80 and a minimum water heating recovery efficiency of 0.87. .... **4**

11.703.3.2 Furnace and/or boiler efficiency is in accordance with one of the following:

(1) Gas and propane heaters:

Per Table 11.703.3.2(1)(a) or 11.703.3.2(1)(b)

Table 11.703.3.2(1)(a)
Gas and Propane Heaters

AFUE	Climate Zone							
	1	2	3	4	5	6	7	8
	POINTS							
≥90% AFUE	0	2	3	6	6	9	10	12
≥92% AFUE	0	2	4	7	8	10	12	14
≥94% AFUE	0	3	4	9	9	12	14	16
≥96% AFUE	1	3	5	10	10	14	16	19
≥98% AFUE	1	3	6	11	12	16	18	21

Table 11.703.3.2(1)(b)
Gas and Propane Heaters for Multifamily Buildings Four or More Stories in Height

AFUE	Climate Zone							
	1	2	3	4	5	6	7	8
	POINTS							
≥90% AFUE	0	4	4	8	8	10	11	13
≥92% AFUE	0	4	4	9	10	11	12	14
≥94% AFUE	0	5	5	10	11	12	14	16
≥96% AFUE	0	5	5	12	12	13	15	17
≥98% AFUE	0	6	6	13	13	14	16	18

GREEN BUILDING PRACTICES	POINTS

(2) Oil furnace:

Per Table 11.703.3.2(2)

Table 11.703.3.2(2)
Oil Furnace

AFUE	Climate Zone							
	1	2	3	4	5	6	7	8
	POINTS							
≥85% AFUE	0	1	2	3	3	4	5	6
≥90% AFUE	0	2	3	6	6	9	10	12

(3) Gas boiler:

Per Table 11.703.3.2(3)

Table 11.703.3.2(3)
Gas Boiler

AFUE	Climate Zone							
	1	2	3	4	5	6	7	8
	POINTS							
≥85% AFUE	0	1	1	2	3	4	4	4
≥90% AFUE	0	1	2	4	6	7	8	6
≥94% AFUE	0	2	3	5	8	9	10	8
≥96% AFUE	0	2	4	6	9	11	12	10

(4) Oil boiler:

Per Table 11.703.3.2(4)

Table 11.703.3.2(4)
Oil Boiler

AFUE	Climate Zone							
	1	2	3	4	5	6	7	8
	POINTS							
≥85% AFUE	0	1	1	3	3	4	4	5
≥90% AFUE	1	2	3	5	6	7	9	10

11.703.3.3 Heat pump heating efficiency is in accordance with Table 11.703.3.3(1) or Table 11.703.3.3(2) or Table 11.703.3.3(3). Refrigerant charge is verified for compliance with manufacturer's instructions utilizing a method in ACCA 5 QI Section 4.3.

Per Table 11.703.3.3(1) or 11.703.3.3(2) or 11.703.3.3(3)

Table 11.703.3.3(1)
Electric Heat Pump Heating

Efficiency	Climate Zone					
	1	2	3	4	5	6-8[a]
	POINTS					
≥8.5 HSPF (11.5 EER)	0	1	1	2	2	2
≥9.0 HSPF (12.5 EER)	0	2	4	5	6	10
≥9.5 HSPF	0	3	7	7	11	18
≥10.0 HSPF	1	5	10	10	15	26
≥12.0 HSPF	1	6	11	11	17	28

| GREEN BUILDING PRACTICES | POINTS |

Table 11.703.3.3(2)
Electric Heat Pump Heating for Multifamily Buildings Four or More Stories in Height

Efficiency	Climate Zone					
	1	2	3	4	5	6-8[a]
	POINTS					
≥8.5 HSPF (11.5 EER)	0	3	4	8	11	13

Table 11.703.3.3(3)
Gas Engine-Driven Heat Pump Heating

Efficiency	Climate Zone					
	1	2	3	4	5	6-8
	POINTS					
≥1.3 COP at 47°F	2	7	11	14	16	18

11.703.3.4 Cooling efficiency is in accordance with Table 11.703.3.4(1) or Table 11.703.3.4(2). Refrigerant charge is verified for compliance with manufacturer's instructions utilizing a method in ACCA 5 QI Section 4.3.

Per Table 11.703.3.4(1) or 11.703.3.4(2)

Table 11.703.3.4(1)
Electric Air Conditioner and Heat Pump Cooling[a]

Efficiency	Climate Zone							
	1	2	3	4	5	6	7	8
	POINTS							
≥15 SEER (12.5 EER)	6	4	2	1	1	1	1	0
≥17 SEER (12.5 EER)	11	9	7	3	3	2	2	0
≥19 SEER (12.5 EER)	19	12	10	6	4	4	4	0
≥21 SEER	26	15	14	8	6	6	5	0
≥25 SEER	29	18	17	10	8	8	6	0

a. Tropical Climate Zone: where none of the occupied space is air conditioned and where ceiling fans are provided for bedrooms and the largest space which is not used as a bedroom, 20 points is awarded.

Table 11.703.3.4(2)
Gas Engine-Driven Heat Pump Cooling

Efficiency	Climate Zone					
	1	2	3	4	5	6-8
	POINTS					
>1.2 COP at 95°F	3	6	3	1	1	0

11.703.3.5 Water source cooling and heating efficiency is in accordance with Table 11.703.3.5. Refrigerant charge is verified for compliance with manufacturer's instructions utilizing a method in ACCA 5 QI Section 4.3.

Per Table 11.703.3.5

Table 11.703.3.5
Water Source Cooling and Heating

Efficiency	Climate Zone					
	1	2	3	4	5	6-8
	POINTS					
≥15 EER, ≥4.0 COP	14	18	22	30	37	37

GREEN BUILDING PRACTICES	M=Mandatory POINTS

11.703.3.6 Ground source heat pump is installed by a Certified Geothermal Service Contractor in accordance with Table 11.703.3.6. Refrigerant charge is verified for compliance with manufacturer's instructions utilizing a method in ACCA 5 QI Section 4.3.

Per Table 11.703.3.6

Table 11.703.3.6
Ground Source Heat Pump[a]

Efficiency	Climate Zone				
	1	2	3	4	5-8
	POINTS				
≥16.0 EER, ≥3.6 COP	1	1	2	16	22
≥24.0 EER, ≥4.3 COP	24	29	22	31	35
≥28.0 EER, ≥4.8 COP	42	46	35	42	44

a. The ground loop is sized to account for the ground conductance and the expected minimum incoming water temperature to achieve rated performance.

11.703.3.7 ENERGY STAR, or equivalent, ceiling fans are installed. *[Points awarded per building.]* 1

[For Tropical Climate Zone and Climate Zones 2B, 3B, and 4B: points awarded per fan where AC is not installed in the dwelling unit or sleeping unit (Max 8 points), and where points awarded in § 11.703.3.8 for these specific climate zones, points shall not be awarded in § 11.703.3.7.]

11.703.3.8 Whole-building or whole-dwelling unit or whole-sleeping unit fan(s) with insulated louvers and a sealed enclosure is installed. *[Points awarded per building.]*

Per Table 11.703.3.8

Table 11.703.3.8
Whole Dwelling Unit Fan

Climate Zone		
1-3, Tropical	4-6	7-8
POINTS		
4	3	0

11.703.4 Duct systems

11.703.4.1 All space heating is provided by a system(s) that does not include air ducts.

Per Table 11.703.4.1

Table 11.703.4.1
Ductless Heating System

Climate Zone					
1	2	3	4	5	6-8
POINTS					
0	2	4	6	8	8

11.703.4.2 All space cooling is provided by a system(s) that does not include air ducts.

Per Table 11.703.4.2

Table 11.703.4.2
Ductless Cooling System

Climate Zone					
1	2	3	4	5	6-8
POINTS					
8	8	4	2	1	0

GREEN BUILDING PRACTICES	POINTS

11.703.4.3 Ductwork is in accordance with all of the following:

(1) Building cavities are not used as return ductwork.

(2) Heating and cooling ducts and mechanical equipment are installed within the conditioned building space.

(3) Ductwork is not installed in exterior walls.

Per Table 11.703.4.3

Table 11.703.4.3
Ducts

Climate Zone					
1	2	3	4	5	6-8
POINTS					
8	10	8	8	8	4

11.703.4.4 Duct Leakage. The entire central HVAC duct system, including air handlers and register boots, is tested by a third party for total leakage at a pressure differential of 0.1 in. w.g. (25 Pa) and maximum air leakage is equal to or less than 6% of the system design flow rate or 4 cu-ft per minute per 100 sq. ft. of conditioned floor area.

Per Table 11.703.4.4

Table 11.703.4.4
Duct Leakage

Ductwork location	Climate Zone					
	1	2	3	4	5	6-8
	POINTS					
ductwork *entirely outside* the building's thermal envelope	4	5	4	3	2	1
ductwork *entirely inside* the building's thermal envelope	1	1	1	1	1	1
ductwork *inside and outside* the building's thermal envelope	3	4	3	2	1	1

Points not awarded if points are taken under § 11.705.6.2.3.

GREEN BUILDING PRACTICES	M=Mandatory POINTS

11.703.5 Water heating system

11.703.5.1 Water heater Uniform Energy Factor (UEF) is in accordance with the following:

[Where multiple systems are used, points awarded based on the system with the lowest efficiency.]

Water heater design is based on only 1 (one) water heater per dwelling unit, based on approved methods from ICC IPC, ASPE, or manufacturer specifications. All table values are based on water heaters with medium water draws as defined by the DOE test procedures (55 gallons per day).

(1) Gas water heating

Per Table 11.703.5.1(1)(a) through 11.703.5.1(1)(e)

Table 11.703.5.1(1)(a)
Gas Water Heating
Storage Water Heater, Rated Storage Volume > 20 Gallons and ≤ 55 Gallons,
Medium Water Draw

Uniform Energy Factor	Climate Zone							
	1	2	3	4	5	6	7	8
	POINTS							
0.65 to <0.78	2	2	2	2	2	2	2	1
≥0.78	3	3	3	3	3	3	3	2

Table 11.703.5.1(1)(b)
Gas Water Heating
Storage Water Heater, Rated Storage Volume > 55 Gallons and ≤ 100 Gallons,
Medium Water Draw

Uniform Energy Factor	Climate Zone							
	1	2	3	4	5	6	7	8
	POINTS							
≥0.78	1	1	1	1	1	1	1	1

Table 11.703.5.1(1)(c)
Gas Water Heating
Storage Water Heater with Input Rate Greater than 75,000 Btu/h (Commercial)

Thermal Efficiency	Climate Zone							
	1	2	3	4	5	6	7	8
	POINTS							
0.90 to < 0.95	6	6	5	3	3	3	3	2
≥0.95	7	7	5	4	4	4	4	2

Table 11.703.5.1(1)(d)
Gas Water Heating
Storage Water Heater with Input Rate Greater than 75,000 Btu/h (Commercial),
In Buildings with High-Capacity Service Water-Heating Systems
(1,000,000 Btu/h or Greater)

Thermal Efficiency	Climate Zone							
	1	2	3	4	5	6	7	8
	POINTS							
0.92 to < 0.95	1	1	1	1	1	1	1	1
≥0.95	2	2	2	2	2	2	2	1

GREEN BUILDING PRACTICES	POINTS

Table 11.703.5.1(1)(e)
Gas Water Heating
Instantaneous Water Heater, Rated Storage Volume < 2 Gallons
and Input Rate of > 50,000 Btu/h, Medium Water Draw

Uniform Energy Factor	Climate Zone							
	1	2	3	4	5	6	7	8
	POINTS							
0.89 to < 0.94	2	2	2	1	1	1	1	1
≥0.94	3	3	2	2	2	2	2	1

(2) Electric water heating

Per Table 11.703.5.1(2)(a) through 11.703.5.1(2)(e)

Table 11.703.5.1(2)(a)
Storage Water Heater, Rated Storage Volume ≥ 20 Gallons and ≤ 55 Gallons, Medium Water Draw

Uniform Energy Factor	Climate Zone							
	1	2	3	4	5	6	7	8
	POINTS							
0.94 to <1.0	1	1	1	1	1	1	1	1
1.0 to <1.5	4	2	2	2	1	1	1	1
1.5 to <2.0	7	4	3	2	2	2	1	1
2.0 to <2.2	14	8	7	5	4	4	2	2
2.2 to <2.5	17	9	8	6	5	4	3	3
2.5 to <3.0	18	12	10	8	6	6	3	3
≥3.0	22	16	13	11	8	8	4	3

Table 11.703.5.1(2)(b)
Storage Water Heater, Rated Storage Volume ≥ 55 Gallons and ≤ 120 Gallons, Medium Water Draw

Uniform Energy Factor	Climate Zone							
	1	2	3	4	5	6	7	8
	POINTS							
2.2 to <2.5	6	4	3	3	2	2	1	1
2.5 to <3.0	7	5	4	3	3	3	2	2
3.0 to <3.5	8	5	5	4	3	3	3	2
≥3.5	9	6	6	5	4	4	3	2

Table 11.703.5.1(2)(c)
Electric Tabletop Water Heating
(Tabletop Water Heater, Rated Storage Volume ≥ 20 Gallons and ≤ 120 Gallons, Medium Water Draw)

Uniform Energy Factor	Climate Zone							
	1	2	3	4	5	6	7	8
	POINTS							
≥0.91	1	1	1	1	1	1	1	1

GREEN BUILDING PRACTICES	POINTS

Table 11.703.5.1(2)(d)
Electric Instantaneous Water Heating[a]
(Instantaneous Electric Water Heater, Rated Storage Volume < 2 Gallons, Medium Water Draw)

Uniform Energy Factor or Thermal Efficiency[b]	Climate Zone							
	1	2	3	4	5	6	7	8
	POINTS							
≥0.97	2	2	2	2	2	2	2	2

a. Applies to any size water heater.
b. Electric instantaneous water heaters have either a Uniform Energy Factor (capacity less than or equal to 12 kW) or a Thermal Efficiency (capacity greater than 12 kW).

Table 11.703.5.1(2)(e)
Electric Grid Enabled Water Heating
(Grid Enabled Storage Water Heater, Rated Storage Volume ≥ 75 Gallons, Medium Water Draw)

Uniform Energy Factor	Climate Zone							
	1	2	3	4	5	6	7	8
	POINTS							
≥0.95	1	1	1	1	1	1	1	1

(3) Oil water heating

Per Table 11.703.5.1(3)

Table 11.703.5.1(3)
Oil Water Heating
(Oil Water Heating, < 50 Gallons, Medium Water Draw)

Uniform Energy Factor	Climate Zone							
	1	2	3	4	5	6	7	8
	POINTS							
≥0.62	1	1	1	1	1	1	1	1

11.703.5.2 Desuperheater is installed by a qualified installer or is pre-installed in the factory.

Per Table 11.703.5.2

Table 11.703.5.2
Desuperheater

Climate Zone						
1	2	3	4	5	6	7-8
POINTS						
23	17	9	7	5	4	2

11.703.5.3 Drain-water heat recovery system is installed. *[Points awarded per building.]* 2

11.703.5.4 Indirect-fired water heater storage tanks heated from boiler systems are installed.................. 1

GREEN BUILDING PRACTICES	POINTS

11.703.5.5 Solar water heater. SRCC (Solar Rating & Certification Corporation) OG 300 rated, or equivalent, solar domestic water heating system is installed. Solar Energy Factor (SEF) as defined by SRCC is in accordance with Table 11.703.5.5(a) and Table 11.703.5.5(b).

Per Table 11.703.5.5(a) or 11.703.5.5(b)

Table 11.703.5.5(a)
Storage Water Heater, Rated Storage Volume of Backup Water Heater is ≥ 0.1 Gallon and ≤ 55 Gallons, Medium Water Draw

SEF	Climate Zone						
	Tropical &1	2	3	4	5	6	7-8
	POINTS						
SEF ≥ 1.3	1	2	3	5	6	7	6
SEF ≥ 1.51	2	2	4	6	9	10	10
SEF ≥ 1.81	2	3	5	9	13	14	14
SEF ≥ 2.31	4	5	8	14	19	21	20
SEF ≥ 3.01	5	7	11	21	27	31	30

Table 11.703.5.5(b)
Storage Water Heater, Rated Storage Volume of Backup Water Heater is >55 Gallons, Medium Water Draw

SEF	Climate Zone						
	Tropical &1	2	3	4	5	6	7-8
	POINTS						
SEF ≥ 1.3	1	1	2	3	4	5	4
SEF ≥ 1.51	1	1	2	4	6	7	7
SEF ≥ 1.81	1	2	4	6	8	10	9
SEF ≥ 2.31	2	3	5	10	13	14	13
SEF ≥ 3.01	4	5	7	14	18	20	20

11.703.6 Lighting and appliances

11.703.6.1 Hard-wired lighting. Hard-wired lighting is in accordance with one of the following:

(1) A minimum percent of the total hard-wired interior luminaires or lamps qualify as ENERGY STAR, DesignLights Consortium (DLC), or applicable equivalent.

Per Table 11.703.6.1(1)

Table 11.703.6.1(1)
Hard-wired Lighting

Minimum percent of fixtures	Climate Zone							
	1	2	3	4	5	6	7	8
	POINTS							
95%	3	3	3	2	2	2	2	2

(2) A minimum of 80% of the exterior lighting wattage has a minimum efficacy of 61 lumens per watt or is solar-powered.. 1

(3) In multifamily buildings, common area lighting power density (LPD) is less than 0.51 Watts per square foot.. 7

GREEN BUILDING PRACTICES	M=Mandatory POINTS

11.703.6.2 Appliances. ENERGY STAR or equivalent appliance(s) are installed:

(1) Refrigerator — Per Table 11.703.6.2(1)

Table 11.703.6.2(1)
Refrigerator

Climate Zone							
1	2	3	4	5	6	7	8
POINTS							
1	1	1	1	1	1	1	1

(2) Dishwasher 1

(3) Washing machine 4

11.703.7 Passive solar design

11.703.7.1 Sun-tempered design. Building orientation, sizing of glazing, and design of overhangs are in accordance with all of the following:... 4

(1) The long side (or one side if of equal length) of the building faces within 20 degrees of true south.

(2) Vertical glazing area is between 5% and 7% of the gross conditioned floor area on the south face [also see § 11.703.7.1(8)] and glazing U-factors meet Table 11.703.2.5.2(a).

(3) Vertical glazing area is less than 2% of the gross conditioned floor area on the west face, and glazing meets Table 11.703.2.5.2(a).

(4) Vertical glazing area is less than 4% of the gross conditioned floor area on the east face, and glazing meets Table 11.703.2.5.2(a).

(5) Vertical glazing area is less than 8% of the gross conditioned floor area on the north face, and glazing meets Table 11.703.2.5.2(a).

(6) Skylights, where installed, are in accordance with the following:

    (a) shades and insulated wells are used, and all glazing meets Table 11.703.2.5.2(a).

    (b) horizontal skylights are less than 0.5% of finished ceiling area.

    (c) sloped skylights on slopes facing within 45 degrees of true south, east, or west are less than 1.5% of the finished ceiling area.

(7) Overhangs, adjustable canopies, awnings, or trellises provide shading on south-facing glass for the appropriate climate zone in accordance with Table 11.703.7.1(7):

Table 11.703.7.1(7)
South-Facing Window Overhang Depth

		Vertical distance between bottom of overhang and top of window sill				
		≤7' 4"	≤6' 4"	≤5' 4"	≤4' 4"	≤3' 4"
Climate Zone	1 & 2 & 3	2' 8"	2' 8"	2' 4"	2' 0"	2' 0"
	4 & 5 & 6	2' 4"	2' 4"	2' 0"	2' 0"	1' 8"
	7 & 8	2' 0"	1' 8"	1' 8"	1' 4"	1' 0"

For SI: 1 in. = 25.4 mm

GREEN BUILDING PRACTICES	M=Mandatory POINTS

(8) The south facing windows have an SHGC of 0.40 or higher.

(9) Return air or transfer grilles/ducts are in accordance with § 11.705.4.

Multifamily Building Note: The site is designed such that at least 40% of the multifamily dwelling or sleeping units have one south facing wall (within 15 degrees) containing at least 50% of glazing for entire unit, Effective shading is required for passive solar control on all south facing glazing. The floor area of at least 15 ft. from the south facing perimeter glazing is massive and exposed to capture solar heat during the day and reradiate at night.

11.703.7.2 Window shading. Automated solar protection or dynamic glazing is installed to provide shading for windows. **1**

11.703.7.3 Passive cooling design. Passive cooling design features are in accordance with at least three of the following: *[1 additional point awarded for each additional item.]* .... **3 [6 max]**

(1) Exterior shading is provided on east and west windows using one or a combination of the following:

    (a) vine-covered trellises with the vegetation separated a minimum of 1 ft. (305 mm) from face of building.

    (b) moveable awnings or louvers.

    (c) covered porches.

    (d) attached or detached conditioned/unconditioned enclosed space that provides full shade of east and west windows (e.g., detached garage, shed, or building).

(2) Overhangs are installed to provide shading on south-facing glazing in accordance with § 11.703.7.1(7).

    Points not awarded if points are taken under § 11.703.7.1.

(3) Windows and/or venting skylights are located to facilitate cross and stack effect ventilation.

(4) Solar reflective roof or radiant barrier is installed in climate zones 1, 2, or 3 and roof material achieves a 3-year aged criteria of 0.50.

(5) Internal exposed thermal mass is a minimum of 3 in. (76 mm) in thickness. Thermal mass consists of concrete, brick, and/or tile fully adhered to a masonry base or other masonry material in accordance with one or a combination of the following:

    (a) A minimum of 1 sq. ft. (0.09 m^2) of exposed thermal mass of floor per 3 sq. ft. (2.8 m^2) of gross finished floor area.

    (b) A minimum of 3 sq. ft. (2.8 m^2) of exposed thermal mass in interior walls or elements per sq. ft. (0.09 m^2) of gross finished floor area.

(6) Roofing material is installed with a minimum 0.75 in. (19 mm) continuous air space offset from the roof deck from eave to ridge.

11.703.7.4 Passive solar heating design. In addition to the sun-tempered design features in § 11.703.7.1, all of the following are implemented: *[Points shall not be awarded in the Tropical Climate Zone]* **4**

(1) Additional glazing, no greater than 12%, is permitted on the south wall. This additional glazing is in accordance with the requirements of § 11.703.7.1.

	M=Mandatory
GREEN BUILDING PRACTICES	**POINTS**

(2) Additional thermal mass for any room with south-facing glazing of more than 7% of the finished floor area is provided in accordance with the following:

    (a) Thermal mass is solid and a minimum of 3 in. (76 mm) in thickness. Where two thermal mass materials are layered together (e.g., ceramic tile on concrete base) to achieve the appropriate thickness, they are fully adhered to (touching) each other.

    (b) Thermal mass directly exposed to sunlight is provided in accordance with the following minimum ratios:

        (i) Above latitude 35 degrees: 5 sq. ft. (0.465 m^2) of thermal mass for every 1 sq. ft. (0.093 m^2) of south-facing glazing.

        (ii) Latitude 30 degrees to 35 degrees: 5.5 sq. ft. (0.51 m^2) of thermal mass for every 1 sq. ft. (0.093 m^2) of south-facing glazing.

        (iii) Latitude 25 degrees to 30 degrees: 6 sq. ft. (0.557 m^2) of thermal mass for every 1 sq. ft. (0.093 m^2) of south-facing glazing.

    (c) Thermal mass not directly exposed to sunlight is permitted to be used to achieve thermal mass requirements of § 11.703.7.4(2) based on a ratio of 40 sq. ft. (3.72 m^2) of thermal mass for every 1 sq. ft. (0.093 m^2) of south-facing glazing.

(3) In addition to return air or transfer grilles/ducts required by § 11.703.7.1(9), provisions for forced airflow to adjoining areas are implemented as needed.

11.705 ADDITIONAL PRACTICES

11.705.1 Application of additional practice points. Points from § 11.705 can be added to points earned in § 11.703 (Prescriptive Path).

11.705.2 Lighting

11.705.2.1 Lighting controls

Percentages for point thresholds are based on lighting not required for means of egress or security lighting as defined by local building codes.

11.705.2.1.1 Interior lighting. In dwelling units or sleeping units, permanently installed interior lighting fixtures are controlled with an occupancy sensor, or dimmer:

(1) greater than 50% to less than 75% of lighting fixtures.. 1

(2) a minimum of 75% of lighting fixtures.. 2

11.705.2.1.2 Exterior lighting. Photo or motion sensors are installed on 75% of outdoor lighting fixtures to control lighting.
[Percentages for point thresholds do not include lighting equipped with photovoltaics.] 1

11.705.2.1.3 Multifamily common areas

(1) In a multifamily building, occupancy sensors, or dimmers are installed in common areas (except corridors and stairwells).

    (a) greater than 50% to less than 75% of lighting fixtures.. 1

    (b) a minimum of 75% of lighting fixtures. 2

GREEN BUILDING PRACTICES	M=Mandatory POINTS

(2) In a multifamily building, occupancy controls are installed to automatically reduce light levels in interior corridors and exit stairwells when the space is unoccupied. Light levels are reduced by:

    (a) greater than 50% to less than 75% or to local minimum requirements **2**

    (b) a minimum of 75% **3**

11.705.2.1.4 In a multifamily building, occupancy controls are installed to automatically reduce light levels in garages and parking structures when the space is unoccupied. Light levels are reduced by:

(1) greater than 50% to less than 75% or to local minimum requirements **2**

(2) a minimum of 75% **3**

11.705.2.2 TDDs and skylights. A tubular daylighting device (TDD) or a skylight that meets the requirements of Table 11.703.2.5.2(a) is installed in rooms without windows.
[Points awarded per building.] **2**

11.705.2.3 Lighting outlets. Occupancy sensors are installed for a minimum of 80% of hard-wired lighting outlets in the interior living space. **1**

11.705.2.4 Recessed luminaires. The number of recessed luminaires that penetrate the thermal envelope is less than 1 per 400 sq. ft. (37.16 m^2) of total conditioned floor area and they are in accordance with § 11.701.4.3.5. .... **1**

11.705.3 Induction cooktop. Induction cooktop is installed. **1**

11.705.4 Return ducts and transfer grilles. Return ducts or transfer grilles are installed in every room with a door. Return ducts or transfer grilles are not required for bathrooms, kitchens, closets, pantries, and laundry rooms. **2**

11.705.5 HVAC design and installation

11.705.5.1 Meet one or both of the following:

(1) HVAC contractor is certified by the Air Conditioning Contractors of America's Quality Assured Program (ACCA/QA) or by an EPA-recognized HVAC Quality Installation Training Oversight Organization (H-QUITO) or equivalent. **1**

(2) HVAC installation technician(s) is certified by North American Technician Excellence, Inc. (NATE) or equivalent. **1**

11.705.5.2 Performance of the heating and/or cooling system is verified by the HVAC contractor in accordance with all of the following: **3**

(1) Start-up procedure is performed in accordance with the manufacturer's instructions.

(2) Refrigerant charge is verified by super-heat and/or sub-cooling method.

(3) Burner is set to fire at input level listed on nameplate.

(4) Air handler setting/fan speed is set in accordance with manufacturer's instructions.

(5) Total airflow is within 10% of design flow.

(6) Total external system static does not exceed equipment capability at rated airflow.

GREEN BUILDING PRACTICES	POINTS

11.705.5.3 HVAC Design is verified by 3rd party as follows:

(1) The ENERGY STAR HVAC Design and Rater Design Review Checklists are completed and correct......... **3**

(2) HVAC Installation is inspected and conforms to HVAC design documents and plans. **3**

11.705.6 Installation and performance verification

11.705.6.1 Third-party on-site inspection is conducted to verify compliance with all of the following, as applicable. Minimum of two inspections are performed: one inspection after insulation is installed and prior to covering, and another inspection upon completion of the building. Where multiple buildings or dwelling units of the same model or sleeping units of the same model are built by the same builder, a representative sample inspection of a minimum of 15% of the buildings or dwelling units or sleeping units is permitted. **3**

(1) Ducts are installed in accordance with the IRC or IMC and ducts are sealed.

(2) Building envelope air sealing is installed.

(3) Insulation is installed in accordance with § 11.701.4.3.2.1.

(4) Windows, skylights, and doors are flashed, caulked, and sealed in accordance with manufacturer's instructions and in accordance with § 11.701.4.3.

11.705.6.2 Testing. Testing is conducted to verify performance.

11.705.6.2.1 Air leakage validation of building or dwelling units or sleeping units. A visual inspection is performed as described in § 11.701.4.3.2(2) and air leakage testing is performed in accordance with ASTM E779, ASTM E1827, or ANSI 380.
[Points awarded only for buildings where building envelope leakage testing is not required by the ICC IECC.]
[Points not awarded if points are taken under § 11.703.2.4.]

(1) A blower door test. **3**

(2) Third-party verification is completed. **5**

11.705.6.2.2 HVAC airflow testing. Balanced HVAC airflows are demonstrated by flow hood or other acceptable flow measurement tool by a third party. Test results are in accordance with the following:

(1) Measured flow at each supply and return register meets or exceeds the requirements in ACCA 5 QI Section 5.2. .... **5**

(2) Total airflow meets or exceeds the requirements in ACCA 5 QI Section 5.2. .... **3**

11.705.6.2.3 HVAC duct leakage testing. One of the following is achieved:
[Points awarded only for buildings where duct leakage testing is not required by ICC IECC.]
[Points not awarded if points are taken under § 11.703.4.4.]

(1) Duct leakage is in accordance with ICC IECC R403.3.3 and R403.3.4. .... **3**

(2) Duct leakage is in accordance with ICC IECC R403.3.3 and R403.3.4, and testing is conducted by an independent third party. **5**

GREEN BUILDING PRACTICES	M=Mandatory POINTS

11.705.6.3 Insulating hot water pipes. Insulation with a minimum thermal resistance (R-value) of at least R-3 is applied to the following, as applicable:
[Points awarded only where these practices are not required by ICC IECC.] 1

- (a) piping 3/4-in. and larger in outside diameter

- (b) piping serving more than one dwelling unit or sleeping unit

- (c) piping located outside the conditioned space

- (d) piping from the water heater to a distribution manifold

- (e) piping located under a floor slab

- (f) buried piping

- (g) supply and return piping in recirculation systems other than demand recirculation systems

11.705.6.4 Potable hot water demand re-circulation system.

11.705.6.4.1 Potable hot water demand re-circulation system is installed in a single-family unit. 1

11.705.6.4.2 Potable hot water demand re-circulation system(s) that serves every unit in a multifamily building is installed in place of a standard circulation pump and control... 2

11.705.7 Submetering system. In multifamily buildings, an advanced electric and fossil fuel submetering system is installed to monitor electricity and fossil fuel consumption for each unit. The device provides consumption information on a monthly or near real-time basis. The information is available to the occupants at a minimum on a monthly basis.. 1

11.706 INNOVATIVE PRACTICES

11.706.1 Energy consumption control. A whole-building, whole-dwelling unit, or whole-sleeping unit device or system is installed that controls or monitors energy consumption. .... **3 max**

(1) programmable communicating thermostat with the capability to be controlled remotely................... 1

(2) energy-monitoring device or system 1

(3) energy management control system 3

(4) programmable thermostat with control capability based on occupant presence or usage pattern 1

(5) lighting control system.. 1

11.706.2 Renewable energy service plan. Renewable energy service plan is provided as follows:

(1) Builder selects a renewable energy service plan provided by the local electrical utility for interim (temporary) electric service, or purchases renewable energy certificates (RECs) to cover electricity used. The builder's local administrative office has renewable energy service or has otherwise been paired with RECs. Green-e Certified (or equivalent) is required for renewable electricity purchases. .. 1

(2) The buyer of the building selects one of the following renewable energy service plans provided by the utility prior to occupancy of the building with a minimum two-year commitment.

- (a) less than 50% of the dwelling's projected electricity and gas use is provided by renewable energy . 1

- (b) greater than or equal to 50% of the dwelling's projected electricity and gas use is provided by renewable energy 2

	M=Mandatory
GREEN BUILDING PRACTICES	**POINTS**

11.706.3 Smart appliances and systems. Smart appliances and systems are installed as follows:
[1 point awarded if at least 3 smart appliances are installed; 1 additional point awarded for 6 or more.]... | 1 [2 max]

(1) Refrigerator

(2) Freezer

(3) Dishwasher

(4) Clothes Dryer

(5) Clothes Washer

(6) Room Air Conditioner

(7) HVAC Systems

(8) Service Hot Water Heating Systems

[Items (7) and (8) are permitted to count as two appliances each for the purpose of awarding points.]

Where points awarded in § 11.706.3, points shall not be awarded in § 11.706.7 and § 11.706.10.

11.706.4 Pumps

11.706.4.1 Pool, spa, and water features equipped with filtration pumps as follows:

(1) Electronically controlled variable-speed pump(s) is installed (full load efficiency of 90% or greater).... | 1

(2) Electronically controlled variable-speed pump(s) is installed (full load efficiency of 90% or greater) in a pool .... | 3

11.706.4.2 Sump pump(s), with electrically commutated motors (ECMs) or permanent split capacitor (PSC) motor, is installed (full load efficiency of 90% or greater). .... | 1

11.706.5 On-site renewable energy system. One of the following options is implemented:

(1) Building is Solar-Ready in compliance with ICC IECC Appendix A Solar Ready Provisions. .... | 1

(2) An on-site renewable energy system(s) is installed on the property. .... | 2 per kW

(3) An on-site renewable energy system(s) and a battery energy storage system are installed on the property.
[2 points awarded per kW or renewable energy system plus 1 per each 2 kWh or battery energy storage system] .... | 2 per kW

Points shall not be awarded in this section for solar thermal or geothermal systems that provide space heating, space cooling, or water heating, points for these systems are awarded in § 11.703. Points awarded in this section shall not be combined with points for renewable energy in another section of this chapter. The solar-ready zone roof area in item (1) is area per dwelling unit. Points in item (2) and (3) shall be divided by the number of dwelling units.

Multifamily Building Note: Conditioned common area and non-residential space is excluded for the purpose of calculating number of units.

11.706.6 Parking garage efficiency. Structured parking garages are designed to require no mechanical ventilation for fresh air requirements. .... | 2

GREEN BUILDING PRACTICES	M=Mandatory POINTS

11.706.7 Grid-interactive electric thermal storage system. A grid-interactive electric thermal storage system is installed.

(1) Grid-Interactive Water Heating System **1**

(2) Grid-Interactive Space Heating and Cooling System... **1**

Where points are awarded in § 11.706.7, points shall not be awarded in § 11.706.3 and § 11.706.10.

11.706.8 Electrical vehicle charging station. A Level 2 (208/240V 40-80 amp) or Level 3 electric vehicle charging station is installed on the building site. (Note: Charging station shall not be included in the building energy consumption.) **2**

11.706.9 CNG vehicle fueling station. A CNG vehicle residential fueling appliance is installed on the building site. The CNG fueling appliances shall be listed in accordance with ANSI/CSA NGV 5.1 and installed in accordance to the appliance manufacturer's installation instructions. (Note: The fueling appliance shall not be included in the building energy consumption.) **1**

11.706.10 Automatic demand response. Automatic demand response system is installed that curtails energy usage upon a signal from the utility or an energy service provider is installed. **1**

Where points are awarded in § 11.706.10, points shall not be awarded in § 11.706.3 and § 11.706.7.

11.706.11 Grid-interactive battery storage system. A grid-interactive battery storage system of no less than 6 kWh of available capacity is installed. **2**

11.706.12 Smart ventilation. A whole-building ventilation system is installed with automatic ventilation controls to limit ventilation during periods of extreme temperature, extreme humidity, and/or during times of peak utility loads and is in accordance with the specifications of ASHRAE Standard 62.2-2010 Section 4. .... **1**

11.706.13 Alternative refrigerant. Use of the following in mechanical space cooling systems for dwellings.

(1) Use alternative refrigerant with a GWP less than 1,000.. **1**

(2) Do not use refrigerants **2**

11.706.14 Third-party utility benchmarking service.

(1) For a multifamily building, the owner has contracted with a third-party utility benchmarking service with at least five (5) years of experience in utility data management and analysis to perform a monthly analysis of whole-building energy and water consumption for a minimum of one (1) year.... **3**

(2) The building owner commits to reporting energy data using EPA's ENERGY STAR Portfolio Manager for a minimum of three (3) years. **1**

11.706.15 Entryway air seal. For multifamily buildings, where not required by the building or energy code, to slow the movement of unconditioned air from outdoors to indoors at the main building entrance, the following is installed:

(1) Building entry vestibule. **2**

(2) Revolving entrance doors. **2**

M=Mandatory

GREEN BUILDING PRACTICES	POINTS

11.801   INDOOR AND OUTDOOR WATER USE

11.801.0 Intent. Implement measures that reduce indoor and outdoor water usage. Implement measures that include collection and use of alternative sources of water. Implement measures that treat water on site.

11.801.1 Mandatory requirements. The building shall comply with § 11.802 (Prescriptive Path) and § 11.803 (Innovative Practices). Points from § 11.804 (Performance Path) shall not be combined with points from § 11.802 (Prescriptive Path) or § 11.803 (Innovative Practices).

11.802   PRESCRIPTIVE PATH

11.802.1 Indoor hot water usage. Indoor hot water supply system is in accordance with one of the practices listed in items (1) through (5). The maximum water volume from the source of hot water to the termination of the fixture supply is determined in accordance with Tables 11.802.1(1) or 11.8021.1(2). The maximum pipe length from the source of hot water to the termination of the fixture supply is 50 ft.

Where more than one water heater or where more than one type of hot water supply system, including multiple circulation loops, is used, points are awarded only for the system that qualifies for the minimum number of points. Systems with circulation loops are eligible for points only if pumps are demand controlled. Circulation systems with timers or aquastats and constant-on circulation systems are not eligible to receive points. Points awarded only if the pipes are insulated in accordance with § 11.705.6.3.

(1)	The maximum volume from the water heater to the termination of the fixture supply at furthest fixture is 128 ounces (1 gallon or 3.78 liters).	8
(2)	The maximum volume from the water heater to the termination of the fixture supply at furthest fixture is 64 ounces (0.5 gallon or 1.89 liters).	12
(3)	The maximum volume from the water heater to the termination of the fixture supply at furthest fixture is 32 ounces (0.25 gallon or 0.945 liters).	20
(4)	A demand controlled hot water priming pump is installed on the main supply pipe of the circulation loop and the maximum volume from this supply pipe to the furthest fixture is 24 ounces (0.19 gallons or 0.71 liters).	24
	(a) The volume in the circulation loop (supply) from the water heater or boiler to the branch for the furthest fixture is no more than 128 ounces (1 gallon or 3.78 liters).	4 Additional
(5)	A central hot water recirculation system is implemented in multifamily buildings in which the hot water line distance from the recirculating loop to the engineered parallel piping system (i.e., manifold system) is less than 30 ft. (9,144 mm) and the parallel piping to the fixture fittings contains a maximum of 64 ounces (1.89 liters) (115.50 cubic in.) (0.50 gallons).	9
(6)	Tankless water heater(s) with at least 0.5 gallon (1.89 liters) of storage are installed, or a tankless water heater that ramps up to at least 110°F within 5 seconds is installed. The storage may be internal or external to the tankless water heater.	1 Additional

GREEN BUILDING PRACTICES

Table 11.802.1(1)
Maximum Pipe Length Conversion Table[a]

Nominal Pipe Size (in.)	Liquid Ounces per Foot of Length	Main, Branch, and Fixture Supply System Volume Category			Branch and Fixture Supply Volume from Circulation Loop
		128 ounces (1 gallons) [per 11.802.1(1)]	64 ounces (0.5 gallon) [per 11.802.1(2)]	32 ounces (0.25 gallon) [per 11.802.1(3)]	24 ounces (0.19 gallon) [per 11.802.1(4)]
		Maximum Pipe Length (feet)			
1/4[b]	0.33	50	50	50	50
5/16[b]	0.5	50	50	50	48
3/8[b]	0.75	50	50	43	32
1/2	1.5	50	43	21	16
5/8	2	50	32	16	12
3/4	3	43	21	11	8
7/8	4	32	16	8	6
1	5	26	13	6	5
1 1/4	8	16	8	4	3
1 1/2	11	12	6	3	2
2	18	7	4	2	1

a. Maximum pipe length figures apply when the entire pipe run is one nominal diameter only. Where multiple pipe diameters are used, the combined volume shall not exceed the volume limitation in § 11.801.1.

b. The maximum flow rate through 1/4 in. nominal piping shall not exceed 0.5 gpm. The maximum flow rate through 5/16 in. nominal piping shall not exceed 1 gpm. The maximum flow rate through 3/8 in. nominal piping shall not exceed 1.5 gpm.

Table 11.802.1(2)
Common Hot Water Pipe Internal Volumes

Size Nominal, In.	Copper Type M	Copper Type L	Copper Type K	CPVC CTS SDR 11	CPVC SCH 40	CPVC SCH 80	PE-RT SDR 9	Composite ASTM F 1281	PEX CTS SDR 9	PP SDR 7.4 F2389	PP SDR 9 F2389
					OUNCES OF WATER PER FOOT OF PIPE						
3/8	1.06	0.97	0.84	N/A	1.17	N/A	0.64	0.63	0.64	N/A	N/A
1/2	1.69	1.55	1.45	1.25	1.89	1.46	1.18	1.31	1.18	1.72	1.96
3/4	3.43	3.22	2.90	2.67	3.38	2.74	2.35	3.39	2.35	2.69	3.06
1	5.81	5.49	5.17	4.43	5.53	4.57	3.91	5.56	3.91	4.41	5.01
1 ¼	8.70	8.36	8.09	6.61	9.66	8.24	5.81	8.49	5.81	6.90	7.83
1 ½	12.18	11.83	11.45	9.22	13.2	11.38	8.09	13.88	8.09	10.77	12.24
2	21.08	20.58	20.04	15.79	21.88	19.11	13.86	21.48	13.86	17.11	19.43

11.802.2 Water-conserving appliances. ENERGY STAR or equivalent water-conserving appliances are installed.

(1) dishwasher 2

(2) clothes washer, or 13

(3) clothes washer with an Integrated Water Factor of 3.8 or less 18

Multifamily Building Note: Washing machines are installed in individual units or provided in common areas of multifamily buildings.

M=Mandatory

GREEN BUILDING PRACTICES	POINTS

11.802.3 Water usage metering. Water meters are installed meeting the following:

(1) Single-Family Buildings: Water Usage Metering:..

    (a) Where not otherwise required by the local AHJ, installation of a meter for water consumed from any source associated with the building or building site... **2 per unique meter**

    (b) Each water meter shall be capable of communicating water consumption data remotely for the dwelling unit occupant and be capable of providing daily data with electronic data storage and reporting capability that can produce reports for daily, monthly, and yearly water consumption. (Fire sprinkler systems are not required to be metered). .... **2 per sensor package**

(2) Multifamily Buildings: Water Usage Metering: ....

    (a) Where not otherwise required by the local AHJ, installation of a meter for water consumed from any source associated with the building or building site... **2 per unique use meter**

    (b) Each water meter shall be capable of communicating water consumption data remotely for the dwelling unit occupant and be capable of providing daily data with electronic data storage and reporting capability that can produce reports for daily, monthly, and yearly water consumption. (Fire sprinkler systems are not required to be metered). .... **2 per sensor package**

[Points earned in § 11.802.3(2) shall not exceed 50% of the total points earned for the Indoor and Outdoor Water Use Category]

11.802.4 Showerheads. Showerheads are in accordance with the following:

(1) The total maximum combined flow rate of all showerheads in a shower compartment with floor area of 2,600 sq. in. or less is equal or less than 2.0 gpm. For each additional 1,300 sq. in. or any portion thereof of shower compartment floor area, an additional 2.0 gpm combined showerhead flow rate is allowed. Showerheads shall comply with ASME A112.18.1/CSA B125.1 and shall meet the performance criteria of the EPA WaterSense Specification for showerheads. Showerheads shall be served by an automatic compensating valve that complies with ASSE 1016/ASME A112.1016/CSA B125.16 or ASME A112.18.1/CSA B125.1 and is specifically designed to provide thermal shock and scald protection at the flow rate of the showerhead.
[4 points awarded for first compartment; 1 point for each additional compartment in dwelling] .... **4 [7 max]**

Points awarded per shower compartment. In multifamily buildings, the average of the points assigned to individual dwelling units or sleeping units may be used as the number of points awarded for this practice, rounded to the nearest whole number.

(2) All shower compartments in the dwelling unit(s) or sleeping unit(s) and common areas meet the requirements of § 11.802.4(1) and all showerheads are in accordance with one of the following:

    (a) maximum of 1.8 gpm.. **6 Additional**

    (b) maximum of 1.5 gpm.. **10 Additional**

(3) Any shower control that can shut off water flow without affecting temperature is installed.
[1 point awarded per shower control] .... **1 [3 max]**

For SI: 1 gallon per minute = 3.785 L/m

	M=Mandatory
GREEN BUILDING PRACTICES	**POINTS**

11.802.5 Faucets

11.802.5.1 Install water-efficient lavatory faucets with flow rates not more than 1.5 gpm (5.68 L/min), tested in compliance with ASME A112.18.1/CSA B125.1 and meeting the performance criteria of the EPA WaterSense High-Efficiency Lavatory Faucet Specification:

(1) Flow rate ≤ 1.5 gpm *[All faucets in a bathroom are in compliance]* .... **1 [3 max]**

[1 point awarded for each bathroom. In multifamily buildings, the average of the points assigned to individual dwelling units or sleeping units may be used as the number of points awarded for this practice, rounded to the nearest whole number.]

(2) Flow rate ≤ 1.20 gpm *[All faucets in a bathroom are in compliance]* .... **2 [6 max]**

[2 Points awarded for each bathroom. In multifamily buildings, the average of the points assigned to individual dwelling units or sleeping units may be used as the number of points awarded for this practice, rounded to the nearest whole number.]

(3) Flow rate ≤ 1.5 gpm for all lavatory faucets in the dwelling unit(s) or sleeping unit(s) .... **6 Additional**

(4) Flow rate ≤ 1.5 gpm for all lavatory faucets in the dwelling unit(s), and at least one bathroom has faucets with flow rates ≤ 1.20 gpm .... **8 Additional**

(5) Flow rate ≤ 1.20 gpm for all lavatory faucets in the dwelling unit(s) .... **12 Additional**

11.802.5.2 Water-efficient residential kitchen faucets are installed in accordance with ASME A112.18.1/CSA B125.1. Residential kitchen faucets may temporarily increase the flow above the maximum rate but not to exceed 2.2 gpm.

(1) All residential kitchen faucets have a maximum flow rate of 1.8 gpm. **3**

(2) All residential kitchen faucets have a maximum flow rate of 1.5 gpm. .... **1 Additional**

11.802.5.3 Self-closing valve, motion sensor, metering, or pedal-activated faucet is installed to enable intermittent on/off operation. *[1 point awarded per fixture]* .... **1 [3 max]**

11.802.5.4 Water closets and urinals are in accordance with the following:

Points awarded for § 11.803.5.4(2) or § 11.802.5.4(3), not both.

(1) Gold and Emerald levels: All water closets and urinals are in accordance with § 11.801.5. .... **M**

(2) A water closet is installed with an effective flush volume of 1.28 gallons (4.85 L) or less in accordance with ASME A112.19.2/CSA B45.1 or ASME A112.19.14 as applicable. Tank-type water closets shall be in accordance with the performance criteria of the EPA WaterSense Specification for Tank-Type Toilets .... **4 [12 max]**

[Points awarded per fixture. In multifamily buildings, the average of the points assigned to individual dwelling units or sleeping units may be used as the number of points awarded for this practice, rounded to the nearest whole number.]

(3) All water closets are in accordance with § 11.802.5.4(2). **17**

(4) All water closets are in accordance with § 11.802.5.4(2) and one or more of the following are installed:

(a) Water closets that have an effective flush volume of 1.2 gallons or less.
[Points awarded per toilet. In multifamily buildings, the average of the points assigned to individual dwelling units or sleeping units may be used as the number of points awarded for this practice, rounded to the nearest whole number.] .... **2 Additional [6 Add'l max]**

GREEN BUILDING PRACTICES	M=Mandatory POINTS

(b) One or more urinals with a flush volume of 0.5 gallons (1.9L) or less when tested in accordance with ASME A112.19.2/CSA B45.1. .... **2 Additional**

(c) One or more composting or waterless toilets and/or non-water urinals. Non-water urinals shall be tested in accordance with ASME A112.19.2/CSA B45.1. .... **12 Additional**

11.802.6 Irrigation systems

11.802.6.1 Where an irrigation system is installed, an irrigation plan and implementation are executed by a qualified professional or equivalent.. **M**

11.802.6.2 Irrigation sprinkler nozzles shall be tested according to ANSI standard ASABE/ICC 802 Landscape Irrigation Sprinkler and Emitter Standard by an accredited third-party laboratory. **6**

11.802.6.3 Drip irrigation is installed... **13 max**

(1) Drip irrigation is installed for all landscape beds. **4**

(2) Subsurface drip is installed for all turf grass areas. **4**

(3) Drip irrigation zones specifications show plant type by name and water use/need for each emitter *[Points awarded only if specifications are implemented.]*.. **5**

11.802.6.4 The irrigation system(s) is controlled by a smart controller or no irrigation is installed. *[Points are not additive.]*

(1) Irrigation controllers shall be in accordance with the performance criteria of the EPA WaterSense program **10**

(2) No irrigation is installed and a landscape plan is developed in accordance with § 11.503.5, as applicable.. **15**

11.802.6.5 Commissioning and water use reduction for irrigation systems. *[Points are not additive per each section.]*

(1) All irrigation zones utilize pressure regulation so emission devices (sprinklers and drip emitters) operate at manufacturer's recommended operating pressure. **3**

(2) Where dripline tubing is installed, a filter with mesh size in accordance with the manufacturer's recommendation is installed on all drip zones.. **3**

(3) Utilize spray bodies that incorporate an in-stem or external flow shut-off device................ **3**

(4) For irrigation systems installed on sloped sites, either an in-stem or external check valve is utilized for each spray body. **3**

(5) Where an irrigation system is installed, a flow sensing device is installed to monitor and alert the controller when flows are outside design range. **3**

11.802.7 Rainwater collection and distribution. Rainwater collection and distribution is provided.

11.802.7.1 Rainwater is used for irrigation in accordance with one of the following:

(1) Rainwater is diverted for landscape irrigation without impermeable water storage **5**

(2) Rainwater is diverted for landscape irrigation with impermeable water storage in accordance with one of the following:

    (a) 50 – 499 gallon storage capacity **5**

GREEN BUILDING PRACTICES	M=Mandatory POINTS

    (b) 500 – 2,499 gallon storage capacity.. **10**

    (c) 2,500 gallon or larger storage capacity (system is designed by a professional certified by the ARCSA or equivalent) **15**

    (d) All irrigation demands are met by rainwater capture (documentation demonstrating the water needs of the landscape are provided and the system is designed by a professional certified by the ARCSA or equivalent). **25**

11.802.7.2 Rainwater is used for indoor domestic demand as follows. The system is designed by a professional certified by the ARCSA or equivalent.

(1) Rainwater is used to supply an indoor appliance or fixture for any locally approved use. *[Points awarded per appliance or fixture.]*.. **5 [15 max]**

(2) Rainwater provides for total domestic demand. Where rainwater is used as potable water the potable rainwater system shall meet the requirements of IRC Sections P2906 and Section P2912. ..... **25**

The following shall also apply:

    (a) The following roof materials shall not be used to collect rainwater: shingles with fire retardant, copper, and materials that contain asbestos. Materials that contain lead, including but not limited to flashings and roof jacks, shall be prohibited.

    (b) Potable water supplies shall be protected against cross connection with rainwater as specified in IRC Section P2902.1.

    (c) Disinfection shall be provided by at least one of the following:

        (i) Ultraviolet (UV) light providing at least 40 mJ/cm2 at 254 nm for the highest water flow rate. A UV sensor with visible alarm, audible alarm, or water shutoff shall be triggered when the UV light is below the minimum at the sensor. In addition, filtration no greater than 5 μm shall be located upstream of the UV light or

        (ii) filtration no greater than 0.2 μm, or

        (iii) other approved disinfection

    (d) Materials and systems that collect, convey, pump, or store rainwater for potable rainwater systems shall comply with NSF 53, NSF 61 or equivalent.

    (e) The quality of the water at the point of use shall be verified in accordance with the requirements of the jurisdiction.

    (f) The rainwater storage shall not admit sunlight.

    (g) Potable rainwater pipe shall not be required to be purple after the point that the water is disinfected.

11.802.8 Sediment filters. Water filter is installed to reduce sediment and protect plumbing fixtures for the whole building or the entire dwelling unit or the sleeping unit. **1**

11.802.9 Water treatment devices.

11.802.9.1 Water Softeners shall not be installed where the supplied water hardness is less than 8.0 grains per gallon measured as total calcium carbonate equivalents. Water softeners shall be listed to NSF 44 and a rated salt efficiency of 3,400 grains of total hardness per 1.0 pound of salt based on

	M=Mandatory
GREEN BUILDING PRACTICES	**POINTS**

sodium chloride equivalency. Devices shall not discharge more than 4.0 gallons of water per 1,000 grains of hardness removed during the service or recharge cycle.

(1) No water softener...	5
(2) Water softener installed to supply softened water only to domestic water heater.	2

11.802.9.2 Reverse Osmosis (R/O) water treatment systems shall be listed to NSF 58 and shall include automatic shut-off valve to prevent water discharge when storage tank is full.

(1) No R/O system..	3
(2) Combined capacity of all R/O systems does not exceed 0.75 gallons.	1

11.802.10 Pools and spas.

11.802.10.1 Pools and Spas with water surface area greater than 36 sq. ft. and connected to a water supply shall have a dedicated meter to measure the amount of water supplied to the pool or spa.

(1) Automated motorized non-permeable pool cover that covers the entire pool surface.	10

11.803   INNOVATIVE PRACTICES

11.803.1 Reclaimed, grey, or recycled water. Reclaimed, grey, or recycled water is used as permitted by applicable code.

Points awarded for either § 11.803.1(1) or § 11.803.1(2), not both.
Points awarded for either § 11. 803.6 or § 11.803.1, not both.

(1) each water closet flushed by reclaimed, grey, or recycled water *[Points awarded per fixture or appliance.]*	5 [20 max]
(2) irrigation from reclaimed, grey, or recycled water on-site...	10
11.803.2 Reclaimed water, greywater, or rainwater pre-piping. Reclaimed, greywater, or rainwater systems are rough plumbed (and permanently marked, tagged or labeled) into buildings for future use.	3 per roughed in system
11.803.3 Automatic leak detection and control devices. One of the following devices is installed. Where a fire sprinkler system is present, ensure the device will be installed to not interfere with the operation of the fire sprinkler system.	2

(1) automatic water leak detection and control devices

(2) automatic water leak detection and shutoff devices

11.803.4 Engineered biological system or intensive bioremediation system. An engineered biological system or intensive bioremediation system is installed and the treated water is used on site. Design and implementation are approved by appropriate regional authority.	20
11.803.5 Recirculating humidifier. Where a humidifier is required, a recirculating humidifier is used in lieu of a traditional "flow through" type.	1
11.803.6 Advanced wastewater treatment system. Advanced wastewater (aerobic) treatment system is installed and treated water is used on site.	20

Points awarded for either § 11.803.6 or § 11.803.1, not both.

GREEN BUILDING PRACTICES	POINTS

11.901 POLLUTANT SOURCE CONTROL

11.901.0 Intent. Pollutant sources are controlled.

11.901.1 Space and water heating options

11.901.1.1 Natural draft furnaces, boilers, or water heaters are not located in conditioned spaces, including conditioned crawlspaces, unless located in a mechanical room that has an outdoor air source, and is sealed and insulated to separate it from the conditioned space(s).
[Points are awarded only for buildings that use natural draft combustion space or water heating equipment.] 5

11.901.1.2 Air handling equipment or return ducts are not located in the garage, unless placed in isolated, air-sealed mechanical rooms with an outside air source. 5

11.901.1.3 The following combustion space heating or water heating equipment is installed within conditioned space:

(1) all furnaces or all boilers

    (a) power-vent furnace(s) or boiler(s).. 3

    (b) direct-vent furnace(s) or boiler(s).. 5

(2) all water heaters

    (a) power-vent water heater(s).. 3

    (b) direct-vent water heater(s).. 5

11.901.1.4 Newly installed gas-fired fireplaces and direct heating equipment is listed and is installed in accordance with the NFPA 54, ICC IFGC, or the applicable local gas appliance installation code. Gas-fired fireplaces within dwelling units or sleeping units and direct heating equipment are vented to the outdoors. Alcohol burning devices and kerosene heaters are vented to the outdoors. .... M

11.901.1.5 Natural gas and propane fireplaces are direct vented, have permanently fixed glass fronts or gasketed doors, and comply with CSA Z21.88/CSA 2.33 or CSA Z21.50/CSA 2.22... 7

11.901.1.6 The following electric equipment is installed:

(1) heat pump air handler in unconditioned space 2

(2) heat pump air handler in conditioned space 5

11.901.2 Solid fuel-burning appliances.

11.901.2.1 Newly installed solid fuel-burning fireplaces, inserts, stoves and heaters are code compliant and are in accordance with the following requirements: .... M

(1) Site-built masonry wood-burning fireplaces are equipped with outside combustion air and a means of sealing the flue and the combustion air outlets to minimize interior air (heat) loss when not in operation.

(2) Factory-built, wood-burning fireplaces are in accordance with the certification requirements of UL 127 and are an EPA Phase 2 Emission Level Qualified Model.

(3) Wood stove and fireplace inserts, as defined in UL 1482 Section 3.8, are in accordance with the certification requirements of UL 1482 and are in accordance with the emission requirements of the EPA Certification and the State of Washington WAC 173-433-100(3).

GREEN BUILDING PRACTICES	M=Mandatory POINTS

(4) Pellet (biomass) stoves and furnaces are in accordance with the requirements of ASTM E1509 or are EPA certified.

(5) Masonry heaters are in accordance with the definitions in ASTM E1602 and IBC Section 2112.1.

(6) Removal of or rendering unusable an existing fireplace or fuel burning appliance that is not in accordance with § 11.901.2.1 or replacement of each fireplace or appliance that is not in accordance with § 11.901.2.1 with a compliant appliance.

11.901.2.2 Fireplaces, woodstoves, pellet stoves, or masonry heaters are not installed. 6

11.901.3 Garages. Garages are in accordance with the following:

(1) Attached garage

    (a) Where installed in the common wall between the attached garage and conditioned space, the door is tightly sealed and gasketed. .... **M 2**

    (b) A continuous air barrier is provided between walls and ceilings separating the garage space from the conditioned living spaces. .... **M 2**

    (c) For one- and two-family dwelling units, a 100 cfm (47 L/s) or greater ducted, or 70 cfm (33 L/s) cfm or greater unducted wall exhaust fan is installed and vented to the outdoors, designed and installed for continuous operation, or has controls (e.g., motion detectors, pressure switches) that activate operation for a minimum of 1 hour when either human passage door or roll-up automatic doors are operated. For ducted exhaust fans, the fan airflow rating and duct sizing are in accordance with ASHRAE Standard 62.2-2007 Section 7.3. 8

(2) A carport is installed, the garage is detached from the building, or no garage is installed. 10

11.901.4 Wood materials. A minimum of 85% of newly installed material within a product group (i.e., wood structural panels, countertops, composite trim/doors, custom woodwork, and/or component closet shelving) is manufactured in accordance with the following: .... **10 max**

(1) Structural plywood used for floor, wall, and/or roof sheathing is compliant with DOC PS 1 and/or DOC PS 2. OSB used for floor, wall, and/or roof sheathing is compliant with DOC PS 2. The panels are made with moisture-resistant adhesives. The trademark indicates these adhesives as follows: Exposure 1 or Exterior for plywood, and Exposure 1 for OSB. **M**

(2) Particleboard and MDF (medium density fiberboard) is manufactured and labeled in accordance with CPA A208.1 and CPA A208.2, respectively. *[Points awarded per product group.]* 2

(3) Hardwood plywood in accordance with HPVA HP-1. *[Points awarded per product group.]* 2

(4) Particleboard, MDF, or hardwood plywood is in accordance with CPA 4.
[Points awarded per product group.] 3

(5) Composite wood or agrifiber panel products contain no added urea-formaldehyde or are in accordance with the *CARB Composite Wood Air Toxic Contaminant Measure Standard*.
[Points awarded per product group.] 4

(6) Non-emitting products. *[Points awarded per product group.]* 4

11.901.5 Cabinets. A minimum of 85% of newly installed cabinets are in accordance with one or both of the following: *[Where both of the following practices are used, only three points are awarded.]*

(1) All parts of the cabinet are made of solid wood or non-formaldehyde emitting materials such as metal or glass. 5

GREEN BUILDING PRACTICES	M=Mandatory POINTS

(2) The composite wood used in wood cabinets are in accordance with CARB Composite Wood Air Toxic Contaminant Measure Standard or equivalent as certified by a program such as but not limited to, those in Appendix B. **3**

11.901.6 Carpets. Carpets are in accordance with the following:

(1) Wall-to-wall carpeting is not installed adjacent to water closets and bathing fixtures. .... **M**

11.901.7 Floor materials. The following types of finished flooring materials are used. The materials have emission levels in accordance with CDPH/EHLB Standard Method v1.1. Product is tested by a laboratory with the CDPH/EHLB Standard Method v1.1 within the laboratory scope of accreditation to ISO/IEC 17025 and certified by a third-party program accredited to ISO 17065, such as, but not limited to, those in Appendix B. *[1 point awarded for every 10% of conditioned floor space using one of the below materials. When carpet cushion meeting the emission limits of the practice is also installed, the percentage of compliant carpet area is calculated at 1.33 times the actual installed area.]* .... **1 [8 max]**

(1) Hard surface flooring: Prefinished installed hard-surface flooring is installed. Where post-manufacture coatings or surface applications have not been applied, the following hard surface flooring types are deemed to comply with the emission requirements of this practice:

   (a) Ceramic tile flooring

   (b) Organic-free, mineral-based flooring

   (c) Clay masonry flooring

   (d) Concrete masonry flooring

   (e) Concrete flooring

   (f) Metal flooring

   (g) Glass

(2) Carpet and carpet cushion are installed.

11.901.8 Wall coverings. When at least 10% of the interior wall surfaces are covered, a minimum of 85% of wall coverings are in accordance with the emission concentration limits of CDPH/EHLB Standard Method v1.1. Emission levels are determined by a laboratory accredited to ISO/IEC 17025 and the CDPH/EHLB Standard Method v1.1 is in its scope of accreditation. The product is certified by a third-party program accredited to ISO 17065, such as, but not limited to, those in Appendix B. **4**

11.901.9 Interior architectural coatings. A minimum of 85% of newly applied interior architectural coatings are in accordance with either § 11.901.9.1 or § 11.901.9.3, not both. A minimum of 85% of architectural colorants are in accordance with § 11.901.9.2.

Exception: Interior architectural coatings that are formulated to remove formaldehyde and other aldehydes in indoor air and are tested and labeled in accordance with ISO 16000-23, Indoor air – Part 23: Performance test for evaluating the reduction of formaldehyde concentrations by sorptive building materials.

11.901.9.1 Site-applied interior architectural coatings, which are inside the waterproofing envelope, are in accordance with one or more of the following: **5**

(1) Zero VOC as determined by EPA Method 24 (VOC content below the detection limit for the method)

(2) GreenSeal GS-11

(3) *CARB Suggested Control Measure for Architectural Coatings* (see Table 11.901.9.1)

Table 11.901.9.1
VOC Content Limits For Architectural Coatings[a,b,c]

Coating Category	LIMIT[d] (g/l)
Flat Coatings	50
Non-flat Coatings	100
Non-flat High-Gloss Coatings	150
Specialty Coatings:	
Aluminum Roof Coatings	400
Basement Specialty Coatings	400
Bituminous Roof Coatings	50
Bituminous Roof Primers	350
Bond Breakers	350
Concrete Curing Compounds	350
Concrete/Masonry Sealers	100
Driveway Sealers	50
Dry Fog Coatings	150
Faux Finishing Coatings	350
Fire Resistive Coatings	350
Floor Coatings	100
Form-Release Compounds	250
Graphic Arts Coatings (Sign Paints)	500
High Temperature Coatings	420
Industrial Maintenance Coatings	250
Low Solids Coatings	120[e]
Magnesite Cement Coatings	450
Mastic Texture Coatings	100
Metallic Pigmented Coatings	500
Multi-Color Coatings	250
Pre-Treatment Wash Primers	420
Primers, Sealers, and Undercoaters	100
Reactive Penetrating Sealers	350
Recycled Coatings	250
Roof Coatings	50
Rust Preventative Coatings	250
Shellacs, Clear	730
Shellacs, Opaque	550
Specialty Primers, Sealers, and Undercoaters	100
Stains	250
Stone Consolidants	450
Swimming Pool Coatings	340
Traffic Marking Coatings	100
Tub and Tile Refinish Coatings	420
Waterproofing Membranes	250
Wood Coatings	275
Wood Preservatives	350
Zinc-Rich Primers	340

a. The specified limits remain in effect unless revised limits are listed in subsequent columns in the table.

b. Values in this table are derived from those specified by the California Air Resources Board, Architectural Coatings Suggested Control Measure, February 1, 2008.

c. Table 11.901.9.1 architectural coating regulatory category and VOC content compliance determination shall conform to the California Air Resources Board Suggested Control Measure for Architectural Coatings dated February 1, 2008.

d. Limits are expressed as VOC Regulatory (except as noted), thinned to the manufacturer's maximum thinning recommendation, excluding any colorant added to tint bases.

e. Limit is expressed as VOC actual.

GREEN BUILDING PRACTICES	POINTS

11.901.9.2 Architectural coating colorant additive VOC content is in accordance with Table 11.901.9.2. *[Points for § 11.901.9.2 are awarded only if base architectural coating is in accordance with § 11.901.9.1.]* .. **1**

Table 11.901.9.2
VOC Content Limits for Colorants

Colorant	LIMIT (g/l)
Architectural Coatings, excluding IM Coatings	50
Solvent-Based IM	600
Waterborne IM	50

11.901.9.3 Site-applied interior architectural coatings, which are inside the waterproofing envelope, are in accordance with the emission levels of CDPH/EHLB Standard Method v1.1. Emission levels are determined by a laboratory accredited to ISO/IEC 17025 and the CDPH/EHLB Standard Method v1.1 is in its scope of accreditation. The product is certified by a third-party program accredited to ISO 17065, such as, but not limited to, those found in Appendix B. **8**

11.901.9.4 When the building is occupied during the remodel, a minimum of 85% of the newly applied interior architectural coatings are in accordance with either § 11.901.9.1 or § 11.901.9.3. .... **M**

11.901.10 Interior adhesives and sealants. Interior low-VOC adhesives and sealants located inside the water proofing envelope: A minimum of 85% of newly applied site-applied products used within the interior of the building are in accordance with one of the following, as applicable.

(1) The emission levels of CDPH/EHLB Standard Method v1.1. Emission levels are determined when tested by a laboratory accredited to ISO/IEC 17025 and the CDPH/EHLB Standard Method v1.1 is in its scope of accreditation. The product is certified by a third-party program accredited to ISO 17065, such as, but not limited to, those found in Appendix B. **8**

(2) GreenSeal GS-36 .... **5**

(3) SCAQMD Rule 1168 in accordance with Table 11.901.10(3), excluding products that are sold in 16-ounce containers or less and are regulated by the California Air Resources Board (CARB) Consumer Products Regulation. **5**

11.901.11 Insulation. Emissions of 85% of newly installed wall, ceiling, and floor insulation materials are in accordance with the emission levels of CDPH/EHLB. Standard Method v1.1. Emission levels are determined by a laboratory accredited to ISO/IEC 17025 and the CDPH/EHLB Standard Method v1.1 is in its scope of accreditation. The product is certified by a third-party program accredited to ISO 17065, such as, but not limited to, those in Appendix B. **4**

11.901.12 Furniture and Furnishings. In a multifamily building, all furniture in common areas shall have VOC emission levels in accordance with ANSI/BIFMA e3-Furniture Sustainability Standard Sections 7.6.1 and 7.6.2, tested in accordance with ANSI/BIFMA Standard Method M7.1. Emission levels are determined by a laboratory accredited to ISO/IEC 17025 and the ANSI/BIFMA Standard Method M7.1 is in its scope of accreditation. Furniture and Furnishings are certified by a third-party program accredited to ISO 17065, such as, but not limited to, those in Appendix B. **2**

11.901.13 Carbon monoxide (CO) alarms. A carbon monoxide (CO) alarm is provided in accordance with the IRC Section R315. .... **M**

GREEN BUILDING PRACTICES	POINTS

Table 11.901.10(3)
Site Applied Adhesive and Sealants VOC Limits[a,b]

ADHESIVE OR SEALANT	VOC LIMIT (g/l)
Indoor carpet adhesives	50
Carpet pad adhesives	50
Outdoor carpet adhesives	150
Wood flooring adhesive	100
Rubber floor adhesives	60
Subfloor adhesives	50
Ceramic tile adhesives	65
VCT and asphalt tile adhesives	50
Drywall and panel adhesives	50
Cove base adhesives	50
Multipurpose construction adhesives	70
Structural glazing adhesives	100
Single ply roof membrane adhesives	250
Architectural sealants	250
Architectural sealant primer	
Non-porous	250
Porous	775
Modified bituminous sealant primer	500
Other sealant primers	750
CPVC solvent cement	490
PVC solvent cement	510
ABS solvent cement	325
Plastic cement welding	250
Adhesive primer for plastic	550
Contact adhesive	80
Special purpose contact adhesive	250
Structural wood member adhesive	140

a. VOC limit less water and less exempt compounds in grams/liter
b. For low-solid adhesives and sealants, the VOC limit is expressed in grams/liter of material as specified in Rule 1168. For all other adhesives and sealants, the VOC limits are expressed as grams of VOC per liter of adhesive or sealant less water and less exempt compounds as specified in Rule 1168.

11.901.14 Building entrance pollutants control. Pollutants are controlled at all main building entrances by one of the following methods:

(1) Exterior grilles or mats are installed in a fixed manner and may be removable for cleaning. 1

(2) Interior grilles or mats are installed in a fixed manner and may be removable for cleaning.................. 1

11.901.15 Non-smoking areas. Environmental tobacco smoke is minimized by one or more of the following:

(1) All interior common areas of a multifamily building are designated as non-smoking areas with posted signage. 1

(2) Exterior smoking areas of a multifamily building are designated with posted signage and located a minimum of 25 ft. from entries, outdoor air intakes, and operable windows. 1

GREEN BUILDING PRACTICES	M=Mandatory POINTS

11.901.16 Lead-safe work practices. For buildings constructed before 1978, lead-safe work practices are used during the remodeling. .... **M**

11.902   POLLUTANT CONTROL

11.902.0 Intent. Pollutants generated in the building are controlled.

11.902.1 Spot ventilation

11.902.1.1 Spot ventilation is in accordance with the following:

(1)   Bathrooms are vented to the outdoors. The minimum ventilation rate is 50 cfm (23.6 L/s) for intermittent operation or 20 cfm (9.4 L/s) for continuous operation in bathrooms.
[1 point awarded only if a window complying with IRC Section R303.3 is provided in addition to mechanical ventilation.] .... **M [1 max]**

(2)   Clothes dryers (except listed and labeled condensing ductless dryers) are vented to the outdoors. ... **M**

(3)   Kitchen exhaust units and/or range hoods are ducted to the outdoors and have a minimum ventilation rate of 100 cfm (47.2 L/s) for intermittent operation or 25 cfm (11.8 L/s) for continuous operation. **8**

11.902.1.2 Bathroom and/or laundry exhaust fan is provided with an automatic timer and/or humidistat: .... **11 max**

(1)   for first device **5**

(2)   for each additional device.. **2**

11.902.1.3 Kitchen range, bathroom, and laundry exhaust are verified to air flow specification. Ventilation airflow at the point of exhaust is tested to a minimum of: **8**

(a)   100 cfm (47.2 L/s) intermittent or 25 cfm (11.8 L/s) continuous for kitchens, and........................ **6**

(b)   50 cfm (23.6 L/s) intermittent or 20 cfm (9.4 L/s) continuous for bathrooms and/or laundry.

11.902.1.4 Exhaust fans are ENERGY STAR, as applicable. .... **12 max**

(1)   ENERGY STAR, or equivalent, fans *[Points awarded per fan.]*................................ **2**

(2)   ENERGY STAR, or equivalent, fans operating at or below 1 sone *[Points awarded per fan.]* **3**

11.902.1.5 Fenestration in spaces other than those identified in 11.902.1.1 through 11.902.1.4 are designed for stack effect or cross-ventilation in accordance with all of the following:.............................. **3**

(1)   Operable windows, operable skylights, or sliding glass doors with a total area of at least 15% of the total conditioned floor area are provided.

(2)   Insect screens are provided for all operable windows, operable skylights, and sliding glass doors.

(3)   A minimum of two operable windows or sliding glass doors are placed in adjacent or opposite walls. If there is only one wall surface in that space exposed to the exterior, the minimum windows or sliding glass doors may be on the same wall.

11.902.1.6 Ventilation for Multifamily Common Spaces. Systems are implemented and are in accordance with the specifications of ASHRAE 62.1 and an explanation of the operation and importance of the ventilation system is included in § 11.1002.1 and § 11.1002.2. .... **3**

GREEN BUILDING PRACTICES	M=Mandatory POINTS

11.902.2 Building ventilation systems

11.902.2.1 One of the following whole building ventilation systems is implemented and is in accordance with the specifications of ASHRAE Standard 62.2-2010 Section 4 and an explanation of the operation and importance of the ventilation system is included in either § 11.1001.1 or § 11.1002.2.
[*Mandatory where the maximum air infiltration rate is less than 5.0 ACH50]... **M***

(1) exhaust or supply fan(s) ready for continuous operation and with appropriately labeled controls....... **3**

(2) balanced exhaust and supply fans with supply intakes located in accordance with the manufacturer's guidelines so as to not introduce polluted air back into the building........................... **6**

(3) heat-recovery ventilator... **7**

(4) energy-recovery ventilator... **8**

(5) Ventilation air is preconditioned by a system not specified above.. **10**

11.902.2.2 Ventilation airflow is tested to achieve the design fan airflow in accordance with ANSI/RESNET/ICC 380 and § 11.902.2.1. .... **4**

11.902.2.3 MERV filters 8 to13 are installed on central forced air systems and are accessible. Designer or installer is to verify that the HVAC equipment is able to accommodate the greater pressure drop of MERV 8 to 13 filters. **2**

11.902.2.4 MERV filters 14 or greater are installed on central forced air systems and are accessible. Designer or installer is to verify that the HVAC equipment is able to accommodate the greater pressure drop of the filter used. **3**

11.902.2.5 All HVAC filter locations are designed such that they are readily accessible to the occupant..... **3**

11.902.3 Radon reduction measures. Radon reduction measures are in accordance with IRC Appendix F or § 11.902.3.1. Radon Zones as identified by the AHJ or, if the zone is not identified by the AHJ, as defined in Figure 9(1). This practice is not mandatory if the existing building has been tested for radon and is accordance with federal and local acceptable limits.

(1) Buildings located in Zone 1

    (a) a passive radon system is installed.. **M**

    (b) an active radon system is installed... **12**

(2) Buildings located in Zone 2 or Zone 3

    (a) a passive or active radon system is installed... **6**

    (b) an active radon system is installed... **12**

11.902.3.1 Radon reduction option. This option requires § 11.902.3.1.1 through § 11.902.3.1.7.

11.902.3.1.1 Soil-gas barriers and base course. A base course in accordance with IRC Section 506.2.2 IRC shall be installed below slabs and foundations. There shall be a continuous gas-permeable base course under each soil-gas retarder that is separated by foundation walls or footings. Between slabs and the base course, damp proofing or water proofing shall be installed in accordance with IRC Section 406. Punctures, tears and gaps around penetrations of the soil-gas retarder shall be repaired or covered with an additional soil-gas retarder. The soil-gas retarder shall be a continuous 6-mil (0.15 mm) polyethylene or an approved equivalent.

GREEN BUILDING PRACTICES	POINTS

11.902.3.1.2 Soil gas collection. There shall be an unobstructed path for soil gas flow between the void space installed in the base course and the vent through the roof. Soil gases below the foundation shall be collected by a perforated pipe with a diameter of not less than 4 in. (10 cm) and not less than 5 ft. (1.5 m) in total length. A tee fitting or equivalent method shall provide two horizontal openings to the radon collection. The tee fitting shall be designed to prevent clogging of the radon collection path. Alternately the soil gas collection shall be by approved radon collection mats or an equivalent approved method.

11.902.3.1.3 Soil gas entry routes. Openings in slabs, soil-gas retarders, and joints such as, but not limited to, plumbing, ground water control systems, soil-gas vent pipes, piping and structural supports, shall be sealed against air leakage at the penetrations. The sealant shall be a polyurethane caulk, expanding foam or other approved method. Foundation walls shall comply with IRC Section 103.2.3. Sumps shall be sealed in accordance with IRC Section 103.2.2. Sump pits and sump lids intended for ground water control shall not be connected to the sub-slab soil-gas exhaust system.

11.902.3.1.4 Soil gas vent. A gas-tight pipe vent shall extend from the soil gas permeable layer through the roof. The vent pipe size shall not be reduced at any location as it goes from gas collection to the roof. Exposed and visible interior vent pipes shall be identified with not less than one label reading "Radon Reduction System" on each floor and in habitable attics.

11.902.3.1.5 Vent pipe diameter. The minimum vent pipe diameter shall be as specified in Table 11.902.3.1.5.

Table 11.902.3.1.5
Maximum Vented Foundation Area

Maximum area vented	Nominal pipe diameter
2,500 ft² (232 m²)	3 in. (7.6 cm)
4,000 ft² (372 m²)	4 in. (10 cm)
Unlimited	6 in. (15.2 cm)

11.902.3.1.6 Multiple vented areas. In dwellings where interior footings or other barriers separate the soil-gas permeable layer, each area shall be fitted with an individual vent pipe. Vent pipes shall connect to a single vent that terminates above the roof or each individual vent pipe shall terminate separately above the roof.

11.902.3.1.7 Fan. Each sub-slab soil-gas exhaust system shall include a fan, or dedicated space for the post-construction installation of a fan. The electrical supply for the fan shall be located within 6 ft. (1.8 m) of the fan. Fan is not required to be on a dedicated circuit.

11.902.3.2 Radon testing. Radon testing is mandatory for Zone 1.

Exceptions: 1) Testing is not mandatory where the authority having jurisdiction has defined the radon zone as Zone 2 or 3; and 2) testing is not mandatory where the occupied space is located above an unenclosed open space.

(1) Testing specifications. Testing is performance as specified in (a) through (j). Testing of a representative sample shall be permitted for multifamily buildings only. **8**

    (a) Testing is performed after the residence passes its airtightness test.

    (b) Testing is performed after the radon control system installation is complete. If the system has an active fan, the residence shall be tested with the fan operating.

GREEN BUILDING PRACTICES	POINTS

(c) Testing is performed at the lowest level within a dwelling unit which will be occupied, even if the space is not finished.

(d) Testing is not performed in a closet, hallway, stairway, laundry room, furnace room, kitchen, or bathroom.

(e) Testing is performed with a commercially available test kit or with a continuous radon monitor that can be calibrated. Testing shall be in accordance with the testing device manufacturer's instructions.

(f) Testing shall be performed by the builder, a registered design professional, or an approved third party.

(g) Testing shall extend at least 48 hours or to the minimum specified by the manufacturer, whichever is longer.

(h) Written radon test results shall be provided by the test lab or testing party. Written test results shall be included with construction documents.

(i) An additional pre-paid test kit shall be provided for the homeowner to use when they choose. The test kit shall include mailing or emailing the results from the testing lab to the homeowner.

(j) Where the radon test result is 4 pCi/L or greater, the fan for the radon vent pipe shall be installed.

(2) Testing results. A radon test done in accordance with § 11.902.3.2(1) and completed before occupancy receives a results of 2 pCi/L or less. 6

11.902.4 HVAC system protection. One of the following HVAC system protection measures is performed. . 3

(1) HVAC supply registers (boots), return grilles, and rough-ins are covered during construction activities to prevent dust and other pollutants from entering the system.

(2) Prior to owner occupancy, HVAC supply registers (boots), return grilles, and duct terminations are inspected and vacuumed. In addition, the coils are inspected and cleaned and the filter is replaced if necessary.

(3) If HVAC systems are to be operated, during construction, all return grilles have a temporary MERV 8 or higher filter installed in a manner ensuring no leakage around the filter.

11.902.5 Central vacuum systems. Central vacuum system is installed and vented to the outside. 3

11.902.6 Living space contaminants. The living space is sealed in accordance with § 11.701.4.3.1 to prevent unwanted contaminants. .... M

11.903 MOISTURE MANAGEMENT: VAPOR, RAINWATER, PLUMBING, HVAC

11.903.0 Intent. Moisture and moisture effects are controlled.

11.903.1 Plumbing

11.903.1.1 Cold water pipes in unconditioned spaces are insulated to a minimum of R-4 with pipe insulation or other covering that adequately prevents condensation. 2

11.903.1.2 Plumbing is not installed in unconditioned spaces. 5

GREEN BUILDING PRACTICES	M=Mandatory POINTS

11.903.2 Duct insulation. Ducts are in accordance with one of the following:

(1) All HVAC ducts, plenums, and trunks are located in conditioned space... **1**

(2) All HVAC ducts, plenums, and trunks are located in conditioned space and all HVAC ducts are insulated to a minimum of R4... **3**

11.903.3 Relative humidity. In climate zones 1A, 2A, 3A, 4A, and 5A as defined by Figure 6(1), equipment is installed to maintain relative humidity (RH) at or below 60% using one of the following:
[Points not awarded in other climate zones.].. **7**

(1) additional dehumidification system(s)

(2) central HVAC system equipped with additional controls to operate in dehumidification mode

11.904   INDOOR AIR QUALITY

11.904.0 Intent. IAQ is protected by best practices to control ventilation, moisture, pollutant sources and sanitation.

11.904.1 Indoor Air Quality (IAQ) during construction. Wood is dry before close-in (§ 11.602.1.7.1(3)), materials comply with emission criteria (§ 11.901.4 - 11.901.11), sources of water infiltration or condensation observed during construction have been eliminated, accessible interior surfaces are dry and free of visible suspect growth (per ASTM D7338 Section 6.3), and water damage (per ASTM D7338 Section 7.4.3)... **2**

11.904.2 Indoor Air Quality (IAQ) post completion. Verify there are no moisture, mold, and dust issues per § 11.602.1.7.1(3), § 11.901.4 - 11.901.11, ASTM D7338 Section 6.3, and ASTM D7338 Section 7.4.3. .. **3**

11.904.3 Microbial growth & moisture inspection and remediation. A visual inspection is performed to confirm the following:

(1) Verify that no visible signs of discoloration and microbial growth on ceilings, walls or floors, or other building assemblies; or if minor microbial growth is observed (less than within a total area of 25 sq. ft.) in homes or multifamily buildings, reference EPA Document 402-K-02-003 (A Brief Guide to Mold, Moisture, and Your Home) for guidance on how to properly remediate the issue. If microbial growth is observed, on a larger scale in homes or multifamily buildings (greater than 25 sq. ft.), reference EPA Document 402-K-01-001 (Mold Remediation in Schools and Commercial Buildings) for guidance on how to properly remediate the issue. .... **M**

(2) Verify that there are no visible signs of water damage or pooling. If signs of water damage or pooling are observed, verify that the source of the leak has been repaired, and that damaged materials are either properly dried or replaced as needed. .... **M**

11.905   INNOVATIVE PRACTICES

11.905.1 Humidity monitoring system. A humidity monitoring system is installed with a mobile base unit that displays readings of temperature and relative humidity. The system has a minimum of two remote sensor units. One remote unit is placed permanently inside the conditioned space in a central location, excluding attachment to exterior walls, and another remote sensor unit is placed permanently outside of the conditioned space. **2**

GREEN BUILDING PRACTICES	M=Mandatory POINTS

11.905.2 Kitchen exhaust. A kitchen exhaust unit(s) that equals or exceeds 400 cfm (189 L/s) is installed, and make-up air is provided. **2**

11.905.3 Enhanced air filtration. Meet all of the following. **2**

(1) Design for and install a secondary filter rack space for activated carbon filters.

(2) Provide the manufacturer's recommended filter maintenance schedule to the homeowner or building manager.

11.905.4 Sound barrier. Provide room-to-room privacy between bedrooms and adjacent living spaces within dwelling units or homes by achieving an articulation index (AI) between 0 and 0.15 per the criteria below. .... **1 SF / 4 MF**

Articulation Index 0 to 0.05 = STC greater than 55 (NIC greater than 47)
Articulation Index 0.05 to 0.15 = STC 52 – 55 (NIC 44 – 47)

11.905.5 Evaporative coil mold prevention. For buildings with a mechanical system for cooling, ultraviolet lamps are installed on the cooling coils and drain pans of the mechanical system supplies. Lamps produce ultraviolet radiation at a wavelength of 254 nm so as not to generate ozone. Lamps have ballasts housed in a NEMA-rated enclosure. **2**

11.905.6 Isolation of areas to be remodeled. To protect unrenovated spaces, meet one of the following: **3 max**

(1) Remodeled space is isolated from unrenovated space by masking of openings and HVAC returns and providing strip doors. **1**

(2) Remodeled space is isolated from unrenovated space by masking of openings and HVAC returns, providing strip doors, and the space is negatively pressurized by ducting exhaust to the exterior. **3**

(2) Remodeled space is isolated from unrenovated space by masking of openings and HVAC returns, providing strip doors, and a dedicated HEPA filtration system is installed. **3**

11.1001 HOMEOWNER'S MANUAL AND TRAINING GUIDELINES FOR ONE- AND TWO-FAMILY DWELLINGS

11.1001.0 Intent. Information on the building's use, maintenance, and green components is provided.

11.1001.1 Homeowner's manual. A homeowner's manual is provided and stored in a permanent location in the dwelling that includes the following, as available and applicable.
[1 Point awarded per two items. Points awarded for non-mandatory items.] .... **1 [8 max]**

(1) A National Green Building Standard certificate with web link and completion document. .... **M**

(2) List of green building features (can include the national green building checklist). .... **M**

(3) Product manufacturer's manuals or product data sheet for newly installed major equipment, fixtures, and appliances including product model numbers and serial numbers. If product data sheet is in the building owners' manual, manufacturer's manual may be attached to the appliance in lieu of inclusion in the building owners' manual. .... **M**

(4) Maintenance checklist.

(5) Information on local recycling and composting programs.

(6) Information on available local utility programs that purchase a portion of energy from renewable energy providers.

GREEN BUILDING PRACTICES	M=Mandatory POINTS

(7) Explanation of the benefits of using energy-efficient lighting systems [e.g., compact fluorescent light bulbs, light emitting diode (LED)] in high-usage areas.

(8) A list of practices to conserve water and energy.

(9) Information on the importance and operation of the home's fresh air ventilation system.

(10) Local public transportation options.

(11) A diagram showing the location of safety valves and controls for major building systems.

(12) Where frost-protected shallow foundations are used, owner is informed of precautions including:

    (a) instructions to not remove or damage insulation when modifying landscaping.

    (b) providing heat to the building as required by the IRC or IBC.

    (c) keeping base materials beneath and around the building free from moisture caused by broken water pipes or other water sources.

(13) A list of local service providers that offer regularly scheduled service and maintenance contracts to ensure proper performance of equipment and the structure (e.g., HVAC, water-heating equipment, sealants, caulks, gutter and downspout system, shower and/or tub surrounds, irrigation system).

(14) A photo record of framing with utilities installed. Photos are taken prior to installing insulation, clearly labeled, and included as part of the building owners' manual.

(15) List of common hazardous materials often used around the building and instructions for proper handling and disposal of these materials.

(16) Information on organic pest control, fertilizers, deicers, and cleaning products.

(17) Information on native landscape materials and/or those that have low-water requirements.

(18) Information on methods of maintaining the building's relative humidity in the range of 30% to 60%.

(19) Instructions for inspecting the building for termite infestation.

(20) Instructions for maintaining gutters and downspouts and importance of diverting water a minimum of 5 ft. away from foundation.

(21) A narrative detailing the importance of maintenance and operation in retaining the attributes of a green-built building.

(22) Where stormwater management measures are installed on the lot, information on the location, purpose, and upkeep of these measures.

(23) For buildings originally built before 1978, the EPA publications "Reducing Lead Hazards When Remodeling Your Home" and "Asbestos in Your Home: A Homeowner's Guide".

(24) Explanation of and benefits from green cleaning in the home.

(25) Retrofit energy calculator that provides baseline for future energy retrofits.

GREEN BUILDING PRACTICES	POINTS

11.1001.2 Training of initial building owners. Initial building owners are familiarized with the role of occupants in achieving green goals. Training is provided to the responsible party(ies) regarding newly installed equipment operation and maintenance, control systems, and occupant actions that will improve the environmental performance of the building. These include:... **M 8**

(1) HVAC filters

(2) thermostat operation and programming

(3) lighting controls

(4) appliances operation

(5) water heater settings and hot water use

(6) fan controls

(7) Recycling and composting practices

(8) Whole-dwelling mechanical ventilation systems

11.1002 CONSTRUCTION, OPERATION, AND MAINTENANCE MANUALS AND TRAINING FOR MULTIFAMILY BUILDINGS

11.1002.0 Intent. Manuals are provided to the responsible parties (owner, management, tenant, and/or maintenance team) regarding the construction, operation, and maintenance of the building. Paper or digital format manuals are to include information regarding those aspects of the building's construction, maintenance, and operation that are within the area of responsibilities of the respective recipient. One or more responsible parties are to receive a copy of all documentation for archival purposes.

11.1002.1 Building construction manual. A building construction manual, including five or more of the following, is compiled and distributed in accordance with § 11.1002.0.
[Points awarded per two items. Points awarded for non-mandatory items.] **1**

(1) A narrative detailing the importance of constructing a green building, including a list of green building attributes included in the building. This narrative is included in all responsible parties' manuals............ **M**

(2) A local green building program certificate as well as a copy of the *National Green Building Standard*, as adopted by the Adopting Entity, and the individual measures achieved by the building. .... **M**

(3) Warranty, operation, and maintenance instructions for all equipment, fixtures, appliances, and finishes... **M**

(4) Record drawings of the building.

(5) A record drawing of the site including stormwater management plans, utility lines, landscaping with common name and genus/species of plantings.

(6) A diagram showing the location of safety valves and controls for major building systems.

(7) A list of the type and wattage of light bulbs installed in light fixtures.

(8) A photo record of framing with utilities installed. Photos are taken prior to installing insulation and clearly labeled.

GREEN BUILDING PRACTICES	M=Mandatory POINTS

11.1002.2 Operations manual. Operations manuals are created and distributed to the responsible parties in accordance with § 11.1002.0. Among all of the operation manuals, five or more of the following options are included. *[Points awarded per two items. Points awarded for non-mandatory items.]* **1**

(1) A narrative detailing the importance of operating and living in a green building. This narrative is included in all responsible parties' manuals. .... **M**

(2) A list of practices to conserve water and energy (e.g., turning off lights when not in use, switching the rotation of ceiling fans in changing seasons, purchasing ENERGY STAR appliances and electronics). ...... **M**

(3) Information on methods of maintaining the building's relative humidity in the range of 30% to 60%.

(4) Information on opportunities to purchase renewable energy from local utilities or national green power providers and information on utility and tax incentives for the installation of on-site renewable energy systems.

(5) Information on local and on-site recycling and hazardous waste disposal programs and, if applicable, building recycling and hazardous waste handling and disposal procedures.

(6) Local public transportation options.

(7) Explanation of the benefits of using compact fluorescent light bulbs, LEDs, or other high-efficiency lighting.

(8) Information on native landscape materials and/or those that have low water requirements.

(9) Information on the radon mitigation system, where applicable.

(10) A procedure for educating tenants in rental properties on the proper use, benefits, and maintenance of green building systems including a maintenance staff notification process for improperly functioning equipment.

(11) Information on the importance and operation of the building's fresh air ventilation system.

11.1002.3 Maintenance manual. Maintenance manuals are created and distributed to the responsible parties in accordance with § 11.1002.0. Between all of the maintenance manuals, five or more of the following options are included. *[Points awarded for non-mandatory items.]* .... **1 per 2 items**

(1) A narrative detailing the importance of maintaining a green building. This narrative is included in all responsible parties' manuals. .... **M**

(2) A list of local service providers that offer regularly scheduled service and maintenance contracts to ensure proper performance of equipment and the structure (e.g., HVAC, water-heating equipment, sealants, caulks, gutter and downspout system, shower and/or tub surrounds, irrigation system).

(3) User-friendly maintenance checklist that includes:

(a) HVAC filters

(b) thermostat operation and programming

(c) lighting controls

(d) appliances and settings

(e) water heater settings

(f) fan controls

	M=Mandatory
GREEN BUILDING PRACTICES	**POINTS**

(4) List of common hazardous materials often used around the building and instructions for proper handling and disposal of these materials.

(5) Information on organic pest control, fertilizers, deicers, and cleaning products.

(6) Instructions for maintaining gutters and downspouts and the importance of diverting water a minimum of 5 ft. away from foundation.

(7) Instructions for inspecting the building for termite infestation.

(8) A procedure for rental tenant occupancy turnover that preserves the green features.

(9) An outline of a formal green building training program for maintenance staff.

(10) A green cleaning plan which includes guidance on sustainable cleaning products.

(11) A maintenance plan for active recreation and play spaces (e.g., playgrounds, ground markings, exercise equipment.

11.1002.4 Training of building owners. Building owners are familiarized with the role of occupants in achieving green goals. On-site training is provided to the responsible party(ies) regarding newly installed equipment operation and maintenance, control systems, and occupant actions that will improve the environmental performance of the building. .... **M 8**

These include:

(1) HVAC filters

(2) thermostat operation and programming

(3) lighting controls

(4) appliances operation

(5) water heater settings and hot water use

(6) fan controls

(7) recycling and composting practices

(8) Whole-dwelling mechanical ventilation system

11.1002.5 Multifamily occupant manual. An occupant manual is compiled and distributed in accordance with § 11.1002.0. *[Points awarded for non-mandatory items.]* .... **1 per 2 items**

(1) NGBS certificate.. **M**

(2) List of green building features .... **M**

(3) Operations manuals for all appliances and occupant operated equipment including lighting and ventilation controls, thermostats, etc. .... **M**

(4) Information on recycling and composting programs

(5) Information on purchasing renewable energy from utility

(6) Information on energy efficient replacement lamps

(7) List of practices to save water and energy

(8) Local public transportation options

(9) Explanation of benefits of green cleaning

GREEN BUILDING PRACTICES	M=Mandatory POINTS

11.1002.6 Training of multifamily occupants. Prepare a training outline, video or website that familiarizes occupants with their role in maintaining the green goals of the project. Include all equipment that the occupant(s) is expected to operate including but not limited to: .... **1 per 2 items**

(1) Lighting controls

(2) Ventilation controls

(3) Thermostat operation and programming

(4) Appliances operation

(5) Recycling and composting

(6) HVAC filters

(7) Water heater setting and hot water use

11.1003 PUBLIC EDUCATION

11.1003.0 Intent. Increase public awareness of the *National Green Building Standard®* and projects constructed in accordance with the NGBS to help increase demand for high-performance homes.

11.1003.1 Public Education. One or more of the following is implemented: .... **2 max**

(1) **Signage.** Signs showing the project is designed and built in accordance with the NGBS are posted on the construction site. **1**

(2) **Certification Plaques.** NGBS certification plaques with rating level attainted are placed in a conspicuous location near the utility area of the home or, in a conspicuous location near the main entrance of a multifamily building. **1**

(3) **Education.** A URL for the NGBS is included on site signage, builder website (or property website for multifamily buildings), and marketing materials for homes certified under the NGBS. **1**

11.1005 INNOVATIVE PRACTICES

11.1005.1 Appraisals. One or more of the following is implemented:

(1) Energy rating or projected usage data is posted in an appropriate location in the home, or public posting so that an appraiser can access the energy data for an energy efficiency property valuation.. **2**

(2) An Appraisal Institute Form 820.05 "Residential Green and Energy Addendum" or Form 821 "Commercial Green and energy Efficient Addendum" that consider NGBS, LEED, ENERGY STAR certifications and equivalent programs, is completed for the appraiser by a qualified professional or builder to use in performing the valuation of the property... **2**

(3) NGBS certification information or one of the Appraisal Institute Forms cited in § 11.1005.1(2) is uploaded to a multiple listing service (MLS) or equivalent database so that appraisers can access it to compare property valuations. **2**

INTENTIONALLY LEFT BLANK.

SECTION 12

CERTIFIED COMPLIANCE PATH FOR SINGLE-FAMILY HOMES, TOWNHOMES, AND DUPLEXES

M=Mandatory

GREEN BUILDING PRACTICES

1200 Substitution of practices. The adopting entity shall be permitted to substitute one or more practices with alternatives that achieve the overall intent of this standard. The determination of intent and equivalency is in the purview of the adopting entity.

1201 LOT DEVELOPMENT

1201.1 Floodplain. Construction shall not occur in a floodplain or construction shall be elevated above the floodplain.

1201.2 Lot slope. Finished grade at all sides of a building shall be sloped to provide a minimum of 6 in. (152 mm) of fall within 10 ft. (3048 mm) of the edge of the building. Where lot lines, walls, slopes, or other physical barriers prohibit 6 in. (152 mm) of fall within 10 ft. (3048 mm), the final grade shall be sloped away from the edge of the building at a minimum slope of 2%.

1201.3 Soil preparation for new plants. Soil shall be tilled or new soil shall be added down 6 in. for new plants and 12 in. for new trees. Soil shall be amended with organic matter, such as mulch or compost, as needed. Long acting sources of nutrients shall be added if the soil is deficient. Alternately, the landscaping plan shall incorporate the jurisdictional Department of Transportation (DOT) specifications (or equal) for soil preparation and amendment for landscape planning. Other approved sources such as University or County agricultural extension services shall be permitted for use.

1201.4 Regionally appropriate vegetation. When an Agency that has jurisdiction has developed a specification for planting, including non-invasive vegetation that is native or appropriate for local growing conditions, vegetation from that specification is selected for the landscaping plan and that landscaping is installed.

1201.5 Protection of natural resources. Any trees or other natural resources that do not conflict with the home construction or finished grading and drainage of the lot and adjacent lots shall be properly protected during construction and all controls shall be removed following construction. The landscape plan shall contain details for the protection and instructions for incorporation of the trees/areas into the final landscape plan.

1202 RESOURCE EFFICIENCY (DURABILITY)

1202.1 Capillary break. A capillary break and vapor retarder shall be installed at concrete slabs in accordance with IRC Sections R506.2.2 and R506.2.3.

1202.2 Foundation drainage. Where required by the IRC for habitable and usable spaces below grade, exterior drain tile shall be installed.

1202.3 Dampproof walls. Dampproof walls shall be provided below finished grade.

1202.4 Sealed crawlspace. 6-mil polyethylene sheeting, or other Class I vapor retarder shall be installed in accordance with § 408.3 or IRC Section 506.

GREEN BUILDING PRACTICES

1202.5 Dry Insulation. Insulation in cavities shall be dry in accordance with manufacturer's instructions before enclosing (e.g., with drywall).

1202.6 Water-resistive barrier. A water-resistive barrier and/or drainage plane system shall be installed in accordance with IRC requirements behind exterior veneer and/or siding.

1202.7 Flashing. Flashing shall be provided as follows to minimize water entry into wall and roof assemblies and to direct water to exterior surfaces or exterior water-resistive barriers for drainage. Flashing details shall be provided in the construction documents and shall be in accordance with the fenestration manufacturer's instructions, the flashing manufacturer's instructions, or as detailed by a registered design professional.

Flashing shall be installed at the following locations, as applicable:

(1) around exterior fenestrations, skylights, and doors

(2) at roof valleys

(3) at building-to-deck, -balcony, -porch, and -stair intersections

(4) at roof-to-wall intersections, at roof-to-chimney intersections, at wall-to-chimney intersections, and at parapets

(5) at ends of and under masonry, wood, or metal copings and sills

(6) above projecting wood trim

(7) at built-in roof gutters

(8) drip edge shall be installed at eave and rake edges

(9) window and door head and jamb flashing is either self-adhered flashing complying with AAMA 711 or liquid applied flashing complying with AAMA 714 and installed in accordance with flashing fenestration or manufacturer's installation instructions.

(10) pan flashing is installed at sills of all exterior windows and doors.

(11) seamless, preformed kickout flashing, or prefabricated metal with soldered seams is provided at all roof-to-wall intersections. The type and thickness of the material used for roof flashing including but not limited kickout and step flashing is commensurate with the anticipated service life of the roofing material.

(12) through-wall flashing is installed at transitions between wall cladding materials, or wall construction types

1202.8 Tile backing materials. Tile backing materials installed under tiled surfaces in wet areas shall be in accordance with ASTM C1178, C1278, C1288, or C1325. Tile shall not be installed over paper-faced drywall in wet areas.

1202.9 Ice and water shield. In areas where there has been a history of ice forming along the eaves causing a backup of water, an ice barrier shall be installed in accordance with the IRC at roof eaves of pitched roofs and shall extend a minimum of 24 in. (610 mm) inside the exterior wall line of the building.

1202.10 Architectural features. Horizontal ledgers shall be sloped away to provide gravity drainage as appropriate for the application.

1202.11 Visible suspect fungal growth. Building materials with visible suspect fungal growth shall not be installed or shall be addressed in accordance with industry recognized guidelines such as ANSI/IICRC S520 Mold Remediation or EPA 402-K-01-001 Table 2: Mold Remediation Guidelines, prior to concealment and

GREEN BUILDING PRACTICES

closing. Porous and semi-porous building materials should be stored in such a manner as to prevent excessive moisture content prior to installation or use. Relative humidity within the structure shall be controlled during construction to minimize the potential for microbial growth.

1202.12 Exterior doors. At least one entry at an exterior door assembly, inclusive of side lights (if any), are covered by one of the following methods to protect the building from the effects of precipitation and solar radiation. Either a storm door or a projection factor of 0.375 minimum is provided. Eastern- and western-facing entries in Climate Zones 1, 2, and 3, as determined in accordance with Figure 6(1) or Appendix A, have either a storm door or a projection factor of 1.0 minimum, unless protected from direct solar radiation by other means (e.g., screen wall, vegetation).

   (a) installing a porch roof or awning

   (b) extending the roof overhang

   (c) recessing the exterior door

   (d) installing a storm door

1202.13 Roof overhangs. Roof overhangs, in accordance with Table 602.1.12, are provided over a minimum of 90% of exterior walls to protect the building envelope.

1202.14 Roof Water discharge. Each downspout shall discharge 5 ft. from building, onto impervious surfaces, into areas designed to infiltrate drainage into the ground, to water vegetation, or into a rain collection system.

1203   ENERGY EFFICIENCY

1203.1 Mandatory requirements. The building shall comply with § 1203.1 through § 1203.9 in addition to one of the following: § 1203.10 (Energy Performance Path); § 1203.11 through § 1203.14 (Energy Prescriptive Path); or § 1203.15 (ERI Target Path). Sampling shall not be permitted for this alternative compliance path.

1203.2 Adopting entity review. A review by the Adopting Entity or approved third party shall be conducted to verify design and compliance with these energy requirements.

1203.3 Duct testing. Ducts shall be pressure tested to determine air leakage by one of the following methods:

(1) Rough-in test: Total leakage shall be measured with a pressure differential of 0.1 in. w.g. (25 Pa) across the system, including the manufacturer's air handler enclosure if installed at the time of the test. Registers shall be taped or otherwise sealed during the test.

(2) Post-construction test: Total leakage shall be measured with a pressure differential of 0.1 in. w.g. (25 Pa) across the entire system, including the manufacturer's air handler enclosure. Registers shall be taped or otherwise sealed during the test.

Exceptions: 1) A duct air-leakage test shall not be required where the ducts and air handlers are located entirely within the building thermal envelope; and 2) A duct air-leakage test shall not be required for ducts serving heat or energy recovery ventilators that are not integrated with ducts serving heating or cooling systems.

A written report of the results of the test shall be signed by the party conducting the test and provided to the code official.

GREEN BUILDING PRACTICES

1203.4 Radiant and hydronic space heating. Where installed as a primary heat source in the building, radiant or hydronic space heating system is designed, installed, and documented, using industry-approved guidelines and standards (e.g., ACCA Manual J, AHRI I=B=R, ACCA 5 QI, or an accredited design professional's and manufacturer's recommendations).

1203.5 Building thermal envelope air sealing. The building thermal envelope is durably sealed to limit infiltration. The sealing methods between dissimilar materials allow for differential expansion and contraction. The following are caulked, gasketed, weather-stripped or otherwise sealed with an air barrier material, suitable film, or solid material:

(a) All joints, seams and penetrations

(b) Site-built windows, doors, and skylights

(c) Openings between window and door assemblies and their respective jambs and framing

(d) Utility penetrations

(e) Dropped ceilings or chases adjacent to the thermal envelope

(f) Knee walls

(g) Walls and ceilings separating a garage from conditioned spaces

(h) Behind tubs and showers on exterior walls

(i) Common walls between dwelling units

(j) Attic access openings

(k) Rim joist junction

(l) Other sources of infiltration

1203.6 Air sealing and insulation. Insulation shall be installed to Grade I. Grade II and Grade III insulation shall not be permitted. Building envelope air tightness and insulation installation shall be verified to be in accordance with the following.

(A) Testing is conducted in accordance with ASTM E 779 using a blower door at a pressure of 1.04 psf (50 pa). Testing is conducted after rough-in and installation of penetrations in the building envelope, including but not limited to penetrations for utilities, electrical, plumbing, ventilation and combustion appliances. Testing is to be conducted under the following conditions:

(a) Exterior windows and doors, fireplace and stove doors are closed, but not sealed;

(b) Dampers are closed, but not sealed, including exhaust, intake, make-up air, backdraft and flue dampers;

(c) Interior doors are open;

(d) Exterior openings for continuous ventilation systems and heat recovery ventilators are closed and sealed;

(e) Heating, cooling, and ventilation systems are turned off;

(f) HVAC duct terminations are not sealed; and

(g) Supply and return registers are not sealed.

(B) Visual inspection. The air barrier and insulation items listed in Table 1203.6(B) shall be field verified by visual inspection.

Table 1203.6(B)
Air Barrier and Insulation Installation

COMPONENT	AIR BARRIER CRITERIA	INSULATION INSTALLATION CRITERIA
General requirements	A continuous air barrier shall be installed in the building envelope. The exterior thermal envelope contains a continuous air barrier. Breaks or joints in the air barrier shall be sealed.	Air-permeable insulation shall not be used as a sealing material.
Ceiling/attic	The air barrier in any dropped ceiling/soffit shall be aligned with the insulation and any gaps in the air barrier shall be sealed. Access openings, drop down stairs or knee wall doors to unconditioned attic spaces shall be sealed.	The insulation in any dropped ceiling/soffit shall be aligned with the air barrier.
Walls	The junction of the foundation and sill plate shall be sealed. The junction of the top plate and the top of exterior walls shall be sealed. Knee walls shall be sealed.	Cavities within corners and headers of frame walls shall be insulated by completely filling the cavity with a material having a thermal resistance of R-3 per inch minimum. Exterior thermal envelope insulation for framed walls shall be installed in substantial contact and continuous alignment with the air barrier.
Windows, skylights and doors	The space between window/doorjambs and framing, and skylights and framing shall be sealed.	
Rim joists	Rim joists shall include the air barrier.	Rim joists shall be insulated.
Floors (including above garage and cantilevered floors)	The air barrier shall be installed at any exposed edge of insulation.	Floor framing cavity insulation shall be installed to maintain permanent contact with the underside of subfloor decking, or floor framing cavity insulation shall be permitted to be in contact with the top side of sheathing, or continuous insulation installed on the underside of floor framing and extends from the bottom to the top of all perimeter floor framing members.
Crawl space walls	Exposed earth in unvented crawl spaces shall be covered with a Class I vapor retarder with overlapping joints taped.	Where provided instead of floor insulation, insulation shall be permanently attached to the crawlspace walls.
Shafts, penetrations	Duct shafts, utility penetrations, and flue shafts opening to exterior or unconditioned space shall be sealed.	
Narrow cavities		Batts in narrow cavities shall be cut to fit, or narrow cavities shall be filled by insulation that on installation readily conforms to the available cavity space.
Garage separation	Air sealing shall be provided between the garage and conditioned spaces.	
Recessed lighting	Recessed light fixtures installed in the building thermal envelope shall be sealed to the drywall.	Recessed light fixtures installed in the building thermal envelope shall be air tight and IC rated.
Plumbing and wiring		Batt insulation shall be cut neatly to fit around wiring and plumbing in exterior walls, or insulation that on installation readily conforms to available space shall extend behind piping and wiring.
Shower/tub on exterior wall	The air barrier installed at exterior walls adjacent to showers and tubs shall separate them from the showers and tubs.	Exterior walls adjacent to showers and tubs shall be insulated.
Electrical/phone box on exterior walls	The air barrier shall be installed behind electrical or communication boxes or air-sealed boxes shall be installed.	
HVAC register boots	HVAC register boots that penetrate building thermal envelope shall be sealed to the subfloor or drywall.	
Concealed sprinklers	When required to be sealed, concealed fire sprinklers shall only be sealed in a manner that is recommended by the manufacturer. Caulking or other adhesive sealants shall not be used to fill voids between fire sprinkler cover plates and walls or ceilings.	

a. In addition, inspection of log walls shall be in accordance with the provisions of ICC-400.

M=Mandatory

GREEN BUILDING PRACTICES

1203.7 High-efficacy lighting. A minimum of 90% of the total hard-wired lighting fixtures or the bulbs in those fixtures qualify as high efficacy or equivalent.

1203.8 Appliances. If installed, refrigerator, dishwasher, and/or washing machine shall be ENERGY STAR or equivalent.

1203.9 Clothes washers. Where installed, clothes washers rated with an IWF (integrated water factor), MEF (modified energy factor), or IMEF (integrated modified energy factor), shall be rated as follows:

(1) Residential Clothes Washers, Front-loading,
     greater than 2.5 cu-ft maximum 3.2 IWF, minimum IMEF 2.76

(2) Residential Clothes Washers, Top-loading,
     greater than 2.5 cu-ft maximum 4.3 IWF, minimum IMEF 2.06

(3) Residential Clothes Washers,
     less than or equal to 2.5 cu-ft maximum 4.2 IWF, minimum IMEF 2.07

1203.10 Energy performance pathway.

1203.10.1 ICC IECC analysis. Energy efficiency features are implemented to achieve energy cost or source energy performance that exceeds the ICC IECC by 7.5%. A documented analysis using software in accordance with ICC IECC Section R405 is required.

1203.10.2 Energy performance analysis. Energy savings levels above the ICC IECC are determined through an analysis that includes improvements in building envelope, air infiltration, heating system efficiencies, cooling system efficiencies, duct sealing, water heating system efficiencies, lighting, and appliances.

1203.11 Energy prescriptive pathway.

1203.11.1 Building envelope. The building thermal envelope complies with § 1203.11.1.1 or § 1203.11.1.2. Exception: Section 1203.11.1.1 is not required for Tropical Climate Zone.

1203.11.1.1 Insulation and fenestration requirements. The building thermal envelope shall meet the requirements of Table 1203.11.1.1 and 1203.11.1.2.

1203.11.1.2 The total UA proposed and baseline calculations are documented where the total proposed building thermal envelope UA is less than or equal to the total baseline UA resulting from multiplying the U-factors in Table 1203.11.1.2 by the same assembly area as in the proposed building. REScheck is deemed to provide UA calculation documentation. SHGC requirements of Table 1203.11.1.1 shall be met.

Table 1203.11.1.1
Insulation and Fenestration Requirements by Component[a]

Climate Zone	Fenestration[b] U-Factor	Skylight[b] U-Factor	Glazed Fenestration SHGC[b,e]	Ceiling R-Value[i]	Wood Frame Wall R-Value	Mass Wall R-Value[i]	Floor R-Value	Basement[c] Wall R-Value	Slab[d] R-Value & Depth	Crawlspace[c] Wall R-Value
1	NR	0.75	0.25	30	13	3/4	13	0	0	0
2	0.40	0.65	0.25	38	13	4/6	13	0	0	0
3	0.32	0.55	0.25	38	20 OR 13+5[h]	8/13	19	5/13[f]	0	5/13
4 except Marine	0.32	0.55	0.40	49	20 OR 13+5[h]	8/13	19	10/13	10, 2 ft	10/13
5 and Marine 4	0.30	0.55	NR	49	20 OR 13+5[h]	13/17	30[g]	15/19	10, 2 ft	15/19
6	0.30	0.55	NR	49	20+5h OR 13+10[h]	15/20	30[g]	15/19	10, 4 ft	15/19
7 and 8	0.30	0.55	NR	49	20+5h OR 13+10[h]	19/21	38[g]	15/19	10, 4 ft	15/19

NR = Not Required

For SI: 1 foot = 304.8 mm.

a. R-values are minimums. U-factors and SHGC are maximums. Where insulation is installed in a cavity that is less than the label or design thickness of the insulation, the installed R-value of the insulation shall be not less than the R-value specified in the table.

b. The fenestration U-factor column excludes skylights. The SHGC column applies to all glazed fenestration.
Exception: In Climate Zones 1 through 3, skylights shall be permitted to be excluded from glazed fenestration SHGC requirements provided that the SHGC for such skylights does not exceed 0.30.

c. "10/13" means R-10 continuous insulation on the interior or exterior of the home or R-13 cavity insulation on the interior of the basement wall. "15/19" means R-15 continuous insulation on the interior or exterior of the home or R-19 cavity insulation at the interior of the basement wall. Alternatively, compliance with "15/19" shall be R-13 cavity insulation on the interior of the basement wall plus R-5 continuous insulation on the interior or exterior of the home.

d. R-5 insulation shall be provided under the full slab area of a heated slab in addition to the required slab edge insulation R-value for slabs. as indicated in the table. The slab edge insulation for heated slabs shall not be required to extend below the slab.

e. There are no SHGC requirements in the Marine Zone.

f. Basement wall insulation is not required in warm-humid locations as defined by ICC IECC Figure R301.1 and ICC IECC Table R301.1.

g. Alternatively, insulation sufficient to fill the framing cavity and providing not less than an R-value of R-19.

h. The first value is cavity insulation, the second value is continuous insulation. Therefore, as an example, "13+5" means R-13 cavity insulation plus R-5 continuous insulation.

i. Mass walls shall be in accordance with ICC IECC Section R402.2.5. The second R-value applies where more than half of the insulation is on the interior of the mass wall.

Table 1203.11.1.2
Equivalent U-Factors[a]

Climate Zone	Fenestration U-Factor	Skylight U-Factor	Ceiling U-Factor	Frame Wall U-Factor	Mass Wall U-Factor[b]	Floor U-Factor	Basement Wall U-Factor	Crawlspace Wall U-Factor
1	0.50	0.75	0.035	0.084	0.197	0.064	0.360	0.477
2	0.40	0.65	0.030	0.084	0.165	0.064	0.360	0.477
3	0.32	0.55	0.030	0.060	0.098	0.047	0.091[c]	0.136
4 except Marine	0.32	0.55	0.026	0.060	0.098	0.047	0.059	0.065
5 and Marine 4	0.30	0.55	0.026	0.060	0.082	0.033	0.050	0.055
6	0.30	0.55	0.026	0.045	0.060	0.033	0.050	0.055
7 and 8	0.30	0.55	0.026	0.045	0.057	0.028	0.050	0.055

a. Non-fenestration U-factors shall be obtained from measurement, calculation, or an approved source.

b. Mass walls shall be in accordance with Section R402.2.5. Where more than half the insulation is on the interior, the mass wall U-factors shall not exceed 0.17 in Climate Zone 1, 0.14 in Climate Zone 2, 0.12 in Climate Zone 3, 0.087 in Climate Zone 4 except Marine, 0.065 in Climate Zone 5 and Marine 4, and 0.57 in Climate Zones 6 through 8.

GREEN BUILDING PRACTICES

1203.12 Space heating and cooling and water heating system efficiencies. The Space Heating and Cooling and Water Heating systems are in accordance with Table 1203.12.

Table 1203.12
Space Heating and Cooling and Water Heating System Efficiencies

Climate Zone	Space Cooling System	Space Heating System - select 1 option from below				Water Heating System - select 1 option from below		
	AC	Gas Furnace	Gas Boiler	ASHP	GSHP or WSHP	Gas Tank WH	Gas Tankless WH	Elec Tank WH
	Min. Req.	Min. Req.	Min. Req.	Min. Req.	Min. Req.	Min. UEF Req.	Min. UEF Req.	Min. UEF Req.
1	15 SEER**	NR	85%	NR	Any	0.78	>.93	>.92
2	15 SEER**	NR	85%	NANR	Any	0.78	>.93	>.92
3	15 SEER**	92%	85%	≥ 8.5 HSPF*	Any	0.78	>.93	>.92
4	15 SEER**	92%	85%	≥ 8.5 HSPF*	Any	0.78	>.93	>.92
5	14 SEER	95%	85%	≥ 8.5 HSPF*	Any	0.78	>.93	>.92
6	14 SEER	95%	85%	≥ 8.5 HSPF*	Any	0.78	>.93	>.92
7	14 SEER	95%	85%	≥ 8.5 HSPF*	Any	0.78	>.93	>.92
8	14 SEER	95%	85%	≥ 8.5 HSPF*	Any	↓	>.93	>.92

* ≥ 8.2 HSPF for single package
**zones 1-4 ≥12.5 EER for split; ≥12 EER for single package
NR = No requirement

1203.13 Duct leakage. The total leakage of the ducts, where measured in accordance with Section R403.3.3, shall be as follows:

(1) Rough-in test: The total leakage shall be less than or equal to 4 cubic feet per minute (113.3 L/min) per 100 sq. ft. (9.29 m^2) of conditioned floor area where the air handler is installed at the time of the test. Where the air handler is not installed at the time of the test, the total leakage shall be less than or equal to 3 cubic feet per minute (85 L/min) per 100 sq. ft. (9.29 m^2) of conditioned floor area.

(2) Postconstruction test: Total leakage shall be less than or equal to 4 cubic feet per minute (113.3 L/min) per 100 sq. ft. (9.29 m^2) of conditioned floor area.

1203.14 High-efficacy lighting. A minimum of 95% of the total hard-wired lighting fixtures or the bulbs in those fixtures qualify as high efficacy or equivalent.

1203.15 ERI target pathway.

1203.15.1 ERI target compliance. Energy efficiency features are implemented to achieve an ERI performance that is 8 points less than the EPA National ERI Target Procedure for ENERGY STAR Certified Homes version 3.0 as computed based on Step 1 of the EPA National ERI Target Procedure. Dwelling ratings shall be submitted to a quality control registry approved by the Adopting Entity for calculating points under this section.

GREEN BUILDING PRACTICES

1204   WATER EFFICIENCY

1204.1 Lavatory faucets. Water-efficient lavatory faucets in bathrooms shall have a maximum flow rate of 1.5 gpm (5.68 L/min), tested at 60 psi (414 kPa) in accordance with ASME A112.18.1/CSA B125.1.

1204.2 Water closets. Water closets shall have an effective flush volume of 1.28 gallons or less and shall be in accordance with the performance criteria of the EPA WaterSense Specification for tank-type toilets.

1204.3 Irrigation systems. Where an irrigation system is installed, one of the following is met:

(1) Drip irrigation is installed for all landscape beds and/or subsurface drip irrigation is installed for all turf grass areas.

(2) Irrigation zones are organized by plant water needs.

(3) The irrigation system(s) is controlled by a climate-based controller or soil moisture controller.

(4) No irrigation is installed.

1204.4 Alternative Compliance Path. Water Rating Index (WRI) needs to achieve a level 70.

1205   INDOOR ENVIRONMENTAL QUALITY

1205.1 Gas-fired fireplaces and direct heating equipment. Gas-fired fireplaces and direct heating equipment is listed and is installed in accordance with the NFPA 54, ICC IFGC, or the applicable local gas appliance installation code. Gas-fired fireplaces within dwelling units and direct heating equipment are vented to the outdoors.

1205.2 Solid fuel-burning fireplaces, inserts, stoves and heaters. Solid fuel-burning fireplaces, inserts, stoves and heaters are code compliant and are in accordance with one or more of the following requirements:

(1) Site-built masonry wood-burning fireplaces use outside combustion air and include a means of sealing the flue and the combustion air outlets to minimize interior air (heat) loss when not in operation.

(2) Factory-built, wood-burning fireplaces are in accordance with the certification requirements of UL 127 and are EPA certified or Phase 2 Qualified.

(3) Wood stove and fireplace inserts, as defined in UL 1482 Section 3.8, are in accordance with the certification requirements of UL 1482 and are in accordance with the emission requirements of the EPA Certification and the State of Washington WAC 173-433-100(3).

(4) Pellet (biomass) stoves and furnaces are in accordance with ASTM E1509 or are EPA certified.

(5) Masonry heaters are in accordance with the definitions in ASTM E1602 and IBC Section 2112.1.

(6) Fireplaces, woodstoves, pellet stoves, or masonry heaters are not installed.

1205.3 Garages. Garages shall be in accordance with "a" or "b":

(a) Attached garage

(1) Doors installed in the common wall between the attached garage and conditioned space are tightly sealed and gasketed; and

(2) A continuous air barrier is provided separating the garage space from the conditioned living spaces.

(b) A carport is installed, the garage is detached from the building, or no garage is installed.

GREEN BUILDING PRACTICES

1205.4 Carpets. Wall-to-wall carpeting shall not be installed adjacent to

(a) water closets and bathing fixtures, and

(b) exterior doors.

1205.5 Carbon monoxide (CO) alarms. A carbon monoxide (CO) alarm shall be provided in accordance with IRC Section R315 in any dwelling unit with a combustion fueled appliance or an attached garage with an opening that communicates with the dwelling unit.

1205.6 Interior architectural coatings. A minimum of 85% of the interior architectural coatings are in accordance with one or more of the following:

(1) Low VOC as determined by EPA Method 24 (VOC content is below the detection limit for the method)

(2) Green Seal GS-11

(3) CARB Suggested Control Measure for Architectural Coatings (see Table 901.9.1).

1205.7 Local ventilation. shall be in accordance with the following:

(1) Bathrooms are vented to the outdoors. The minimum tested ventilation rate is 50 cfm (23.6 L/s) for intermittent operation or 20 cfm (9.4 L/s) for continuous operation in bathrooms. Exhaust fans are ENERGY STAR, or equivalent.

(2) Kitchen exhaust units and/or range hoods are ducted to the outdoors and have a minimum ventilation rate of 100 cfm (47.2 L/s) for intermittent operation or 25 cfm (11.8 L/s) for continuous operation.

(3) Bathroom and kitchen exhaust ventilation rates are tested to meet minimum ventilation rates or ducts are installed to meet the prescriptive requirements in IRC Table M1504.2.

1205.8 Whole Dwelling Ventilation. One of the following whole dwelling ventilation systems shall be implemented and shall be in accordance with the specifications of ASHRAE Standard 62.2-2010 Section 4. An explanation of the operation and importance of the ventilation system shall be included in the homeowner's manual practice.

(1) exhaust air ventilation system equipped with outdoor air ducts and intake(s) for ventilation air.

(2) exhaust air ventilation system equipped with outdoor air ducts and intake(s) for ventilation air and with automatic ventilation controls to limit ventilation air during periods of extreme temperature, extreme humidity and/or during times of peak utility loads.

(3) supply air ventilation system.

(4) supply air ventilation system equipped with automatic ventilation controls to limit ventilation air during periods of extreme temperature, extreme humidity and/or during times of peak utility loads.

(5) balanced air ventilation system with exhaust and supply fan(s) with supply intakes located in accordance with the manufacturer's guidelines to not introduce polluted air back into the building.

(6) heat-recovery ventilator.

(7) balanced air ventilation system with exhaust and supply fan(s) with automatic ventilation controls to limit ventilation air during periods of extreme temperature, extreme humidity and/or during times of peak utility loads, and with intakes located in accordance with the manufacturer's guidelines to not introduce polluted air back in to the building.

(8) energy-recovery ventilator

M=Mandatory

GREEN BUILDING PRACTICES

1205.9 Radon control. Radon control measures are installed in accordance with 902.3 for Zone 1 as defined in Figure 9(1).

(a) a passive radon system is installed, or

(b) an active radon system is installed

1205.10 Kitchen exhaust. If a kitchen exhaust unit(s) that equals or exceeds 400 cfm (189 L/s) is installed, make-up air shall be provided.

1205.11 MERV filters. Minimum 8 MERV filters shall be installed on central forced air systems and are accessible.

1205.12 HVAC system protection. One of the following HVAC system protection measures shall be performed.

(a) HVAC supply registers (boots), return grilles, and rough-ins are covered during construction activities to prevent dust and other pollutants from entering the system.

(b) Prior to owner occupancy, HVAC supply registers (boots), return grilles, and duct terminations are inspected and vacuumed. In addition, the coils are inspected and cleaned, and the filter is replaced if necessary.

1206   HOMEOWNER OPERATION AND MAINTAINANCE

1206.1 Homeowner's manual. A homeowner's manual shall be provided. The homeowner's manual shall include all items below:

(1) A National Green Building Standard certificate with a web link and completion document.

(2) List of green building features (can include the National Green Building Standard checklist).

(3) Product manufacturer's manuals or product data sheet for installed major equipment, fixtures, and appliances. If product data sheet is in the building owners' manual, manufacturer's manual may be attached to the appliance in lieu of inclusion in the building owners' manual.

(4) Maintenance checklist.

(5) Information on the importance and operation of the home's fresh air ventilation system.

(6) Provide information on regionally-appropriate vegetation from the local authority with jurisdiction.

(7) A narrative detailing the importance of maintenance and operation of the green building features from the National Green Building Standard checklist in retaining the attributes of a green-built home.

(8) Where stormwater management measures are installed on the lot, information on the location, purpose, and upkeep of these measures.

M=Mandatory

GREEN BUILDING PRACTICES	

1206.2 Training of initial homeowners. Initial homeowners shall be familiarized with the role of occupants in achieving green goals. Training is provided to the responsible party(ies) regarding equipment operation and maintenance, control systems, and occupant role. These include:

(1) HVAC filters

(2) Water heater settings

(3) Whole-house ventilation systems

(4) Operation of household equipment

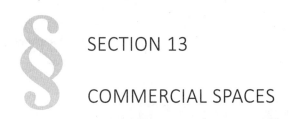

SECTION 13

COMMERCIAL SPACES

GREEN BUILDING PRACTICES

13.101 INTENT AND SCOPE

13.101.1 Intent. This chapter shall provide green requirements for the non-residential portion(s) of a mixed-use building.

13.101.2 Scope. The provisions of this Chapter shall apply to the design, construction, addition, and alteration of non-residential portion(s) of a mixed-use building.

13.102 COMPLIANCE

13.102.1 Compliance. The non-residential portion(s) of a mixed-use building shall comply with all provisions of this chapter as applicable. The provisions of this Chapter are mandatory.

13.102.1.1 Core and shell compliance. The exterior air barrier, insulation, air sealing, and fenestration, are verified to the requirements of this chapter at the time of certification.

13.102.1.2 Full mixed-use building compliance. Residential and non-residential spaces are verified to the requirements of this standard at the time of certification. The residential portions of the building are verified to the requirements of Chapters 5 through 10 of this Standard. The non-residential portion(s) of the building must comply with the requirements of this chapter.

13.102.1.3 Additions and alterations. The provisions of this Chapter shall only apply to areas of the building that are exposed or created during the remodel of mixed-use building(s) complying with § 305, Green Remodeling.

13.102.1.4 Alternate compliance. Non-residential portions of a building shall comply with ICC IgCC Section 501.3.7.2 and Chapters 6 through 10.

Exception: Section 6.3.1 of the ICC IgCC.

13.103 BICYCLE PARKING

13.103.1 Bicycle parking. Bicycle parking shall comply with § 13.103.1.1 through § 13.103.1.2

13.103.1.1 Minimum number of spaces. The minimum number of required bicycle parking spaces shall be 4 parking spaces.

Exceptions: 1) The number of bicycle parking spaces shall be allowed to be reduced subject to Adopting Entity approval; 2) bicycle parking shall not be required where the total non-residential conditioned space in the building is less than 1,000 sq. ft.; and 3) The minimum number of spaces shall be permitted to be reduced by the authority having jurisdiction based on the occupants expected use of public transit or walking to the building.

13.103.1.2 Location. The bicycle parking must be located on the same building site or within the building. It must be located within 100 ft. of, and visible from, the main entrance.

GREEN BUILDING PRACTICES

13.104 RESOURCE EFFICIENCY

13.104.1 Enhanced durability.

13.104.1.1 Capillary break. A capillary break and vapor retarder shall be installed under the concrete slabs in accordance with IBC Sections 1907, excluding exception #3 and 1805.2.1.

13.104.1.2 Foundation drainage. Where required by the IBC for habitable and usable spaces below grade, exterior drain tile is installed.

13.104.1.3 Dampproof walls. Walls that retain earth, and encloses interior space are required to be dampproof per IBC Section 1805.

13.104.1.4 Water-resistive barrier. Where required by the IBC, a water-resistive barrier and/or drainage plane system is installed behind exterior cladding.

13.104.1.5 Flashing. Flashing is provided as follows to minimize water entry into wall and roof assemblies and to direct water to exterior surfaces or exterior water-resistive barriers for drainage. Flashing details are provided in the construction documents and are in accordance with the fenestration manufacturer's instructions, the flashing manufacturer's instructions, or as detailed by a registered design professional.

Flashing is installed at the following locations, as applicable unless in conflict with manufacturer's installation instructions:

(1) Around exterior fenestrations, skylights, and doors;

(2) At roof valleys;

(3) At all building-to-deck, -balcony, -porch, and -stair intersections;

(4) At roof-to-wall intersections, at roof-to-chimney intersections, at wall-to-chimney intersections, and at parapets;

(5) At ends of and under masonry, wood, or metal copings and sills;

(6) Above projecting wood trim;

(7) At built-in roof gutters;

(8) Drip edge is installed at eave and rake edges;

(9) Window and door head and jamb flashing is either self-adhered or liquid applied;

(10) Flashing is installed at exterior windows and doors;

(11) Through-wall flashing is installed at transitions between wall cladding materials or wall construction types; and

(12) Flashing is installed at the expansion joint in stucco walls.

13.104.1.6 Tile backing materials. Tile backing materials installed under tiled surfaces in wet areas are in accordance with ASTM C1178, C1278, C1288, or C1325. Tile shall not be installed over paper-faced gypsum board in wet areas.

13.104.1.7 Ice barrier. In areas where there has been a history of ice forming along the eaves causing a backup of water, an ice barrier is installed in accordance with the IBC at roof eaves of pitched roofs and extends a minimum of 24 in. (610 mm) inside the exterior wall line of the building.

GREEN BUILDING PRACTICES

13.104.1.8 Architectural features. Architectural features that increase the potential for water intrusion are avoided, and must comply with the following:

(1) Horizontal ledgers are sloped away to provide gravity drainage as appropriate for the application.

(2) No roof configurations that create horizontal valleys in roof design, unless directed to a drain on a flat roof.

(3) No recessed windows and architectural features that trap water on horizontal surfaces

13.104.1.9 Moisture control measures. Moisture control measures for newly installed materials are in accordance with the following:

(1) Building materials with visible mold are not installed or are cleaned or encapsulated prior to concealment and closing.

(2) Insulation in cavities is dry in accordance with manufacturer's installation instructions when enclosed (e.g., with drywall).

13.104.2 Construction material and waste management plan. A written construction waste management plan is posted at the jobsite and implemented.

13.104.3 Core and shell material selection. The core and shell of the non-residential portion of the building must contain similar green material selections of the residential portion of the building and must comply with the additional provisions of this section.

13.104.3.1 Material selection. At least six of these sections must be met from the following:

(1) Biobased products § 606.1

(2) Wood-based products § 606.2

(3) Manufacturing energy § 606.3

(4) Resource-efficient materials § 608.1

(5) Regional materials § 609.1

(6) Product LCA § 610.1.2.1

(7) Building assembly LCA § 610.1.2.2

(8) Manufacturer's environmental management system concepts § 612.1

(9) Sustainable products § 612.2

(10) Salvaged materials § 603.2

(11) Product declarations § 611.1.1 and § 611.1.2

(12) Recycled content § 604.1

13.104.4 Recycling and composting. A readily accessible space(s) adequate to accommodate the recycling and composting containers for materials accepted in local recycling/composting programs is provided and identified on the floorplan.

GREEN BUILDING PRACTICES

13.105 ENERGY EFFICIENCY

13.105.1 Building thermal envelope insulation. The non-residential portion of the building must comply with the insulation requirements of ICC IECC Sections C402.1 through C402.3 as applicable, and § 13.105.1.1. A UA tradeoff shall be allowed for § 13.105.1 and § 13.105.2 is equal to or less than the ICC IECC UA.

Maximum UA. For ICC IECC residential, the total building UA is less than or equal to the total maximum UA as computed by 2015 ICC IECC Section R02.1.5. For ICC IECC commercial, the total UA is less than or equal to the sum of the UA for 2015 ICC IECC Tables C402.1.4 and C402.4, including the U-factor times the area and C-factor or F-factor times the perimeter. The total UA proposed and baseline calculations are documented. REScheck or COMcheck is deemed to provide UA calculation documentation.

13.105.1.1 Insulation installation. Insulation installed in the thermal envelope shall be visually inspected for compliance with Grade I installation. Grade II insulation is only permitted where exterior continuous insulation is installed. Grade III insulation installation is not permitted.

13.105.2 Building thermal envelope fenestration. The non-residential portion of the building shall be in accordance with the requirements of the ICC IECC Section C402.4 as applicable.

13.105.3 Building thermal envelope air sealing. The building thermal envelope is durably sealed to limit infiltration. The sealing methods between dissimilar materials allow for differential expansion and contraction. The following are caulked, gasketed, weather-stripped or otherwise sealed with an air barrier material, suitable film, or solid material:

(1) All joints, seams and penetrations

(2) Site-built windows, doors and skylights

(3) Openings between window and door assemblies and their respective jambs and framing

(4) Utility penetrations

(5) Dropped ceilings or chases adjacent to the thermal envelope

(6) Knee walls

(7) Walls and ceilings separating the garage from conditioned spaces

(8) Behind tubs and showers on exterior walls

(9) Cantilevers

(10) Attic access openings

(11) Rim joists junction

(12) Other sources of infiltration

13.105.3.1 Air barrier verification. If not previously verified, the air barrier shall be visually inspected to demonstrate compliance with Table 701.4.3.2(2) and shall comply with the requirements of ICC IECC C402.5.

13.105.4 Energy metering. Energy metering shall be provided for each tenant individually for the non-residential portions of the building.

Exception: non-residential spaces under 10,000 sq. ft.

13.105.5 Efficiency of HVAC equipment. HVAC equipment shall meet the minimum efficiency requirements listed in ICC IECC Tables C403.3.2(1) through C403.3.2(7).

GREEN BUILDING PRACTICES

13.105.6 Efficiency of Service Water Heating equipment. Service Water Heating equipment shall meet the minimum efficiency requirements listed in ICC IECC Table C404.2.

13.105.7 Lighting. The total interior lighting power allowance shall be less than the total lighting power allowance in accordance with ICC IECC Section C405.3.2.

13.105.8 Commissioning.

13.105.8.1 Mechanical and service water heating systems. Mechanical and service water heating systems shall comply with ICC IECC Section C408.2.

13.105.9 Calculation of heating and cooling loads. Design loads associated with heating, ventilating and air conditioning of the building shall be determined in accordance with ASHRAE/ACCA Standard 183 or by an approved equivalent computational procedure and using the design parameters specified in ICC IECC Chapter 3. Heating and cooling loads shall be adjusted to account for load reductions that are achieved where energy recovery systems are utilized in the HVAC system in accordance with the ASHRAE HVAC Systems and Equipment Handbook or an approved equivalent computational procedure.

13.105.10 Duct air sealing. Ductwork shall be constructed in accordance with the IMC.

13.105.11 Heated-water circulation and temperature maintenance. Where installed, heated-water circulation systems shall be in accordance with § 13.105.11.1. Heat trace temperature maintenance systems shall be in accordance with § 13.105.11.2. Controls for hot water storage shall be in accordance with § 13.105.11.3. Automatic controls, temperature sensors, and pumps shall be in a location that is accessible. Manual controls shall be in a location with ready access.

13.105.11.1 Circulation systems. Heated-water circulation systems shall be provided with a circulation pump. The system return pipe shall be a dedicated return pipe, or a cold water supply pipe. Gravity and thermos-syphon circulation systems shall be prohibited. Controls for circulation hot water system pumps shall start the pump based on the identification of a demand for hot water. The controls shall automatically turn off the pump when the water in the circulation loop is at the desired temperature and when there is not a demand for hot water.

13.105.11.2 Heat trace systems. Electric heat trace systems shall comply with ICC IECC 505.1. Controls for such systems shall be able to automatically adjust the energy input to the heat tracing to maintain the desired water temperature in the piping in accordance with the times when heated water is used in the occupancy. Heat trace shall be arranged to be turned off automatically when there is not a demand for hot water.

13.105.11.3 Controls for hot water storage. The controls on pumps that circulate water between a water heater and a heated water storage tank shall limit the operation of the pump from the heating cycle startup to not greater than 5 minutes at the end of the cycle.

13.105.12 Energy options. Non-residential portions of the building shall comply with one of the three options below:

13.105.12.1 Energy requirements shall be met if modeling in accordance with C407 shows a 10% reduction in energy from the ICC IECC.

13.105.12.2 Energy requirements shall be met if modeling in accordance with ASHRAE 90.1 Appendix G shows a 10% reduction in energy cost from the prescribed levels.

13.105.12.3 Energy requirements shall be met if at least two options in ICC IECC Section C406 are met.

GREEN BUILDING PRACTICES

13.106 WATER EFFICIENCY AND CONSERVATION

13.106.1 Fitting and fixture consumption. Plumbing fixtures and fixture fittings shall comply with the maximum flow rates specified in Table 13.106.1. Plumbing fixtures and fixture fittings in Table 13.106.1 shall have a manufacturer's designation for flow rate.

Exceptions: The following fixtures and devices shall not be required to comply with the reduced flow rates in Table 13.106.1: 1) Clinical sinks having a maximum water consumption of 4.5 gallons (17 L) per flush; 2) service sinks faucets, tub fillers, pot fillers, laboratory faucets, utility faucets, and other fittings designed primarily for filling operations; and 3) Fixtures, fittings, and devices whose primary purpose is safety.

TABLE 13.106.1
MAXIMUM FLOW RATES AND FLUSH VOLUMES FOR
FIXTURES AND FIXTURES FITTING

FIXTURE OR FIXTURE FITTING TYPE	MAXIMUM FLOW RATE OR FLUSH VOLUME
Showerhead[a]	2.0 gpm at 80 psi
Lavatory faucet and bar sink-private	1.5 gpm at 60 psi
Lavatory faucet-public (metering)	0.25 gpc[b] at 60 psi
Lavatory faucet-public (non-metering)	0.5 gpm at 60 psi
Kitchen faucet-private[e]	1.8 gpm at 60 psi
Kitchen and bar sink faucets in other than dwelling units and guest rooms	2.2 gpm at 60 psi
Urinal	0.5 gpf or nonwater urinal
Water closet	1.28 gpf[c]
Prerinse Spray Valves	1.3 gpm
Drinking Fountains (manual)	0.7 gpm[d]
Drinking Fountains (metered)	0.25 gpc[b,d]

a. Includes hand showers, body sprays, and rainfall panels.
b. Gallons per cycle.
c. Dual flush water closets in public bathrooms shall have a maximum full flush of 1.28.
d. Bottle filling stations associated with drinking fountains shall not have limitations for flow rate.
e. Kitchen faucets may temporarily increase the flow above the maximum rate but not to exceed 2.2 gpm.

13.106.2 Once-through cooling for appliances and equipment. Once-through or single-pass cooling with potable or municipal reclaimed water is prohibited.

13.106.3 Clothes washers. Clothes washers rated with an IWF (integrated water factor), MEF (modified energy factor), or IMEF (integrated modified energy factor), shall be rated as follows:

(1) Residential Clothes Washers, Front-loading,
greater than 2.5 cu-ft maximum 3.2 IWF minimum IMEF 2.76

(2) Residential Clothes Washers, Top-loading,
greater than 2.5 cu-ft maximum 4.3 IWF, minimum IMEF 2.06

(3) Residential Clothes Washers,
less than or equal to 2.5 cu-ft maximum 4.2 IWF, minimum IMEF 2.07

(4) Commercial Clothes Washers, maximum 4.0 IWF, minimum MEF 2.20

GREEN BUILDING PRACTICES

13.106.4 Food Service.

13.106.4.1 Dipper wells. The water supply to a dipper well shall have a shutoff valve and flow control valve. The maximum flow shall not exceed 1 gpm (3.78 lpm) at a supply pressure of 60 psi (413.7 kPa). The dipper well shall have a manufacturer's designation of flow rate.

13.106.4.2 Food waste disposal. The disposal of food wastes that are collected as part of preparing ware for one or more of the following shall accomplish washing:

(1) A food strainer (scrapper) basket that is emptied into a trash can.

(2) A garbage grinder where the water flow into the food waste disposer is controlled by a load sensing device such that the water flow does not exceed 1 gpm under no-load operating conditions and 8 gpm under full-load operating conditions.

(3) A pulper or mechanical strainer that uses no more than 2 gpm of potable water.

13.106.4.3 Pre-rinse spray heads. Food service pre-rinse spray heads shall have a manufacturers designation of flow rate, shall comply with the maximum flow rate in Table 1305.1, and shall shut off *automatically* when released.

13.106.4.4 Hand washing faucets. Faucets for hand washing sinks in food service preparation and serving areas shall be self-closing.

13.106.5. Water softeners. Water softeners shall comply with § 13.106.5.1 through § 13.106.5.3.

13.106.5.1 Demand initiated regeneration. Water softeners shall be equipped with demand-initiated regeneration control systems. Such control systems shall automatically initiate the regeneration cycle after determining the depletion, or impending depletion of softening capacity.

13.106.5.2 Water consumption. Water softeners shall have a maximum water consumption during regeneration of 5 gal (18.9 L) per 1000 grains of hardness removed as measured in accordance with NSF 44.

13.106.5.3 Waste connections. Wastewater from water softener regeneration shall not discharge to reclaimed, greywater or rainwater water collection systems and shall discharge in accordance with the ICC IPC.

13.106.6 Heat exchangers. Once-through or single-pass cooling with potable or municipal reclaimed water is prohibited. Heat exchangers shall be connected to a recirculating water system such as a chilled water loop, cooling tower loop, or similar recirculating system.

13.107 INDOOR AIR QUALITY

13.107.1 Carpets. Carpeting is not installed adjacent to water closets and bathing and or shower fixtures.

13.107.1.1 Entry. The primary entryway from the outdoors shall include one of the following:

(1) Permanent walk-off mat that allows access for cleaning (e.g., grating with catch basin); or

(2) Roll-out mat that will be maintained on a weekly basis by a contracted service.

13.107.2 Prohibited materials. The use of the following materials shall be prohibited:

(1) Asbestos-containing materials

(2) Urea-formaldehyde foam insulation

GREEN BUILDING PRACTICES

13.107.3 Product emissions. At least five types of the following product categories must meet their respective section of the Standard referenced below:

(1) Wood materials § 901.4

(2) Cabinets § 901.5

(3) Floor materials § 901.7

(4) Wall coverings § 901.8

(5) Interior architectural coatings § 901.9

(6) Interior adhesives and sealants § 901.10

(7) Insulation § 901.11

13.107.4 Fireplaces and appliances. Where located within buildings, fireplaces, solid fuel-burning appliances, vented decorative gas appliances, vented gas fireplace heaters and decorative gas appliances for installation in fireplaces shall comply with § 13.107.4.1 through § 13.107.4.5.

13.107.4.1 Venting and combustion air. Fireplaces and fuel-burning appliances shall be vented to the outdoors and shall be provided with combustion air provided from the outdoors in accordance with the International Mechanical Code and the International Fuel Gas Code. Solid-fuel-burning fireplaces shall be provided with a means to tightly close off the chimney flue and combustion air openings when the fireplace is not in use.

13.107.4.2 Wood-fired appliances. Wood stoves and wood-burning fireplace inserts shall be listed and, additionally, shall be labeled in accordance with the applicable requirement.

(1) Site-built masonry wood-burning fireplaces use outside combustion air and include a means of sealing the flue and the combustion air outlets to minimize interior air (heat) loss when not in operation.

(2) Factory-built, wood-burning fireplaces are in accordance with the certification requirements of UL 127.

(3) Wood stove and fireplace inserts, as defined in UL 1482 Section 3.8, are in accordance with the certification requirements of UL 1482.

13.107.4.3 Biomass appliances. Biomass fireplaces, stoves and inserts shall be listed and labeled in accordance with ASTM E 1509 or UL 1482. Biomass furnaces shall be listed and labeled in accordance with CSA B366.1 or UL 391. Biomass boilers shall be listed and labeled in accordance with CSA B366.1 or UL 2523.

13.107.4.4 Gas-fireplaces. Gas-fired fireplaces and direct heating equipment is listed and is installed in accordance with the NFPA 54, ICC IFGC, or the applicable local gas appliance installation code. Gas-fired fireplaces within dwelling units and direct heating equipment are vented to the outdoors.

13.107.4.5 Unvented. Unvented room heaters and unvented decorative appliances, including alcohol burning, shall be prohibited.

13.107.5 Protection of HVAC system openings. HVAC supply and return duct and equipment openings shall be protected during dust-producing operations of construction.

13.107.6 Garages. Attached garages are in accordance with the following:

(1) Doors installed in the common wall between the attached garage and conditioned space are tightly sealed and gasketed.

(2) A continuous air barrier is provided separating the garage space from the conditioned spaces.

13.107.7 Spot Ventilation. Exhaust systems shall be provided in accordance with ICC IMC Chapter 5 or ASHRAE 62.1.

13.107.8 Building Ventilation Systems.

13.107.8.1 Building Ventilation. Ventilation shall be provided to non-residential spaces in accordance with ICC IMC Chapter 4 or ASHRAE 62.1.

13.107.8.2 Air filters. Air filters with a minimum MERV rating of 6 are installed on central forced air systems and are accessible.

13.107.9 Radon system. Commercial spaces in building located in Zone 1 shall comply with § 902.3.

13.108 OPERATION, MAINTENANCE, AND BUILDING OWNER EDUCATION

13.108.1 Operation and maintenance manuals for tenants. Manuals are provided to the initial tenants of the non-residential space regarding the operation and maintenance of the building. Paper or digital format manuals are to include information regarding those aspects of the building's maintenance and operation that are within the area of responsibilities of the respective tenant. One or more responsible parties are to receive a copy of all documentation for archival purposes.

(1) A narrative detailing the importance of operating in a green building. This narrative is included in all responsible parties' manuals.

(2) A list of practices to conserve water and energy which require maintenance.

(3) Information on opportunities to purchase renewable energy from local utilities or national green power providers.

(4) Information on local and on-site recycling and hazardous waste disposal programs.

(5) Local public transportation options for employees.

13.108.2 Tenant finish out manual. Manuals are provided to the tenants of the non-residential space prior to the start of construction regarding the design and construction of the non-residential portion of the building. Paper or digital format manuals are to include information regarding those aspects of the design and construction that are within the area of responsibilities of the respective tenant. One or more responsible parties are to receive a copy of all documentation for archival purposes.

(1) Provisions of this Chapter verified at the time of building Certification for the respective space that shall be maintained as part of the Tenant Finish Out

(2) Provisions of this Chapter NOT verified at the time of building Certification for the respective space that shall be included in the Tenant Finish Out Construction Documents.

(3) A list of minimum green building material specifications that are to be included in the Tenant Finish Out Construction Documents based on the materials that were installed in the residential portion of the building.

INTENTIONALLY LEFT BLANK.

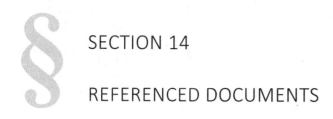

SECTION 14

REFERENCED DOCUMENTS

1401 GENERAL

1401.1 This chapter lists the codes, tandards, and other documents that are referenced in various sections of this Standard. The codes, standards, and other documents are listed herein indicate the promulgating agency of the document, the document identification, the effective date and title, and the section or sections of this Standard that reference the document. Unless indicated otherwise, the first printing of the document is referenced.

1401.2 The application of the referenced documents shall be as specified in § 102.2.

1402 REFERENCED DOCUMENTS

ACCA – Air Conditioning Contractors of America | www.acca.org

DOCUMENT	DATE	TITLE	SECTION
Manual D	2016	*Residential Duct Systems*	701.4.2.3, 11.701.4.2.3,
Manual J	2016	*Residential Load Calculation, Eighth Edition, Version 2.1*	701.4.1.1, 701.4.1.2, 703.3.0, 11.701.4.1.1, 11.701.4.1.2, 11.703.3.0, 1203.4
Manual S	2014	*Residential Equipment Selection*	701.4.1.1, 703.3.0, 11.701.4.1.1, 11.703.3.0
5 QI	2015	*HVAC Quality Installation Specification*	701.4.1.2, 703.3.3, 703.3.4, 703.3.5, 703.3.6, 705.6.2.2(1), 705.6.2.2(2), 11.701.4.1.2, 11.703.3.3, 11.703.3.4, 11.703.3.5, 11.703.3.6, 11.705.6.2.2(1), 11.705.6.2.2(2), 1203.4

AFF – American Forest Foundation, Inc. | www.forestfoundation.org

DOCUMENT	DATE	TITLE	SECTION
2010-2015 AFF Standards	2010	American Tree Farm System Standards for Sustainability for Forest Certification, including Performance Measures and Field Indicators	606.2(a), 11.606.2(a),

AAMA – American Architectural Manufacturers Association | www.aamanet.org

DOCUMENT	DATE	TITLE	SECTION
711	2013	The Voluntary Specification for Self-Adhering Flashing Used for Installation of Exterior Wall Fenestration Products	602.1.9(2), 11.602.1.9(2), 1202.7(9)
714	2015	Voluntary Specification for Liquid Applied Flashing Used to Create a Water-Resistive Seal around Exterior Wall Openings in Buildings	602.1.9(2), 11.602.1.9(2), 1202.7(9)
AAMA/WDMA/CSA 101/I.S.2/A440 UP3	2008		701.4.3.4, 11.701.4.3.4,

AHRI – Air-Conditioning, Heating, and Refrigeration Institute | www.ahrinet.org

DOCUMENT	DATE	TITLE	SECTION
I=B=R	2009	Heat Loss Calculation Guide	701.4.1.2, 11.701.4.1.2, 1203.4

ASCE – American Society of Civil Engineers | www.asce.org

DOCUMENT	DATE	TITLE	SECTION
32-01	2001	Design and Construction of Frost-Protected Shallow Foundations	202

ASHRAE – American Society of Heating, Refrigeration, Air-conditioning Engineers| www.ashrae.org

DOCUMENT	DATE	TITLE	SECTION
ASHRAE 62.1	2016	Ventilation for Acceptable Indoor Air Quality	902.1.6, 11.902.1.6, 13.107.7, 13.107.8.1
ASHRAE/ACCA 183	2007 (RA 2017)	Peak Cooling and Heating Load Calculations in Buildings Except Low-Rise Residential	13.105.9

ASME – American Society of Mechanical Engineers | www.asme.org

DOCUMENT	DATE	TITLE	SECTION
A112.18.1/CSA B125.1	2012	*Plumbing Supply Fittings*	802.4(1), 802.5.1, 802.5.2, 11.802.4(1), 11.802.5.1, 11.802.5.2
A112.19.2/CSA B45.1	2013	*Vitreous China Plumbing Fixtures and Hydraulic Requirements for Water Closets and Urinals*	802.5.4(2), 802.5.4(4)(b), 802.5.4(4)(c), 11.802.5.4(2), 11.802.5.4(4)(b), 11.802.5.4(4)(c)
A112.19.14	2013	*Six-Liter Water Closets Equipped with a Dual Flushing Device*	802.5.4(2), 11.802.5.4(2)

ASSE – American Society of Sanitary Engineering | www.asse-plumbing.org

DOCUMENT	DATE	TITLE	SECTION
1016/ASME A112.1016/CSA B125.16	2011	*Automatic Compensation Valves for Individual Showers and Tub/Shower Combinations*	802.4(1), 11.802.4(1)

ASTM – ASTM International, Inc. | www.astm.org

DOCUMENT	DATE	TITLE	SECTION
C1178	2013	*Standard Specification for Coated Glass Mat Water-Resistant Gypsum Backing Panel*	602.1.11, 11.602.1.11, 1202.8, 13.104.1.6
C1278 – 07a/1278M – 07a	2011	*Standard Specification for Fiber-Reinforced Gypsum Panel*	602.1.11, 11.602.1.11, 1202.8, 13.104.1.6
C1288	2010	*Standard Specification for Discrete Non-Asbestos Fiber-Cement Interior Substrate Sheets*	602.1.11, 11.602.1.11, 1202.8, 13.104.1.6
C1325-08b	2008	*Standard Specification for Non-Asbestos Fiber-Mat Reinforced Cementitious Backer Units*	602.1.11, 11.602.1.11, 1202.8, 13.104.1.6
C1371	2010	*Standard Test Method for Determination of Emittance of Materials Near Room Temperature Using Portable Emissometers*	703.2.3, 11.703.2.3
D7338	2010	*Standard Guide for Assessment of Fungal Growth in Buildings*	904.1, 904.2, 11.904.1, 11.904.2

ASTM – ASTM International, Inc. | www.astm.org (Continued)

DOCUMENT	DATE	TITLE	SECTION
D7612	2015	*Standard Practice for Categorizing Wood and Wood-Based Products According to Their Fiber Sources*	606.2(h), 11.606.2(h)
E283	2012	*Standard Test Method for Determining Rate of Air Leakage Through Exterior Windows, Curtain Walls, and Doors Under Specified Pressure Differences Across the Specimen*	701.4.3.5, 11.701.4.3.5,
E779	2010	*Standard Test Method for Determining Air Leakage Rate by Fan Pressurization*	705.6.2.1, 11.705.6.2.1
E1509	2012	*Standard Specification for Room Heaters, Pellet Fuel-Burning Type*	901.2.1(4), 11.901.2.1(4), 1205.2(4)
E1602	2010	*Standard Guide for Construction of Solid Fuel Burning Masonry Heaters*	901.2.1(5), 11.901.2.1(5), 1205.2(4)
E1827	2011	*Standard Test Methods for Determining Airtightness of Buildings Using an Orifice Blower Door*	705.6.2.1, 11.705.6.2.1
E1980	2011	*Standard Practice for Calculating Solar Reflectance Index of Horizontal and Low Sloped Opaque Surfaces*	505.2(1)(b), 602.2(3), 11.505.2(1)(b), 11.602.2(3)
E2273	2011	*Standard Test Method for Determining the Drainage Efficiency of Exterior Insulation and Finish Systems (EIFS) Clad Wall Assemblies*	602.1.9(5)(b), 11.602.1.9(5)(b)
E2921	2013	*Standard Practice for Minimum Criteria for Comparing Whole Building Life Cycle Assessments for Use with Building Codes and Rating Systems*	610.1.1, 610.1.1(1), 11.610.1.1, 11.610.1.1(1),

BOMA – Building Owners and Managers Association International | www.boma.org

DOCUMENT	DATE	TITLE	SECTION
Z65.4	2010	Multi-Unit Residential Buildings: Standard Methods of Measurement	601.1, 11.601.1

CARB – California Air Resources Board | www.arb.ca.gov

DOCUMENT	DATE	TITLE	SECTION
	2007	*Composite Wood Air Toxic Contaminant Measure Standard*	901.4(5), 901.5(2), 11.901.4(5), 11.901.5(2)
	2008	*Suggested Control Measure for Architectural Coatings*	901.9.1(3), 11.901.9.1(3), 1205.6(3)
	2011	*The California Consumer Products Regulations*	901.10(3), 11.901.10(3)

CDPH – California Department of Public Health | www.cdarb.ca.gov

DOCUMENT	DATE	TITLE	SECTION
	2010	*Standard Method for the Testing and Evaluation of Volatile Organic Chemical Emissions from Indoor Sources Using Environmental Chambers Version 1.1.*	901.7, 901.8, 901.9.3, 901.10(1), 901.11, 11.901.7, 11.901.8, 11.901.9.3, 11.901.10(1), 11.901.11, 12.1.901.7, 12.1.901.8, 12.1.901.9.2, 12.11.901.10(1)

CPA – Composite Panel Association | www.pbmdf.com

DOCUMENT	DATE	TITLE	SECTION
A208.1	2009	*Particleboard Standard*	901.4(2), 11.901.4(2)
A208.2	2009	*MDF Standard*	901.4(2), 11.901.4(2)
CPA 4	2011	*The Eco-Certified Composite™ (ECC) Standard*	901.4(4), 11.901.4(4)

CSA – CSA International | www.csa-international.org

DOCUMENT	DATE	TITLE	SECTION
6.19	2011	*Residential Carbon Monoxide Alarming Devices*	
CSA Z21.50/ CSA 2.22	2014	*Vented Gas Fireplaces w/ Addenda b*	901.1.5, 11.901.1.5
CSA Z21.88/ CSA 2.33	2014	*Vented Gas Fireplace Heaters*	901.1.5, 11.901.1.5
Z809	2013	*Sustainable Forest Management Requirements and Guidance (SFM)*	606.2(b), 11.606.2(b)
B366.1	2007	*Solid-Fuel-Fired Central Heating Appliances*	13.107.4.3

DOC/NIST – United States Department of Commerce / National Institute of Standards and Technology | www.nist.gov

DOCUMENT	DATE	TITLE	SECTION
PS 1-09	2010	*Construction and Industrial Plywood*	901.4(1), 11.901.4(1)
PS 2-10	2011	*Performance Standard for Wood-based Structural-use Panels*	901.4(1), 11.901.4(1)

DOE – U.S. Department of Energy | www.energy.gov

DOCUMENT	DATE	TITLE	SECTION
v. 4.6.1	2015	*REScheck*	703.1.1.1, 703.2.1, 11.703.1.1.1, 11.703.2.1, 1203.11.1.2, 13.105.1
v. 4.4.0	2015	*COMcheck*	703.1.1.1, 703.2.1, 11.703.1.1.1, 11.703.2.1, 1203.11.1.2, 13.105.1

EPA – Environmental Protection Agency | www.epa.gov

DOCUMENT	DATE	TITLE	SECTION
Burn Wise	2012	*EPA Qualified Wood-Burning Fireplace Program Partnership Agreement*	901.2(2), 11.901.2(2)
EPA 402-K-01-001	2008	*Mold Remediation in Schools and Commercial Buildings*	904.3(1), 11.904.3(1), 1202.11
EPA 402-K-02-003	2012	*A Brief Guide to Mold, Moisture and Your Home*	904.3(1), 11.904.3(1)
EPA 747-K-97-001	1997	*Reducing Lead Hazards When Remodeling Your Home*	11.1001.1(23)
Method 24	2000	*Determination of Volatile Matter Content, Water Content, Density, Volume Solids, and Weight Solids of Surface Coatings*	901.9.1(1), 11.901.9.1(1), 1205.6(1)
	1990	*Asbestos in the Home: A Homeowner's Guide*	11.1001.1(23)
	2013	*Smart Location Database, NGBS: Points for Smart Location Practices* https://epa.maps.arcgis.com/home/item.html?id=9508f9295c144b9fb392d33b18b569e3	405.6(7), 405.6(8), 501.2(4), 11.501.2(3)

ENERGY STAR® Documents

DOCUMENT	DATE	TITLE	SECTION
	September 1, 2018	*National ERI Target Procedure, ENERGY STAR Certified Homes, Version 3 (Rev. 09)*	701.1, 701.1.3, 704.1, 704.2, 1203.15.1
	September 1, 2018	*National Program Requirements ENERGY STAR Certified Homes, Version 3 (Rev. 09)*	701.1.4
	September 1, 2018	*National Program Requirements ENERGY STAR Certified Homes, Version 3.1 (Rev. 09)*	701.1.4
	January 1, 2015	*ENERGY STAR Multifamily High Rise Version 1 (Rev 03)*	701.1.4

EPA – Environmental Protection Agency | www.epa.gov (continued)

ENERGY STAR® Documents (Continued)

DOCUMENT	DATE	TITLE	SECTION
	January 1, 2014	*ENERGY STAR Program Requirements for Clothes Washers, Version 7.0*	703.6.2(3), 802.2(2), 11.703.6.2(3), 11.802.2(3)
	January 20, 2013	*ENERGY STAR Program Requirements for Dishwashers, Version 5.2*	703.6.2(2), 802.2(1), 11.703.6.2(2), 11.802.2(1)
	December 1, 2009	*ENERGY STAR Program Requirements for Geothermal Heat Pumps – Eligibility Criteria Version 3.1*	703.3.6, 11.703.3.6
	April 1, 2012	*ENERGY STAR Program Requirements for Luminaires, Version 1.2*	703.6.1(1), 11.703.6.1(1)
	April 28, 2014	*ENERGY STAR Program Eligibility Criteria for Residential Refrigerators and/or Freezers, Version 5*	703.6.2(1), 11.703.6.2(1)
	April 1, 2012	*ENERGY STAR Program Requirements for Residential Ceiling Fans – Eligibility Criteria Version 3.0*	703.3.7, 11.703.3.7
	April 1, 2012	*ENERGY STAR Program Requirements for Residential Ventilating Fans – Eligibility Criteria Version 3.2*	902.1.4(1), 902.1.4(2), 11.902.1.4(1), 11.902.1.4(2)
	January 17, 2014	*ENERGY STAR Program Requirements for Residential Windows, Doors, and Skylights – Eligibility Criteria Version 6.0*	703.2.5.2.1, 11.703.2.5.2.1
	2012	*ENERGY STAR Program Requirements for Roof Products – Eligibility Criteria Version 2.3*	602.2(1), 11.602.2(1)

WaterSense Documents

DOCUMENT	DATE	TITLE	SECTION
	May 20, 2014	*WaterSense Specification for Tank-Type Toilets, Version 1.2*	802.5.4(2), 12.3.801.6
	November 3, 2011	*WaterSense Specification for Weather-Based Irrigation Controllers, Version 1.0*	802.6.4(1), 11.802.6.4(1)
	December 9, 2014	*WaterSense Water Budget Approach Version 1.02*	403.6(4), 503.5(4), 11.503.5(4)
	October 1, 2007	*WaterSense High-Efficiency Lavatory Faucet Specification Version 1.0*	802.5.1, 11.802.5.1
	March 4, 2010	*WaterSense Specification for Showerheads Version 1.0*	802.4(1), 11.802.4(1)

FSA – Forest Stewardship Council | www.fsc.org

DOCUMENT	DATE	TITLE	SECTION
FSC-STD-01-001 (Version 4-0) EN	2013	FSC Principles and Criteria for Forest Stewardship v5	606.2(c), 11.606.2(c)

GS – Green Seal | www.greenseal.org

DOCUMENT	DATE	TITLE	SECTION
GS-11	2013	Paints and Coatings 3.1	901.9.1(2), 11.901.9.1(2), 1205.6(2)
GS-36	2013	Adhesives for Commercial Use 2.1	901.10(2), 11.901.10(2),

HPVA – Hardwood Plywood Veneer Association | www.hpva.org

DOCUMENT	DATE	TITLE	SECTION
HP-1	2009	American National Standard for Hardwood and Decorative Plywood	901.4(3), 11.901.4(3)

HUD – U.S. Department of Housing and Urban Development | www.hud.gov

DOCUMENT	DATE	TITLE	SECTION
24 CFR, Part 3280	2014	Manufactured Home Construction and Safety Standards	202

ICC – International Code Council | www.iccsafe.org

DOCUMENT	DATE	TITLE	SECTION
A117.1	2017	Accessible and Usable Buildings and Facilities	611.3
IBC	2018	International Building Code	202, 602.1.1.1, 602.1.3.1, 602.1.8, 602.1.13, 613.2, 901.2.1(5), 1001.1(12)(b), 11.602.1.1.1, 11.602.1.3.1, 11.602.1.8, 11.602.1.13, 11.613.2, 11.901.2.1(5), 11.1001.1(12)(b), 1205.2(5), 13.104.1.1, 13.104.1.2, 13.104.1.3, 13.104.1.4, 13.104.1.6

ICC – International Code Council | www.iccsafe.org (Continued)

DOCUMENT	DATE	TITLE	SECTION
ICC-400	2012	*Standard on the Design and Construction of Log Structures*	Table 701.4.3.2(2)
IECC	2018	*International Energy Conservation Code*	610.1.1(2), 701.1.4, 701.1.6(1), 701.1.6(6)(a), 701.4.3.3, 702.2.1, 702.2.2, 702.2.3, 703.1.1.1, 703.1.1.2, 703.1.2, 703.1.3, 703.2.1, 705.6.2.1, 705.6.2.3(1), 705.6.2.3(2), 705.6.3, 706.5(1), 11.610.1.1(2), 11.701.4.0, 11.701.4.3.3, 11.703.1.1.1, 11.703.1.1.2, 11.703.1.2, 11.703.1.3, 11.703.2.1, 11.705.6.2.1, 11.705.6.2.3(1), 11.705.6.2.3(2), 11.705.6.3, 11.706.5(1), 1203.10.1, 1203.10.2, 13.105.1, 13.105.3.1, 13.105.5, 13.105.6, 13.105.7, 13.105.8.1, 13.105.9, 13.105.11.2, 13.105.12.1, 13.105.12.3
IFGC	2018	*International Fuel Gas Code*	901.1.4, 11.901.1.4, 1205.1, 13.107.4.4

ICC – International Code Council | www.iccsafe.org   (Continued)

DOCUMENT	DATE	TITLE	SECTION
IgCC	2018	*International Green Construction Code*	301.1.1, 304.2, 701.1.5, 13.102.1.4
IMC	2018	*International Mechanical Code*	705.6.1(1), 11.705.6.1(1), 13.105.10, 13.107.7, 13.107.8.1
IRC	2018	*International Residential Code*	202, 602.1.1.1, 602.1.3.1, 602.1.4.2(1), 602.1.4.2(2), 602.1.8, 602.1.13, 705.6.1(1), 902.1.1(1), 902.3, 1001.1(12)(b), 11.602.1.1.1, 11.602.1.3.1, 11.602.1.4.2(1), 11.602.1.4.2(2), 11.602.1.8, 11.602.1.13, 11.705.6.1, 11.902.1.1(1), 11.902.3, 11.1001.1(12)(b), 1202.1, 1202.4
IPC	2018	*International Plumbing Code*	703.5.1, 11.703.5.1, 13.106.5.3
IWUIC	2018	*International Wildlife Urban Interface Code*	503.1(8), 11.503.1(8)

IA – Irrigation Association & American Society of Irrigation Consultants | www.irrigation.com

DOCUMENT	DATE	TITLE	SECTION
	2014	*Landscape Irrigation Best Management Practices*	403.6(15)

ISO – International Organization for Standardization | www.iso.org

DOCUMENT	DATE	TITLE	SECTION
14025	2006	*Environmental labels and declarations – Type III environmental declarations – Principles and procedures*	611.1.1, 611.1.2, 11.611.1.1, 11.611.1.2
14044	2006	*Environmental management – Life cycle assessment – Requirements and guidelines*	610.1.1, 610.1.2, 11.610.1.1, 11.610.1.2,
14001	2004	*Environmental management systems – Requirements with guidance for use*	612.1, 11.612.1
16000-23	2009	*Indoor air – Part 23: Performance test for evaluating the reduction of formaldehyde concentrations by sorptive building materials*	901.9, 11.901.9
17025	2005	*General requirements for the competence of testing and calibration laboratories*	901.7, 901.8, 901.9.3, 901.10(1), 901.11, 901.12 11.901.7, 11.901.8, 11.901.9.3, 11.901.10(1), 11.901.11, 11.901.12
17065	2012	*Conformity assessment – Requirements for bodies certifying products, processes and services*	612.2, 901.7, 901.8, 901.9.3, 901.10(1), 901.11, 901.12, 11.612.2, 11.901.7, 11.901.8, 11.901.9.3, 11.901.10(1), 11.901.11, 11.901.12
21930	2007	*Sustainability in building construction – Environmental declaration of building products*	611.1.1, 611.1.2, 11.611.1.1, 11.611.1.2

Home Innovation | Home Innovation Research Labs | www.HomeInnovation.com

DOCUMENT	DATE	TITLE	SECTION
Z765	2013	Single-Family Residential Buildings - Square Footage - Method for Calculating	601.1, 11.601.1

KCMA – Kitchen Cabinet Manufacturers Association | www.kcma.org

DOCUMENT	DATE	TITLE	SECTION
ANSI/KCMA A161.1	2012	Performance and Construction Standard for Kitchen and Vanity Cabinets	602.1.15, 11.602.1.15

NFPA – National Fire Protection Association | www.nfpa.org

DOCUMENT	DATE	TITLE	SECTION
54	2012	National Fuel Gas Code	901.1.4, 11.901.1.4, 1205.1, 13.107.4.4

NFRC – National Fenestration Rating Council | www.nfrc.org

DOCUMENT	DATE	TITLE	SECTION
400	2010	Procedure for Determining Fenestration Product Air Leakage	701.4.3.4, 11.701.4.3.4

NSF – NSF International | www.nsf.org

DOCUMENT	DATE	TITLE	SECTION
NSF/ANSI 140	2013	Sustainable Carpet Assessment	612.2(1), 11.612.2(1)
NSF/ANSI 332	2012	Sustainability Assessment for Resilient Floor Coverings	612.2(2), 11.612.2(2)
NSF/ANSI 342	2012	Sustainability Assessment for Wallcovering Products	612.2(4), 11.612.2(4)

NWFA – National Wood Flooring Association | www.nwfa.org

DOCUMENT	DATE	TITLE	SECTION
	2011	Responsible Procurement Program	606.2(f), 11.606.2(f)

PEFC – Pan European Forest Council | www.pefc.org

DOCUMENT	DATE	TITLE	SECTION
GL 2	2011	PEFC Council Minimum Requirements Checklist	606.2(d) & (g), 11.606.2(d) & (g)

RESNET – Residential Energy Services Network| www.resnet.us

DOCUMENT	DATE	TITLE	SECTION
ANSI/RESNET/ICC 380	2018	Standard for Testing Airtightness of Building Enclosures, Airtightness of Heating and Cooling Air Distribution Systems, and Airflow of Mechanical Ventilation Systems	902.2.2, 705.6.2.1, 11.705.6.2.1, 11.902.2.2

SAE – SAE International | https://www.sae.org

DOCUMENT	DATE	TITLE	SECTION
J1772_201001	2010	Electric Vehicle and Plug in Hybrid Vehicle Conductive Charge Coupler	505.6, 11.505.6

SCAQMD – South Coast Air Quality Management District | www.aqmd.gov

DOCUMENT	DATE	TITLE	SECTION
Rule 1168	2011	Adhesive and Sealant Applications	901.10(3), 11.901.10(3)

SRCC – Solar Rating and Certification Corporation | www.solar-rating.org

DOCUMENT	DATE	TITLE	SECTION
OG 300	2014	Operating Guidelines and Minimum Standards for Certifying Solar Water Heating Systems	703.5.5, 11.703.5.5

SFI – Sustainable Forestry Initiative, Inc. | www.sfiprogram.org

DOCUMENT	DATE	TITLE	SECTION
2010-2014 Standard	2010	Sustainable Forestry Initiative Standard (SFIS)	606.2(e), 11.606.2(e)

TCIA – Tree Care Industry Association | www.tcia.org

DOCUMENT	DATE	TITLE	SECTION
A300	2001	Standards for Tree Care Operations - Tree, Shrub and Other Woody Plant Maintenance - Standard Practices	503.1(6), 11.503.1(6)

TCNA – Tile Council of North America | www.tileusa.com

DOCUMENT	DATE	TITLE	SECTION
A138.1	2011	Green Squared: American National Standard Specifications for Sustainable Ceramic Tiles, Glass Tiles, and Tile Installation Materials	612.2(7), 11.612.2(7)

UL – Underwriters Laboratories Inc. | www.ul.com

DOCUMENT	DATE	TITLE	SECTION
127	2011	Factory-Built Fireplaces	901.2.1(2), 11.901.2.1(2)
181	2013	The Standard for Safety for Factory-Made Air Ducts and Air Connectors	701.4.2.1, 11.701.4.2.1
1482	2011	Solid-Fuel Type Room Heaters	901.2.1(3), 11.901.2.1(3), 1205.2(3), 13.107.4.2(3)
100	2012	Interim Sustainability Requirements for Gypsum Boards and Panels	612.2(5), 11.612.2(5)
102	2012	Standard for Sustainability for Door Leafs	612.2(6), 11.612.2(6)
2985	2015	Sustainability Outline for Thermal Insulation	612.2(3), 11.612.2(3)
391	2010	Standard for Solid-Fuel and Combination Fuel Central and Supplementary Furnaces	13.107.4.3
2523	2009	Standard for Solid Fuel-Fired Hydronic Heating Appliances, Water Heaters, and Boilers	13.107.4.3

USDA – U.S. Department of Agriculture | www.usda.gov

DOCUMENT	DATE	TITLE	SECTION
7 CFR Part 2902	2014	Designation of Biobased Items for Federal Procurement; Final Rule	606.1(h)

WSL – Washington State Legislature | www.leg.wa.gov

DOCUMENT	DATE	TITLE	SECTION
WAC 173-433-100(3)	2014	Solid Fuel Burning Devices - Emission Performance Standards	901.2.1(3), 11.901.2.1(3), 1205.2(3)

APPENDIX A:

CLIMATE ZONES

A101.1 Applicability of Appendix A. Appendix A is part of this Standard. Text identified as "User Note" is not considered part of this Standard.

A101.2 Scope. The provisions contained in Appendix A provide the criteria necessary for complying with the climate-specific provisions of this Standard.

TABLE A200
CLIMATE ZONES, MOISTURE REGIMES, AND WARM-HUMID
DESIGNATIONS BY STATE, COUNTY AND TERRITORY

Key: A – Moist, B – Dry, C – Marine. Absence of moisture designation indicates moisture regime is irrelevant. Asterisk (*) indicates a warm-humid location.

ALABAMA
3A Autauga*
2A Baldwin*
3A Barbour*
3A Bibb
3A Blount
3A Bullock*
3A Butler*
3A Calhoun
3A Chambers
3A Cherokee
3A Chilton
3A Choctaw*
3A Clarke*
3A Clay
3A Cleburne
3A Coffee*
3A Colbert
3A Conecuh*
3A Coosa
3A Covington*
3A Crenshaw*
3A Cullman
3A Dale*
3A Dallas*
3A DeKalb

3A Elmore*
3A Escambia*
3A Etowah
3A Fayette
3A Franklin
3A Geneva*
3A Greene
3A Hale
3A Henry*
3A Houston*
3A Jackson
3A Jefferson
3A Lamar
3A Lauderdale
3A Lawrence
3A Lee
3A Limestone
3A Lowndes*
3A Macon*
3A Madison
3A Marengo*
3A Marion
3A Marshall
2A Mobile*
3A Monroe*
3A Montgomery*

3A Morgan
3A Perry*
3A Pickens
3A Pike*
3A Randolph
3A Russell*
3A Shelby
3A St. Clair
3A Sumter
3A Talladega
3A Tallapoosa
3A Tuscaloosa
3A Walker
3A Washington*
3A Wilcox*
3A Winston

ALASKA
7   Aleutians East
7   Aleutians West
7   Anchorage
8   Bethel
7   Bristol Bay
7   Denali
8   Dillingham
8   Fairbanks North
    Star

7   Haines
7   Juneau
7   Kenai Peninsula
7   Ketchikan
    Gateway
7   Kodiak Island
7   Lake and
    Peninsula
7   Matanuska-
    Susitna
8   Nome
8   North Slope
8   Northwest Arctic
7   Prince of Wales-
    Outer Ketchikan
7   Sitka
7   Skagway-Hoonah
    Angoon
8   Southeast
    Fairbanks
7   Valdez-Cordova
8   Wade Hampton
7   Wrangell-
    Petersburg
7   Yakutat
8   Yukon-Koyukuk

ARIZONA
5B Apache
3B Cochise
5B Coconino
4B Gila
3B Graham
3B Greenlee
2B La Paz
2B Maricopa
3B Mohave
5B Navajo
2B Pima
2B Pinal
3B Santa Cruz
4B Yavapai
2B Yuma

ARKANSAS
3A Arkansas
3A Ashley
4A Baxter
4A Benton
4A Boone
3A Bradley
3A Calhoun

(continued)

TABLE A200 – Continued
CLIMATE ZONES, MOISTURE REGIMES, AND WARM-HUMID DESIGNATIONS
BY STATE, COUNTY AND TERRITORY

Key: A – Moist, B – Dry, C – Marine. Absence of moisture designation indicates moisture regime is irrelevant.
Asterisk (*) indicates a warm-humid location.

4A Carroll	3A Perry	3C Marin	5B Boulder	6B Rio Blanco
3A Chicot	3A Phillips	4B Mariposa	5B Broomfield	7 Rio Grande
3A Clark	3A Pike	3C Mendocino	6B Chaffee	7 Routt
3A Clay	3A Poinsett	3B Merced	5B Cheyenne	6B Saguache
3A Cleburne	3A Polk	5B Modoc	7 Clear Creek	7 San Juan
3A Cleveland	3A Pope	6B Mono	6B Conejos	6B San Miguel
3A Columbia*	3A Prairie	3C Monterey	6B Costilla	5B Sedgwick
3A Conway	3A Pulaski	3C Napa	5B Crowley	7 Summit
3A Craighead	3A Randolph	5B Nevada	6B Custer	5B Teller
3A Crawford	3A Saline	3B Orange	5B Delta	5B Washington
3A Crittenden	3A Scott	3B Placer	5B Denver	5B Weld
3A Cross	4A Searcy	5B Plumas	6B Dolores	5B Yuma
3A Dallas	3A Sebastian	3B Riverside	5B Douglas	
3A Desha	3A Sevier*	3B Sacramento	6B Eagle	**CONNECTICUT**
3A Drew	3A Sharp	3C San Benito	5B Elbert	5A (all)
3A Faulkner	3A St. Francis	3B San Bernardino	5B El Paso	
3A Franklin	4A Stone	3B San Diego	5B Fremont	**DELAWARE**
4A Fulton	3A Union*	3C San Francisco	5B Garfield	4A (all)
3A Garland	3A Van Buren	3B San Joaquin	5B Gilpin	
3A Grant	4A Washington	3C San Luis Obispo	7 Grand	**DISTRICT OF**
3A Greene	3A White	3C San Mateo	7 Gunnison	**COLUMBIA**
3A Hempstead*	3A Woodruff	3C Santa Barbara	7 Hinsdale	4A (all)
3A Hot Spring	3A Yell	3C Santa Clara	5B Huerfano	
3A Howard		3C Santa Cruz	7 Jackson	**FLORIDA**
3A Independence	**CALIFORNIA**	3B Shasta	5B Jefferson	2A Alachua*
4A Izard	3C Alameda	5B Sierra	5B Kiowa	2A Baker*
3A Jackson	6B Alpine	5B Siskiyou	5B Kit Carson	2A Bay*
3A Jefferson	4B Amador	3B Solano	7 Lake	2A Bradford*
3A Johnson	3B Butte	3C Sonoma	5B La Plata	2A Brevard*
3A Lafayette*	4B Calaveras	3B Stanislaus	5B Larimer	1A Broward*
3A Lawrence	3B Colusa	3B Sutter	4B Las Animas	2A Calhoun*
3A Lee	3B Contra Costa	3B Tehama	5B Lincoln	2A Charlotte*
3A Lincoln	4C Del Norte	4B Trinity	5B Logan	2A Citrus*
3A Little River*	4B El Dorado	3B Tulare	5B Mesa	2A Clay*
3A Logan	3B Fresno	4B Tuolumne	7 Mineral	2A Collier*
3A Lonoke	3B Glenn	3C Ventura	6B Moffat	2A Columbia*
4A Madison	4C Humboldt	3B Yolo	5B Montezuma	2A DeSoto*
4A Marion	2B Imperial	3B Yuba	5B Montrose	2A Dixie*
3A Miller*	4B Inyo		5B Morgan	2A Duval*
3A Mississippi	3B Kern	**COLORADO**	4B Otero	2A Escambia*
3A Monroe	3B Kings	5B Adams	6B Ouray	2A Flagler*
3A Montgomery	4B Lake	6B Alamosa	7 Park	2A Franklin*
3A Nevada	5B Lassen	5B Arapahoe	5B Phillips	2A Gadsden*
4A Newton	3B Los Angeles	6B Archuleta	7 Pitkin	2A Gilchrist*
3A Ouachita	3B Madera	4B Baca	5B Prowers	2A Glades*
		5B Bent	5B Pueblo	

(continued)

2020 NATIONAL GREEN BUILDING STANDARD®

TABLE A200 – Continued
CLIMATE ZONES, MOISTURE REGIMES, AND WARM-HUMID DESIGNATIONS
BY STATE, COUNTY AND TERRITORY

Key: A – Moist, B – Dry, C – Marine. Absence of moisture designation indicates moisture regime is irrelevant.
Asterisk (*) indicates a warm-humid location.

2A Gulf*	2A Washington*	2A Decatur*	3A Lee*	3A Taylor*
2A Hamilton*		3A DeKalb	2A Liberty*	3A Telfair*
2A Hardee*	**GEORGIA**	3A Dodge*	3A Lincoln	3A Terrell*
2A Hendry*	2A Appling*	3A Dooly*	2A Long*	2A Thomas*
2A Hernando*	2A Atkinson*	3A Dougherty*	2A Lowndes*	3A Tift*
2A Highlands*	2A Bacon*	3A Douglas	4A Lumpkin	2A Toombs*
2A Hillsborough*	2A Baker*	3A Early*	3A Macon*	4A Towns
2A Holmes*	3A Baldwin	2A Echols*	3A Madison	3A Treutlen*
2A Indian River*	4A Banks	2A Effingham*	3A Marion*	3A Troup
2A Jackson*	3A Barrow	3A Elbert	3A McDuffie	3A Turner*
2A Jefferson*	3A Bartow	3A Emanuel*	2A McIntosh*	3A Twiggs*
2A Lafayette*	3A Ben Hill*	2A Evans*	3A Meriwether	4A Union
2A Lake*	2A Berrien*	4A Fannin	2A Miller*	3A Upson
2A Lee*	3A Bibb	3A Fayette	2A Mitchell*	3A Turner
2A Leon*	3A Bleckley*	4A Floyd	3A Monroe	4A Walker
2A Levy*	2A Brantley*	3A Forsyth	3A Montgomery*	3A Walton
2A Liberty*	2A Brooks*	4A Franklin	3A Morgan	2A Ware*
2A Madison*	2A Bryan*	3A Fulton	4A Murray	3A Warren
2A Manatee*	3A Bulloch*	4A Gilmer	3A Muscogee	3A Washington
2A Marion*	3A Burke	3A Glascock	3A Newton	2A Wayne*
2A Martin*	3A Butts	2A Glynn*	3A Oconee	3A Webster*
1A Miami-Dade*	3A Calhoun*	4A Gordon	3A Oglethorpe	3A Wheeler*
1A Monroe*	2A Camden*	2A Grady*	3A Paulding	4A White
2A Nassau*	3A Candler*	3A Greene	3A Peach*	4A Whitfield
2A Okaloosa*	3A Carroll	3A Gwinnett	3A Pickens	3A Wilcox*
2A Okeechobee*	4A Catoosa	4A Habersham	2A Pierce*	3A Wilkes
2A Orange*	2A Charlton*	4A Hall	3A Pike	3A Wilkinson
2A Osceola*	2A Chatham*	3A Hancock	3A Polk	3A Worth*
2A Palm Beach*	3A Chattahoochee*	3A Haralson	3A Pulaski*	
2A Pasco*	4A Chattooga	3A Harris	3A Putnam	**HAWAII**
2A Pinellas*	3A Cherokee	3A Hart	3A Quitman*	1A (all)*
2A Polk*	3A Clarke	3A Heard	4A Rabun	
2A Putnam*	3A Clay*	3A Henry	3A Randolph*	**IDAHO**
2A Santa Rosa*	3A Clayton	3A Houston*	3A Richmond	5B Ada
2A Sarasota*	2A Clinch*	3A Irwin*	3A Rockdale	6B Adams
2A Seminole*	3A Cobb	3A Jackson	3A Schley*	6B Bannock
2A St. Johns*	3A Coffee*	3A Jasper	3A Screven*	6B Bear Lake
2A St. Lucie*	2A Colquitt*	2A Jeff Davis*	2A Seminole*	5B Benewah
2A Sumter*	3A Columbia	3A Jefferson	3A Spalding	6B Bingham
2A Suwannee*	2A Cook*	3A Jenkins*	4A Stephens	6B Blaine
2A Taylor*	3A Coweta	3A Johnson*	3A Stewart*	6B Boise
2A Union*	3A Crawford	3A Jones	3A Sumter*	6B Bonner
2A Volusia*	3A Crisp*	3A Lamar	3A Talbot	6B Bonneville
2A Wakulla*	4A Dade	2A Lanier*	3A Taliaferro	6B Boundary
2A Walton*	4A Dawson	3A Laurens*	2A Tattnall*	6B Butte
				6B Camas

(continued)

TABLE A200 – Continued
CLIMATE ZONES, MOISTURE REGIMES, AND WARM-HUMID DESIGNATIONS
BY STATE, COUNTY AND TERRITORY

Key: A – Moist, B – Dry, C – Marine. Absence of moisture designation indicates moisture regime is irrelevant.
Asterisk (*) indicates a warm-humid location.

5B Canyon	4A Clay	4A Marion	**INDIANA**	5A Lake
6B Caribou	4A Clinton	5A Marshall	5A Adams	5A La Porte
5B Cassia	5A Coles	5A Mason	5A Allen	4A Lawrence
6B Clark	5A Cook	4A Massac	5A Bartholomew	5A Madison
5B Clearwater	4A Crawford	5A McDonough	5A Benton	5A Marion
6B Custer	5A Cumberland	5A McHenry	5A Blackford	5A Marshall
5B Elmore	5A DeKalb	5A McLean	5A Boone	4A Martin
6B Franklin	5A De Witt	5A Menard	4A Brown	5A Miami
6B Fremont	5A Douglas	5A Mercer	5A Carroll	4A Monroe
5B Gem	5A DuPage	4A Monroe	5A Cass	5A Montgomery
5B Gooding	5A Edgar	4A Montgomery	4A Clark	5A Morgan
5B Idaho	4A Edwards	5A Morgan	5A Clay	5A Newton
6B Jefferson	4A Effingham	5A Moultrie	5A Clinton	5A Noble
5B Jerome	4A Fayette	5A Ogle	4A Crawford	4A Ohio
5B Kootenai	5A Ford	5A Peoria	4A Daviess	4A Orange
5B Latah	4A Franklin	4A Perry	4A Dearborn	5A Owen
6B Lemhi	5A Fulton	5A Piatt	5A Decatur	5A Parke
5B Lewis	4A Gallatin	5A Pike	5A De Kalb	4A Perry
5B Lincoln	5A Greene	4A Pope	5A Delaware	4A Pike
6B Madison	5A Grundy	4A Pulaski	4A Dubois	5A Porter
5B Minidoka	4A Hamilton	5A Putnam	5A Elkhart	4A Posey
5B Nez Perce	5A Hancock	4A Randolph	5A Fayette	5A Pulaski
6B Oneida	4A Hardin	4A Richland	4A Floyd	5A Putnam
5B Owyhee	5A Henderson	5A Rock Island	5A Fountain	5A Randolph
5B Payette	5A Henry	4A Saline	5A Franklin	4A Ripley
5B Power	5A Iroquois	5A Sangamon	5A Fulton	5A Rush
5B Shoshone	4A Jackson	5A Schuyler	4A Gibson	4A Scott
6B Teton	4A Jasper	5A Scott	5A Grant	5A Shelby
5B Twin Falls	4A Jefferson	4A Shelby	4A Greene	4A Spencer
6B Valley	5A Jersey	5A Stark	5A Hamilton	5A Starke
5B Washington	5A Jo Daviess	4A St. Clair	5A Hancock	5A Steuben
	4A Johnson	5A Stephenson	4A Harrison	5A St. Joseph
ILLINOIS	5A Kane	5A Tazewell	5A Hendricks	4A Sullivan
5A Adams	5A Kankakee	4A Union	5A Henry	4A Switzerland
4A Alexander	5A Kendall	5A Vermilion	5A Howard	5A Tippecanoe
4A Bond	5A Knox	4A Wabash	5A Huntington	5A Tipton
5A Boone	5A Lake	5A Warren	4A Jackson	5A Union
5A Brown	5A La Salle	4A Washington	5A Jasper	4A Vanderburgh
5A Bureau	4A Lawrence	4A Wayne	5A Jay	5A Vermillion
5A Calhoun	5A Lee	4A White	4A Jefferson	5A Vigo
5A Carroll	5A Livingston	5A Whiteside	4A Jennings	5A Wabash
5A Cass	5A Logan	5A Will	5A Johnson	5A Warren
5A Champaign	5A Macon	4A Williamson	4A Knox	4A Warrick
4A Christian	4A Macoupin	5A Winnebago	5A Kosciusko	4A Washington
5A Clark	4A Madison	5A Woodford	5A Lagrange	5A Wayne

(continued)

2020 NATIONAL GREEN BUILDING STANDARD®

TABLE A200 – Continued
CLIMATE ZONES, MOISTURE REGIMES, AND WARM-HUMID DESIGNATIONS
BY STATE, COUNTY AND TERRITORY

Key: A – Moist, B – Dry, C – Marine. Absence of moisture designation indicates moisture regime is irrelevant.
Asterisk (*) indicates a warm-humid location.

5A Wells	6A Hancock	5A Tama	4A Franklin	4A Pottawatomie
5A White	6A Hardin	5A Taylor	4A Geary	4A Pratt
5A Whitley	5A Harrison	5A Union	5A Gove	5A Rawlins
	5A Henry	5A Van Buren	5A Graham	4A Reno
IOWA	6A Howard	5A Wapello	4A Grant	5A Republic
5A Adair	6A Humboldt	5A Warren	4A Gray	4A Rice
5A Adams	6A Ida	5A Washington	5A Greeley	4A Riley
6A Allamakee	5A Iowa	5A Wayne	4A Greenwood	5A Rooks
5A Appanoose	5A Jackson	6A Webster	5A Hamilton	4A Rush
5A Audubon	5A Jasper	6A Winnebago	4A Harper	4A Russell
5A Benton	5A Jefferson	6A Winneshiek	4A Harvey	4A Saline
6A Black Hawk	5A Johnson	5A Woodbury	4A Haskell	5A Scott
5A Boone	5A Jones	6A Worth	4A Hodgeman	4A Sedgwick
6A Bremer	5A Keokuk	6A Wright	4A Jackson	4A Seward
6A Buchanan	6A Kossuth		4A Jefferson	4A Shawnee
6A Buena Vista	5A Lee	**KANSAS**	5A Jewell	5A Sheridan
6A Butler	5A Linn	4A Allen	4A Johnson	5A Sherman
6A Calhoun	5A Louisa	4A Anderson	4A Kearny	5A Smith
5A Carroll	5A Lucas	4A Atchison	4A Kingman	4A Stafford
5A Cass	6A Lyon	4A Barber	4A Kiowa	4A Stanton
5A Cedar	5A Madison	4A Barton	4A Labette	4A Stevens
6A Cerro Gordo	5A Mahaska	4A Bourbon	5A Lane	4A Sumner
6A Cherokee	5A Marion	4A Brown	4A Leavenworth	5A Thomas
6A Chickasaw	5A Marshall	4A Butler	4A Lincoln	5A Trego
5A Clarke	5A Mills	4A Chase	4A Linn	4A Wabaunsee
6A Clay	6A Mitchell	4A Chautauqua	5A Logan	5A Wallace
6A Clayton	5A Monona	4A Cherokee	4A Lyon	4A Washington
5A Clinton	5A Monroe	5A Cheyenne	4A Marion	5A Wichita
5A Crawford	5A Montgomery	4A Clark	4A Marshall	4A Wilson
5A Dallas	5A Muscatine	4A Clay	4A McPherson	4A Woodson
5A Davis	6A O'Brien	5A Cloud	4A Meade	4A Wyandotte
5A Decatur	6A Osceola	4A Coffey	4A Miami	
6A Delaware	5A Page	4A Comanche	5A Mitchell	**KENTUCKY**
5A Des Moines	6A Palo Alto	4A Cowley	4A Montgomery	4A (all)
6A Dickinson	6A Plymouth	4A Crawford	4A Morris	
5A Dubuque	6A Pocahontas	5A Decatur	4A Morton	**LOUISIANA**
6A Emmet	5A Polk	4A Dickinson	4A Nemaha	2A Acadia*
6A Fayette	5A Pottawattamie	4A Doniphan	4A Neosho	2A Allen*
6A Floyd	5A Poweshiek	4A Douglas	5A Ness	2A Ascension*
6A Franklin	5A Ringgold	4A Edwards	5A Norton	2A Assumption*
5A Fremont	6A Sac	4A Elk	4A Osage	2A Avoyelles*
5A Greene	5A Scott	5A Ellis	5A Osborne	2A Beauregard*
6A Grundy	5A Shelby	4A Ellsworth	4A Ottawa	3A Bienville*
5A Guthrie	6A Sioux	4A Finney	4A Pawnee	3A Bossier*
6A Hamilton	5A Story	4A Ford	5A Phillips	3A Caddo*

(continued)

TABLE A200 – Continued
CLIMATE ZONES, MOISTURE REGIMES, AND WARM-HUMID DESIGNATIONS
BY STATE, COUNTY AND TERRITORY

Key: A – Moist, B – Dry, C – Marine. Absence of moisture designation indicates moisture regime is irrelevant.
Asterisk (*) indicates a warm-humid location.

2A Calcasieu*	3A Tensas*	4A Howard	5A Hillsdale	7 Schoolcraft
3A Caldwell*	2A Terrebonne*	4A Kent	7 Houghton	5A Shiawassee
2A Cameron*	3A Union*	4A Montgomery	6A Huron	5A St. Clair
3A Catahoula*	2A Vermilion*	4A Prince George's	5A Ingham	5A St. Joseph
3A Claiborne*	3A Vernon*	4A Queen Anne's	5A Ionia	5A Tuscola
3A Concordia*	2A Washington*	4A Somerset	6A Iosco	5A Van Buren
3A De Soto*	3A Webster*	4A St. Mary's	7 Iron	5A Washtenaw
2A East Baton Rouge*	2A West Baton Rouge*	4A Talbot	6A Isabella	5A Wayne
3A East Carroll	3A West Carroll	4A Washington	5A Jackson	6A Wexford
2A East Feliciana*	2A West Feliciana*	4A Wicomico	6A Kalamazoo	
2A Evangeline*	3A Winn*	4A Worcester	6A Kalkaska	**MINNESOTA**
3A Franklin*			5A Kent	7 Aitkin
3A Grant*	**MAINE**	**MASSACHUSETTS**	7 Keweenaw	6A Anoka
2A Iberia*	6A Androscoggin	5A (all)	6A Lake	7 Becker
2A Iberville*	7 Aroostook		5A Lapeer	7 Beltrami
3A Jackson*	6A Cumberland	**MICHIGAN**	6A Leelanau	6A Benton
2A Jefferson*	6A Franklin	6A Alcona	5A Lenawee	6A Big Stone
2A Jefferson Davis*	6A Hancock	6A Alger	5A Livingston	6A Blue Earth
2A Lafayette*	6A Kennebec	5A Allegan	7 Luce	6A Brown
2A Lafourche*	6A Knox	6A Alpena	7 Mackinac	7 Carlton
3A La Salle*	6A Lincoln	6A Antrim	5A Macomb	6A Carver
3A Lincoln*	6A Oxford	6A Arenac	6A Manistee	7 Cass
2A Livingston*	6A Penobscot	7 Baraga	6A Marquette	6A Chippewa
3A Madison*	6A Piscataquis	5A Barry	6A Mason	6A Chisago
3A Morehouse	6A Sagadahoc	5A Bay	6A Mecosta	7 Clay
3A Natchitoches*	6A Somerset	6A Benzie	6A Menominee	7 Clearwater
2A Orleans*	6A Waldo	5A Berrien	5A Midland	7 Cook
3A Ouachita*	6A Washington	5A Branch	6A Missaukee	6A Cottonwood
2A Plaquemines*	6A York	5A Calhoun	5A Monroe	7 Crow Wing
2A Pointe Coupee*		5A Cass	5A Montcalm	6A Dakota
2A Rapides*	**MARYLAND**	6A Charlevoix	6A Montmorency	6A Dodge
3A Red River*	4A Allegany	6A Cheboygan	5A Muskegon	6A Douglas
3A Richland*	4A Anne Arundel	7 Chippewa	6A Newaygo	6A Faribault
3A Sabine*	4A Baltimore	6A Clare	6A Oakland	6A Fillmore
2A St. Bernard*	4A Baltimore (city)	5A Clinton	6A Oceana	6A Freeborn
2A St. Charles *	4A Calvert	6A Crawford	6A Ogemaw	6A Goodhue
2A St. Helena*	4A Caroline	6A Delta	7 Ontonagon	7 Grant
2A St. James*	4A Carroll	6A Dickinson	6A Osceola	6A Hennepin
2A St. John the Baptist*	4A Cecil	5A Eaton	6A Oscoda	6A Houston
2A St. Landry*	4A Charles	6A Emmet	6A Otsego	7 Hubbard
2A St. Martin*	4A Dorchester	5A Genesee	5A Ottawa	6A Isanti
2A St. Mary*	4A Frederick	6A Gladwin	6A Presque Isle	7 Itasca
2A St. Tammany*	5A Garrett	7 Gogebic	6A Roscommon	6A Jackson
2A Tangipahoa*	4A Harford	6A Grand Traverse	5A Saginaw	7 Kanabec
		5A Gratiot	6A Sanilac	6A Kandiyohi

(continued)

2020 NATIONAL GREEN BUILDING STANDARD®

TABLE A200 – Continued
CLIMATE ZONES, MOISTURE REGIMES, AND WARM-HUMID DESIGNATIONS
BY STATE, COUNTY AND TERRITORY

Key: A – Moist, B – Dry, C – Marine. Absence of moisture designation indicates moisture regime is irrelevant.
Asterisk (*) indicates a warm-humid location.

7 Kittson	7 Wadena	3A Lafayette	3A Yalobusha	4A Henry
7 Koochiching	6A Waseca	3A Lamar*	3A Yazoo	4A Hickory
6A Lac qui Parle	6A Washington	3A Lauderdale		5A Holt
7 Lake	6A Watonwan	3A Lawrence*	**MISSOURI**	4A Howard
7 Lake of the Woods	7 Wilkin	3A Leake	5A Adair	4A Howell
6A Le Sueur	6A Winona	3A Lee	5A Andrew	4A Iron
6A Lincoln	6A Wright	3A Leflore	5A Atchison	4A Jackson
6A Lyon	6A Yellow Medicine	3A Lincoln*	4A Audrain	4A Jasper
7 Mahnomen		3A Lowndes	4A Barry	4A Jefferson
7 Marshall	**MISSISSIPPI**	3A Madison	4A Barton	4A Johnson
6A Martin	3A Adams*	3A Marion*	4A Bates	5A Knox
6A McLeod	3A Alcorn	3A Marshall	4A Benton	4A Laclede
6A Meeker	3A Amite*	3A Monroe	4A Bollinger	4A Lafayette
7 Mille Lacs	3A Attala	3A Montgomery	4A Boone	4A Lawrence
6A Morrison	3A Benton	3A Neshoba	5A Buchanan	5A Lewis
6A Mower	3A Bolivar	3A Newton	4A Butler	4A Lincoln
6A Murray	3A Calhoun	3A Noxubee	5A Caldwell	5A Linn
6A Nicollet	3A Carroll	3A Oktibbeha	4A Callaway	5A Livingston
6A Nobles	3A Chickasaw	3A Panola	4A Camden	5A Macon
7 Norman	3A Choctaw	2A Pearl River*	4A Cape Girardeau	4A Madison
6A Olmsted	3A Claiborne*	3A Perry*	4A Carroll	4A Maries
7 Otter Tail	3A Clarke	3A Pike*	4A Carter	5A Marion
7 Pennington	3A Clay	3A Pontotoc	4A Cass	4A McDonald
7 Pine	3A Coahoma	3A Prentiss	4A Cedar	5A Mercer
6A Pipestone	3A Copiah*	3A Quitman	5A Chariton	4A Miller
7 Polk	3A Covington*	3A Rankin*	4A Christian	4A Mississippi
6A Pope	3A DeSoto	3A Scott	5A Clark	4A Moniteau
6A Ramsey	3A Forrest*	3A Sharkey	4A Clay	4A Monroe
7 Red Lake	3A Franklin*	3A Simpson*	5A Clinton	4A Montgomery
6A Redwood	3A George*	3A Smith*	4A Cole	4A Morgan
6A Renville	3A Greene*	2A Stone*	4A Cooper	4A New Madrid
6A Rice	3A Grenada	3A Sunflower	4A Crawford	4A Newton
6A Rock	2A Hancock*	3A Tallahatchie	4A Dade	5A Nodaway
7 Roseau	2A Harrison*	3A Tate	4A Dallas	4A Oregon
6A Scott	3A Hinds*	3A Tippah	5A Daviess	4A Osage
6A Sherburne	3A Holmes	3A Tishomingo	5A DeKalb	4A Ozark
6A Sibley	3A Humphreys	3A Tunica	4A Dent	4A Pemiscot
6A Stearns	3A Issaquena	3A Union	4A Douglas	4A Perry
6A Steele	3A Itawamba	3A Walthall*	4A Dunklin	4A Pettis
6A Stevens	2A Jackson*	3A Warren*	4A Franklin	4A Phelps
7 St. Louis	3A Jasper	3A Washington	4A Gasconade	5A Pike
6A Swift	3A Jefferson*	3A Wayne*	5A Gentry	4A Platte
6A Todd	3A Jefferson Davis*	3A Webster	4A Greene	4A Polk
6A Traverse	3A Jones*	3A Wilkinson*	5A Grundy	4A Pulaski
6A Wabasha	3A Kemper	3A Winston	5A Harrison	5A Putnam

(continued)

TABLE A200 – Continued
CLIMATE ZONES, MOISTURE REGIMES, AND WARM-HUMID DESIGNATIONS
BY STATE, COUNTY AND TERRITORY

Key: A – Moist, B – Dry, C – Marine. Absence of moisture designation indicates moisture regime is irrelevant.
Asterisk (*) indicates a warm-humid location.

5A Ralls	5B Lander	**NEW MEXICO**	6A Clinton	6A Tompkins
4A Randolph	5B Lincoln	4B Bernalillo	5A Columbia	6A Ulster
4A Ray	5B Lyon	5B Catron	6A Cortland	6A Warren
4A Reynolds	5B Mineral	3B Chaves	6A Delaware	5A Washington
4A Ripley	5B Nye	4B Cibola	5A Dutchess	5A Wayne
4A Saline	5B Pershing	5B Colfax	5A Erie	4A Westchester
5A Schuyler	5B Storey	4B Curry	6A Essex	6A Wyoming
5A Scotland	5B Washoe	4B DeBaca	6A Franklin	5A Yates
4A Scott	5B White Pine	3B Dona Ana	6A Fulton	
4A Shannon		3B Eddy	5A Genesee	**NORTH**
5A Shelby	**NEW HAMPSHIRE**	4B Grant	5A Greene	**CAROLINA**
4A St. Charles	6A Belknap	4B Guadalupe	6A Hamilton	4A Alamance
4A St. Clair	6A Carroll	5B Harding	6A Herkimer	4A Alexander
4A Ste. Genevieve	5A Cheshire	3B Hidalgo	6A Jefferson	5A Alleghany
4A St. Francois	6A Coos	3B Lea	4A Kings	3A Anson
4A St. Louis	6A Grafton	4B Lincoln	6A Lewis	5A Ashe
4A St. Louis (city)	5A Hillsborough	5B Los Alamos	5A Livingston	5A Avery
4A Stoddard	6A Merrimack	3B Luna	6A Madison	3A Beaufort
4A Stone	5A Rockingham	5B McKinley	5A Monroe	4A Bertie
5A Sullivan	5A Strafford	5B Mora	6A Montgomery	3A Bladen
4A Taney	6A Sullivan	3B Otero	4A Nassau	3A Brunswick*
4A Texas		4B Quay	4A New York	4A Buncombe
4A Vernon	**NEW JERSEY**	5B Rio Arriba	5A Niagara	4A Burke
4A Warren	4A Atlantic	4B Roosevelt	6A Oneida	3A Cabarrus
4A Washington	5A Bergen	5B Sandoval	5A Onondaga	4A Caldwell
4A Wayne	4A Burlington	5B San Juan	5A Ontario	3A Camden
4A Webster	4A Camden	5B San Miguel	5A Orange	3A Carteret*
5A Worth	4A Cape May	5B Santa Fe	5A Orleans	4A Caswell
4A Wright	4A Cumberland	4B Sierra	5A Oswego	4A Catawba
	4A Essex	4B Socorro	6A Otsego	4A Chatham
MONTANA	4A Gloucester	5B Taos	5A Putnam	4A Cherokee
6B (all)	4A Hudson	5B Torrance	4A Queens	3A Chowan
	5A Hunterdon	4B Union	5A Rensselaer	4A Clay
NEBRASKA	5A Mercer	4B Valencia	4A Richmond	4A Cleveland
5A (all)	4A Middlesex		5A Rockland	3A Columbus*
	4A Monmouth	**NEW YORK**	5A Saratoga	3A Craven
NEVADA	5A Morris	5A Albany	5A Schenectady	3A Cumberland
5B Carson City (city)	4A Ocean	6A Allegany	6A Schoharie	3A Currituck
5B Churchill	5A Passaic	4A Bronx	6A Schuyler	3A Dare
3B Clark	4A Salem	6A Broome	5A Seneca	3A Davidson
5B Douglas	5A Somerset	6A Cattaraugus	6A Steuben	4A Davie
5B Elko	5A Sussex	5A Cayuga	6A St. Lawrence	3A Duplin
5B Esmeralda	4A Union	5A Chautauqua	4A Suffolk	4A Durham
5B Eureka	5A Warren	5A Chemung	6A Sullivan	3A Edgecombe
5B Humboldt		6A Chenango	5A Tioga	4A Forsyth

(continued)

TABLE A200 – Continued
CLIMATE ZONES, MOISTURE REGIMES, AND WARM-HUMID DESIGNATIONS
BY STATE, COUNTY AND TERRITORY

Key: A – Moist, B – Dry, C – Marine. Absence of moisture designation indicates moisture regime is irrelevant.
Asterisk (*) indicates a warm-humid location.

4A Franklin	3A Rowan	6A LaMoure	4A Clermont	5A Morgan
3A Gaston	4A Rutherford	6A Logan	5A Clinton	5A Morrow
4A Gates	3A Sampson	7 McHenry	5A Columbiana	5A Muskingum
4A Graham	3A Scotland	6A McIntosh	5A Coshocton	5A Noble
4A Granville	3A Stanly	6A McKenzie	5A Crawford	5A Ottawa
4A Greene	4A Stokes	7 McLean	5A Cuyahoga	5A Paulding
4A Guilford	4A Surry	6A Mercer	5A Darke	5A Perry
4A Halifax	4A Swain	6A Morton	5A Defiance	5A Pickaway
4A Harnett	4A Transylvania	7 Mountrail	5A Delaware	4A Pike
4A Haywood	3A Tyrrell	7 Nelson	5A Erie	5A Portage
4A Henderson	3A Union	6A Oliver	5A Fairfield	5A Preble
4A Hertford	4A Vance	7 Pembina	5A Fayette	5A Putnam
3A Hoke	4A Wake	7 Pierce	5A Franklin	5A Richland
3A Hyde	4A Warren	7 Ramsey	5A Fulton	5A Ross
4A Iredell	3A Washington	6A Ransom	4A Gallia	5A Sandusky
4A Jackson	5A Watauga	7 Renville	5A Geauga	4A Scioto
3A Johnston	3A Wayne	6A Richland	5A Greene	5A Seneca
3A Jones	4A Wilkes	7 Rolette	5A Guernsey	5A Shelby
4A Lee	3A Wilson	6A Sargent	4A Hamilton	5A Stark
3A Lenoir	4A Yadkin	7 Sheridan	5A Hancock	5A Summit
4A Lincoln	5A Yancey	6A Sioux	5A Hardin	5A Trumbull
4A Macon		6A Slope	5A Harrison	5A Tuscarawas
4A Madison	**NORTH DAKOTA**	6A Stark	5A Henry	5A Union
3A Martin	6A Adams	7 Steele	5A Highland	5A Van Wert
4A McDowell	7 Barnes	7 Stutsman	5A Hocking	5A Vinton
3A Mecklenburg	7 Benson	7 Towner	5A Holmes	5A Warren
5A Mitchell	6A Billings	7 Traill	5A Huron	4A Washington
3A Montgomery	7 Bottineau	7 Walsh	5A Jackson	5A Wayne
3A Moore	6A Bowman	7 Ward	5A Jefferson	5A Williams
4A Nash	7 Burke	7 Wells	5A Knox	5A Wood
3A New Hanover*	6A Burleigh	7 Williams	5A Lake	5A Wyandot
4A Northampton	7 Cass		4A Lawrence	
3A Onslow*	7 Cavalier	**OHIO**	5A Licking	**OKLAHOMA**
4A Orange	6A Dickey	4A Adams	5A Logan	3A Adair
3A Pamlico	7 Divide	5A Allen	5A Lorain	3A Alfalfa
3A Pasquotank	6A Dunn	5A Ashland	5A Lucas	3A Atoka
3A Pender*	7 Eddy	5A Ashtabula	5A Madison	4B Beaver
3A Perquimans	6A Emmons	5A Athens	5A Mahoning	3A Beckham
4A Person	7 Foster	5A Auglaize	5A Marion	3A Blaine
3A Pitt	6A Golden Valley	5A Belmont	5A Medina	3A Bryan
4A Polk	7 Grand Forks	4A Brown	5A Meigs	3A Caddo
3A Randolph	6A Grant	5A Butler	5A Mercer	3A Canadian
3A Richmond	7 Griggs	5A Carroll	5A Miami	3A Carter
3A Robeson	6A Hettinger	5A Champaign	5A Monroe	3A Cherokee
4A Rockingham	7 Kidder	5A Clark	5A Montgomery	3A Choctaw

(continued)

TABLE A200 – Continued
CLIMATE ZONES, MOISTURE REGIMES, AND WARM-HUMID DESIGNATIONS
BY STATE, COUNTY AND TERRITORY

Key: A – Moist, B – Dry, C – Marine. Absence of moisture designation indicates moisture regime is irrelevant.
Asterisk (*) indicates a warm-humid location.

4B Cimarron	3A Ottawa	4C Marion	5A Huntingdon	3A Allendale*
3A Cleveland	3A Pawnee	5B Morrow	5A Indiana	3A Anderson
3A Coal	3A Payne	4C Multnomah	5A Jefferson	3A Bamberg*
3A Comanche	3A Pittsburg	4C Polk	5A Juniata	3A Barnwell*
3A Cotton	3A Pontotoc	5B Sherman	5A Lackawanna	3A Beaufort*
3A Craig	3A Pottawatomie	4C Tillamook	5A Lancaster	3A Berkeley*
3A Creek	3A Pushmataha	5B Umatilla	5A Lawrence	3A Calhoun
3A Custer	3A Roger Mills	5B Union	5A Lebanon	3A Charleston*
3A Delaware	3A Rogers	5B Wallowa	5A Lehigh	3A Cherokee
3A Dewey	3A Seminole	5B Wasco	5A Luzerne	3A Chester
3A Ellis	3A Sequoyah	4C Washington	5A Lycoming	3A Chesterfield
3A Garfield	3A Stephens	5B Wheeler	6A McKean	3A Clarendon
3A Garvin	4B Texas	4C Yamhill	5A Mercer	3A Colleton*
3A Grady	3A Tillman		5A Mifflin	3A Darlington
3A Grant	3A Tulsa	**PENNSYLVANIA**	5A Monroe	3A Dillon
3A Greer	3A Wagoner	5A Adams	4A Montgomery	3A Dorchester*
3A Harmon	3A Washington	5A Allegheny	5A Montour	3A Edgefield
3A Harper	3A Washita	5A Armstrong	5A Northampton	3A Fairfield
3A Haskell	3A Woods	5A Beaver	5A Northumberland	3A Florence
3A Hughes	3A Woodward	5A Bedford	5A Perry	3A Georgetown*
3A Jackson		5A Berks	4A Philadelphia	3A Greenville
3A Jefferson	**OREGON**	5A Blair	5A Pike	3A Greenwood
3A Johnston	5B Baker	5A Bradford	6A Potter	3A Hampton*
3A Kay	4C Benton	4A Bucks	5A Schuylkill	3A Horry*
3A Kingfisher	4C Clackamas	5A Butler	5A Snyder	3A Jasper*
3A Kiowa	4C Clatsop	5A Cambria	5A Somerset	3A Kershaw
3A Latimer	4C Columbia	6A Cameron	5A Sullivan	3A Lancaster
3A Le Flore	4C Coos	5A Carbon	6A Susquehanna	3A Laurens
3A Lincoln	5B Crook	5A Centre	6A Tioga	3A Lee
3A Logan	4C Curry	4A Chester	5A Union	3A Lexington
3A Love	5B Deschutes	5A Clarion	5A Venango	3A Marion
3A Major	4C Douglas	6A Clearfield	5A Warren	3A Marlboro
3A Marshall	5B Gilliam	5A Clinton	5A Washington	3A McCormick
3A Mayes	5B Grant	5A Columbia	6A Wayne	3A Newberry
3A McClain	5B Harney	5A Crawford	5A Westmoreland	3A Oconee
3A McCurtain	5B Hood River	5A Cumberland	5A Wyoming	3A Orangeburg
3A McIntosh	4C Jackson	5A Dauphin	4A York	3A Pickens
3A Murray	5B Jefferson	4A Delaware		3A Richland
3A Muskogee	4C Josephine	6A Elk	**RHODE ISLAND**	3A Saluda
3A Noble	5B Klamath	5A Erie	5A (all)	3A Spartanburg
3A Nowata	5B Lake	5A Fayette		3A Sumter
3A Okfuskee	4C Lane	5A Forest	**SOUTH**	3A Union
3A Oklahoma	4C Lincoln	5A Franklin	**CAROLINA**	3A Williamsburg
3A Okmulgee	4C Linn	5A Fulton	3A Abbeville	3A York
3A Osage	5B Malheur	5A Greene	3A Aiken	

(continued)

TABLE A200 – Continued
CLIMATE ZONES, MOISTURE REGIMES, AND WARM-HUMID DESIGNATIONS
BY STATE, COUNTY AND TERRITORY

Key: A – Moist, B – Dry, C – Marine. Absence of moisture designation indicates moisture regime is irrelevant.
Asterisk (*) indicates a warm-humid location.

SOUTH DAKOTA

6A Aurora	6A McPherson	4A Dickson	4A Overton	2A Bexar*
6A Beadle	6A Meade	3A Dyer	4A Perry	3A Blanco*
5A Bennett	5A Mellette	3A Fayette	4A Pickett	3B Borden
5A Bon Homme	6A Miner	4A Fentress	4A Polk	2A Bosque*
6A Brookings	6A Minnehaha	4A Franklin	4A Putnam	3A Bowie*
6A Brown	6A Moody	4A Gibson	4A Rhea	2A Brazoria*
6A Brule	6A Pennington	4A Giles	4A Roane	2A Brazos*
6A Buffalo	6A Perkins	4A Grainger	4A Robertson	3B Brewster
6A Butte	6A Potter	4A Greene	4A Rutherford	4B Briscoe
6A Campbell	6A Roberts	4A Grundy	4A Scott	2A Brooks*
5A Charles Mix	6A Sanborn	4A Hamblen	4A Sequatchie	3A Brown*
6A Clark	6A Shannon	4A Hamilton	4A Sevier	2A Burleson*
5A Clay	6A Spink	4A Hancock	3A Shelby	3A Burnet*
6A Codington	6A Stanley	3A Hardeman	4A Smith	2A Caldwell*
6A Corson	6A Sully	3A Hardin	4A Stewart	2A Calhoun*
6A Custer	5A Todd	4A Hawkins	4A Sullivan	3B Callahan
6A Davison	5A Tripp	3A Haywood	4A Sumner	2A Cameron*
6A Day	6A Turner	3A Henderson	3A Tipton	3A Camp*
6A Deuel	5A Union	4A Henry	4A Trousdale	4B Carson
6A Dewey	6A Walworth	4A Hickman	4A Unicoi	3A Cass*
5A Douglas	5A Yankton	4A Houston	4A Union	4B Castro
6A Edmunds	6A Ziebach	4A Humphreys	4A Van Buren	2A Chambers*
6A Fall River		4A Jackson	4A Warren	2A Cherokee*
6A Faulk	**TENNESSEE**	4A Jefferson	4A Washington	3B Childress
6A Grant	4A Anderson	4A Johnson	4A Wayne	3A Clay
5A Gregory	4A Bedford	4A Knox	4A Weakley	4B Cochran
6A Haakon	4A Benton	3A Lake	4A White	3B Coke
6A Hamlin	4A Bledsoe	3A Lauderdale	4A Williamson	3B Coleman
6A Hand	4A Blount	4A Lawrence	4A Wilson	3A Collin*
6A Hanson	4A Bradley	4A Lewis		3B Collingsworth
6A Harding	4A Campbell	4A Lincoln	**TEXAS**	2A Colorado*
6A Hughes	4A Cannon	4A Loudon	2A Anderson*	2A Comal*
5A Hutchinson	4A Carroll	4A Macon	3B Andrews	3A Comanche*
6A Hyde	4A Carter	3A Madison	2A Angelina*	3B Concho
5A Jackson	4A Cheatham	4A Marion	2A Aransas*	3A Cooke
6A Jerauld	3A Chester	4A Marshall	3A Archer	2A Coryell*
6A Jones	4A Claiborne	4A Maury	4B Armstrong	3B Cottle
6A Kingsbury	4A Clay	4A McMinn	2A Atascosa*	3B Crane
6A Lake	4A Cocke	3A McNairy	2A Austin*	3B Crockett
6A Lawrence	4A Coffee	4A Meigs	4B Bailey	3B Crosby
6A Lincoln	3A Crockett	4A Monroe	2B Bandera	3B Culberson
6A Lyman	4A Cumberland	4A Montgomery	2A Bastrop*	4B Dallam
6A Marshall	4A Davidson	4A Moore	3B Baylor	3A Dallas*
6A McCook	4A Decatur	4A Morgan	2A Bee*	3B Dawson
	4A DeKalb	4A Obion	2A Bell*	4B Deaf Smith

(continued)

TABLE A200 – Continued
CLIMATE ZONES, MOISTURE REGIMES, AND WARM-HUMID DESIGNATIONS
BY STATE, COUNTY AND TERRITORY

Key: A – Moist, B – Dry, C – Marine. Absence of moisture designation indicates moisture regime is irrelevant.
Asterisk (*) indicates a warm-humid location.

3A Delta	2A Hays*	3A Llano*	3B Reeves	2B Webb
3A Denton*	3B Hemphill	3B Loving	2A Refugio*	2A Wharton*
2A DeWitt*	3A Henderson*	3B Lubbock	4B Roberts	3B Wheeler
3B Dickens	2A Hidalgo*	3B Lynn	2A Robertson*	3A Wichita
2B Dimmit	2A Hill*	2A Madison*	3A Rockwall*	3B Wilbarger
4B Donley	4B Hockley	3A Marion*	3B Runnels	2A Willacy*
2A Duval*	3A Hood*	3B Martin	3A Rusk*	2A Williamson*
3A Eastland	3A Hopkins*	3B Mason	3A Sabine*	2A Wilson*
3B Ector	2A Houston*	2A Matagorda*	3A San Augustine*	3B Winkler
2B Edwards	3B Howard	2B Maverick	2A San Jacinto*	3A Wise
3A Ellis*	3B Hudspeth	3B McCulloch	2A San Patricio*	3A Wood*
3B El Paso	3A Hunt*	2A McLennan*	3A San Saba*	4B Yoakum
3A Erath*	4B Hutchinson	2A McMullen*	3B Schleicher	3A Young
2A Falls*	3B Irion	2B Medina	3B Scurry	2B Zapata
3A Fannin	3A Jack	3B Menard	3B Shackelford	2B Zavala
2A Fayette*	2A Jackson*	3B Midland	3A Shelby*	
3B Fisher	2A Jasper*	2A Milam*	4B Sherman	**UTAH**
4B Floyd	3B Jeff Davis	3A Mills*	3A Smith*	5B Beaver
3B Foard	2A Jefferson*	3B Mitchell	3A Somervell*	6B Box Elder
2A Fort Bend*	2A Jim Hogg*	3A Montague	2A Starr*	6B Cache
3A Franklin*	2A Jim Wells*	2A Montgomery*	3A Stephens	6B Carbon
2A Freestone*	3A Johnson*	4B Moore	3B Sterling	6B Daggett
2B Frio	3B Jones	3A Morris*	3B Stonewall	5B Davis
3B Gaines	2A Karnes*	3B Motley	3B Sutton	6B Duchesne
2A Galveston*	3A Kaufman*	3A Nacogdoches*	4B Swisher	5B Emery
3B Garza	3A Kendall*	3A Navarro*	3A Tarrant*	5B Garfield
3A Gillespie*	2A Kenedy*	2A Newton*	3B Taylor	5B Grand
3B Glasscock	3B Kent	3B Nolan	3B Terrell	5B Iron
2A Goliad*	3B Kerr	2A Nueces*	3B Terry	5B Juab
2A Gonzales*	3B Kimble	4B Ochiltree	3B Throckmorton	5B Kane
4B Gray	3B King	4B Oldham	3A Titus*	5B Millard
3A Grayson	2B Kinney	2A Orange*	3B Tom Green	6B Morgan
3A Gregg*	2A Kleberg*	3A Palo Pinto*	2A Travis*	5B Piute
2A Grimes*	3B Knox	3A Panola*	2A Trinity*	6B Rich
2A Guadalupe*	3A Lamar*	3A Parker*	2A Tyler*	5B Salt Lake
4B Hale	4B Lamb	4B Parmer	3A Upshur*	5B San Juan
3B Hall	3A Lampasas*	3B Pecos	3B Upton	5B Sanpete
3A Hamilton*	2B La Salle	2A Polk*	2B Uvalde	5B Sevier
4B Hansford	2A Lavaca*	4B Potter	2B Val Verde	6B Summit
3B Hardeman	2A Lee*	3B Presidio	3A Van Zandt*	5B Tooele
2A Hardin*	2A Leon*	3A Rains*	2A Victoria*	6B Uintah
2A Harris*	2A Liberty*	4B Randall	2A Walker*	5B Utah
3A Harrison*	2A Limestone*	3B Reagan	2A Waller*	6B Wasatch
4B Hartley	4B Lipscomb	2B Real	3B Ward	3B Washington
3B Haskell	2A Live Oak*	3A Red River*	2A Washington*	5B Wayne

(continued)

2020 NATIONAL GREEN BUILDING STANDARD®

TABLE A200 – Continued
CLIMATE ZONES, MOISTURE REGIMES, AND WARM-HUMID DESIGNATIONS
BY STATE, COUNTY AND TERRITORY

Key: A – Moist, B – Dry, C – Marine. Absence of moisture designation indicates moisture regime is irrelevant.
Asterisk (*) indicates a warm-humid location.

5B Weber

VERMONT
6A (all)

VIRGINIA
4A (all)

WASHINGTON
5B Adams
5B Asotin
5B Benton
5B Chelan
4C Clallam
4C Clark
5B Columbia
4C Cowlitz
5B Douglas
6B Ferry
5B Franklin
5B Garfield
5B Grant
4C Grays Harbor
4C Island
4C Jefferson
4C King
4C Kitsap
5B Kittitas
5B Klickitat
4C Lewis
5B Lincoln
4C Mason
6B Okanogan
4C Pacific
6B Pend Oreille
4C Pierce
4C San Juan
4C Skagit
5B Skamania
4C Snohomish
5B Spokane
6B Stevens
4C Thurston
4C Wahkiakum
5B Walla Walla

4C Whatcom
5B Whitman
5B Yakima

WEST VIRGINIA
5A Barbour
4A Berkeley
4A Boone
4A Braxton
5A Brooke
4A Cabell
4A Calhoun
4A Clay
5A Doddridge
5A Fayette
4A Gilmer
5A Grant
5A Greenbrier
5A Hampshire
5A Hancock
5A Hardy
5A Harrison
4A Jackson
4A Jefferson
4A Kanawha
5A Lewis
4A Lincoln
4A Logan
5A Marion
5A Marshall
4A Mason
4A McDowell
4A Mercer
5A Mineral
4A Mingo
5A Monongalia
4A Monroe
4A Morgan
5A Nicholas
5A Ohio
5A Pendleton
4A Pleasants
5A Pocahontas
5A Preston
4A Putnam

5A Raleigh
5A Randolph
4A Ritchie
4A Roane
5A Summers
5A Taylor
5A Tucker
4A Tyler
5A Upshur
4A Wayne
5A Webster
5A Wetzel
4A Wirt
4A Wood
4A Wyoming

WISCONSIN
6A Adams
7 Ashland
6A Barron
7 Bayfield
6A Brown
6A Buffalo
7 Burnett
6A Calumet
6A Chippewa
6A Clark
6A Columbia
6A Crawford
6A Dane
6A Dodge
6A Door
7 Douglas
6A Dunn
6A Eau Claire
7 Florence
6A Fond du Lac
7 Forest
6A Grant
6A Green
6A Green Lake
6A Iowa
7 Iron
6A Jackson
6A Jefferson

6A Juneau
6A Kenosha
6A Kewaunee
6A La Crosse
6A Lafayette
7 Langlade
7 Lincoln
6A Manitowoc
6A Marathon
6A Marinette
6A Marquette
6A Menominee
6A Milwaukee
6A Monroe
6A Oconto
7 Oneida
6A Outagamie
6A Ozaukee
6A Pepin
6A Pierce
6A Polk
6A Portage
7 Price
6A Racine
6A Richland
6A Rock
6A Rusk
6A Sauk
7 Sawyer
6A Shawano
6A Sheboygan
6A St. Croix
7 Taylor
6A Trempealeau
6A Vernon
7 Vilas
6A Walworth
7 Washburn
6A Washington
6A Waukesha
6A Waupaca
6A Waushara
6A Winnebago
6A Wood

WYOMING
6B Albany
6B Big Horn
6B Campbell
6B Carbon
6B Converse
6B Crook
6B Fremont
5B Goshen
6B Hot Springs
6B Johnson
6B Laramie
7 Lincoln
6B Natrona
6B Niobrara
6B Park
5B Platte
6B Sheridan
7 Sublette
6B Sweetwater
7 Teton
6B Uinta
6B Washakie
6B Weston

U.S. TERRITORIES

AMERICAN SAMOA
1A (all)*

GUAM
1A (all)*

**NORTHERN
MARIANA ISLANDS**
1A (all)*

PUERTO RICO
1A (all)*

VIRGIN ISLANDS
1A (all)*

A201.1 Tropical climate zone. The tropical climate zone shall be defined as:

(1)   Hawaii, Puerto Rico, Guam, American Samoa, U.S. Virgin Islands, Commonwealth of Northern Mariana Islands

(2)   Islands in the area between the Tropic of Cancer and the Tropic of Capricorn

A300   INTERNATIONAL CLIMATE ZONES

A301 International climate zones. The climate *zone* for any location outside the United States shall be determined by applying Table A301(1) and then Table A301(2).

TABLE A301(1)
INTERNATIONAL CLIMATE ZONE DEFINITIONS

MAJOR CLIMATE TYPE DEFINITIONS
Marine (C) Definition – Locations meeting all four criteria: 1. Mean temperature of coldest month between -3°C (27°F) and 18°C (65°F) 2. Warmest month mean <22°C (72°F) 3. At least four months with mean temperatures over 10°C (50°F) 4. Dry season in summer. The month with the heaviest precipitation in the cold season has at least three times as much precipitation as the month with the least precipitation in the rest of the year. The cold season is October through March in the Northern Hemisphere and April through September in the Southern Hemisphere.
Dry (B) Definition—Locations meeting the following criteria: Not marine and P_{in} <0.44 × (TF - 19.5)   [P_{cm}<2.0 × (TC + 7) in SI units] where: P_{in} = Annual precipitation in inches (cm) T = Annual mean temperature in °F (°C)
Moist (A) Definition – Locations that are not marine and not dry.
Warm-humid Definition – Moist (A) locations where either of the following wet-bulb temperature conditions shall occur during the warmest six consecutive months of the year: 1. 67°F (19.4°C) or higher for 3,000 or more hours; or 2. 73°F (22.8°C) or higher for 1,500 or more hours

For SI: °C = [(°F)-32]/1.8; 1 in. = 2.54 cm.

TABLE A301(2)
INTERNATIONAL CLIMATE ZONE DEFINITIONS

ZONE NUMBER	THERMAL CRITERIA	
	IP Units	**SI Units**
1	9000 <CDD50°F	5000 < CDD10°C
2	6300 < CDD50°F ≤ 9000	3500 < CDD10°C ≤ 5000
3A and 3B	4500 < CDD50°F ≤ 6300 AND HDD65°F ≤ 5400	2500 < CDD10°C ≤ 3500 AND HDD18°C ≤ 3000
4A and 4B	CDD50°F ≤ 4500 AND HDD65°F ≤ 5400	CDD10°C ≤ 2500 AND HDD18°C ≤ 3000
3C	HDD65°F ≤ 3600	HDD18°C ≤ 2000
4C	3600 < HDD65°F ≤ 5400	2000 < HDD18°C ≤ 3000
5	5400 < HDD65°F ≤ 7200	3000 < HDD18°C ≤ 4000
6	7200 < HDD65°F ≤ 9000	4000 < HDD18°C ≤ 5000
7	9000 < HDD65°F ≤ 12600	5000 < HDD18°C ≤ 7000
8	12600 < HDD65°F	7000 < HDD18°C

For SI: °C = [(°F)-32]/1.8

2020 NATIONAL GREEN BUILDING STANDARD®

APPENDIX B:

EXAMPLES OF THIRD-PARTY PROGRAMS FOR INDOOR ENVIRONMENTAL QUALITY

B100   SCOPE AND APPLICABILITY

B101.1 Applicability of Appendix B. Appendix B is not part of this Standard.

B101.2 Scope. Appendix B provides examples of third-party programs for indoor environmental quality that can be used to demonstrate compliance with the applicable provisions of this Standard.

D200   CONFORMANCE

TABLE B200(1) Examples of Third-party Certification Programs	
Related Section of Standard	**Examples of Third-party Certification Programs Compliant with the Corresponding Section**
901.5 Cabinets	Kitchen Cabinet Manufacturers Association (KCMA) Environmental Stewardship Program (ESP)
901.6 Carpets	Carpet and Rug Institute's (CRI) Green Label Plus Indoor Air Quality Program
901.7 Hard-surface flooring	UL GREENGUARD Gold Resilient Floor Covering Institute's FloorScore Indoor Air Certification Program
901.8 Wall coverings	UL GREENGUARD Gold Scientific Certification Systems (SCS) Indoor Advantage Gold Program
901.9 Architectural coatings	UL GREENGUARD Gold Scientific Certification Systems (SCS) Indoor Advantage Gold Program Green Seal-11 Standard for Paints and Coatings UL 2768
901.10 Adhesives and sealants	UL GREENGUARD Scientific Certifications Systems (SCS) Indoor Advantage Gold Program Carpet and Rug Institute's (CRI) Green Label Plus Indoor Air Quality Program Resilient Floor Covering Institute's FloorScore Indoor Air Certification Program Green Seal-36 Standard for Adhesives for Commercial Use
901.11 Insulation	UL GREENGUARD Gold Scientific Certifications Systems (SCS) Indoor Advantage Gold Program
901.12 Furniture and Furnishing	UL GREENGUARD Gold Scientific Certifications Systems (SCS) Indoor Advantage Gold Program BIFMA level certification where 7.6.1 and 7.6.2 are proven to be achieved

TABLE B200(2) Contact Information for the Example Third-party Certification Programs	
Third-party Certification Program	**Contact Information for the Program Administrator**
Kitchen Cabinet Manufacturers Association (KCMA) Environmental Stewardship Program (ESP)	*Kitchen Cabinet Manufacturers Association* *1899 Preston White Drive* *Reston, VA 20191* *www.kcma.org* *(703) 264-1690*
Carpet and Rug Institute's (CRI) Green Label Plus Indoor Air Quality Program	*Carpet and Rug Institute* *730 College Drive* *Dalton, Georgia 30720* *United States of America* *http://www.carpet-rug.org* *(706) 278-3176*
UL GREENGUARD Gold	*Underwriters Laboratories Inc. 333 Pfingsten Road* *Northbrook, IL 60062-2096* *www.ul.com* *(877) 854-3577*
Resilient Floor Covering Institute's FloorScore Indoor Air Certification Program	*Resilient Floor Covering Institute* *115 Broad Street, Suite 201* *LaGrange, Georgia 30240* *http://www.rfci.com*
Scientific Certification Systems (SCS) Indoor Advantage Gold Program	*Scientific Certification Systems* *2000 Powell Street, Suite 600* *Emeryville, California 94608* *http://www.scscertified.com* *(510) 452-8000*
Green Seal-11 Standard for Paints and Coatings	*Green Seal* *1001 Connecticut Avenue, NW, Suite 827* *Washington, DC 20036-5525* *http://www.greenseal.org/* *(202) 872-6400*
UL 2768	*Underwriters Laboratories Inc.* *333 Pfingsten Road* *Northbrook, IL 60062-2096* *www.ul.com* *(877) 854-3577*

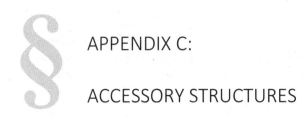

APPENDIX C:

ACCESSORY STRUCTURES

C100   SCOPE AND APPLICABILITY

C101.1 Applicability of Appendix C. Appendix C is part of this Standard. Text identified as "User Note" is not considered part of this Standard.

C101.2 Scope. The provisions contained in Appendix C provide the criteria necessary for complying with Section 306 for accessory structures.

C201   CONFORMANCE

C201.1 Conformance. Accessory structures that meet all applicable requirements of Appendix C shall be designated as *conforming*. The *conforming* designation for the accessory structure is separate from the rating achieved by the residential buildings located on the same site or lot. Where residential buildings located on the same lot have not achieved a rating in accordance with this Standard, the accessory structures shall not be eligible for designation under this Appendix. Each accessory structure shall seek a separate designation of *conforming* based on the rules established by the Adopting Entity in accordance with Section E202. The residential building shall not receive points for any practices implemented only for the accessory structure.

C202   CONFORMANCE CRITERIA

C202 Conformance Criteria. Accessory structures shall implement practices from Chapters 5 through 10 in accordance with Sections C202.1 through C202.7.

C202.1 The practices that are mandatory for the residential building shall also be mandatory for the accessory structure unless these practices are exempt under Sections C202.5 or C202.7.

C202.2 All land development practices associated with construction of the accessory structure shall comply with the land development practices for the residential building located on the same lot.

C202.3 For the accessory structures that use the same basic construction and mechanical systems as the residential buildings, the design and construction of the accessory structures shall meet the practices, or the intent of the practices, implemented to achieve compliance for the residential building located on the same site or lot.

C202.4 For the accessory structures that use basic construction or mechanical systems that are different from the residential buildings, the design and construction of the accessory structures shall meet the intent of the practice implemented to achieve compliance for the residential building located on the same site or lot.

C202.5 Where the residential buildings located on the same site or lot include construction methods or systems that do not have functionally-equivalent methods or systems as part of the accessory structure, the accessory structure does not need to comply with any of the practices implemented for the residential building with regard to such construction methods or systems.

> **User note:** Examples of the practices that may be exempt from implementation in accessory structures include, but are not limited to:
>
> 1) *Section 601.1 Conditioned floor area.*
>
> 2) *Section 601.5 Prefabricated components – accessory structure is not required to be modular if the residential building is modular.*
>
> 3) *Section 601.6 Stacked stories – accessory structures are not required to have more than one story if the residential building is more than one story.*
>
> 4) *Section 602.2 Roof surfaces – if the residential building has a landscaped roof, the accessory structure is not required to have a landscaped roof.*
>
> 5) *Chapter 7 Energy efficiency – unconditioned spaces in the accessory structure are not required to comply with Chapter 7.*
>
> 6) *Section 902.3 Radon control except for habitable space.*

C202.6 Where the accessory structure includes construction methods or systems that do not have functionally-equivalent counterparts as part of the residential buildings located on the same site or lot, the Adopting Entity shall review such construction methods and systems and shall establish an approach for meeting the overall intent of the Standard with regard to the minimum acceptable threshold.

C202.7 Where the use of the accessory structure does not necessitate the implementation of a specific practice in the same manner as the practice applies to the residential building, such practice for the accessory structure may be exempted by the Adopting Entity.

> **User note:** Examples of the practices that may be exempted from implementation in accessory structures include, but are not limited to:
>
> 1) *Section 602.1.14 Ice barrier – if the accessory structure does not contain conditioned space, ice barrier is not required.*

APPENDIX D:

WATER RATING INDEX

D101.1 Intent. Provide a flexible method to quantify home water use efficiency as a single number.

D101.2 Scope. The Water Rating Index (WRI) is a performance calculation for water use efficiency, including both indoor and outdoor water use.

D101.3 Capabilities. The WRI calculation shall include the following capabilities

(1) Both new and existing construction.

(2) One or more of the following building types:

    (a) One- and two-family dwellings.

    (b) Townhouses not more than three stories above grade in height.

    (c) Multifamily buildings as a whole building; or individual dwelling units provided each unit has a separate water meter.

(3) Three types of WRI rating reports shall be available:

    (a) Preliminary reports with WRI from plans.

    (b) Final reports with WRI with field verification. The final reports shall be formatted to be compared side-by-side with the preliminary reports.

    (c) Existing dwellings WRI with field-verified existing conditions.

(4) Building water use shall be reduced based on the water capture and reuse. Where a specific type of water capture and reuse would violate local laws or ordnances, the amount of water capture and reuse for that specific type shall be zero.

    (a) The water types for capture and reuse shall be:

        (i) Rainwater, which is natural precipitation that falls on a structure.

        (ii) Sitewater, which is natural precipitation that falls on the ground, softscapes, and hardscapes.

        (iii) Greywater, which is untreated wastewater that has not come into contact with toilet waste, kitchen sink waste, dishwasher waste or similarly contaminated sources:

            (1) Only wastewater from bathtubs, showers, lavatories, and clothes washers shall be used in the greywater offset calculation.

            (2) If no filtration/purification system and properly sized tank is present, then greywater shall only be used outdoors as subsurface irrigation.

        (iv) Blackwater, which is the liquid and waterborne waste that would be permitted without special treatment into either the public sewer or a private sewage disposal system.

    (b) Water offset credit for rainwater, sitewater, and greywater use indoors shall require filtration, purification and properly sized tanks. Blackwater shall not offset indoor water.

D101.4 Process. The following shall be required as part of a WRI implementation:

(1) Trained WRI Verifiers shall provide field verifications, ratings and the associated reports.

(2) At minimum training shall include:

   (a) Confirmation of contract documents including building drawings, site drawings, landscape drawings, specifications, cut sheets, and approved final submittals.

   (b) Visual confirmation of installed site material, fixtures, and equipment.

   (c) Physical field testing of installed fixtures and equipment.

   (d) Ability to utilize a tool that incorporates this WRI calculation.

D101.5 Compute Water Rating Index. The WRI is an overall rating for the home on an annual basis. The WRI shall be computed as a percentage of the combined indoor and outdoor water use in relation to the combined indoor and outdoor water baseline.

$$\text{WRI} = 100 * (\text{IndoorUse} + \text{OutdoorUse}) / (\text{IndoorBaseline} + \text{OutdoorBaseline})$$

This Appendix species which parameters input to the WRI shall be verified from plans and/or field inspection. Variables with the subscript "verified" shall be verified.

D101.6 Indoor Water. The WRI

(1) Indoor water calculations for annual Baseline and annual Use shall be as follows:

IndoorBaseline = [ToiletWater$_{\text{(baseline)}}$ + ShowerWater$_{\text{(baseline)}}$ + BathtubWater$_{\text{(baseline)}}$ + LavatoryWater$_{\text{(baseline)}}$ + FaucetWater$_{\text{(baseline)}}$ + DishWasherWater$_{\text{(baseline)}}$ + ClothesWasherWater$_{\text{(baseline)}}$ + StructuralWasteWater$_{\text{(baseline)}}$ + OtherWaterUse$_{\text{(baseline)}}$] * 365 days/year

IndoorUse = [ToiletWater$_{\text{(verified)}}$ + ShowerWater$_{\text{(verified)}}$ + BathtubWater$_{\text{(verified)}}$ + LavatoryWater$_{\text{(verified)}}$ + FaucetWater$_{\text{(verified)}}$ + DishWasherWater$_{\text{(verified)}}$ + ClothesWasherWater$_{\text{(verified)}}$ + StructuralWasteWater$_{\text{(verified)}}$ + OtherWaterUse$_{\text{(verified)}}$] - IndoorWaterReuseCredit$_{\text{(verified)}}$

(2) NumOccupants = bedrooms + 1

(3) Baseline water for each device in Table 1 shall be:

   (a) Baseline$_{\text{(device)}}$ = VolumePerOccupant$_{\text{(device)}}$ * NumOccupants

   (b) For dishwasher and clothes washer, if it is verified that there is no hookup
   Baseline$_{\text{(device)}}$ = 0

(4) Verified use for each device in Table 1 shall be:

   (a) Verified$_{\text{(device)}}$ = VerifiedFlowRate$_{\text{(device)}}$ * UseFactor * NumOccupants

   (b) A thermostatic control value (TSV) on all showerheads shall be verified, otherwise the shower shall assume no TSV for all showerheads

   (c) For bathtub, dishwasher and clothes washer, if it is verified that there is no hookup
   Verified$_{\text{(device)}}$ = 0

TABLE 1.
WATER USE FOR BASELINE AND VERIFIED DEVICES

Device	Baseline Volume Per Occupant gallons / day / occupant	Uses for Verified Devices and units
Toilet	8	5 uses / day / occupant
Shower	13.455	5.382 or 4.7035 with TSVs minutes / day / occupant at device flow rate
Bathtub	1.414	same as the baseline gallons / day / occupant
Lavatory	2.75	1.25 minutes / day / occupant at device flow rate
Faucet	8.8	4 minutes / day / occupant at device flow rate
Dishwasher	1.69	0.26 uses / day / occupant
Clothes Washer	7.41	0.78 uses / day / occupant

(5) Structural waste, which is the water volume in the pipe between the hot water source and the plumbing fixture or appliance plus the extra volume needed to heat the pipe as hot water is delivered to its use.

    (a) VerifiedStructuralWaste (gallons), shall be field measured as the water volume collected until the temperature of the water equals 100°F at the furthest fixture for a domestic hot water system.

        (i) This test shall be performed before any other tests in order to avoid preheating the pipes. This test shall use an apparatus with a thermometer and water container.

        (ii) If there is more than one domestic hot water system, all systems shall be tested for structural waste with the worst performing system entered into the calculation.

    (b) BaselineStructuralWaste (gallons/day) is approximated based on the house size and configuration. The pipe length is estimated as a horizontal length plus a vertical length.

        (i) EstimatedHorizontalPipe = SQRT(HouseFootprint) * 2
which is the pipe length estimated as the distance between two opposite corners of square with same area as house, assuming the pipe went along the length and width of the square.

        (ii) EstimatedVerticalPipe = NumberOfFloors * FloorHeight

        Except:

            (1) Add half floor height for one story house with crawlspace and water heater on first floor or in garage

            (2) Add half floor height for 1 story with slab

            (3) Subtract 1 floor height for 2 story slab on grade

        (iii) EstimatedTotalPipe = EstimatedHorizontalPipe + EstimatedVerticalPipe

    (iv) BaselineStructuralWaste = EstimatedTotalPipe * WaterVolumePerPipeLength

    Variables

       (1) HouseFootprint - sf of the exterior conditioned space on the ground floor

         (a) Exception: the attached garage's sf shall be included if a water heater is located in the garage

       (2) FloorToFloorHeight, average floor to floor height (ft) WaterVolumePerPipeLength is gallons per ft pipe from Table 2, based on the predominate type of pipe. For existing homes, the value of 0.025 shall be used when the predominant type of pipe is not known

TABLE 2.
GALLONS OF WATER PER FOOT OF PIPE

Pipe Material	3/8"	1/2"	3/4"	1"
K (fat wall copper)	0.007	0.011	0.023	0.040
L (medium wall copper)	0.008	0.012	0.025	0.043
M (skinny wall copper)	0.008	0.013	0.027	0.045
CPVC	N/A	0.010	0.021	0.035
PEX	0.005	0.009	0.019	0.031

(c) PreliminaryStructuralWaste (gallons) is the estimated structural waste volume for a building when there is no built construction to verify but a preliminary estimate is necessary to create a comparison to the baseline. This estimate shall be the same as BaselineStructuralWaste, except that the EstimatetedHorizonatalPipe shall be replaced with the PreliminaryHorizontalPipe computed as:

PreliminaryHorizontalPipe = horizontal measurement of the straight-line distance from the water heater to the furthest hot-water-using fixture on the plans

(6) Other types of water use. OtherWaterUse (gallons/day) - other water fixture use for fixtures verified to be present

   (a) The baseline is zero, when device is not present

   (b) OtherWaterUse sums the water use for fixtures that are present

   (c) OtherWaterUse includes:

     (i) Water use per manufacturer (gallons/day)

       (1) Water softeners

       (2) Humidifiers

       (3) Evaporative coolers

       (4) Water filters, except reverse osmosis

     (ii) Reverse osmosis water use shall be as specified by the manufacturer or shall default to a water waste of 4 times the water consumption

     (iii) Fountains and spas – water loss (gallons/day) = pan evaporation rate * area

     (iv) VerifiedLeaks shall be included as a direct use item. The baseline is no leaks. Leaks are included in both baseline and actual if verified as present for existing or final ratings.

     (v) Where there are multiple fixtures or appliances of the same type, the baseline fixtures and appliances shall be assumed to all be of the same type, flow rate and water use rate.

(7) Master bath adjustment. This item shall apply where there is a master bath. If the flow rate of the individual toilet, lavatory, or shower devices varies, then water use in the master bath and outside the master bath shall be computed separately.

(a) For each device type, average the device-type flow rates. Compute two separate device-type-averages, one average for the master bath and one average for outside the master bath.

(b) Device-type uses are divided as follows:

(i) For each device the total number of uses shall be as given in Table 1, with the uses divided between the master bath and outside the master bath.

(ii) For master bath toilets and lavatories assume 2 uses each for 2 occupants, for a total of 4 uses per day. For master bath showers assume 1 use each for 2 occupants for a total of 2 uses per day.

(iii) Assume the remaining uses in Table 1 are outside the master bath.

(c) For both the master bath and outside the master bath compute water use as the device-type average times the number of uses.

(d) Add the device water use to ToiletWater, LavatoryWater and ShowerWater as appropriate in the IndoorUse equation in item #1.

(8) Other appliances. For other appliances: If there is more than one of a specific type of appliance, then the worst-case appliance water use shall be used in the ApplianceFlowRate $_{(device)}$.

Defaults - If cut sheets or internet information is available for either dishwashers or clothes washers, that information shall supersede these defaults.

TABLE 4.
DEFAULTS FOR CLOTHES WASHERS AND DISHWASHERS

Clothes Washer	9.5 IWF, 4 CF (ft^2)
Dishwasher	6.5 gallon/cycle

D101.7 Water Capture for Potential Reuse. This calculates the water available for reuse for each month.

(1) RainwaterCapture, GreywaterCapture, and BlackwaterCapture shall be computed for each month.

(a) RainwaterCapture$_{(month)}$ - gallons/month, includes roofwater and sitewater.

= [(RoofwaterArea * RoofSurfaceCapture) + (SitewaterArea * SiteSurfaceCapture)] * 0.623 (gallons/sq ft of 1 in of rain) * DaysInMonth$_{(month)}$

(i) RainwaterArea$_{(roof)}$ and RainwaterArea$_{(site)}$ – Verified Rainwater capture areas for the roof and site in sq ft. Where there is no rainwater capture, these areas shall be zero

(ii) SiteSufaceCapture – Site surface affects water capture as specified in Table 6. Site surface shall be verified. Where there are multiple site surface types, the area-weighted average shall be used.

TABLE 6.
SITE SURFACE FRACTION CAPTURED

Surface	Capture
Asphalt	0.83
Concrete	0.88
Brick	0.78
Patios, stone or other pavers	0.88
Unknown (also default)	0.50

(iii) RoofSurfaceCapture – Roof surface affects water capture as specified in Table 7. Roof surface shall be verified. Where there are multiple roof surface types, the area-weighted average shall be used.

TABLE 7.
ROOF SURFACE FRACTION CAPTURED

Surface	Capture
Asphalt/sloped	0.90
Concrete or Tile/sloped	0.90
Metal/sloped	0.95
Tar & Gravel/sloped	0.80
Membrane/sloped	0.90
Concrete or Tile/flat	0.81
Foam & Gravel/flat	0.62
Foam/flat	0.90
Membrane/flate	0.90
Uknown (also default)	0.50

(b) GreywaterCapture$_{(month)}$ - in gallons/month

= (ShowerWater$_{(verified)}$ + BathtubWater$_{(verified)}$ + LavatoryWater$_{(verified)}$ + ClothesWasherWater$_{(verified)}$) * DaysInMonth$_{(month)}$

(c) BlackwaterCapture$_{(month)}$ - in gallons/month

= (ToiletWater$_{(verified)}$ + FaucetWater$_{(verified)}$) * DaysInMonth$_{(month)}$

(d) To get credit for reuse of captured rainwater, greywater and blackwater:

(i) Tank size shall be 90% of nominal size to provide a safety factor.

(ii) Capture systems shall include filtration and purification for reuse indoors or above ground irrigation.

(iii) Capture water credit for each month shall be no more than the tank size or the captured water available – whichever is less.

(iv) Any remaining unused captured water can be carried over to the following month but not in excess of the tank size.

(v) Reuse of rainwater, greywater and blackwater shall not receive credit in violation of ordinances or other regulations.

D101.8 Outdoor Calculations. The annual outdoor water use shall be calculated as follows:

OutdoorUse = LandscapeWaterUse + NonLandscapeWaterUse

OutdoorBaseline$_{(month)}$ = Evapotranspiration$_{(month)}$ * LandscapeWaterArea$_{(total)}$ * 0.623 (gallons/sq ft of 1 in of rain) where LandscapeWaterArea$_{(total)}$ is the total of all the areas that are planted, irrigated, hand-watered or have a water feature like a pool.

(1) LandscapeWaterUse – Is the annual outdoor water use for landscaping. It sums the monthly water use for each landscape zone into the LandscapeWaterUse

(a) Water use shall be increased for an IrrigationEfficiency of less than 1, as specified in Table 8

(b) Water use shall be adjusted based on the irrigation controller, as some controllers conserve water by adjusting for weather or soil conditions

LandscapeWaterUse = For each month that is a water month and for each landscape zone sum

([Evapotranspiration$_{(month)}$ * PlantFractionEvapotranspiration$_{(zone)}$] - EffectiveRainfall$_{(month)}$) * LandscapeArea$_{(zone)}$ *
(1 - IrrigationControllerReduction)$_{(zone)}$ / IrrigationEfficiency$_{(zone)}$) * 0.623 (gallons/sq ft of 1 in of rain)

(a) Multiple physical zones with the same values for Evapotranspiration, IrrigationEfficiency and IrrigationControllerReduction shall be permitted to be combined into one zone with LandscapeArea being the sum of the areas of those zones

(2) Months shall be water-months as follows based on approved long-term climate data which includes frost days and average last frost

(a) To define the watering months, take the number of frost days in a year, divide by twelve, and round to the nearest whole month

(b) The month with the average last frost is the beginning of the watering months

(3) If an irrigation system is installed, the verifiers shall verify that the irrigation emitters and zones are operational

(4) Variables:

(a) LandscapeArea$_{(zone)}$ - verified landscape zone(s) with specific verified area

(b) Defaults – If the landscaping cannot be verified then the verifier shall use an automatic minimum of 10% of the LandscapeWaterArea$_{(total)}$. Where the plants cannot be verified, the verifier shall assume plants with the highest water requirements and no irrigation

(c) IrrigationEfficiency$_{(zone)}$ – The efficiency of a specific type of irrigation, a number between 0 and 1

TABLE 8.
IRRIGATION EFFICIENCY

Only hand irrigation	1
Drip – standard	.7
Drip – micro	.8
Drip – press comp	.9
Fixed spray	.65
Micro spray	.7
Rotor	.7
Rotary nozzle	.75
Spray	.55
Flood	1
Direct injection/root	1

(d) IrrigationControllerReduction$_{(zone)}$ is irrigation water reduction based on a verified weather-based irrigation controller:

(i) An irrigation controller that integrates rain sensors shall be a 10% IrrigationControllerReduction

(ii) An irrigation controller that integrates daily weather tracking shall be a 10% IrrigationControllerReduction

(iii) Both i and ii, which shall be a 20% IrrigationControllerReduction

(5) Evapotranspiration(month) - Monthly evapotranspiration (ETo)

    (a) Approved long-term evapotranspiration data with a least a monthly resolution shall be used to define monthly evapotranpiration rates for specific locations

    (b) PlantFractionEvapotranspiration(zone) – which is from the highest water using plant in that zone

    (c) For purposes of identifying plant water demand, an approved resource shall be used to identify plant type

TABLE 9.
RELATIVE WATER USE BY PLANT TYPE

Plant Type	Plant Fraction of Evapotranspiration
Turf, cool season grasses adapted to temperatures from 65° to 75°F.	0.8
Turf, warm season grasses adapted to temperatures from 80° to 95°F	0.6
Annual flowers	0.8
Woody plants and herbaceous perennials, wet plants adapted to ≥20 in. of annual precipitation	0.7
Woody plants and herbaceous perennials, dry plants adapted to 10 to 20 in. of annual precipitation	0.5
Desert plants plants adapted to <10 in. of annual precipitation	0.3
Home food crops	1.0

(6) NonLandscapeWaterUse shall be the sum of outdoor exposed pools, spas, and fountains, if any

    (a) The water requirement for outdoor uncovered pools, spas, or fountains is 70% of the evapotranspiration (ETo). The water demand is the same covered or uncovered.

    Exception: Pools with motorized covers shall use 40% of the evapotranspiration.

    (b) The baseline assumes uncovered pools, spas or fountains only if present for the proposed.

D101.9 Water Cost Calculations. Where water costs are calculated the water cost shall be obtained from the authority having jurisdiction.

(1) All indoor and outdoor water use shall be included in the water cost calculation. This includes items for which there is no industry accepted baseline efficiency as specified in the Indoor Calculations section of this appendix.

INDEX